MONOGRAPHS OF THE SOCIETY

P9-EDU-347

Serial No. 233, Vol. 58, Nos. 3–4, 1993

CONTENTS

ABSTRACT

Savage-Rumbaugh, E. Sue; Murphy, Jeannine; Sevcik, Rose A.; Brakke, Karen E.; Williams, Shelly L.; and Rumbaugh, Duane M. Language Comprehension in Ape and Child. With Commentary by Elizabeth Bates; and a Reply by E. Sue Savage-Rumbaugh. *Monographs of the Society for Research in Child Development*, 1993, **58**(3–4, Serial No. 233).

Previous investigations of the linguistic capacities of apes have focused on the ape's ability to produce words, and there has been little concern for comprehension. By contrast, it is increasingly recognized that comprehension precedes production in the language development of normal human children, and it may indeed guide production. It has been demonstrated that some species can process speech sounds categorically in a manner similar to that observed in humans. Consequently, it should be possible for such species to comprehend language if they have the cognitive capacity to understand word-referent relations and syntactic structure. Popular theories of human language acquisition suggest that the ability to process syntactic information is unique to humans and reflects a novel biological adaptation not seen in other animals.

The current report addresses this issue through systematic experimental comparisons of the language comprehension skills of a 2-year-old child and an 8-year-old bonobo (*Pan paniscus*) who was raised in a language environment similar to that in which children are raised but specifically modified to be appropriate for an ape. Both subjects (child and bonobo) were exposed to spoken English and lexigrams from infancy, and neither was trained to comprehend speech. A common caretaker participated in the rearing of both subjects. All language acquisition was through observational learning. Without prior training, subjects were asked to respond to the same 660 novel sentences. All responses were videotaped and scored for accuracy of comprehension of the English language.

The results indicated that both subjects comprehended novel requests and simple syntactic devices. The bonobo decoded the syntactic device of word recursion with higher accuracy than the child; however, the child tended to do better than the bonobo on the conjunctive, a structure that places a greater burden on short-term memory. Both subjects performed as well on sentences that required the ability to reverse word order as they did on sentences that did not require this capacity.

These results are discussed in light of a model of the evolution of language that suggests that the potential for language comprehension preceded the appearance of speech by several million years at minimum. The onset of speech is linked to the appearance of fully adapted bipedalism, which necessitated reorientation of the laryngeal tract and made closure of the soft palate possible. For the first time, such closure permitted mammals to easily produce sounds that could be interpreted by the mammalian auditory system in a categorical manner. When these sounds were paired with the previously extant capacity to produce vowels, it became possible to form "bounded vowels" or sound units that could readily be discriminated as units by the auditory system. It is suggested that this physical adaptation allowed the extant cognitive capacity of the hominids to embark on a speech-like mode of communication.

I. INTRODUCTION:
OF LANGUAGE, APES, AND MEN

This *Monograph* reports one study within an ongoing project designed to examine the linguistic and cognitive competencies of nonhuman primates, which was begun in 1972 by Duane M. Rumbaugh of Georgia State University in cooperation with the Yerkes Regional Primate Research Center of Emory University. The research reported here was conducted at the Language Research Center, established in 1980 by Georgia State University. Since the inception of the project, five *Pan troglodytes* (Lana, Sherman, Austin, Panpanzee, and Mercury), five *Pan paniscus* (Matata, Kanzi, Mulika, Panbanisha, and Tamuli), and three *Homo sapiens* (Nathaniel, Alia, and Katie) have served, and continue to serve, as subjects in long-term studies of language acquisition skills.

One of the most intriguing results to date from this long-term effort has been the observation that, given appropriate rearing conditions, speech comprehension spontaneously emerges in apes (Savage-Rumbaugh, 1986; Savage-Rumbaugh, McDonald, Sevcik, Hopkins, & Rubert, 1986; Savage-Rumbaugh, Romski, Hopkins, & Sevcik, 1989; Savage-Rumbaugh, Sevcik, Rumbaugh, & Rubert, 1985). Initially, it appeared that this capacity was limited to a single species (*Pan paniscus*) and to single words. However, continued exposure to speech and the addition of multiple subjects reared in identical environments have led to two important conclusions. (*a*) Comprehension of novel complex utterances and some syntactic structures begins to appear around 5 years of age. (*b*) For *Pan paniscus, Pan troglodytes,* and *Homo sapiens,* it is the age of the exposure to speech and the nature of the environment that are the critical variables with regard to the emergence of speech comprehension (Savage-Rumbaugh, Brakke, & Hutchins, 1992).

As with children, the early emergence of complex language understanding is a phenomenon that is tightly linked to contextually specific real-world knowledge. It is this knowledge that is increasingly employed to help make sense of the multiple novel utterances that are directed to the child or, in our case, the ape. Consequently, our previous attempts to document the emergence and existence of the comprehension of novel utterances and syn-

1

tactic structures have been confined, of necessity, to natural settings in which the language directed to the ape has not been experimentally manipulated (Savage-Rumbaugh, 1987). These studies attempted to eliminate all obvious contextual information, and they strongly suggested that an ability to comprehend novel utterances and complex syntactic devices (e.g., "If you don't want the juice, put it back in") was present. However, since the ape's knowledge of preceding real-world events may have made it possible to deduce, at least partially, the speaker's intended meaning, it was difficult to determine how much comprehension was dependent on linguistic input alone.

The current *Monograph* attempts to push the data envelope further by reporting the results of a comparative study of a bonobo (Kanzi) and a child (Alia) in an experimental setting that was designed to permit deliberate manipulation of the speech input and to afford control of the real-world environment while nonetheless preserving much of the flavor of the "natural speech interaction" to which the ape and the child were accustomed. At the outset of the study, the feasibility of the current technique had not been established. Rather, it emerged during the actual testing of the subjects as they became increasingly sophisticated "test takers." However, the nature of the research question ("Can they comprehend novel utterances?") made it imperative to present only unique sentences and to collect data throughout this process. Additionally, since the overall competency of the subjects was not known prior to the collection of this data set, the sophistication of the sentences presented to the subjects increased across time as it became apparent that they could process more complex material.

The research reported here has taken place within an intellectual climate that has been at best highly skeptical. In part, this is because previous studies of ape language fell prey to heavy criticism that studies of signing apes did not effectively counter. However, it is also the case that, while many scientists are comfortable with our current understanding of the biological relation between human and ape, there still exists a distinct tendency to discount the implications of this biological kinship for complex behavior. Claims of cognitive contiguity between human and ape still evoke in many scientists a quick reaction of disgust, as if humankind in general is not yet comfortable with the image of itself as being part ape. Following the position laid down by Terrace, Pettito, Sanders, and Bever (1979), those who view the gap between human and animal cognition as unbridgeable and unassailable have recently dominated cognitive and linguistic research.

APE LANGUAGE IN HISTORICAL PERSPECTIVE

Studies of the linguistic abilities of apes began with the work of Furness (1916), who attempted to teach a young orangutan to speak. The orang quickly acquired a number of different sounds, which it appeared to produce voluntarily and in appropriate settings. The study was terminated unexpectedly, however, owing to the orang's death. Sometime later, Kellogg and Kellogg (1933) attempted to follow up this work by obtaining a young orangutan for purposes of rearing it with their 9½-month-old son, Donald. They sought to shed light on the manner in which heredity and environment exert their conjoint influence on the development of the young primate organism, observing,

> Without doubt, one of the most significant tests which could be applied to a problem of this nature would be to put to rigid experimental proof the stories of the "wild" children themselves. To accomplish this end it would be necessary to place a normal human infant in uncivilized surroundings and to observe and record its development *as it grew up* in this environment. Such an experiment should throw important light upon the precise influence of outside stimulation in the development of the young baby. Yet obviously, in spite of all the scientific zeal which could be brought to bear upon an undertaking of this kind, it would be both legally dangerous and morally outrageous to carry out.
>
> Although it would be impossible, therefore, to duplicate the conditions under which these foundlings are reported to have been discovered, it would be possible and practical, it occurred to us, to reverse these conditions. Instead of placing a child in a typical animal environment, why not place an animal in a typical human environment: Why not give one of the higher primates exactly the environmental advantages which a young child enjoys and then study the development of the resulting organism? . . .
>
> If such an experiment were to produce valid results, it would admit of no halfway measures. To carry it out in any comprehensive manner one would have to obtain an infant anthropoid ape, as young as possible, and rear it in every respect as a child is reared. (p. 11)

Unable to obtain an orangutan, they secured a 7½-month-old female chimpanzee, whom they named Gua, from the Anthropoid Experiment Station of Yale University (the forerunner of the Yerkes Primate Center). Gua was co-reared with Donald for the following 9 months. According to Kellogg and Kellogg (1933), "Neither of the subjects was to be systematically drilled in any behavior which is learned *incidentally* in the normal course of the upbringing of a civilized human" (p. 188). Gua quickly mastered navigation of the house, learning to open a swing door at 8 months, to release a door latch by 10 months, to unhook window screens by 10½ months, and to unlock the front door by 13 months, all well in advance of the human child, whose locomotor behavior was still restricted to a walker during this time. Both were toilet trained, with Donald acquiring this skill about 15 days

3

sooner than Gua. Gua proved able to discover how to extract her hand from a loop and to position a chair so as to obtain a cookie much more rapidly than Donald. She learned to eat with a spoon by 13½ months, whereas Donald did not achieve this feat until age 17½ months. Gua also proved more advanced than Donald in learning to use a hoe to rake a desired item into reach, although both required some instruction in this task. Tests of spatial memory, using a delayed-response paradigm, indicated that Donald could negotiate delays of only 9 min at 10½ months of age, whereas Gua could negotiate delays of 30 min at 8 months of age.

Gua also proved sensitive to human speech, first exhibiting differential responses to "no" and to "kiss." By 9½ months she displayed a total of seven distinctive responses to speech stimuli, whereas at 12½ months Donald evinced only two. By 12½ months Gua evinced comprehension of 21 different requests, while Donald, then 14½ months of age, was responding to 20 different requests. Donald's comprehension then began to overtake Gua's. Only 1 month later he understood 32 distinctive requests, while Gua responded properly to 28. By the end of the study, Donald comprehended 68 requests and Gua 58. In both cases, the responses were limited to utterances that they heard frequently, such as "Take Gua's hand" or "Supper's ready," and that, for the most part, were action oriented and did not entail selection of a single object from a group of objects. Many of them (e.g., "Close the drawer") were uttered in a particular context (i.e., after a drawer had just been opened); consequently, the interpretation was greatly simplified. When specific attempts were made to teach Donald and Gua to select an object on command from an arbitrary array of three items, both failed to learn the task, even after 100 training trials.

The next major step in language work with apes was taken by Hayes and Hayes (1951), who also obtained a young female ape from Yerkes and reared it in their home. However, unlike the Kelloggs, the Hayeses had no children of their own and thus devoted their full attention to Viki's development from 3 days to 7 years of age, when she died of viral encephalitis. Extensive psychological testing was carried out with Viki throughout her life and was carefully documented both in writing (Hayes & Hayes, 1951, 1952a, 1953b, 1954; Hayes & Nissen, 1971; Hayes, Thompson, & Hayes, 1953a, 1953b) and through an excellent cinematographic record (Hayes & Hayes, 1950, 1952b, 1953a).

The work with Viki revealed that chimpanzees were capable of far more human-like intellectual feats than previously thought possible. She demonstrated excellent picture recognition and could even imitate actions she saw in photographs. She could sort both photographs and objects into different conceptual categories and expertly employed all manner of household implements, including a needle and thread. One area of great difficulty for Viki was to imitate a series of tabletop tapping motions. Viki could differentiate between one tap and two taps by 3½ years of age, but she never correctly imitated three or four taps, even when tested at 6½ years of age. By comparison, most 3-year-old children could perform this task, and by 4½ years of age all human subjects do so quite easily (Hayes & Nissen, 1971).

Unlike the Kelloggs, Keith and Cathy Hayes made extensive efforts to develop vocal speech in their ape subject. After waiting 5 months for Viki to show some signs of babbling or any progress at all toward speech, the Hayeses decided to begin formal speech training. They began to withhold milk, asking Viki to speak. She was able to produce food barks in anticipation of receiving the milk, but she could not actually speak on command. However, they continued this effort, and at 10 months of age Viki suddenly became able to produce a breathy "ahh" sound whenever she was asked to speak. Viki also spontaneously used this sound to request all manner of things that she desired, but she did not appear to be able to vary the sound to any significant degree. Consequently, the Hayeses began to mold her lips to form an "m," releasing them as Viki said "ahh," thereby enabling her to produce the word "Ma Ma." Viki shortly became able to make this sound by pressing her lips together on her own. As with her previous "ahh" sound, this new word was used for all manner of things that Viki desired and did not appear to function as a name for Cathy Hayes. By a similar process, Viki learned to produce "Papa," "cup," and "up," although there was still no clear evidence that she employed these words to refer to their English referents.

Like Gua, Viki also appeared to understand a large number of phrases in context; however, unlike the Kelloggs, Keith and Cathy Hayes recognized the difficulties of measuring comprehension. Cathy Hayes (1951) observed,

> Of all the questions we are asked by new acquaintances, the one we dread most to hear is: "How many words does Viki understand?" A definite answer is next to impossible for a number of reasons: (1) Failure to obey a command is not a test of comprehension in our contrary Viki. (2) She understands in a fluctuating way—some days she "knows" a word perfectly, other days not at all. (3) Any list of understood words can be endlessly lengthened by including variations of the basic form. (4) Almost any expression includes a great deal more than the words themselves; and these other elements of the language complex—situation, gesture, the inflection, pitch, and loudness of the speaker's voice—are so bound up with the words as we commonly use them, that it is very hard to say for sure just what an animal (or a person) is responding to. (p. 224)

In some cases, Viki responded to utterances if they fit the situation or the expected routine, but if they did not, she gave no evidence of comprehension. Thus, it seemed that the situation cued Viki to listen for certain commands, and, within a given situation, once she expected to hear a certain set of requests ("Take your diaper off," "Get on the potty," "Flush the potty," etc.), it was possible to vary the order of the commands and still have Viki respond appropriately. However, if a request occurred that was completely out of context (e.g., "Do you want to go to the show?" in the midst of the potty routine), Viki gave no evidence of understanding what was said. Attempts to teach her to respond reliably to a number of different alternatives ("Show me your nose, your eyes, your ears," etc.) met with the same defeat that Kellogg and Kellogg (1933) had experienced with Gua.

The next major effort to inculcate language in an ape was undertaken by Gardner and Gardner (1971). Taking their cue from Viki's difficulties with vocal sounds, the Gardners decided to teach Washoe ASL (American sign language for the deaf). The Gardners obtained Washoe from the wild when she was approximately 1 year of age. Washoe, a common chimpanzee (*Pan troglodytes*), was raised by student caretakers in a house trailer located in the Gardners' back yard. No one was allowed to use spoken language around Washoe, only signs. One or more students were with Washoe during her waking hours, and signing was integrated into all daily activities. Washoe could hear perfectly well; however, the Gardners reasoned that she might well have a great deal more neurological control over her hands than over her vocal-laryngeal apparatus and that, if exposed to signs at an early age, she might acquire them spontaneously, as do hearing children of deaf parents. This hunch proved to be spectacularly successful. Although Washoe rarely acquired signs simply by observing her caretakers, as do human children, the Gardners could nonetheless teach signs by molding Washoe's hands into the proper configuration, as hands are far more manipulable than vocal tracts. By 36 months of age Washoe produced 85 different signs in the appropriate contextual situations and had begun to combine them as well. Rarely, however, did she make subject-verb (SV) or verb-object (VO) combinations. Instead, she tended to add words like "hurry," "more," "up," "food," "please," and "gimme" to nouns.

The Gardners' approach was taken up by one of their students with four additional apes (Fouts, 1973, 1975) and by others with gorillas (Patterson, 1978) and orangutans (Miles, 1983). These additional studies supported the Gardners' initial conclusions that signs were much more readily acquired by apes than spoken language, that molding greatly enhanced the rate of sign acquisition, and that apes generalized their signs to exemplars not utilized during training.

Shortly after the Gardners' breakthrough with Washoe, David Premack (1971) and Duane Rumbaugh (Rumbaugh, Gill, & von Glasersfeld, 1973) reported that nonvocal symbol systems effectively permitted chimpanzees to "talk." Premack (1971) utilized magnetized plastic chips placed on a metal board outside the cage of his subject, Sarah. Rumbaugh, von Glasersfeld, et al. (1973) used geometric symbols embossed on keys that lighted when depressed by their subject, Lana. Unlike Washoe, Lana was taught to string symbols together from her earliest training; hence, the majority of her utterances exhibited a sentence-like quality and were termed "stock sentences" by Rumbaugh. However, Lana also began to form sentences that she had not been trained to produce. In the early 1970s, it seemed that, regardless of the type of symbol system employed, if apes were given some alternative to speech, they were able to learn symbols.

Rumbaugh's approach was utilized by a group of researchers in Japan (Asano, Kojima, Matsuzawa, Kubota, & Murofushi, 1982). Working with a chimpanzee named Ai, they replicated Rumbaugh's work on color and object classification with a similar lexical keyboard system (Matsuzawa, 1985a). They also found that Ai developed spontaneous word-order preferences (Matsuzawa, 1989), that she was able to label numbers up to six (Matsuzawa, 1985b; Matsuzawa, Asano, Kubota, & Murofushi, 1986), and that she could construct her symbols from the elements of which they were composed (Matsuzawa, 1989).

However, language work with apes soon became the recipient of a strong critique. Premack's subject Sarah's competence with linguistic primitives could in many instances be reduced to simpler tasks. Although Premack attributed concepts such as "name of," "negation," etc. to many of Sarah's feats, close analysis of the actual problems faced by Sarah revealed that conditional match-to-sample strategies could often account for her performance (Savage-Rumbaugh & Rumbaugh, 1979; Savage-Rumbaugh, Rumbaugh, & Boysen, 1980; Terrace, 1979).

Additionally, the tasks presented to Sarah were noncommunicative in nature; consequently, the skills she exhibited could never be tested in the service of communication. Sarah's "language" was embodied as an abstract formal system without communicative value. At best, it illustrated that apes are capable of solving complex conceptual tasks, but the relation between Sarah's performance on such tasks and language as utilized by human speakers remained vague.

Lana's sentences were attacked by Terrace, Straub, Bever, and Seidenberg (1977) and by Thompson and Church (1980), who maintained that Lana had acquired, not a syntactic system, but rather sets of chained associative responses that could be interchanged at various branching points. Terrace et al. (1977) demonstrated that pigeons could learn a four-element associative chain (A → B → C → D) and implied that Lana's communications could be interpreted as a more elaborate version of the same associative process (Straub, Seidenberg, Bever, & Terrace, 1979; Straub & Terrace, 1981). Pate and Rumbaugh (1983) responded by presenting sentences constructed by Lana for which associative models could not readily account;

nonetheless, it was difficult to grant Lana full communicative competence as she also generated sentences that were semantically uninterpretable (Savage-Rumbaugh et al., 1980).

The strongest attack, however, was that leveled against the Gardners by Terrace et al. (1979). After attempting to replicate the Gardners' work with a chimpanzee named Nim, Terrace et al. concluded that Washoe's "language-like" utterances could be accounted for by attempts to imitate the experimenter's utterances. On reviewing videotapes of Nim's signing sessions, Terrace et al. demonstrated that many of his multisign utterances were preceded by similar utterances on the part of his teachers. Terrace also analyzed segments of a film distributed by the Gardners, in which he identified the existence of the same phenomenon in Washoe's behavior.

Since the Gardners had no record of the signs directed to Washoe by experimenters, they were unable to provide data to refute these claims satisfactorily. Instead, they focused on replicating their work with additional chimpanzee subjects (Gardner, Gardner, & Van Cantfort, 1989). In an exhaustive account of this work, however, they failed to mention either the issue of "imitation" or Terrace's critique, and they made no attempt to determine whether utterances directed toward the chimpanzees affected their ensuing signs. They did show that their new subjects (Moja, Dar, and Tatu) passed blind tests similar to those given to Washoe. Such tests clearly implied that the chimpanzees could recognize and respond to photographs by producing the appropriate sign under conditions that precluded cuing. However, Terrace et al. (1979) never challenged the validity of these tests—their critique was directed at Washoe's ability to form semantically meaningful and grammatically correct sentences without imitating her caretakers. Unfortunately, the Gardners continued to fail to address this issue straightforwardly.

Fouts, Fouts, and Van Cantfort (1989) have attempted to respond to these critiques by studying the signs that Loulis (Washoe's adopted infant) has acquired from other signing chimpanzees and by looking at gestures within the second group of chimpanzees raised by the Gardners (Fouts & Fouts, 1989; Fouts, Fouts, & Schoenfeld, 1984). While this work suggested that the apes signed to one another with no human present, it was not altogether clear how these gestures differed in function from the many nonverbal gestures and "body language" that the chimpanzees employ as well. Fout's analysis focused on the issues of addressee, number of signs, and number of conversational turns rather than on sign content, leaving open the questions of why the chimpanzees gesture to one another and what type of communicational gain they achieve through the use of such gestures.

Shortly before the controversies outlined above emerged, the first language study with co-reared apes (Savage-Rumbaugh, 1979; Savage-Rumbaugh & Rumbaugh, 1978) began with two young chimpanzees, Sherman and Austin. Unlike all previous ape studies, the subjects in this case were males. Moreover, they were maintained in social housing (with two additional chimpanzees) throughout the evening and early morning hours as well as whenever they were not engaged in linguistic tasks, rather than being reared by human caretakers or being left alone. The decision to rear Sherman and Austin as members of a social group was taken to ensure the development of appropriate social bonds and behaviors characteristic of their species and to avoid the difficulties that apes reared solely among humans encountered on being reintroduced to members of their own species.

The Sherman and Austin project incorporated the lexical keyboard system used with Lana; however, the problems encountered as a result of Lana's "stock phrases" were avoided by training single words rather than combinations. The problems of imitation were overcome by focusing on peer communications rather than experimenter/subject communications (Savage-Rumbaugh, Rumbaugh, & Boysen, 1978a, 1978b). Additionally, since the experimenter's utterances took place at the lexical keyboard, a permanent record was created of the input to the apes along with their output. This permitted an ongoing, accurate measure of the level and influence of imitation, which proved to be very low and well within the range shown by children (Greenfield & Savage-Rumbaugh, 1984). More important, the issues of intentional communication, reference, and semantics were treated as primary and those of syntax as secondary. Finally, because of the emphasis on peer communication, receptive competence was an important part of the research effort from the outset. All previous studies of ape language had taken receptive competence more or less for granted, assuming that it was extant whenever production appeared. Nonetheless, no systematic, controlled measures of receptive capacities were taken by the Gardners or by Terrace and his colleagues. Consequently, assertions that Washoe and Nim understood far more than they produced were unsubstantiated by data.

The work with Sherman and Austin quickly revealed that productive and receptive competencies were not necessarily synonymous (Savage-Rumbaugh, 1984c; Savage-Rumbaugh & Rumbaugh, 1978; Savage-Rumbaugh et al., 1978a, 1978b, 1980). In order to demonstrate comprehension, it was necessary for the ape, as listener, to engage in a set of actions that corresponded properly to each utterance. The reward, which was more closely linked to symbol use during production, vanished when the ape had to listen to and carry out the requests of others. "Language use" had to become more than producing symbols for "tickle" or "time-eat" and having one's wishes granted in response. Comprehension required responding appropriately when someone else indicated that *she* wanted to be tickled or that *he* wanted a banana.

By beginning with single words, emphasizing receptive competence, minimizing imitation, and focusing on peer communication among co-reared male chimpanzees, the Sherman and Austin project began on a very different footing than any of its predecessors had. Consequently, the data produced by this effort did not come under as severe an attack as earlier studies had. However, neither did this study receive the attention given to those others. In part, many researchers erroneously viewed it as a replication of the Lana effort. Others (Seidenberg & Pettito, 1979, 1987) failed to recognize the value of experimentally demonstrating the range of competencies required for single word use and questioned the relevance of such demonstrations for language (Sugarman, 1983). Still others (Sebeok & Umiker-Sebeok, 1980) worried about possible cuing. Each of these issues was systematically addressed (Rumbaugh, 1981; Rumbaugh & Savage-Rumbaugh, 1980; Savage-Rumbaugh, 1986, 1987; Savage-Rumbaugh, Romski, Sevcik, & Pate, 1983; Savage-Rumbaugh & Rumbaugh, 1982; Savage-Rumbaugh & Sevcik, 1984).

The work with Sherman and Austin demonstrated the following: (*a*) apes can comprehend symbols, but production does not lead spontaneously to comprehension; (*b*) in order to function "representationally," the symbols learned by apes must become decontextualized and freed for use in novel situations; (*c*) apes can use symbols to communicate with each other *if* they develop skills of joint attention and *if* their environment places a premium on cooperation; (*d*) apes can make informative statements regarding their *intended* future actions; and (*e*) referential comprehension and usage are *prerequisites* to the development of syntactic competence (Savage-Rumbaugh, 1982, 1984a, 1984c, 1986, 1988; Savage-Rumbaugh, Pate, Lawson, Smith, & Rosenbaum, 1983). However, by this time, the field of psychology had become centered on cognitive models that assumed that any similarities that exist between human and ape cognition are of little value unless apes can be shown to be capable of syntax (Klix, 1982; Macphail, 1982, 1985).

Nonetheless, work with Sherman and Austin firmly established chimpanzees' ability to use symbols in a representational manner (Savage-Rumbaugh, 1981) and their ability to use a symbol system for intraspecies communication (Savage-Rumbaugh, 1986). The controls against cuing used in these studies were extensive and left little doubt that "Clever Hans" could be excised from the data by sound experimental procedures.[1] This work also

---

[1] "Clever Hans" was a horse who supposedly learned to count. However, it was eventually discovered that the horse was responding to unintentional nonverbal cues given off by his trainer. The horse merely struck the ground with his foot until the trainer signaled

indicated that the ape's capacity for representational processes extended far beyond symbols. Sherman and Austin recognized themselves on television and asked to have the television turned on so they could see themselves, engaged in imaginary play with puppets, attempted to "talk" using the same breathy sound employed by Viki, sorted photographs, played with their shadows, learned to operate a slide projector, and began using a joystick to touch a target after only a few demonstrations.

The next major advance in the field of ape language occurred when a new species, the bonobo, was exposed to language. Bonobos had not been utilized in previous studies because they are extremely rare both in the wild and in captivity. Bonobos are indigenous only to Zaire, where they are vanishing rapidly as the forest is depleted for food. They have no regularly patrolled national park, and adults are often eaten by local people and infants sold as pets. Robert Yerkes (Yerkes & Learned, 1925), the first psychologist to have investigated the intellectual and communicative capacity of this species, concluded that the single bonobo that he studied was considerably more intelligent and communicative than any chimpanzee.

Bonobos are more affiliative than common chimpanzees; they also tend to engage in upright posture frequently and to use eye contact, iconic gestures, and vocalization more frequently than other apes during intraspecies communication (Savage & Bakeman, 1978; Savage-Rumbaugh, 1984b; Savage-Rumbaugh & Wilkerson, 1978; Savage, Wilkerson, & Bakeman, 1977). Unlike common chimpanzees, bonobo females are sexually receptive throughout their cycle and utilize sexual activity to form and maintain social bonds. Wild groups tend to contain a nearly equal number of males and females, and food sharing and co-feeding, especially with plant foods, are very common. Among the nonhuman primates, bonobos manifest an unusually high degree of interindividual tolerance; mothers permit other adults, both male and female, to carry and play with infants, and males share food with infants frequently (Kano, 1980, 1982; Kuroda, 1980, 1984).

The first bonobo exposed to language was Matata, a wild-caught adult female. In spite of intensive efforts across a 4-year period, Matata failed to master any representational use of symbols (Savage-Rumbaugh, Rumbaugh, & McDonald, 1985). However, her son, Kanzi, began to acquire symbols by observing the efforts to train his mother, even though he was not rewarded for doing so and no efforts were made to teach him. Not only did he learn the geometric symbols that were so difficult for his mother, but he also began to evince an understanding of spoken language. By 5 years of age

---

him to stop. The horse's response was simple in that all it required was either to continue striking the ground or to stop. Consequently, such cues as relaxing the shoulders when the correct count had been reached sufficed to indicate to the horse that it was time to stop.

he spontaneously produced combinations that revealed a sensitivity to English word order as well as the capacity to invent and assign grammatical rules (Greenfield & Savage-Rumbaugh, 1990, 1991). Kanzi's rearing and the nature of his language use are described in more detail in Chapters IV and V. More than any previous ape, the nature and scope of Kanzi's language acquisition has paralleled that of the human child, suggesting that the capacity for language is much more highly evolved in the bonobo than field studies have revealed to date.

In Chapter II of this *Monograph* we review the issues surrounding the manner in which symbols come to function as referential vehicles and provide an overview of the literature on language comprehension in children. Chapter III addresses the question of how it is that apes come to learn symbols without training and relates observations on apes to language acquisition in normal children. The underrated importance of comprehension is heavily emphasized here; we attempt to show how speech is laid down on a vast substratum of real-world knowledge by caretakers who both act to evoke that knowledge and simultaneously map it through speech input. In Chapter IV, we discuss the "innateness debate" and respond to the view that man and man alone is biologically equipped for the cognitive task of language. The issue of human vocal speech capacity and why it seems to be unique to our species is also addressed. The methodology and the results of the current study are presented in Chapters V and VI, respectively. In the final chapter, we attempt to place these findings within a broader evolutionary perspective, and we also offer partial guidelines for translating our current understanding of cognitive and linguistic processes into a phylogenetic and evolutionary framework.

II. THE CAPACITY TO USE WORDS AS REFERENTS

The capacity to use words to refer to events, objects, locations, relations, etc. is so ubiquitous a part of human language that it was treated in a peripheral manner in many of the early accounts of language acquisition (Bloom, 1973; Brown, 1973; Greenfield & Smith, 1976; McNeil, 1970). Nonetheless, philosophers have noted that reference is a fundamental component of language and that any comprehensive theory of language acquisition must eventually address this difficult issue (Gauker, 1990; Quine, 1960). It remains to be explained how it is that a child (or an ape for that matter) determines which bits of sounds are words and where one word begins and another ends and also how children come to understand that words refer to particular objects, events, emotions, etc., even though adults fail to set up specific, invariable relations between what they say and what is happening in the world.

Quine (1960) posed the "dilemma" of reference as one of needing to determine which of the myriad properties of objects is being denoted by a given word; for example, how is the child to know that the word "apple" denotes the whole fruit, as opposed to its color, its texture, its taste, etc. However, there is more to understanding the process of reference than Quine's "dilemma." Even if it is true that children have, or develop, a bias to interpret initial terms as referring to whole objects (Golinkoff, 1991), there still remains the greater problem that the ways in which a word is used at times A, B, C, etc. are not the same. For example, our data reveal people saying such diverse things to Kanzi as, "He's having a ball," "No, you cannot have a ball now," "Where's your ball?" "Kanzi hid his ball," "Kanzi, don't bite the ball," "Yes, I'll slap your ball," "Do you want to play ball keep-away?" "Kanzi left his ball at the A-frame," etc. In many of these cases no ball is present, so the issue of how the properties of a ball are to be paired with the word *ball* is replaced by that of ascertaining how it is that Kanzi knows that it is any property whatsoever of a ball that is being referenced by such diverse productions.

These issues have only recently begun to be addressed systematically by child language researchers (Bates, Thal, & Marchman, 1991; Golinkoff, 1991; Lock, 1980, 1991). While there is a growing consensus that subcomponents of language use and acquisition such as intentionality, rule learning, imitation, fast associative mapping, and sequencing need to be better understood, there is as yet no generally accepted explanation of the conditions that are sufficient and necessary for language acquisition. Other than the need for exposure to a language-using model, there is little agreement as to what is required for a child to learn that words and sentences refer to a complex and shifting panoply of objects, events, places, emotions, etc.

In some regards, the issue of "reference" has been more clearly addressed by studies of apes (Gauker, 1990; Savage-Rumbaugh, 1986, 1990) precisely because one may not assume that apes use words in the same manner as children. Consequently, it has been necessary to devise means of comparing the relative capacities of ape and child in a manner that objectifies and defines *reference* in a measurable way (Savage-Rumbaugh & Brakke, 1990).

Adopting a strict view of reference, Gauker (1990) has argued that no single set of relations can be said to hold between a symbol and an event, object, action, etc. Indeed, virtually every sentence constructs a *new set of relations* between words and the world. Gauker insists, therefore, that "reference" cannot be viewed as a set of word-referent relations that a child should memorize, as if she were learning a dictionary.

Gauker suggests abandoning the concept of reference, offering in its place a neural-net account of language acquisition. The concept of reference is less problematic, however, if we view the use of words as an attempt to bring about a certain behavior or set of beliefs in the listener. Word-use skills are seen as a set of abilities that the child utilizes, based on her past experiences with words, to bring about desired future events and/or beliefs in others (which presumably will themselves lead to desired actions at some point). It is the link between previous perceived utterances of a word such as *apple* and the events surrounding its usage, in all their variability, that determines when and how a person will use *apple* in the future. This perspective assumes that children (and apes) remember, contrast, and compare usages they have heard across different instances. From this process of comparison arises a "percept" of acceptable uses that defines "expected outcomes" for each word or group of words. When novel outcomes are desired, they lead to the production of novel utterances by pulling bits and pieces of utterances associated with previous similar outcomes together to form the new utterance. This "new utterance" is then reformulated according to grammatical rules so that it can be easily processed by listeners, who need some rules as they try to process information that flows rapidly through a fading auditory channel.

As Gauker notes, such a process-oriented perspective of reference has been utilized to describe the behavior of apes as they learn symbols (Savage-Rumbaugh, 1986, 1991). This perspective has the advantage of externalizing the symbol acquisition process so that one can measure what the ape knows about the symbols it is using at various points in time, rather than simply waiting to see if an ape can produce grammatically correct sentences in order to determine if it "has" language, as Terrace et al. (1979) attempted to do. In other words, if one focuses on the kinds of things that apes have learned to accomplish with symbols and/or combinations of symbols, rather than assessing the nature of their internalized "referents," one then has a direct basis for measuring linguistic competence.

Consequently, work with apes has revealed that, when they are taught simple "namelike" associations such as "see a banana, make the sign for banana," they display extremely limited symbol use. This is because associative, "namelike" training does not enable them to encounter the variety of effects that symbols can have in normal linguistic exchanges. For example, apes trained in this way do not respond appropriately to messages of others regarding the state of the bananas, the absence of the bananas, the location of the bananas, etc. (Savage-Rumbaugh, 1981; Savage-Rumbaugh, Pate, et al., 1983; Savage-Rumbaugh, Romski, et al., 1983). Therefore, the fact that apes acquire "namelike" associations implies neither that they can use such "names" appropriately in a wide variety of linguistic exchanges nor that they understand these names as used by others (Savage-Rumbaugh, 1984a, 1984c; Savage-Rumbaugh & Brakke, 1990). Even the ability to produce associative responses to different exemplars of the same item illustrates only the ape's capacity for *perceptual* generalization (Savage-Rumbaugh et al., 1980). Perceptual generalization cannot tell us about the linguistic knowledge associated with symbol usages in typical conversation because it is not the ability to "name" different exemplars that is critical to language but rather the ability to understand that a word such as *ball* has a common meaning whether one says "It's my ball," "Go hide the ball," or "Where did you leave the ball?"

It is easy to train an ape to say *apple* in order to get an apple but difficult to teach it to use *apple* to describe a food that it is not allowed to eat, a food that it sees someone else eating, a food that it does not like, a food that is found in a particular location, etc. Such usages, common in children, are seen in apes only when symbols are "decontextualized" from the events associated with symbol learning. It then becomes possible for the ape to recognize that the symbol *apple* can be employed to indicate something about a particular fruit that has little to do with the "reward value" of receiving an apple.

When many symbols become decontextualized, any new symbols that are encountered provoke a search for a "common kernel referent" of sorts.

That is, the principle that each symbol is associated with only part of the situation in which it occurs is derived by children and can be derived by apes. Once language learners develop means of determining the "kernel referent," new symbols will be assigned to the "most likely" new referent on the first trial. Thus, children will tend to pair new words with new objects when the new words are uttered in the presence of a mixture of old and new objects. Once children have learned that words are often associated with whole objects and that each different object has a different name, it becomes self-evident to them that "known words" refer to the recognizable objects and unknown words to new objects (Golinkoff, 1991).

Like children, once Sherman and Austin were sufficiently sophisticated in their use of symbols to decontextualize new symbols from the events immediately following them, they could also assign novel names to new foods on a first-trial basis (Savage-Rumbaugh, 1986). This ability to assign a new word to a new object rapidly has been termed "fast mapping" in human children. When such fast mapping occurs, it can be concluded that the child or ape has recognized that the world can be profitably parceled into symbol units for the purposes of communication.

It may seem surprising that an ape or a child would assign a new name to a new object. However, if one looks at what must be naturally occurring during *comprehension,* it becomes clear that children (and apes in certain experimental rearing environments) are being constantly bombarded with new symbols and must attempt to assign appropriate referents to them in some manner. Hence, once children and apes have learned that the world is parceled into symbols, it is probable that, on being confronted with new objects, events, etc., they will invent new symbols of their own.

LANGUAGE COMPREHENSION IN CHILDREN

Single Word Comprehension

Although the processes of symbol acquisition and decontextualization take place in the receptive domain in normal children, the vast majority of studies of child language have focused exclusively on production, owing to the difficulties of determining exactly what very young children comprehend. Nonetheless, to the extent that they can be carried out appropriately, studies of receptive capacities should provide a more accurate picture of a child's language skills than studies of production. Production requires a complex orchestration of planned motor skills whose limited level of development is likely to make it difficult for the young child to demonstrate her full knowledge. As anyone who has learned a second language is aware, one's comprehension can readily outpace one's productive capacity.

Studies of comprehension have focused on both single words (Benedict, 1979; Cuvo & Riva, 1980; Goldin-Meadow, Seligman, & Gelman, 1976; Golinkoff, Hirsh-Pasek, Cauley, & Gordon, 1987; Huttenlocher, 1974; Snyder, Bates, & Bretherton, 1981) and syntax (Bates et al., 1984; Chapman & Kohn, 1978; Chapman & Miller, 1975; de Villiers & de Villiers, 1973; Fraser, Bellugi, & Brown, 1963; Golinkoff et al., 1987; Hirsh-Pasek & Golinkoff, 1991; Lempert, 1978; Lovell & Dixon, 1967; Roberts, 1983; Sachs & Truswell, 1978; Shipley, Smith, & Gleitman, 1969; Strohner & Nelson, 1974). Without exception, studies looking at the acquisition of single words in natural environments have found that comprehension precedes and outpaces production, frequently by a rather large gap. The precedence of comprehension at this stage exists regardless of whether investigators utilize maternal interviews alone (Snyder et al., 1981), maternal interviews accompanied by natural observation (Benedict, 1979), or actual tests with an array of objects (Goldin-Meadow et al., 1976) as measurement devices.

Children begin to show evidence of single-word comprehension around 9 months of age and by 1-1 comprehend 50 words while producing less than 10 (Benedict, 1979; Snyder et al., 1981). By 2 years of age, children can reportedly handle an array of 70 different objects by selecting the correct one on request if properly attentive and motivated (Goldin-Meadow et al., 1976). Noun comprehension generally precedes verb comprehension, and children with the highest rates of noun comprehension also evince early language production. However, children often comprehend words that they do not use, especially verbs. This discrepancy seems to result naturally from the fact that caretakers typically use verbs to initiate action on the child's part (e.g., "Wash your hands" or "Go potty"). The child needs to understand such terms but has little reason to use them to initiate action in others.

Generally, investigators have maintained that, before a word qualifies as "comprehended," it must be understood in more than one context; however, formal tests that include controls for inadvertent cuing and proper randomization have yet to be employed. Golinkoff et al. (1987) recently introduced a new method of measuring language comprehension that entails monitoring a child's glance in response to linguistic input. While they have employed controls against inadvertent cuing, Golinkoff et al. have not, however, used this technique to map the extent of single-word comprehension; rather, they have sought simply to validate the technique before applying it to issues of syntactic comprehension.

While there is agreement that single-word comprehension precedes single-word production, there is uncertainty regarding the degree to which these two skills overlap. Snyder et al. (1981) found that the correlation between productive and receptive vocabularies was only .29. However, Goldin-Meadow et al. (1976) found that "there was no child who was correct on any given item on the production test and failed that same item on the comprehension test" (p. 193). This discrepancy can be accounted for by the fact that some words are imitated in context but not used in a truly innovative manner. Children imitate words they do not know; however, words that are part of a child's truly functional vocabulary are well comprehended before they are employed in the service of communication.

The finding that comprehension precedes production at the single-word level is robust and apparently holds for language-delayed subjects (Gibson & Ingram, 1983), as well as apes (Savage-Rumbaugh et al., 1986), as long as language is not trained but rather acquired naturally through observing others. In fact, under such circumstances, both language-delayed subjects and apes evince a much greater discrepancy between comprehension and production than normal children, presumably because the motor skills involved make production a difficult task for language-delayed subjects and an almost impossible one for apes. Gibson and Ingram (1983) found that, while a language-delayed child at 2 years of age had a receptive vocabulary of 183 words, his functional productive vocabulary was only eight words. Similarly, a 2-year-old bonobo reared in a naturalistic language environment was found to comprehend 70 words while producing only four (Savage-Rumbaugh et al., 1986).

Although production lags behind comprehension in all studies of naturalistic language acquisition, this does not seem to be true when direct attempts are made to teach words. Whether the subject population consists of normal children (Rice, 1980), language-delayed children (Cuvo & Riva, 1980), or apes (Savage-Rumbaugh, 1986), attempts to teach words have typically led to a very different language acquisition profile. In such cases, production appears first, and comprehension may not occur at all. This is because it is the productive response that is trained, as such responses are more readily elicited and measured than comprehension. Consequently, subjects in such tasks learn associatively rather than referentially and do not generalize productive responses to either novel contexts or comprehension tasks unless they entered the training task with extant comprehension skills (Guess & Baer, 1973; Rice, 1980; Romski & Sevcik, 1991; Romski, Sevcik, & Pate, 1988; Savage-Rumbaugh, 1986).

The fact that such subjects can produce a name yet cannot select that named item from an array on request has been taken by some as evidence for the separateness of the comprehension and the production subsystems. However, in order to arrive at word comprehension under normal circumstances, a child (or an ape) must understand what is being said in a number of complex settings and determine the common content that permits use of the same word. This decoding process necessitates referential understanding and decontextualization in order to assess the intent of the speaker (Savage-Rumbaugh, 1991). Production training does not foster the referential decoding processes; instead, it causes the subject to attempt to remember what to say when shown a particular object and consequently results in minimal transfer to other situations or communicative processes.

By contrast, when training emphasizes comprehension, particularly comprehension in seminatural settings, production occurs as a spontaneous by-product of such training (Oviatt, 1980; Rice, Buhr, & Nemeth, 1990; Rice & Woodsmall, 1988; Savage-Rumbaugh, 1991; Whitehurst & Valdez-Menchaca, 1988). This phenomenon is quite robust and seems to hold even for unconventional methods of word acquisition (Oviatt, 1980; Rice et al., 1990) as well as for different species (Savage-Rumbaugh, 1991). Interestingly, Whitehurst and Valdez-Menchaca (1986) found that, while comprehension of new words (selected from another language) emerged spontaneously in seminatural settings, production of these words did not occur unless reinforcement was provided, suggesting that some of the apparent discrepancies between these two subsystems are motivational rather than functional. The fact that comprehension did *not* require reinforcement supports the view that comprehension is the driving force underlying all language acquisition and that the motivation for comprehension lies in the listener's desire to predict what the speaker is going to do as a consequence of having produced a particular utterance (for a more complete account of this view, see Savage-Rumbaugh, 1991).

Sentence Comprehension

Comprehension of sentences has proved to be more difficult to measure than single-word comprehension; consequently, conclusions have differed as a result of the techniques selected. Most studies of sentence comprehension have attempted to determine the order in which children master the skills of imitation, comprehension, and production as well as the order in which they come to comprehend various grammatical constructions (Bever, 1970; Cocking & McHale, 1981; de Villiers & de Villiers, 1973; Fraser et al., 1963; Golinkoff et al., 1987; Hirsh-Pasek & Golinkoff, 1991; Lempert, 1978; Lovell & Dixon, 1967; Roberts, 1983; Sachs & Truswell, 1978; Shipley et al., 1969). Other studies have been more theoretically oriented, focusing on the kinds of processing strategies that underlie the comprehension process (Bates et al., 1984; Chapman & Kohn, 1978; Chapman & Miller, 1975; Hakuta, 1982; Slobin & Bever, 1982; Strohner & Nelson, 1974). The emphasis on processing strategies, rather than order of skill emergence, reflects attempts to respond to claims regarding the existence of language universals (Pinker, 1981).

A number of different techniques have been used to measure sentence comprehension, including requiring children to interpret line drawings or photographs (Fraser et al., 1963), asking them to act out sentences with puppets (Bever, 1970), and measuring direction of gaze in response to video material depicting competing sentence interpretations (Golinkoff et al., 1987). In a critique of these different methodologies, Cocking and McHale (1981) demonstrated that picture-based tasks were more difficult for children than object-based tasks. In addition, the only studies that employed any form of control for inadvertent cuing were those by Golinkoff et al. (1987) and Hirsh-Pasek and Golinkoff (1991). When children were asked to select objects from an array and carry out a sentence, the items in the array were often limited to those that were appropriate to the sentence. No investigators videotaped the responses of the subjects. Typically, observers simply scored each child as correct or incorrect while observing his or her response, and frequently only one observer was employed. In some cases the mother was asked to present the sentence, while in other cases experimenters were employed to do so.

Only Shipley et al. (1969) attempted to provide a running description of what children actually did in response to sentences. They used audiotape to provide a narrative account of the child's actions. Two observers then listened to the tape and, on the basis of the description they heard, judged whether the child responded accurately. As a result of this unusual attention to detail, the report of Shipley et al., unlike those of other investigators, notes that children between 18 and 33 months of age do not always respond directly to the sentence as presented. Sometimes subjects responded by doing something that was not related to the sentence before carrying out the request. Sometimes they merely looked at or touched an item corresponding to a key word in the sentence, sometimes they gave a verbal reply in place of responding to the sentence, sometimes they repeated the sentence, and sometimes they made a response that was relevant to what was said but not completely accurate. And, of course, sometimes they responded appropriately to the sentence.

Within the age range studied by Shipley et al. (1969), two different developmental levels emerged. The youngest subjects tended to be holophrastic; that is, when they listened to a whole sentence and responded, they treated the sentence as a word. When given a chance to respond to single-word commands versus well-formed commands embedded in complete sentence frames, they were much more likely to respond to the single words and ignore the sentences. By contrast, telegraphic speakers (generally those producing multiword utterances) tended to respond more often and more appropriately when they were presented with well-formed sentences than when they heard only single words.

Most of the work on sentence comprehension has shown that English-speaking children between 2 and 3 years of age respond appropriately to active sentences and are sensitive to word-order cues (Bates et al., 1984; de Villiers & de Villiers, 1973; Golinkoff et al., 1987; Hirsh-Pasek & Golinkoff,

1991; Lovell & Dixon, 1967; Roberts, 1983; Sachs & Truswell, 1978; Strohner & Nelson, 1974). Comprehension of the passive construction is much more difficult and seems to develop piece by piece between 4 and 7 years of age (Bever, 1970; de Villiers & de Villiers, 1973; Fraser et al., 1963; Lempert, 1978; Lovell & Dixon, 1967; Roberts, 1983; Sachs & Truswell, 1978; Strohner & Nelson, 1974).

Other grammatical markers have received less attention; however, the work of Lovell and Dixon (1967) found that affirmative-negative utterances ("The girl is cooking"/"The girl is not cooking") were readily comprehended by most children at 2-6. By 3–4 years of age most children comprehended subject-object distinctions when they were presented in the active voice ("The train bumps the car"/"The car bumps the train") and the distinction between the present progressive and the future ("The girl is drinking"/ "The girl will drink"). By 5–6 years most children reliably responded to mass noun and count noun distinctions ("some chicken"/"a chicken"), the singular-plural distinction as marked by third-person pronouns ("his wagon"/"their wagon"), the present progressive versus past tense distinction ("The paint is spilling"/"The paint spilled"), and the singular-plural distinction as marked by the copula ("is"/"are"). The oldest subjects in this study were 7 years of age, and even by that age the majority of them did not show comprehension of the subject-object distinction in the passive voice ("The car is bumped by the train"/"The train is bumped by the car") or comprehension of the indirect-direct object word-order distinction ("The girl shows the cat the dog"/"The girl shows the dog the cat"). Without exception, all the tested grammatical structures were imitated before they were comprehended, and they were comprehended before they were produced (Fraser et al., 1963; Lovell & Dixon, 1967). However, only two pairs of sentences were tested for each grammatical construction, and the test materials consisted of line drawings. Conceivably, tests that are less abstract could reveal comprehension of some of these structures at earlier ages.

Using mean length of utterance (MLU) rather than age as the independent variable, de Villiers & de Villiers (1973) found that children with an MLU between 1 and 1.5 were unable to use word order at all in sentence comprehension tasks. Those with an MLU between 1.6 and 3 could comprehend word-order distinctions presented in the active voice but not in the passive voice. However, when MLU reached 3, reversible passives were comprehended. Children who have attained an MLU of 1.5 are producing a large number of multiword utterances that appear to follow the constraints of English word order rather closely; thus, de Villiers and de Villiers contend that production of word-order constraints *precedes* comprehension. Similarly, testing children with MLUs of 1.8, 2.4, and 2.9, Chapman and Miller (1975) concluded that grammatical production precedes comprehension.

The conflicting findings regarding the relative timing of comprehension and production skills with respect to word order appear to arise from differences in the measurement of production. De Villiers and de Villiers (1973) did not test productive competence directly but rather compared performance on a comprehension task (which was tested) with MLU. Children with an MLU of 1.5 are producing multiword utterances; however, such utterances rarely include full SVO (subject-verb-object) constructions. Instead, most multiword utterances consist of SV, VO, or SO constructions. By contrast, sentence comprehension tests of word order require the child to appreciate the full SVO construction, a much more difficult task. Chapman and Miller (1975) did test for both production and comprehension; however, they counted incomplete productions (such as SV, VO, or SO constructions) as correct responses as long as these constructions followed English word order. In their comprehension task, however, complete SVO understanding was required.

The apparent conflict between the majority of studies—which have found that comprehension precedes production at the multiword level as well as at the single-word level—and those that have concluded the opposite seems to be a function of whether production requires full SVO sentences or whether partial sentences are acceptable. When partial sentences are counted as correct only for production, production appears to precede comprehension. However, when similar requirements are used for both skills, comprehension is found to precede production without exception.

A number of investigators (Bates et al., 1984; Bloom, 1978; Chapman & Kohn, 1978; Chapman & Miller, 1975) have noted that appropriate comprehension may be facilitated by semantic strategies (meaning relations) or event probabilities rather than word order and that these factors often coincide in the natural setting, thus providing "multiple cues" to sentence interpretation. The notion of "language universals" as advanced by the field of linguistics has raised the issue of which of the strategies outlined above young children use as they learn to comprehend language. Pinker (1981) has argued that, "for case inflected languages, children will utter sentences in the dominant word order, and will use the dominant word order as a cue in comprehending sentences, before they have mastered their language's morphology" (p. 78).

On this view, it is the innate structure, part of the universal linguistic heritage of our species, that permits children to interpret language. Such linguistic universals "bootstrap" the entrance into the linguistic system, thereby permitting the child to gain a toehold that will allow him ultimately to decode the syntactic nuances that characterize his particular language. Cross-linguistic studies do not tend to support this view (Bates et al., 1984; Hakuta, 1982; Slobin & Bever, 1982). Hakuta (1982) found that word order and inflectional cues are acquired simultaneously by young Japanese children, thus ruling out the primacy of word order suggested by Pinker. Slobin and Bever (1982) found that Hungarian children acquire the nominative/ accusative distinction by 2-6 but do not acquire word-order distinctions until 4 years. Bates et al. (1984) found that Italian children rely preferentially on semantic cues rather than word order, even at 5 years of age. By contrast, American children begin to respond to word-order cues by 2 years of age. Sinclair and Bronckart (1972) found that French children tend to rely heavily on event probabilities, as contrasted with word order, even at 7 years of age. Thus, the conclusion offered by Bates et al. (1984)—"that children are sensitive from the beginning to the information value of cues in their particular language" (p. 351)—seems inescapable.

Not until the field of linguistics adequately integrates all the strategies constantly being employed by speakers and listeners during real dialogues will a satisfying account of the development of linguistic competence emerge. The current emphasis on model sentences, typified by those that occur in text only, cannot account for how children go about the process of language acquisition.

III. LEARNING HOW WORDS WORK: ROUTINES OF TALKING COUPLED WITH DOING

Early ape language studies were predestined to fail because of a common fundamental methodological flaw: they concentrated on production to the virtual exclusion of comprehension. Although some investigators paid lip service to the importance of comprehension, they did not systematically test or measure it. Attempts to teach apes to talk when they did not understand the language in which they were addressed inevitably led to ambiguous performances and muddled conclusions.

Comprehension is a far more effective medium through which to "figure out how language works" than is language production. Children do not learn language by talking; they learn it by listening. Moreover, the talking from which they learn is directed toward them, and they are expected to attempt to respond to it appropriately. When human children and apes are treated in a similar manner, both species respond by learning how to (*a*) decode sounds into word units, (*b*) map these word units onto real-world cause-and-effect relations, (*c*) reconstruct the rules governing the combinatorial usages of different classes of these word units, and (*d*) use these relations and units in a productive manner to change the behavior of others so as to suit their own interests (Greenfield & Savage-Rumbaugh, 1990, 1991; Savage-Rumbaugh, 1988, 1990). How do they manage to do all this?

A number of different accounts of how children acquire language have been offered during the past decade (Bates, Benigni, Bretherton, Camaioni, & Volterra, 1979; Bates, Bretherton, & Snyder, 1988; Bruner, 1983; Greenfield & Smith, 1976; Lock, 1980; Nelson, 1985, 1986; Peters, 1983). All these accounts stress the role of learning and, to a greater or lesser extent, the role of the caretaker. None directly address the role of motivation beyond assuming that children strive to acquire language because they are predisposed to want to be like "grown-ups." Hence, the role of "reward," or the value of what children may be able to communicate and how communication may change the nature and form of interindividual interactions, has yet to be addressed.

By contrast, investigators of language acquisition in apes cannot take it for granted that the young ape is preprogrammed to want to act like "grown-up" human models. Hence, the question of the functional-motivational aspects of language must be addressed from the outset. Under certain conditions, the answers to this question that are obtained by working with apes can have direct relevance to the phenomenon of language acquisition in our own species. If it is the case that language is something that we, as humans, learn because it is beneficial to us to do so, rather than something that is a closely constrained manifestation of genetic programming (like our opposable thumbs), then what is learned by studying apes should, in some measure, tell us something about language in ourselves.

ACQUIRING LANGUAGE THROUGH INTERINDIVIDUAL ROUTINES

The account of language acquisition presented below is based on observational data collected on four different apes, all of whom acquired language by observing models who spoke and pointed to lexical symbols while rearing the animals in a culturally enriched environment. It is also based on observational data collected on two human children who were reared half of each day in a similar environment, although not with the apes.

Symbol acquisition in the four apes and the two children began with the learning of routines. These were not experimental protocols but rather structured sequences of events that emerged naturally out of everyday life. The apes' and the children's daily interactions with caretakers, while not experimentally programmed, can be described as a series of "interindividual routines" that became ever more complex and interchangeable with maturation and experience.

The term *interindividual routine* is used to mean a more or less regularly sequenced set of interindividual interactions that occur in a relatively similar manner on different occasions. The sequence of interactions may vary, as may the words used in connection with the interactions; however, each routine is carried out for a specific purpose. An "interindividual routine" is analogous in some respects to the ethological term *behavioral pattern*. It can take place only between two or more parties; that is, interindividual routines exist only in the interplay of organized patterns of interaction between partners. Similarly, the mating dances or dueting between birds of various species occur only when there are two participants. The intertwined patterns serve to synchronize the behavioral-emotional states of these organisms.

Interindividual routines are always embedded within larger behavioral contexts, which some authors have referred to as schema or scripts (Nelson, 1986; Schank & Abelson, 1977). These larger contexts are encoded linguistically as goals (the restaurant schema, the birthday party schema, etc.) and reflect events in which two or more participants engage. Each script has a sort of "skeleton" set of events that identifies it. Each script also has nodes or branching points that can be utilized by any of the participants to control the flow of events within the script into one or more of the many nested subroutines that make up the main script. "Routines" are inherent in all social behavior in that we are always engaging in a slightly modified version of some pattern of behavior that occurred previously. However, mother-infant routines are highly repetitive and rhythmic (Stern, Beebe, Jaffe, & Bennett, 1977) in that mothers tend to repeat behaviors, including the same vocalizations, over and over. Such behavior is maintained by sustained engagement and increased smiling on the part of the infant.

Events such as changing diapers, getting ready to go outdoors, taking a bath, riding in the car, looking at a book, blowing bubbles, putting items in the backpack, visiting with other apes, playing a game of tickle, and traveling down various trails in the forest are all interindividual routines, each with a large, if not infinite, number of potentially nested subroutines. It is important to note that the ape may be a willing or an unwilling participant in such routines.

Recognizing Routines

The learning of interindividual routines occurs regardless of whether the child or the ape actively seeks to carry out the routine or finds it reinforcing. For example, if she does not know what is happening to her, a young child or ape who is walking about, playing, climbing, and exploring her world may be startled and irritated when someone waves a white thing around, pulls her down, and begins forcibly separating her body from the warm and comfortable cloth tucked in her groin. If, however, she recognizes that action as the "diaper-changing routine," she will stop protesting and allow herself to be placed on the changing mat when she sees the clean diaper being held up in the caretaker's hand as a signal of his intent. If the caretaker always executes the diaper removal and replacement in the same calm manner, the youngster will lie still, knowing what to expect. If, however, a new caretaker tries to grab her feet or lift her in a manner she has never experienced during previous "diaper-changing routines," she will startle and wiggle away because she no longer finds the world predictable and is uncertain as to what the future actions of the other party will be within this routine.

The "diaper-changing routine" will be truncated when one or the other of the partners is unable to interact in the "expected way." The caretaker will likely conclude that the youngster "did not want to have her diapers changed," thereby attributing the failure of the interindividual interaction to the "emotional desires" of the child or the ape. However, it is not the emotional state of either the infant or the caretaker that causes an interindividual routine to fail; rather, it is their inability to join behaviors in a smooth manner and to pass each change of interacter-cum-interactant seamlessly back and forth. When the regular caretaker returns, the interaction will proceed smoothly, according to its past history, because both participants know what to expect of each other and when to carry out their roles, just as do players in an orchestra. Each sort of interindividual routine is something like a delicate dance with many different scores, the selection of which is being constantly negotiated while the dance is in progress, rather than in advance. Experienced partners know what turns the dance may take, and, more important, they have developed subroutines for negotiating what to do when one or both partners falter in the routine.

Caretakers unconsciously utilize frequent and sometimes exaggerated postural, gestural, and verbal markers when engaging in interactions with very young children or apes. (When these markers occur in the vocal domain, they are referred to as "motherese" because of their exaggerated style.) The markers are critical from a communicative standpoint because their purpose is to amplify or make obvious the signals of transition between various components of a given routine or changes from one routine to another. From the ape's or the child's perspective, "preferred caretakers" are those whose use of marking signals is finely tuned to the infant's abilities to comprehend these transitional indicators. Moreover, the timing and the form of transitional markers employed by effective caretakers will differ as a function of the child's or the ape's increasing ability to translate them.

Fostering Understanding of Routines

For example, the simple game of blowing bubbles has, at minimum, the following components: (*a*) finding the bubbles, (*b*) opening the bubble jar, (*c*) getting the bubble wand out of the bubble jar, (*d*) blowing bubbles, and (*e*) watching or attempting to pop the bubbles. Both participants may take turns at any of these activities. Additionally, some components are often added by the children or the apes themselves, such as drinking the bubble liquid or pouring it on the floor. Moreover, since all routines develop spontaneously, each interindividual interaction sequence inevitably differs somewhat on each new occasion.

The bubble-blowing routine may be announced with some statement such as "Let's play with the bubbles," "Let's find the bubbles," "Would you like the bubbles," etc., made while pointing to the "bubbles" lexigram. A young child or ape who has never seen bubbles before will display no response to such verbal markers. Noting this, the caretaker will tend to adopt more direct measures to signal her intentions, for example, pointing to the bubble jar or holding the jar in front of the ape. Once the child or ape has attended to the bubble bottle, he may spontaneously attempt to reach for or to open it, as he is naturally curious. However, at a young age, he will probably not hold the bubble jar carefully or show any anticipation that the liquid inside may spill. On opening the jar, he may taste the substance, but he will do little more on his own. However, the caretaker will demonstrate the bubble wand with statements such as "Oh look, what is this in the bottle?" uttered *just as* she notes that the child or the ape is looking at the bubble wand and perhaps trying to take it out. The caretaker may then say "Let's have a look at it" *just before* taking the wand out of the bottle and "Watch what it does" *just before* blowing bubbles. If the child or ape pops the bubbles, the caretaker will comment on this action. The caretaker may also comment on his *intention* of popping bubbles just prior to doing so.

In general, the caretakers best able to foster the development of communicative skills are those who vocally and gesturally mark their own actions *prior to* engaging in them in a way that the child or ape can understand. They then wait for the latter to show signs of willingness to cooperate. When this is done carefully, the child or ape is prepared for what will happen next and learns to recognize the caretaker's signal at the joints of the interchange.

Lock (1991) has described a similar phenomenon while observing differences in the methods that caretakers employ when picking up babies. Some caretakers announce their intent to pick up the child vocally and gesturally (by holding their hands out toward the infant) and then wait for the infant to make some appropriate response, such as waving his arms toward them, stiffening his body and looking toward them, etc. Other mothers simply announce the behavior and then get on with picking up the baby, rather than waiting for the latter to engage in a behavior that could be viewed as a signal that he is ready to be picked up.

In either case, the *initial* "ready" signals of the infant are accidental because the baby neither understands what the caretaker is about to do nor knows how to signal the caretaker that he is ready to be picked up. However, babies whose caretakers wait for the emergence of a contingent signal are the ones who quickly learn to use that signal to indicate to the mother that they anticipate her intent. Similarly, when such babies do not want to be picked up, they can withhold the "I'm ready" signal. Either way, the babies have a degree of control over what happens to them by virtue of the caretaker having sought to make her picking-up action integrated with, and contingent on, the behavior of the baby. Babies who have not experienced such contingent "picking-up" behavior do not develop a signal between themselves and the caretaker that indicates their readiness to be picked up.

While "picking up" is one small routine, it is possible that caretakers who do not signal and wait for the baby to produce a response in this context are less inclined to do so in other contexts as well. A child who has experienced less contingent interactions might be more prone to view the social world as something to which she constantly needs to adjust, rather than as something over which she has a significant degree of control. As Ainsworth (1973, 1979) and Lamb (1981a, 1981b) have noted, the security of a child's attachment is related to the caretaker's sensitivity and responsiveness to the child's signals. The less sensitive the caretakers, the less the child is able to relate to and control her world through a competent intermediary.

While effective caretakers tend to mark their own actions prior to engaging in them, they often mark the ape or child's actions vocally as the action is happening or as it becomes visually evident that it is going to happen. Furthermore, they set the behavioral occasion for the action by arranging events so that it will be virtually inevitable that the child or the ape will carry out a particular action; then they mark that action vocally just before it occurs.

In addition, effective caretakers closely monitor the child or ape to determine whether the verbal marker has been understood; if not, they drop back to a gestural marker, and, if that fails, they actually perform the action to which they are referring, but in an elaborated manner that signals communication about the action as it is taking place. The way in which these verbal and gestural markers are timed and interdigitated with interindividual interactions sets the stage for the development of the autonomy of the marker from the event that it is marking.

As children or apes begin to learn all about what is done while playing with bubbles, they also learn to respond to the vocal markers that accompany such play. Instead of simply grasping and tasting, they begin to look for the bubble wand and orient it in front of their mouths. Later, they try to pucker their lips and finally learn to expel air. If the air is aimed properly, they may even blow some bubbles. Not only is the act of blowing bubbles itself acquired, but knowledge of the gestural, vocal, and lexical markers also begins to appear. On hearing the word *bubbles,* children or apes can be observed directing a glance toward the jar of bubbles even before it has been singled out or displayed by the caretaker.

Thus, as routines are learned, behavioral changes occur in the child or ape that suggest that she has learned the main components of the routine. More important, once a routine and its markers are understood, the child or ape can begin to use the latter to initiate the routine and thus play a part in determining the course of events. At first, such initiations will be limited and "primitive" in the sense that they are usually action based and context dependent. For example, the child or ape may see the bottle of bubbles among other toys, pick it up, and look at the caretaker. By selecting the bubbles from other things, she conveys a desire to execute the "bubble-blowing" routine. Later, she may simply point to the bubbles and look at the caretaker. Still later, she will say "bubbles" or point to the "bubbles" lexigram and turn to the caretaker.

In so doing, children or apes begin the move from the role of a responder during routines to that of a primitive initiator and then to that of a symbolic communicator capable of announcing their intentions to another party. The process occurs very naturally, without the caretaker intentionally or knowingly structuring the transition from passive receptive comprehension to active productive knowledge and use. This appears to happen more rapidly with routines that are most clearly structured and effectively marked. It is important that the marker precede the routine or the changes in the components of the routine. Verbal, gestural, or action markers that merely overlay a routine (such as repeatedly commenting "bubbles" while pointing to a jar of bubbles) are not acquired as effectively as markers that signal changes between routines or changes within a given routine.

An Illustrative Example

Examples of some of these strategies can be seen by noting the events that occur as a mother (JM [Jeannine Murphy]) is making lemonade with two children, one 1½ years and the other 3½ years of age. (This incident was videotaped in our lab as part of regular weekly taping sessions.) The mother first divides the task into roles appropriate to the competencies of each child. In addition, the younger child is placed in one side of the sink, which prevents her from wandering about and helps direct attention to the task. The task is broken down into the following components: opening the lemonade can, obtaining a pitcher, pouring the contents of the can into the pitcher, and adding water. The younger child continually tries to insert components of a washing routine by washing her hands or washing other items in the sink, as these are both routines that she associates with being at the sink. The older child stays with the lemonade-making routine and does not interpose such "off-task" intrusions.

The mother starts the procedure with the older child by announcing, "Nathaniel's gonna open it, and you're gonna pour it in." She then instructs the older child to "Pull it out" while he is pulling the strip of plastic that opens the can. When it is not done correctly, the mother emphasizes "out" vocally but does nothing more than make her vocal instructions more explicit; the assumption that the older child can understand verbal instructions is clear.

The caretaker then turns to the younger child and says, "We need this thing Alia," *just before* taking the pitcher from Alia and putting it in the sink, where it can be filled with water. (The mother unconsciously is verbally describing her own imminent action while simultaneously using a gesture to draw Alia's attention to the object that is to be moved. She waits to relocate the object until the child's attention is focused on it.) Next, the mother comments, "You get to pour it in here," while gesturing again to the pitcher and just prior to handing Alia the can of lemonade. She then immediately guides Alia to pour the lemonade properly into the pitcher, thus helping Alia manifest the action that has just been encoded on both the verbal and the gestural levels. (Here the mother unconsciously is describing the child's imminent action and is structuring the situation so that the action that she has verbally marked becomes highly probable.)

After focusing Alia's attention first on the water by turning it on, then on the empty lemonade can by holding it in front of her, the mother comments, "OK, put the water in the cup." (Here the mother seems to realize that both the water and the empty can will orient Alia's attention and that she will then pour the water into the pitcher. Again the mother unconsciously has behaviorally set the stage for the child's action and then verbally encoded that action, just prior to the time the child is highly likely to emit that action.) The mother then steadies the cup for Alia and helps her carry out the action that she has just encoded both verbally and gesturally.

Alia then tries to initiate a change in the routine with the sponge by saying, "Le ash" (a version, presumably, of "Let's wash"), and picking up the sponge. (Alia has thus attempted to use a vocal marker to make the routine take a direction of her choosing.) The mother says, "No," and uses the lemonade can to push Alia's sponge away and back toward the sink's edge. (In so doing, the mother unconsciously interposes the central object of her routine, the lemonade can, into Alia's field of vision and uses it to move the object of Alia's proposed routine, the sponge, out of her field of vision.) Alia ignores this and insists on putting the sponge under the water. The mother removes the sponge from Alia's hand and then says, "Do you want to wash, or do you want to do the lemonade?" while ostensibly offering both the can of lemonade and the sponge as choices for Alia. However, the mother unconsciously crosses her hands just before she utters this sentence so that the lemonade can is directly in Alia's field of vision and the sponge is again slightly removed from it. (The verbal "choice" that Alia is given is thus summarily preempted by the physical choice that she is simultaneously offered. The manner in which the two objects are presented is such that Alia's choice is likely to be the one that continues the routine of lemonade making.) Alia takes the lemonade can and in so doing gets "back on task" while ostensibly having made her own choice.

The role of the mother in the process of transmitting interindividual routines is similar to that described by Bruner (1973, 1983), Lock (1980), and Nelson (1985). However, it is important to note the ways in which the model being presented here differs from accounts in which the role of the mother as a creative force in the "scaffolding" and "ratcheting" of the communicative process is stressed. Here it is emphasized that the process is driven, not by the mother's desire to increase the child's competencies, but by the *joint need* of the mother and the child to coordinate interindividual interactions within routines. To the degree that the mother unconsciously is scaffolding or ratcheting the process, it is not out of a conscious desire to teach the child. Rather, these behaviors emerge because they are necessary to make the interindividual interactions with the child or ape "successful" in the sense that they are coordinated and that both participants act smoothly together. It is the verbal and nonverbal segmental markers that allow this coordination to take place.

Because these segmental markers permit the recipient to predict what is going to happen next, they become valuable skills to acquire. In this model, the "driving force" behind language acquisition is not the caretaker; rather, it is the desire of the child or ape accurately to predict what is going to happen to him or her next that motivates the attention toward the acquisition of vocal and gestural transition markers.

REFERENCE REVISITED

Given that the ape (or child) is attending to the routine, how does it learn that the caretaker is using the word *bubbles* to refer to the jar and/or the bubbles themselves rather than to the act of puffing air, the taste of the soapy liquid, the opening of the bottle, the many other indeterminate referents in the situation, or even to the whole routine itself? Indeed, how does the child or ape come to acquire the idea that a word such as *bubbles* should refer to anything at all rather than just occurring as a piece of the routine?

Part of the answer to this question is hidden in what happens as segments of the routine are negotiated and marked. For example, after the bubble bottle has been grasped, the caretaker may say, "You open the bubbles." If this is not understood, she may place the bottle in the ape's hand and show how to start opening it, repeating the marker "You open the bubbles" and thus engaging him in the subroutine of opening, within the larger routine of blowing bubbles. The marker will continue to be repeated in various forms, along with increasingly explicit action guides and aid, until the next event in the routine is performed. By linking the word *bubbles* to the activity of selecting the bottle from other objects *and* to the activity of acting on the bottle to open it, the word *bubbles* comes to be associated with the one element common to these different action forms.

Thus, the relation of any given routine to other routines aids the development of reference. There are, for example, routines with bubbles that do not involve blowing, such as "putting the bubbles in the backpack" for the purpose of later play. During this routine, the word *bubbles* and the lexigram for *bubbles* may be repeatedly employed while the caretaker is looking for the bubbles and announcing to the ape that such is the goal of their actions. Once the bottle is found, it will be placed in the backpack and not mentioned again for some time. Thus, the word *bubbles* functions in two ways: to initiate a search for the bubble bottle and to initiate a game with it. It may also be used in other routines such as "hide the bubbles" or "put the bubbles in the bath water." In all these instances, the single commonality is the word *bubbles* and the bottle of bubbles. Thus, knowledge of specific referents comes, not from a single routine, but from a group of intermeshed routines that have overlapping markers. It also comes from the application of the marker to actions that the caretaker intends of the ape, such as "helping find the bubbles." While the ape may not know initially that it is expected to search for the bubbles, it will begin to recognize that actions other than finding the bubbles do not suffice when it is asked to "find the bubbles."

IV. THE INNATENESS DEBATE

POOR RELATIVES OR RICH RELATIONS?

Apes are our closest living relatives (Sarich, 1983). On the basis of biochemical data, it has recently been suggested that *Homo* and the African apes should share the genus nomenclature *Pan* (Sibley & Ahlquist, 1984, 1987). For the three species of African apes—gorilla (*Gorilla gorilla*), chimpanzee (*Pan troglodytes*), and bonobo (*Pan paniscus*)—currently available data indicate that both species of *Pan* share more DNA sequences with *Homo* than they do with *Gorilla* (Andrews & Martin, 1987; Bishop & Friday, 1986; Sibley & Ahlquist, 1984, 1987). The estimated date of divergence between *Homo* and *Pan* is now placed at 4–6 million years ago (Sibley & Ahlquist, 1987). Oldowan stone tools appear in the archaeological record a bit later, at 2–3 million years, or roughly coincident with the point at which the bonobo and the chimpanzee diverged from one another (Harris, 1983; Sarich, 1984).

The close biological connection between *Homo* and *Pan* has raised a variety of evolutionary questions that center around the rapid evolution in brain size that began at the point of *Homo-Pan* divergence. The human brain is approximately three times larger than the ape brain but resembles it in major anatomical detail (Le Gros Clark, 1978). Endocast studies and measurements of modern brains indicate that the left temporal gyral area (which controls fluent speech in humans) experienced significant enlargement relative to the right temporal area about 2–3 million years ago (Falk, 1983).

The evolutionary implications of these observations suggest that perhaps some anatomical change occurred around 2–3 million years ago that made the appearance of proto-language possible. However, data from modern humans illustrate that language can be located in either hemisphere (Calvin & Ojemann, 1980) and may also be present in hydrocephalics, whose brains are much reduced in size and grossly abnormal in structure. Further complicating the picture is the clear evidence from direct electrical stimulation of the brains of epileptic patients (obtained prior to surgery) that language can be localized in dramatically different areas in different individuals (Calvin & Ojemann, 1980).

LANGUAGE: THE ACQUIRED VERSUS INNATE DEBATE

Differential localization of linguistic function suggests that language may be an acquired skill, developed and organized individually by each person through interactions with others. Studies of language development in infants reveal different styles of language acquisition, particularly when one looks at individual cases rather than merging group data to create "norms" that fail to portray any given infant in the sample (Bates et al., 1991; Lock, 1991). Children have been characterized as adopting one of two basic approaches to language acquisition. Some appear to be "expressive learners," who concentrate on whole phrases and emotive topics, while others are "concept learners," who focus on single words and content-loaded topics. However, even a single child will display different styles when learning different languages, indicating that such styles may reflect more about the child's exposure than about any innate predispositions (Bates et al., 1991).

The strongest argument for viewing language as an "innate" skill, unique to humans, has been set forth by Chomsky (1988). This view asserts that the formal aspects of syntactic constructions must be prewired because currently described learning mechanisms do not successfully account for the appearance of formal syntactic operators that characterize all languages (recursion, combination, etc.). Parents do not frequently correct children's syntactic errors, thus raising the question of how a child comes to learn that what he has said is wrong (Brown & Hanlon, 1970; Hirsh-Pasek, Treiman, & Schneiderman, 1984). This observation has been referred to as the argument from "negative evidence," and it relies on an analysis of the types of errors that young children do and do not make while acquiring language and on the assertion that relatively little correction is given to children during the process (Gleason, 1989). Phrasal movement or relative clauses, for example, seem to cause few difficulties as such errors are almost nonexistent among young language learners. Since parents are not observed to train such skills, Chomsky (1988) concluded that, at minimum, there must exist a prewired "parsing device" that switches on during development. While the basic components of this parsing device are not yet fully specified, the field of linguistics is devoted to pursuing this task.

The "innate account" of language thus rests on a default premise—that, since no alternative theory currently explains the observed phenomena, the innate account is accepted by default. Some have termed this postulate the "smoking gun" of learnability theory (Gleason, 1989; Pinker, 1984), for if it falls, the rest of the theory loses credibility. There is increasing evidence to suggest that parents do in fact reformulate or query children after ungrammatical utterances (Demetras, Post, & Snow, 1986; Hirsh-Pasek et al., 1984; Penner, 1987). However, the effectiveness of such feedback is widely debated (Pinker, 1987a, 1987b) on the grounds that it still provides no input regarding the internal linguistic structure that the child is thought to need in order to produce syntactically correct sentences.

Could there be a plausible alternative account of how a child can avoid such linguistic mistakes? If children learned to understand much of what others are saying before they attempted to speak, it is possible that some performance errors would never occur, as many of these mistakes would have already occurred and been corrected while children were attempting to comprehend what was said to them. Children do not need to produce ungrammatical sentences, and have their errors corrected, in order to comprehend language. Moreover, children must begin the route into language by attempting to understand what it is that others are saying. To do so, they must somehow start to decode both words and sentences (Peters, 1983).

Chomsky (1988) noted that children rarely, if ever, make relative clause errors that entail splitting a sentence in an uninterpretable manner. For example, a child might say, "Let's eat the cake what I baked," confusing the syntactic marker *what* with *that*. However, errors such as "Let's cake the eat what I baked" do not seem to occur. The fact that one type of error occurs often and the other essentially not at all is surprising only if one assumes that the child must construct sentences in order to learn how to use them.

If we look at typical circumstances in which a child is expected to comprehend complex syntactic structures, such as relative clauses, we find that, in most "natural cases," the situation itself leads children to avoid interpretive errors. A mother may, for example, present a child with two cakes after the child has watched her bake one of them, say, "Let's eat the cake that I baked," and then extend that cake toward the child. It is reasonable to assume that the child's knowledge of the immediate "baking history" of the cake will permit her to draw inferences about what the mother is saying. Furthermore, children are also likely to select the object that is extended to them. If, even with all these cues, the child should still attempt to take the wrong cake, her choice is most likely to be corrected by the parent, who will show her which cake to eat.

Thus, the contextual situation can easily be seen as biasing the child toward the correct interpretation of complex syntactic structures such as relative clauses. Moreover, "behavioral correction" (such as reoffering the correct cake) is likely to be employed if the child finds the contextual information insufficient to decode the sentence. Such "behavioral correction" of miscomprehension has not, in the past, been viewed as a means of language instruction. However, caretakers must constantly engage in some means of "behavioral explanation" of their linguistic intent when children do not understand what is said to them. Consequently, when correct comprehension of relative clauses precedes their production, it is not surprising that children do not make such errors as "Let's cake the eat what I baked."

The kinds of errors that do occur in children's speech (such as "I goed downstairs" or "Nobody don't likes me") do not reflect a failure of language comprehension in the sense that such a sentence as "Let's cake the eat what I baked" does. The "typical childish errors" are easily interpretable by adults and indeed sound "cute" precisely because they are readily interpretable. Such errors reflect overgeneralization of marking rules rather than errors in the general structural organization of the sentence. The fact that severe structural errors rarely occur can be taken as evidence that the child has worked out the general structural principles during attempts to comprehend sentences before trying to utter them.

It has also been shown that intonation and timing cues help mark phrasal contours and that children can, in some cases, separate phrases before they are able to differentiate single words (Morgan, 1986; Peters, 1983). Thus, comprehension of syntactic structure seems to precede the onset of single-word speech and guide the development of such speech (Golinkoff et al., 1987). Children do not appear to be building up a complex grammar out of single-word units and an innate parsing device. Rather, they seem to be pulling apart the syntactic structure inherent in the speech around them, through the help of speakers who mark these syntactic units by their intonation and use of phrasing.

While it is increasingly recognized that language comprehension precedes language production, the implications of this fact for language acquisition are often overlooked (Snyder et al., 1981). If the intricacies of syntactic structure are deduced by listening to others, we should expect to find little need for parents to correct their child's speech. Instead, what parents would need to correct would be children's misunderstandings of what they heard. An adequate theory of how language is acquired, then, is likely to depend more on an analysis of errors of comprehension than on an analysis of errors of production. The cognitive burden of interpreting novel sentences constructed by other speakers is already equivalent in many ways to that of constructing sentences oneself. It may be even greater in some cases since the listener has no "insider's knowledge" of what the speaker is attempting to say.

The "innateness hypothesis" fails to take into account the many opportunities that children have for both making errors and receiving corrections in the realm of language comprehension. Until these are better understood, the conclusion that children do not receive the feedback needed to enable them to construct syntactic structures without a "language acquisition device" remains speculative.

THE SPEECH-PROCESSING CAPACITIES OF OTHER SPECIES

Data from nonhuman primate species are critical to the debate surrounding the "innateness" issue. If closely related species can learn language or are in fact using a language-like system already, then the "innate hypothesis" must be either expanded to include species other than humans or abandoned in favor of explanations that rely more heavily on the learned components of language skills.

In the 1970s and early 1980s, it was widely assumed that animals other than humans were unable to process speech at the phonemic level. This view was based on the theory (Fodor, 1983; Lieberman, 1975) that the neural components of the productive and receptive systems co-evolve in all animals and that, consequently, human infants are born with specialized mechanisms dedicated to processing speech sounds and formal syntactic structures. According to this theory, it is not possible for other animals to hear the speech signal in the same manner as humans because they do not possess a "speech module" designed to decode the complex and intricate sounds that typify human speech. Similarly, it is thought to be impossible for humans to decode the vocal signals of other animals, such as dolphins, because our auditory receptors are not designed to process their sounds. This perspective defines animal species as irrevocably separated from one another by a genetic inability to process communication signals belonging to other species. The popularity of this position stems, in part, from its intuitively appealing postulate of supposed biological structures (the "speech module" and the "language acquisition device") that set man clearly apart from all other creatures, a position supported by the Judaeo-Christian cultural context in which this perspective evolved and holds sway.

Recent evidence has tended not to support this view. It has been found, for example, that both chinchillas and monkeys can be taught to make /da/-/ta/ discriminations. Having learned these distinctions, they then evince categorically bounded perceptions similar to those found with humans (Kuhl & Miller, 1975; Waters & Wilson, 1976). Categorically bounded perceptions are those in which the percept that an auditory stimulus has changed from exemplar A (e.g., /ta/) to exemplar B (e.g., /da/) is based on "psychophysical characteristics" of stimulus processing rather than on definable physical attributes. Like Waters and Wilson, who used macaques, Kuhl and Miller (1978) extended these findings to bilabial pairs (/ba/-/pa/) and velar contrasts (/ga/-/ka/) using chinchillas. Taken together, these studies indicate that the natural phonetic boundaries of at least chinchillas and macaque monkeys are similar to human phonetic boundaries.

A second area of investigation has addressed the question of whether animals are able to perceive similarities among phonemes produced by different speakers. Examples of the phoneme /ba/ can sound quite different when produced by speakers of different ages, sexes, and cultural backgrounds; nonetheless, most speakers have little difficulty identifying them as the same sound. Monkeys who were asked to judge different phonemic pairs as the same or different did poorly when pairs were taken from the same phonemic category (i.e., different sounding examples of /ba/) but performed well when pairs were taken from different phonemic categories (i.e., /ba/ vs. /pa/), just as do human subjects (Kuhl, 1987; Kuhl & Padden, 1982, 1983). As Kuhl (1987) has argued, these results suggest that, "in the evolution of language, the choice of the particular phonetic units used in communication was strongly influenced by the extent to which the units were ideally suited to the (extant) auditory system" (p. 336).

SPECIES SPECIFICITY OF THE LANGUAGE ACQUISITION DEVICE

A third area of study has attempted to extend the investigation of animals' ability to discriminate speech sounds to discrimination of words and sentences in bonobos (Savage-Rumbaugh, Sevcik, Brakke, Rumbaugh, & Greenfield, 1990). However, this work differs methodologically from that of Kuhl and others cited above in that these animals are not taught specific auditory discrimination tasks but instead acquire word and sentence comprehension naturally, much as children do, by virtue of being reared in a language-rich environment.

Conclusions regarding the linguistic capacities of apes were initially compromised by the fact that the ape vocal tract is shaped differently from that of man. Instead of bending sharply, the ape vocal tract curves gently downward. Consequently, apes cannot position their supralaryngeal tracts properly to produce all the phonemic sounds characteristic of human speech (Lieberman, 1968). Apes could perhaps construct a language using sounds that they can produce, but if this has occurred, it has gone unrecognized. Researchers have yet to determine the analogue of phonemic components (if any exists) in the vocal repertoires of any nonhuman primates (Snowdon, 1988, in press). Lacking any knowledge of the "sound units" that they might utilize, it is nearly impossible to look for the analogues of words and/or sentences in other species.

The approach that we have taken with a group of apes (three bonobos or pygmy chimpanzees [*Pan paniscus*] and one common chimpanzee [*Pan troglodytes*]) has been quite different. By exposing them to a spoken language

39

shortly after birth and intentionally avoiding attempts to train or teach language, the "speech-rich" environment of the young child was replicated with another species. As with children, language was used as a communicative instrument in all interactions. In addition, people spoke to the apes as they pointed to symbols, thus providing both visual and auditory input, on the assumption that, if bonobos could not discriminate the units of the auditory signal, they could rely instead on the visually distinct symbols.

In general, the rearing environment was designed to promote communication about topics of interest to apes. Food was dispersed at identifiable locations in a 55-acre wooded area, and most of the day was spent traveling from one food source to another, playing and resting just as would be the case in the apes' natural environment. Human companions accompanied the apes at all times, using both speech and geometric symbols to communicate their intentions regarding travel, play, rest, etc. and encouraging the apes to attend to these communications. The apes, like children, were cared for as needed and allowed to play and interact socially with persons and other apes as they desired.

This environment was intentionally designed as an informal, relaxed setting in which apes could be given the opportunity to hear and see people talk about things that were of particular interest to them. Such opportunities were not experimentally structured but rather occurred spontaneously within the daily events of traveling in the forest in search of food. Communications differed constantly and were always linked to the current context. For example, if dogs or turtles appeared in the woods, they would become, for a short period of time, the topic of conversation. Later, it might be the snake on the path or the ice in the cooler at "Lookout Point" if it were a hot day. It was the events of the moment that determined the topics of conversation rather than an experimental protocol. Experimenters did not decide which words, if any, an ape should learn. This was left up to the individual ape, and, in general, the apes' first words reflected their own particular interests.

Table 1 lists the first 10 words acquired by different bonobos reared in this environment. There is no single word that is common to all three animals among these first 10 items, even though all were exposed to essentially the same vocabulary and the same environment. More interesting than the specific lexical items, however, was the way in which the words were learned. Because the speech plus symbol keyboard system (described in the next chapter) both simplified the topology of the response and provided extensive opportunity for observational learning, ape subjects readily acquired symbols without reward or training (Savage-Rumbaugh et al., 1986). Not only were the lexigrams learned, but comprehension of the spoken words also occurred, typically preceding the learning of lexical symbols.

Kanzi, a bonobo, was the first ape to demonstrate that rearing in this

TABLE 1

FIRST 10 WORDS ACQUIRED BY DIFFERENT APE SUBJECTS

Kanzi	Mulika	Panbanisha
Orange	Milk	Milk
Peanut	Key	Chase
Banana	T-room	Open
Apple	Surprise	Tickle
Bedroom	Juice	Grape
Chase	Water	Bite
Austin	Grape	Dog
Sweet potato	Banana	Surprise
Raisin	Go	Yogurt
Ball	Staff office	Soap

environment was sufficient to produce spontaneous acquisition of lexical and vocal symbols and that "symbol training" was not required (Savage-Rumbaugh, Rumbaugh, & McDonald, 1985). Two additional bonobos (Mulika and Panbanisha) and one common chimpanzee (Panpanzee) have also learned symbols without training, indicating that Kanzi's ability was unique neither to him nor to his species (Savage-Rumbaugh et al., 1992).

The communicative effect produced by a combination of words, with or without syntax, is different, in a way that is not often discussed, from that which can occur with single words. The production of novel combinatorial utterances is a powerful communicative process that characterizes all languages. The appearance of "sequenced words" antedates the emergence of syntax proper and, like syntax, serves to create new meanings that are not simply an additive result of the separate words.

For example, two-word utterances, such as "Car trailer" or "Grouproom Matata" (both produced by Kanzi), convey novel meanings that the individual components could never generate if uttered alone. Additionally, these utterances can convey their novel meaning regardless of the order of their components and of whether this order is "fixed" according to any rule-based syntactic system. When Kanzi produced the combination "Car trailer," he was inside the car and employed this utterance as a means of indicating that he wanted to be driven to the trailer rather than walking there. He followed the utterance with a gesture toward the trailer and the steering wheel of the car. Had Kanzi said "car" alone, this single symbol utterance would have been interpreted as a comment about being in the car and would have simply been acknowledged. Had he said "trailer" alone, the caretaker would probably have simply got out of the car and walked with Kanzi to the trailer since it was a very short distance to drive. However, by saying "Car trailer," Kanzi produced a novel meaning and brought about a set of events that otherwise would not have been likely to occur (i.e., taking the car to the trailer).

Kanzi similarly produced the combination "Grouproom Matata" to convey something different than either symbol could convey alone. Kanzi was in the grouproom and had just heard Matata (his mother), who was in another room, vocalize. Typically, if Kanzi wanted to visit Matata, he would simply say "Matata" and gesture toward her room. However, on this occasion, by producing the combination he indicated that he wanted Matata to come to the grouproom where he was instead of going to visit her. In response to this utterance, the caretaker asked, "Do you want Matata to come to the grouproom?" Kanzi answered with loud positive vocal noises, directed first to the experimenter, then to Matata. He seemed to be announcing something about his intent to Matata. Had Kanzi said only "grouproom," his utterance would have been interpreted as a comment on his location, just as "car" would have been in the preceding example. However, because it is not possible to take a room somewhere (a piece of real-world knowledge assumed to be known by both Kanzi and the caretaker), it was surmised that Kanzi wanted Matata to come to the grouproom. Kanzi's vocalization in response to the caretaker's inquiry affirmed his intent. These sorts of combinatorial processes characterized Kanzi's utterances even though the majority of his productions were still single words.

Words such as *Matata* and *grouproom* can be uttered in any order, and the relational meaning will remain clear and will convey a different message than either word uttered alone. The novel meaning conveyed by such a two-word utterance is possible because both listener and speaker assume that a new relation is made manifest by putting two words together (Savage-Rumbaugh, 1990).

An analysis of Kanzi's combinations reveals not only that he can communicate novel information but also that he follows, as well as invents, simple syntactic rules. He tends to follow the ordering strategies of English syntax. For example, action-object combinations are more frequent than object-action combinations. He has also invented an ordering rule of his own for action-action combinations (Greenfield & Savage-Rumbaugh, 1991).

The language comprehension of these four ape subjects (Kanzi, Mulika, Panbanisha, and Panpanzee) contrasts dramatically with that of five other ape subjects (Lana, Sherman, Austin, Matata, and Tamuli) who were reared in a similar environment but whose exposure to language began at a much later age. None of the animals who began language training after 2½ years of age acquired symbols without extensive and explicit training (Rumbaugh, 1977; Savage-Rumbaugh, Sevcik, et al., 1985). More important, none of the "late exposure" animals developed auditory comprehension of more than a few spoken words even by 9 years of age, while all the "early exposure" animals comprehended 40 or more spoken words by 2½ years of age. The fact that age of exposure is a critical variable in language learning in both apes and humans suggests that the brains of young animals are developing language-activated circuitry that is "exposure biased" at a very early age and that equivalent opportunities for the brain to replicate that circuitry at a later age may not exist (Greenough, Black, & Wallace, 1987; Rumbaugh, Hopkins, Washburn, & Savage-Rumbaugh, 1991).

V. METHODS OF THE CURRENT STUDY

The data presented in this *Monograph* contrast the ability of a bonobo (Kanzi) and of a normal 2-year-old child (Alia) to comprehend novel English sentences in which both lexical units and syntactic construction were systematically varied on each trial. Unlike previous ape-child comparisons that have used the "idealized child," this study sought to test the capacities of an actual human child and of an ape in precisely the same manner. Moreover, the rearing histories of both subjects were known to be sufficiently similar as to make the comparison valid.

Both subjects were exposed to a similar linguistic environment from infancy, but neither was "trained" to talk. Both had similar experiences with lexigrams (i.e., geometric symbols that serve as words in our laboratory). Additionally, both subjects shared a primary caregiver, Jeannine Murphy (JM), who was the mother of the child and whose language input and caretaking behavior were similar for both subjects. The subjects were not "playmates," however. Kanzi's peers were apes and Alia's other children. The primary caregiver worked full time with Kanzi before Alia was born and part of each day thereafter.

Testing comprehension can be arduous as the cooperation of very young children and apes is difficult to secure in a test setting that eliminates contextual cuing. Because comprehension is a "hidden skill" that can be made manifest only by exposing the subject to specific linguistic input, it is necessary to present a wide variety of materials in order to gain an understanding of the subject's competency. It is also critical that such testing not become routine, or the subject will not be likely to listen closely and attempt to interpret the sentence. For purposes of the current study, both subjects were presented with a large number of novel sentences to determine the extent to which they comprehended utterances based on speech cues alone. The sentences were presented in spoken English and in a normal voice. Both relative clauses and word-order reversals were utilized to investigate comprehension of specific syntactic devices.

The goals of the study were simple. Given (*a*) that both a bonobo and a child had learned to comprehend some language and to use symbols, (b) that this knowledge had been imparted to them in a similar manner (in part, even, by the same caretaker), and (c) that the language comprehension skills of both subjects were imperfectly understood, a systematic means of evaluating and comparing these two subjects on the dimension of language competency was sought. The most reasonable comparison lay in the domain of receptive ability because the ape was not anatomically compromised relative to the child in this skill, at least not with regard to pitch perception. A nonformal test situation was selected because it provided the best means of pressing both subjects to their limit in a way that was natural for them and did not require depriving them of food, toys, etc.; nor did it require them to perform correctly for a reward. Since the competencies of both subjects were understood only in a general way prior to this systematic comparison, we selected a wide variety of sentences in order to determine whether these subjects could respond appropriately to novel utterances by integrating the information given by the words in a semantically meaningful manner. Syntactic questions inevitably arose also because syntactic structures were employed in the novel utterances presented. However, the goal of the study was not to provide a definitive picture of these subjects' syntactic competencies but rather to develop a better understanding of the forms of syntactic markers, if any, to which the subjects were becoming sensitive.

SUBJECTS

The subjects were Kanzi (born October 28, 1980), a male bonobo 8 years of age, and Alia (born July 26, 1987), a human female between 1½ and 2 years of age. Kanzi was exposed to human language and to lexigrams from age 6 months, while still with his bonobo mother. Kanzi's caretakers (Sue Savage-Rumbaugh [SSR], Rose Sevcik, Kelly McDonald, JM, Phillip Shaw, and Elizabeth Rubert) typically talked to him in natural English and pointed to lexigrams as they spoke. Kanzi began to evince speech comprehension at 2 years of age and spontaneously employed lexigrams for communicative purposes at age 2½ years.

Kanzi was raised by his mother, Matata, until he was 2½ years old. During this time, Kanzi's mother participated in symbol instruction studies, but Kanzi did not—he merely accompanied her. At age 2½, he was separated from Matata for 4 months while she was housed with a breeding male. At that time, it became clear that Kanzi had learned the symbols that his mother had been attempting to acquire, even though he had received no specific training. Consequently, a decision was made not to train him with additional symbols but rather to determine what he could learn on his own.

One or more of the previously noted caretakers was with Kanzi throughout each day, up to the time of the present study. Kanzi was allowed to accompany these caretakers into the 50 acres of forest surrounding the laboratory and to visit immediately adjacent locations. In the forest, Kanzi could find foods at many predictable locations, just as he might in the wild. These locations were replenished daily. Kanzi's caretakers always attempted to do things that were of interest to him and to talk to him in a natural manner. They also carried with them a large symbol board and pointed to symbols as they spoke to Kanzi. If the words they were saying were not on the symbol board, they simply continued talking without pointing to any symbols. (Indoors, Kanzi's symbol board was attached to a speech synthesizer so that he could "talk" aloud by pressing the symbols.)

Kanzi spent a great deal of time outdoors during the warm months of the year, traveling and playing in the woods. In the winter, he played with toys, painted, helped cook, watched television, visited people in other parts of the indoor building, played with other apes at the facility, and even traveled by car (to keep warm) through the woods. All these activities were accompanied by language in any way that seemed natural to the caretakers.

Kanzi was not required to use any symbols in order to get food or other desirable items; however, he was asked to watch when others used the symbol board. Kanzi learned to comprehend individual spoken words that were of interest to him and to associate these words with the symbols on the board without any specific training (Savage-Rumbaugh, 1986). His comprehension of speech was not limited to that of those who cared for him but extended to most clear speakers and even to synthesized speech (Savage-Rumbaugh, 1988; for a more detailed account of Kanzi's language development, see Savage-Rumbaugh et al., 1990).

Alia was exposed to English from birth and to lexigram symbols from 3 months of age. Her mother (JM) pointed to lexigrams as she spoke to Alia, just as was done with Kanzi. JM also participated in Kanzi's rearing and employed speech patterns and lexical use patterns in a similar manner for both subjects. She served as one of Kanzi's caretakers from 8:00 A.M. until 1:00 P.M. During the afternoon, she brought her daughter to a modified double-wide mobile home located approximately 300 feet from the main laboratory facility, where she set up an indoor environment similar to Kanzi's and engaged Alia in similar games. Alia watched many of the same videotapes that Kanzi saw, worked at many of the same computer-based video tasks, and traveled to a number of the same locations surrounding the laboratory, including some of those in the woods. Alia did not find food in the forest, as did Kanzi, nor did she interact directly with the apes, although she saw them through the window often and watched them on tape regularly.

Alia comprehended 32 spoken words at 13 months of age in a formal test that required her to select a photograph from an array when she heard the spoken word. (Similar tests are reported elsewhere for Kanzi; see Savage-Rumbaugh et al., 1990.) She spontaneously employed lexigram symbols at 7½ months of age, several months before producing intelligible spoken words, which she did at 11 months. Her first spoken word was *jazz* (for *shoes*). By 13 months, she produced 26 intelligible words with demonstrated comprehension. The Bayley test of motor and cognitive development (Bayley, 1969), administered at 1 year, 21 days, indicated that Alia was 3–5 months advanced for her age, placing her 1 standard deviation above the mean. Her mean length of utterance (MLU) was 1.91 morphemes at the beginning of the tests reported here. By the end of the current study, it had risen to 3.19. (Kanzi's MLU was 1.15 at 5 years of age and remained there throughout the period covered by this study.)

The tests of comprehension skill took place across 9 months (from May 18, 1988, to February 25, 1989) for Kanzi and across 6 months (from January 30, 1989, to July 19, 1989) for Alia. Kanzi's testing was interrupted for 5 months and Alia's for 3 months, in both cases owing to experimenters having to take unrelated leaves of absence.

DESIGN AND PROCEDURE

Location

The subjects were tested in different buildings approximately 300 feet apart. Kanzi was tested in the main laboratory area, where he was reared, while Alia was tested in the double-wide mobile home, where she had spent each weekday afternoon with her mother from 3 months of age. Both subjects knew the names of most of the rooms in these areas and were intimately familiar with the general floor plans shown in Figure 1 and with the typical furnishings of their test area. Objects were placed in a group a few feet in front of each subject. Prior to each day's testing, objects were also placed in other rooms if any of the test sentences in that session required the subjects to retrieve objects from other areas.

Whenever available, additional personnel who were familiar to the subjects were asked to be present so that test sentences that required the subject to act on or with another animate could be presented. These persons sat at a distance of 3–10 feet from the subjects. In Kanzi's case they were generally located behind him, whereas in Alia's case they sat to her left because the mobile-home floor plan made it difficult to locate someone behind Alia. Alia's 4-year-old brother, Nathaniel, was present throughout all test sessions, and her younger sister, Katie, was present in the later ones. Kanzi's siblings and mother were present in adjacent rooms throughout his test sessions.

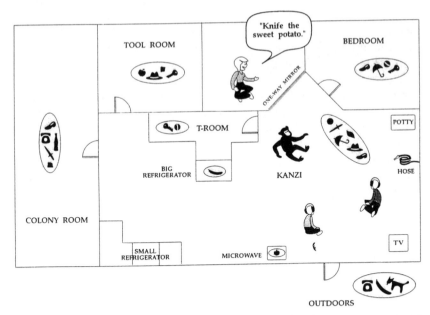

Fig. 1a.—Figures 1a and 1b depict the basic layout of the test environment for Kanzi and for Alia, respectively. Both subjects were very familiar with the various named locations in their respective test settings. Alia was separated from the experimenter only by a large one-way mirror. The experimenter's voice carried over the mirror, and Alia could walk around it. For the majority of the blind trials, Kanzi was separated from the experimenter by a steel door with a ¼-inch lexan one-way mirror. This made it more difficult for him to hear the experimenter.

SSR conducted the tests with Kanzi; Alia was tested by JM. Neither experimenter was aware of the responses of the other subject on the test trials; thus, knowledge of what Kanzi did could not have influenced Alia's results, or vice versa.

Pretest

Prior to administration of the spoken English test sentences, both subjects were tested with individual words to ensure that they comprehended most of the words to be employed in the sentences. In general, novel test sentences were limited to words that the subjects comprehended on this pretest. Occasionally, words that were not a part of the pretest appeared in a sentence. Alia and Kanzi's vocabularies overlapped for the majority of items, but, whenever a word used with Kanzi was not known by Alia, substitution of an appropriate word from the same vocabulary class was made for

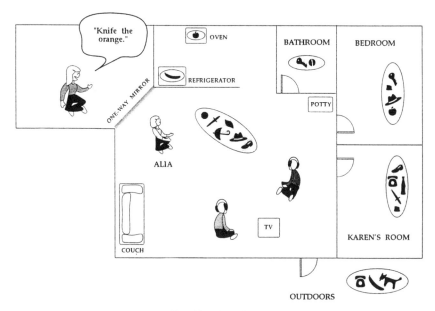

FIG. 1*b*.—See Fig. 1*a*

her in the test sentence. The test was begun with Kanzi, and each sentence was presented to Kanzi before it was presented to Alia.

Test Environment

Both subjects were allowed free access to food during the test, and both were allowed to play between trials. Trials were never started unless the subject indicated a willingness to participate; consequently, it was important to maintain a cooperative attitude in both subjects. Because the experimenters also participated in their rearing, both subjects were accustomed to cooperating with them on a daily basis, and the experimenters were accustomed to determining their moods and facilitating a cooperative attitude. In spite of this, both subjects often balked and occasionally refused to participate in the test. Generally, such disruptions were handled by engaging in another activity for a short period of time and then requesting participation in the test once again.

Nonblind Trials

The test was divided into two parts, blind and nonblind trials. We recognized that results indicating linguistic comprehension on the part of either subject would be suspect if either Kanzi's caretaker or Alia's mother were visible to the subject. It was important to determine how well each subject could respond to the sentence when no linguistically competent partner was available to provide helpful gestures, glances, or other means of nonverbal assistance. Consequently, it was important to present sentences from behind a one-way mirror so as to preclude any unintentional nonverbal communication with the subject.

However, neither subject was accustomed to responding to requests produced by a disembodied voice. Both found it odd that their caretaker should hide under a blanket or behind a mirror and then ask them to do something. Even after they realized that this was to be her behavior and that they were still supposed to do as she asked, both subjects seemed to feel somewhat ill at ease. Both also attempted to do things that they were not normally allowed to do, so as to determine whether they could be seen. Kanzi was far more adamant in this regard than Alia. Consequently, the "nonblind" portion of the test was used to familiarize the subjects with the expectancies generated by the test-setting procedure (i.e., sitting quietly and listening to the experimenter, attempting to do what the experimenter asked, and playing or eating between trials). It was helpful for the experimenter to be visible during this portion of the test in order to initiate the cooperative participation and maintain the attention of the subject. Blind control trials were slowly introduced during this period, and both subjects learned that they were expected to listen and to attempt to carry out the instructions in the sentence. They also learned that, if they did not know what to do, the experimenter would help them. Attempts to keep the atmosphere playful and to engage the subject in the game "what will the experimenter say next?" were constantly maintained.

It proved necessary to query both subjects about their state with such questions as, "Are you ready now?" Alia typically indicated readiness by saying "Yes" or "OK," while Kanzi did so by producing a sound that resembled "Un huh" or "Ready" with regard to intonational contour. On some trials, he gestured toward the experimenter to indicate readiness. Whenever the subject could not carry out a request correctly, the experimenter provided help and scored the data accordingly. From the subjects' viewpoint, they were always "correct," but at some times they needed more help than at others.

During the nonblind portion of the test, the experimenter sat in front of the subject and, using spoken English alone, asked the subjects to carry out a particular action on a group of randomly selected objects placed in front of them. During the early trials of this portion, sentences were sometimes broken down so as to make them easier to understand. Thus, for example, in saying, "Get the paper . . . put the paper in the backpack," the experimenter intentionally waited until the subject had selected the first object (the paper) before uttering the second part of the sentence. Overall, 29 such sentences were administered during the nonblind segment of data collection.

Blind Trials

Once the subject was comfortable and responding well in the nonblind test situation, the experimenter moved behind a one-way mirror and remained there both while saying the sentence and while the subject carried out the requested action. If the subject's response was incorrect or only partially correct, the experimenter helped the subject as needed until the request was accurately carried out. The blind phase was begun after 244 trials for Kanzi but after only 180 trials for Alia. However, for purposes of data analysis, only trials subsequent to the 244th are treated as "blind" trials for both subjects.

As noted earlier, both subjects initially refused to respond to a request from a party that could not be seen; however, continued urging sufficed to overcome the apparent "strangeness" of the blind testing, and both willingly began to reply to the requests of the invisible experimenter. That the experimenter came out from behind the screen to help carry out a sentence if the subject was hesitant or incorrect appeared to be important in eliciting both subjects' willingness to cooperate. It also proved necessary to speak to the subjects from behind the one-way mirror using a natural conversational style, as though the test were a game of sorts in which they were allowed to participate. If the experimenter started to speak in a more formal manner, both subjects tended to stop attending.

Throughout the test, some of the requests referred to activities involving other persons. Initially, such persons covered their eyes so that they could not see what the subject was doing. However, since both subjects hesitated to carry out actions toward people who kept their eyes covered and were unresponsive, it proved necessary during the early blind trials to permit these persons to behave as appropriate recipients when the action was specifically directed to them (as, for instance, in the request "Can you give Liz a shot?"). Note, however, that these individuals were located well away from the subject and spaced far apart; additionally, they kept their eyes covered until the subject had selected the correct object and approached them. (This technique was employed for approximately the first 100 blind trials with Kanzi. In Alia's case, for approximately the first 300 blind trials these persons were placed well away from the array, and Alia did not generally look toward them while responding unless directed to do so by the experimenter on that trial. They did not cover their eyes as Alia became uncomfortable when everyone else in the room hid their eyes.)

TABLE 2

MEAN NUMBER OF OBJECTS AND AGENTS IN THE ARRAYS FACING KANZI AND ALIA

| | KANZI | | ALIA | |
| | Objects | Agents | Objects | Agents |
TRIALS				
1–100	18	3	5	2
101–200	13	2	4	2
201–300	7	3	6	2
301–400	8	3	7	3
401–500	9	3	7	3
501–600	12	3	8	3
601–end	12	3	8	3

For both Kanzi and Alia, in all subsequent trials such persons were equipped with radio headphones that transmitted loud music. This prevented them from hearing the target sentence but nonetheless permitted seeing the subject and smiling in order to indicate their willingness to engage in an activity when approached by the subject.

While blind conditions were utilized as a standard procedure to prevent inadvertent cuing, neither subject typically looked for cues, and failure to carry out the request appropriately did not prompt the subjects to do so either.

Sentence Construction

Objects were selected and displayed randomly for both subjects. Initially, Kanzi would not search through a large array of objects systematically before carrying out an action; consequently, the majority of his errors—particularly in the nonblind trials—resulted from a failure to examine all the objects in front of him. The array was subsequently decreased, and this problem disappeared. Because of Kanzi's difficulty, the arrays presented to Alia were smaller. The mean number of objects and agents included in arrays facing each subject (grouped by blocks of 100 trials) are shown in Table 2. When found in other locations, at least three objects were placed at each site prior to the test session.

Sentences were generated by taking a random selection of objects, locations, and agents and forming requests from this array; the structure of the sentences was varied systematically (see below). In order to preclude the criticism that the subjects' responses were determined by the constituents of the array itself rather than by the sentence that was presented, multiple sentences were given for each array. For example, the sentences "Go vacuum Liz," "Go put some soap on Liz," "Rose is gonna chase Kanzi," "Put on the monster mask and scare Linda," "I want Kanzi to grab Rose," "Take the mushrooms to Matata," and "Kanzi is going to chase Rose" were all presented while the array in front of Kanzi consisted of the following items: monster mask, ball, bunny puppet, sweet potato, melon, soap, umbrella, straw, toothbrush, toy gorilla, hose, vacuum, mushrooms, two televisions, and a shoe. The persons in the room were Liz, Linda, Rose, and Kelly, and the available locations were tool room, colony room, microwave, refrigerator, outdoors, and potty. (A complete list of the options available on each trial is available from the authors on request.)

In the majority of instances, the requests were for actions that the subjects were unlikely to have encountered in their daily environment. Thus, "Can you make the snake bite the doggie?" was judged to be an unusual request because the referents for *snake* and *doggie* were toy animals, whereas in Kanzi and Alia's experience these words had been used to refer to the real snakes in the woods and to the real dogs that lived at the laboratory. It was highly improbable that either subject would have previously heard anyone speak of a snake biting a dog; however, both probably would have heard someone caution that a snake or a dog could bite them. Similarly, since no one ever cooked lettuce, neither subject would ever have been asked, "Take the lettuce out of the microwave," or have heard someone say, "Wash the hotdogs," since that is not what is done with hotdogs.

In any case, both Alia and Kanzi's experience prior to these test trials had been limited to hearing sentences in meaningful contexts. Thus, if someone had asked one of them to put hotdogs in the pan, it was in the course of cooking; if someone had told them to watch out for a snake that might bite, it was because a snake lying on the trail in front of them appeared ready to bite. Previous linguistic experiences were thus real and meaningful, providing both subjects with an intrinsic reason to understand the sentence spoken to them; this factor was lacking during the test trials.

Test Differences between Subjects

Overall, Kanzi received 244 nonblind trials, followed by 416 blind ones, and Alia received 180 nonblind trials, followed by 410 blind ones. Since the order of the requests in both conditions was random, those that Alia failed to receive varied randomly across sentence types. Alia had fewer nonblind trials than Kanzi because her testing was interrupted by the birth of a sibling, and the latter portion of the nonblind segment was dropped so as to conclude her testing within a reasonable time frame.

Sentence Types

The requests were classified into 13 types and subtypes according to the different interpretive demands that they placed on the subject. The number of sentences within each type differs because these structural groupings emerged while the data were being collected. Thus, for example, when it became apparent that the subjects could take an object to a location, it became important to determine whether they could also go to a specified location and retrieve an object. Similarly, when we found that they could put object X in object Y, it was then necessary to determine whether they were responding to X and Y as key words to initiate the "put" routine or integrating the information about the object with that carried by the verb. Consequently, sentences that asked them to "Give X and Y" were introduced. Because it was important to avoid consecutive repetitions of a given sentence type, additional exemplars of previous types were presented as new types were introduced. As a result, some sentence types are overrepresented in the data set, whereas others are underrepresented either because they were difficult to fit into the current test model or because the subject's vocabulary was not sufficiently developed to permit many novel constructions. The various sentence types are described below.

Type 1

Type 1A: Put object X *in/on transportable object* Y (e.g., "Put the ball on the pine needles"; see Fig. 2).—These sentences required that the subject construct a relation of adjacency between two objects, X and Y. Both X and Y were movable; consequently, actions of this type could be reversed. Objects X and Y were related by the verb *put* and by a preposition. The prepositions *in* and *on* were used to denote the spatial relations of X and Y. However, neither subject responded differentially to specific prepositions in a consistent manner. They generally placed X in, on, or next to Y, treating all prepositions as conveying "adjacent" placement information. Because the goal of type 1A requests was to determine whether the subjects understood that the sentence required them to construct a relation between X and Y (as opposed to acting independently on X and Y), not to determine whether they fully comprehended the prepositions, they were scored as having responded correctly if they placed X and Y in any adjacent relation.

Type 1B: Put object X *in nontransportable object* Y (e.g., "Put the ice water in the potty"; see Fig. 3).—These requests were very similar to type 1A sentences except that one of the objects was large and bulky, not something that typically would be moved. The distinction between types 1A and 1B was made to allow an analysis taking into account the transportability of the objects, as a similar analysis had been done in evaluating sentence compre-

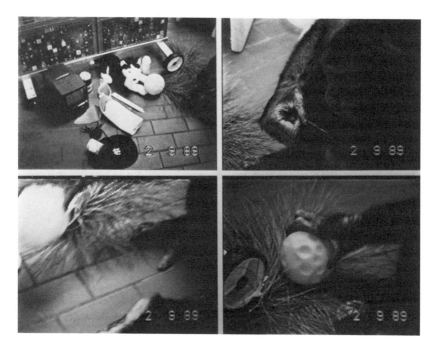

FIG. 2.—This figure illustrates the array immediately in front of Kanzi (top left), Kanzi listening to the type 1A sentence "Put your ball on the pine needles" (top right), and Kanzi immediately picking up the ball (bottom left) and placing it on the branch of pine needles (bottom right).

hension in dolphins by Schusterman and Gisiner (1988). These authors point out that requests involving a nontransportable object are simpler because errors of inverting the object-object relation cannot occur—for example, while one can "put the melon in the potty," one cannot "put the potty in the melon." The nontransportables used in the current study were car, Fourtrax (an off-road vehicle), potty, vacuum, cabinet, trash receptacle, television, microwave, door, hose, and refrigerator.

Type 2

Type 2A: Give (or show) object X *to animate* A (e.g., "Give the lighter to Rose").—These requests required that the subject show or give an object to a person or other animate. For purposes of the test, the "other animates" were toy representations of living animals such as dogs, snakes, gorillas, etc.; hence, these items were also "objects" in the sense that the "animate" qualities that they possessed had to be endowed by the subjects' imagination.

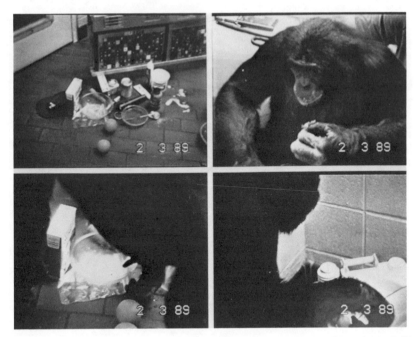

FIG. 3.—This figure illustrates the array immediately in front of Kanzi (top left), Kanzi listening to the type 1B sentence "Put the ice water in the potty" (the potty was listed as a nontransportable object) (top right), and Kanzi picking up the bowl of ice water (bottom left) and pouring it into the potty (bottom right).

(Both subjects did engage in pretend behaviors with these toys and treated them as "animates.") It should be noted that both Kanzi and Alia learned the words *dog* and *snake* as a result of encounters with real dogs and snakes. They learned *bunny* as the name of a Sesame Street–type character that appeared in the lab and on videotape from time to time, but the "bunny" used in the test was a hand puppet that only marginally resembled the "bunny" they were accustomed to seeing. However, both subjects transferred the terms from the real objects to the inanimate ones and proceeded to make the inanimate objects act out the sentences as they understood them without special training or help. *Show* and *give* were summed together for purposes of analysis because it was difficult to differentiate the subjects' responses to them.

Type 2B: Give object X *and object* Y *to animate* A (e.g., "Give the peas and the sweet potatoes to Kelly"; see Fig. 4).—These requests were equivalent to type 2A sentences except that the subjects were asked to give or show two objects instead of one. These trials were included as controls to determine whether the mere mention of two objects would cause the subjects to at-

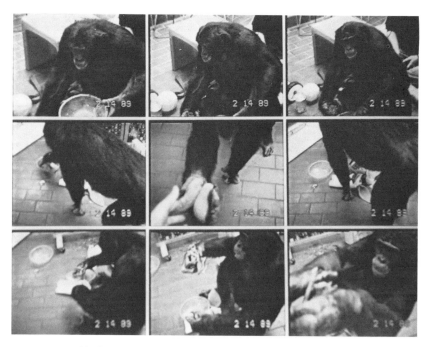

FIG. 4.—This figure illustrates Kanzi listening to the type 2B sentence "Give Kelly the peas and the sweet potatoes" (top three frames), Kanzi selecting the sweet potatoes and handing them to Kelly (who is videotaping him) (middle left and center frames), then selecting the peas after the experimenter has added "and the peas" and giving Kelly the peas as well (middle right and bottom three frames).

tempt to relate them in some manner. That is, on hearing two key words such as *doggie* and *ball* in the sentence "Show me the doggie and the ball," would they try, for example, to put the ball on the doggie? If the subjects were to attempt to construct some type of relation between X and Y in response to these sentences, it would indicate that they were not responding to the verb and the relation it specified in either type 2A or type 2B sentences but instead were responding in some manner to "key words" as a part of a generalized expectancy of the test.

Different responses to *doggie* and *ball* in response to type 2B and 2D (see below) sentences would indicate that the subjects were able to construct a relation of transfer with two objects when the verb *give* was employed and a relation of adjacency between the same two objects when the verb *put* was used; this would imply that the verb could function to control the relation of the objects to each other or to control the relation of both objects to the recipient.

Type 2C: (Do) action A on animate A (e.g., "Give Rose a hug"; see

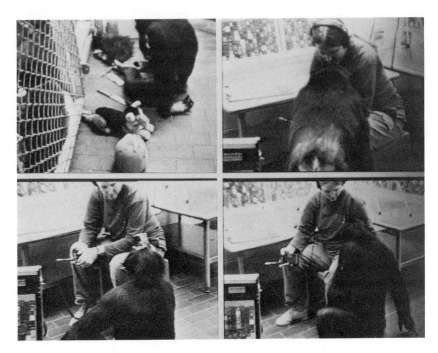

Fig. 5.—This figure illustrates, first, the array immediately in front of Kanzi as he listens to the type 2C sentence "Give Rose a hug" (top left). He does not act on the array; instead he goes directly to Rose and attempts to press his cheek against her (top right). However, she is looking down and listening to loud music (so as not to provide any input to Kanzi); consequently, it is difficult for him to "hug" her. Kanzi then sits down and taps her gently on the arm (bottom left). Rose looks over at Kanzi and moves her arms into a more open position (bottom right). Kanzi presses his cheek and chest against Rose's body, but he is hesitant to put his arms around her since she still does not understand what he is doing.

Fig. 5).—The requests in this group required only that the subjects execute a simple action on a recipient; no object was involved. Verbs used in these sentences were *bite, chase, groom, hammer, hide, hug, play, scare, slap, tickle, wash,* and *vacuum.* The purpose of including sentences of this form was to provide a contrast with sentences of type 2B, in which the basic person-object relation was one of giving or showing. Could the subjects respond to verbs that specified other types of relationships to animates?

Type 2D: (Do) action A *on animate* A *with object* X (e.g., "Get Rose with the snake"; see Fig. 6).—These sentences expanded the action-animate format of type 2C to request that the subject act on the recipient (who could be a person, a pretend animate, or the subjects themselves) with an object. Verbs employed in this sentence type were *brush, feed, get, hide, hit, put, scare, take, tickle, throw,* and *wash.* In the simple action-animate format of type 2C

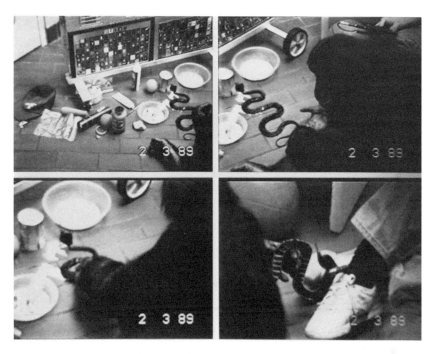

Fig. 6.—This figure illustrates the array immediately in front of Kanzi (top left), Kanzi listening to the type 2D sentence "Get Rose with the snake" (top right), and Kanzi picking up the snake and tossing it toward Rose (bottom left), who kicks back at it with her foot.

requests, the relationship between the verb and the animate is fully specified by the utterance of each word; that is, there is no alternative interpretation of a sentence such as "Tickle Kelly" given that the subject understands the words *tickle* and *Kelly*. In type 2D sentences, other interpretations do present themselves. For example, "Hit the dog with the stick" could result in hitting the stick with the (toy) dog or in hitting the dog with the stick. Thus, while type 2C sentences ask whether the subjects can relate a verb and a recipient in a manner that is intrinsically inherent in the semantic content of the words, type 2D sentences ask whether they can use the verb to construct a complex relationship between object and recipient that is specified only by the complete sentence alone and that is not inherent in the semantics of its specific elements.

Type 3

(Do) action A *on object* X *(with object* Y*)* (e.g., "Knife the sweet potato"; see Figs. 7, 8).—The following verbs appeared in type 3 sentences: *bite, eat,*

FIG. 7.—This figure illustrates the array in front of Kanzi (top left), Kanzi listening to the type 3 sentence "Knife the sweet potatoes" (top right), and Kanzi picking up the knife (bottom left) and repeatedly stabbing the sweet potatoes (bottom right).

feed, hammer, hide, knife, open, play, slap, squeeze, throw, wash, and *vacuum.* In contrast to the verbs of more general movement, such as *show, put,* etc., all these verbs specify a particular type of action that was to be carried out on an object. These sentences generally requested that the action take place on a single object.

The nature of the relationship between objects X and Y is not inherent in the semantic content of the words themselves. That is, the sweet potato could act on the knife, or vice versa. Thus, these requests could not be correctly executed simply by responding to key words without understanding the intended relationship between items carried by the syntactic structure of the sentence.

Type 4

Announce information (e.g., "The surprise is hiding in the dishwasher").—These sentences differ from all others in that they did not re-

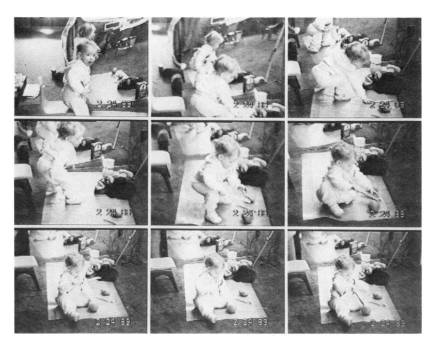

FIG. 8.—This figure illustrates, first, Alia starting toward the array, having just heard the type 3 sentence "Can you knife the orange?" Alia bends over, picks up the knife, goes to the orange, and attempts to poke it, in much the same manner as Kanzi poked at the sweet potato with the knife.

quest a specific action but simply provided the subject with information. Although constructed in a variety of syntactic forms, they are lumped together here as a group since their purpose was not to investigate syntactic features but to determine whether the subjects would respond appropriately if the statement was not in a request format. In their everyday lives, most of the sentences heard by Kanzi and Alia functioned to provide information rather than to make requests; the latter were employed extensively during this test simply because this format provides the clearest assay of what it was that the subject understood about any given sentence.

Information that was of interest and designed to promote some response was presented to the subjects in order to determine whether they would respond to statements as they would to requests. This information was limited to two forms: announcements either of where an object was hidden or that another party was about to engage in a tickle or a chase game with them.

Fig. 9.—This figure illustrates the array in front of Kanzi (top left), Kanzi listening to the type 5A sentence "Take the snake outdoors" (top right), and Kanzi picking up the snake (bottom left) and then putting it down on a log outdoors (bottom right).

Type 5

Type 5A: Take object X *to location* Y (e.g., "Take the snake outdoors"; see Fig. 9).—These sentences required the subject to take an object to a specified location or, in some cases, to an animate. The type 5A requests were similar to the type 1B requests. However, type 5A sentences generally employed distinct spatial entities, such as *bedroom, outdoors,* etc., rather than bulky objects, such as *vacuum* and *refrigerator.* Also, most type 5A sentences employed the verb *take,* while type 1B sentences employed the verb *put.*

Type 5B: Go to location Y *and get object* X (e.g., "Go to the refrigerator and get a banana"; see Fig. 10).—These sentences requested that the subject go to a particular location and "get" an object. Between six and nine different words indicating locations were employed during each session. For Kanzi, these included *bedroom, cabinet, colony room, dishwasher, hammock, hose, microwave, outdoors, play yard, refrigerator, television, tool room, trash bin,* and *T-room* (a room shaped like the letter *T*). For Alia, they included *bedroom,*

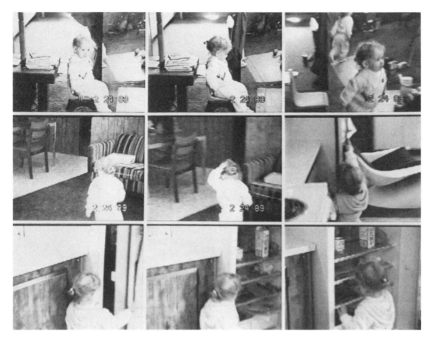

FIG. 10.—This figure illustrates Alia waiting for the sentence by the one-way mirror, Alia listening to the type 5B sentence "Go to the refrigerator and get a banana," Alia heading off in response to the sentence (her back can be seen in the one-way mirror), Alia on her way to the refrigerator, Alia trying to open the refrigerator, Alia looking in the refrigerator tentatively, and Alia selecting a banana from the refrigerator.

couch, Karen's room, kitchen, living room, outdoors, oven, refrigerator, and *television.*

Three or more objects were placed in each of these locations so that, when the subjects traveled to the correct place, they had to remember and retrieve the requested item, not simply any item that was there. Additionally, these objects were not ones usually found at that place. For example, although many objects were stored in the T-room, potatoes were not. Thus, the sentence "Go to the T-room and get the potato" could not be carried out simply by listening to the word *potato* and traveling to a place where potatoes were always found. Furthermore, the central positioning of the immediate array of objects was such that the other objects could not be seen prior to traveling to the indicated location. Thus, the subjects could not simply look around for the mentioned object and then retrieve it without really understanding where they were to go.

In order to determine whether the subjects were simply responding to

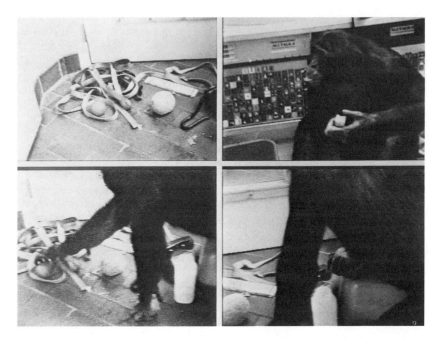

Fig. 11a.—Of Figs. 11a and 11b, Fig. 11a illustrates the array immediately in front of Kanzi (top left) as he listens to the control type 5B sentence "Go to the bedroom and get the tomato" (top right). Kanzi responds by picking up the tomato from the array (bottom left) and looking at it (bottom right). In Fig. 11b, the experimenter asks Kanzi to put this tomato down, which he does by tossing it on the floor (top left). The experimenter repeats the sentence. Kanzi then responds by immediately stepping over the keyboard (top right) and going into the bedroom (bottom left). The bedroom lexigram can be seen on the door as Kanzi approaches the array of objects in the bedroom. In the final scene (bottom right), Kanzi steps back over the keyboard carrying a tomato from the bedroom in his left hand.

the object and the location terms without integrating the information carried by the verb, a control set of sentences was presented in which the item to be retrieved from the distal location was duplicated in the central array. It was possible for the subjects to err on such trials by acting on the object in front of them, perhaps by taking it to the designated location and then returning with it. For instance, "Go to the bedroom and get a tomato," when a tomato was also in the central array could well result in such behavior (see Fig. 11).

It is important to note that, while these control trials present the subjects with the decision of whether to act on the object in front of them or go to another place to look for it, all type 5B sentences were *semantically ambiguous*. This is because the type 5B format implied, but did not actually specify, which of the duplicate objects was to be "retrieved." Thus, the

Fig. 11b.—See Fig. 11a

subject could interpret the sentence as a request to go to a location, then return and "get" the object in the central array; to do so would not violate the syntactic constraints of the type 5B format. Consequently, in order completely to specify which object was to be acted on (the one in the immediate or the one in the distal array), type 5C sentences were also given.

Type 5C: Go get object X *that's in location* Y (e.g., "Go get the carrot that's in the microwave"; see Fig. 12).—By adding the embedded phrasal modifier *that's*, the object of choice was clarified as the one in the distal location. Type 5C requests were not initially included in the test as they were thought to be grammatically too complex for these subjects. However, during an attempt to correct an error on a type 5B control sentence, the phrasal modifier *that's* was employed. On hearing it, Kanzi stopped acting on the object in front of him and went to the distal location to retrieve the specified object. Consequently, type 5C sentences were added to determine whether this was a reliable skill for either subject.

As was the case with type 5B requests, in some instances the object to be retrieved was found only in the distal location, but on type 5C control trials the specified object was found in both the immediate and the distal array (e.g., "Go get the melon that's in the bedroom," with a melon in the

Fig. 12a.—Of Figs. 12a and 12b, Fig. 12a illustrates the array immediately in front of Kanzi (top left) as he listens to the type 5C sentence "Go get the carrot that's in the microwave" (top right). Kanzi does not even look at the array for a carrot, but instead turns at once and heads for the microwave (bottom left). Kanzi has moved so rapidly that the cameraperson finds him already at the microwave opening the door by the time she has followed him to the kitchen area (bottom right). In Fig. 12b, Kanzi can be seen reaching into the microwave and selecting a carrot (from among other items) (top left and right), looking at the carrot as he takes it out of the microwave (bottom left), and returning with it in the final scene (bottom right). In this scene, the experimeter is behind the reflective mirror surface in front of the small couch to which Kanzi is returning.

array directly in front of Kanzi and also one in the potty; see Fig. 13). Trials of this type did not permit an ambiguous interpretation and thus could be contrasted with the ambiguous type 5B control trials.

Type 6

Make pretend animate A *do action* A *on recipient* Y (e.g., "Make the doggie bite the snake"; see Fig. 14).—These requests made use of toy objects such as a dog, a snake, a bunny, and so on. The pretend animates were employed only for test purposes, and, as noted earlier, neither subject was specifically taught to transfer from real to pretend exemplars for purposes of this test, although both did so readily. Both subjects understood the application of

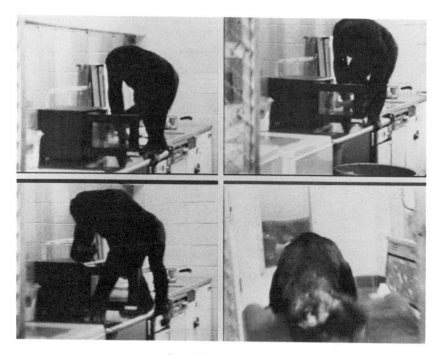

Fig. 12b.—See Fig. 12a

these terms to toys as a form of "pretending" and treated these toys very differently than they would treat the real animal. Additionally, their treatment was appropriate; for example, they patted and hugged the dog but held the snake gingerly.

Type 7

All other sentence types.—The final grouping included 11 sentences that differed from all the above and did not form a single category of their own. Seven of these 11 entailed two verbs, and each verb was associated with a different object or recipient. Thus, this grouping, although small, represented more complex sentences than any other grouping in the data base.

DATA COLLECTION

Scoring Responses

All trials were videotaped, except for instances where the camera malfunctioned or the subject moved out of view too rapidly. Sixty trials were

FIG. 13.—This figure illustrates the array immediately in front of Kanzi (top left) as he listens to the control type 5C sentence "Get the melon that's in the potty" (top right). (The large round object on the left of the array is the melon.) Kanzi starts toward the potty at once, walking past and in fact stepping over the melon that is in the array in order to reach the potty (bottom left). He takes the melon out of the potty, smelling it as he does so (bottom right).

not recorded for Kanzi and 57 for Alia; all occurred during the nonblind condition.

The subjects' performance was coded on all trials in real time by each experimenter according to a simple tripartite code: correct, partly correct, incorrect.

Correct

When the subjects carried out the request appropriately, even if doing something else they wanted to do first, they were scored as correct. (For example, Kanzi brushed himself before brushing the toy dog as requested, and Alia placed a sparkler in the clay before she put it on the ball.) We judged in such cases that the sentence was understood but that a preferred action was carried out before responding directly to the request. In some cases, the experimenter had to repeat or rephrase the original instruction as the subjects became distracted by engagement in their own activity. On still other occasions, the subjects became so engrossed in their own activities that it was necessary to intervene and then repeat the sentence. All such trials were scored as "correct" if the subjects carried out the request *immediately* after their own initial actions or after the experimenter succeeded in focusing their attention on the sentence itself.

Partially Correct

Subjects were scored as "partially correct" if they attempted to carry out the request but appeared to understand it only in part. For example, when asked to "Bite the rock," Kanzi bit the stick; when asked to "Vacuum the ball," Alia put oil on the ball instead. As with correct trials, subjects often did something they preferred to do prior to carrying out the request in these instances as well. However, in contrast to responses coded "correct," after the experimenter repeated the sentence or intervened to remove a distracting object, the request was still not carried out appropriately. On incorrect and partially correct trials, the experimenter often repeated and/ or rephrased the sentence several times in an attempt to help the subject, but to no avail. The experimenter then showed the subject the correct action and, if needed, helped the subject carry it out. Thus, subjects were typically asked to continue trying until the request was carried out; sometimes they did this quickly and on their own, and at other times they needed assistance from the experimenter. However, they were eventually correct in most instances and were told so on each trial. On some occasions, the subjects continued to insist that they were carrying out the request correctly despite the experimenter's attempts to help them correct their error. Regardless of whether they were eventually correct or not, if their response before the experimenter intervened was incorrect or appropriate only for a portion of the sentence, that trial was not scored as correct.

Both subjects also occasionally added something extra in responding to the request. These "elaborations," which may have reflected a partial misunderstanding or been an intentional addition to the requested actions, occurred on trials in which all other sentence constituents were responded to appropriately as well as on trials in which some constituent of the sentence was not responded to appropriately. For example, when Alia was asked to "Go get the carrot that's in the oven," she brought back the carrot as well as some soap. In our coding schema, returning from a location with an additional item did not detract from a correct code if the subjects indicated in some manner that they wanted to play with or to consume the extra object. However, if they simply returned with more than one item and gave all such items to the experimenter, they were scored as having made an object error.

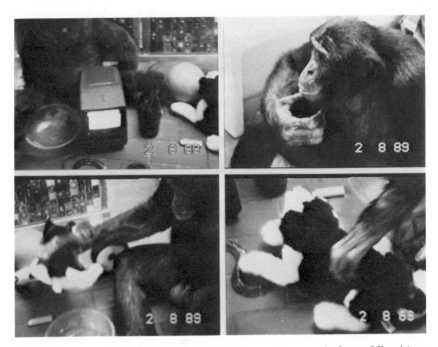

FIG. 14a.—Of Figs. 14a and 14b, Fig. 14a illustrates the array in front of Kanzi (top left) as he listens to the type 6 sentence "Make the doggie bite the snake" (top right). First, Kanzi picks up the doggie and puts it on top of the snake (bottom left and right). Next, in Fig. 14b, he picks up the snake and looks at it (top left and right), then opens the dog's mouth and inserts the snake's head (bottom left and right).

Incorrect

As noted above, incorrect scores were given when the subjects failed to complete any portion of the sentence correctly.

Interobserver Reliability: Tripartite Code

Kanzi's responses were coded in real time by Sue Savage-Rumbaugh (SSR), and Alia's were similarly coded by Jeannine Murphy (JM). However, to ensure the accuracy of the real-time code, the videotape was scored by a third person, Lisa Conger (LC). LC had not worked with Kanzi and was unfamiliar with apes in general. Her initial coding consisted of a determination as to whether the subjects correctly completed all parts of the request, executed it partially, or were completely wrong. She also made a judgment as to whether any behavior on the part of SSR or JM (such as repeating a sentence) may have helped the subject perform the sentence correctly.

Fig. 14*b.*—See Fig. 14*a*

Interobserver percentage agreement for the tripartite code (correct, partly correct, or incorrect) was computed for randomly selected trials for each subject. SSR coded 386 randomly selected trials from videotape of Kanzi. Another observer, Linda Gilmore (LG), coded 326 randomly selected trials from videotape of Alia. Percentage agreement on the judgment of correct, partially correct, or incorrect response was .98 for Kanzi and .89 for Alia. Percentage agreement on judgments that behaviors on the part of the experimenter may have helped the subject was .83 for Kanzi and .64 for Alia.

Expanded Coding System

Subsequently, SSR reviewed the tapes to determine what types of events may have led to discrepant ratings on judgment codes. This review indicated that both SSR and JM made frequent inferences as to whether Kanzi and Alia were cooperating, attending, purposefully ignoring them, etc. These determinations were based on extensive knowledge of these subjects as individuals. For example, when asked to "Put the raisins in the yogurt," Alia became interested in her reflection in the mirror and slapped at it before carrying out the sentence. The "mirror slapping" was not interpreted by JM as an attempt to respond to the sentence. Similarly, when asked to "Go to the bedroom and get the milk," Kanzi ate some mushrooms first, then carried out the sentence. SSR did not interpret Kanzi's mushroom consumption as an indication that he misunderstood the sentence.

On other occasions of actual or potential disagreement, the subjects' initial actions were focused on an item mentioned in the sentence, but the nature of the action differed from the requested one. For example, when asked to "Knife the doggie," Kanzi began to play with the toy dog and continued to do so until the sentence was repeated. When asked to "Put the pine needles in the ball," Alia only played with the ball until the experimenter asked, "Do you see the pine needles?" and repeated the sentence. In such cases, some judgment as to whether the subject was ignoring the sentence or did not understand it had to be made.

Thus, a second coding system was designed, and a more complete transcription of the subjects' responses was made for all trials by additional observers. Linda McGarrah (LM) transcribed Kanzi's data, and Shane Keating (SK) and LG transcribed Alia's data. These transcriptions also included information about the behavior of the experimenters prior to the subjects' response to the sentence. The revised coding scheme, presented in Table 3, took this information into account.

Unlike the simpler tripartite code, the revised scheme broke down correct trials into a number of different categories for the purpose of determining whether different behaviors on the part of SSR and JM during sentence presentation may have led to differing performances by Kanzi and Alia. Consequently, such things as whether SSR or JM repeated the sentence, redirected the subjects' attention, or asked the subject not to engage in a tangential activity were noted.

Two persons, SSR and Shelly Williams (SW), independently assigned the codes shown in the Appendix on the basis of these written transcriptions. Whenever the transcription appeared inadequate to determine what the code should be, SSR or SW reviewed the videotape. Cohen's kappa was computed to determine SSR and SW's agreement with regard to their interpretations of the transcriptions. The kappa value was .72 for Kanzi and .83 for Alia.

These codes, along with a full description of the events on each blind trial, are presented in the Appendix. In preparing the Appendix, it was found that the transcriptions made for the purpose of assigning codes did not always provide a sufficiently detailed description of everything that occurred. These transcriptions were made to permit code assignment rather than to detail each and every event. Consequently, all the blind trials were

TABLE 3

CRITERIA FOR CODING SUBJECTS' RESPONSES TO REQUESTS

Code and Type of Response	Response
Correct:	
C	S carries out the request immediately and correctly
C1–C5	S first hesitates or engages in a tangential activity, then . . .
C1	S carries out the request correctly
C2	E repeats the request; S carries it out promptly
C3	E rewords and may repeat the request; S carries it out promptly
C4	S's involvement in the tangential activity interferes with his/her ability to attend; E insists the activity stop and then repeats the request; S carries it out promptly
C5	Asked to retrieve a distal object, S attends to its duplicate in the immediate array; E redirects attention to the distal object; S retrieves it promptly
Partially correct:	
PC	S is partially correct in carrying out the request
OE	S retrieves more objects than requested
I	S carries out the act in inverse order but is correct with regard to all other components of the request
Incorrect:	
W	S is incorrect with regard to all aspects of the request
NR	S does not respond or refuses to respond
M	Mistrial (an item mentioned in the request was unavailable)

NOTE.—S = subject. E = experimenter. Illustrative examples of each type of code are found in the Appendix.

reviewed for a third time, and a *complete* verbatim description of every action or utterance on the part of the experimenters and subjects was provided for Kanzi by SSR and for Alia by JM.

It is important to note that, although different observers coded the data, it was nonetheless the case that the real-time decisions made by SSR and JM affected all subsequent data coding. When they believed that the subjects' responses indicated a lack of attention, they typically waited, re-presented the sentence, urged the subject to respond, or sometimes directed the subjects' attention to an object that was not easy to see. When they believed that the subjects' failures to respond resulted from lack of comprehension, they typically began to engage in behaviors designed to help the subjects rather than encouraging them to go ahead. Consequently, these real-time interpretations of the subjects' reactions determined how soon and what type of help was given when the subjects did not carry out a request fairly quickly after it was made.

TABLE 4

SENTENCES PRESENTED TWICE TO KANZI

Sentence	First Code	Second Code
1. Can you put the apple in the hat?	I	C
2. Put the ball in the oil	C	I
3. Put the ball on the potty	I	I
4. Hide the ball	C	C
5. Give your ball a shot	C	C
6. Take the ball to the T-room	C	C
7. Take the ball to the bedroom	C	C
8. Make the doggie bite the ball	C	I
9. Put the ball in the bowl	C	C
10. Give the doggie some carrots	I	I
11. Put the clay on the vacuum	C	C
12. Take your collar outdoors	C	C
13. Go to the colony room and get the orange	C	I
14. Put the ball on the doggie	C	C
15. Give the doggie the pine needles	C	C
16. Hide the gorilla	C	C
17. Take the keys and open the T-room	C	C
18. Throw the ball to Liz	C	C
19. Put the milk in the water	C	C
20. Put the mushrooms in the cabinet	C	C
21. Put the oil in the backpack	I	C
22. Take the potato to the bedroom	C	C
23. Take the rock outdoors	I	C
24. Take the doggie outdoors	C	C
25. Take the sparklers outdoors	C	C
26. Put the rubber bands in the plastic bag	I	I
27. Put the sparklers on the TV	I	C
28. Eat the raisins	C	C
29. Put the pine needles on the TV	C	C
30. Put the telephone on the TV	C	C
31. Put your ball on the rock	C	C
32. Put some paint on the dog	I	C
33. Can you put the soap in the umbrella?	C	C
34. Put the melon in the tomatoes	I	I
35. Put the doggie on the vacuum	C	C
36. Knife your ball	C	C
37. Take the umbrella to the T-room	I	I
38. Can you put the blanket on the doggie?	C	C

NOTE.—C = any correct code: C1, C2, C3, C4, or C5. I = any incorrect code: PC, OE, I, W, NR, or M.

Test-Retest Reliability

In order to provide a measure of validity, 38 randomly selected requests were presented twice to Kanzi to determine whether the response could be replicated (see Table 4). These repeated presentations were separated by several weeks or months, and, in each case, the array of objects differed from the first to the second presentations. On 79% of the second-presentation trials, Kanzi did as well as or better than he had done originally, suggesting that his performance was relatively stable across time. Most of these sentences were also repeated for Alia; however, she was developing so rapidly during the test period that test-retest reliability was not expected in her case. In all instances of repeated administration, only the performance on the first occasion was included as part of the final data base, except for two trials on which both presentations were included. (In this case, the trial was given a second time because neither Kanzi nor Alia would attempt the requested action on a can of milk that was not open. The can was opened, the trial was re-presented later, and both trials were included in the data base.)

VI. RESULTS:
KANZI AND ALIA'S PERFORMANCE
ON DIFFERENT SENTENCE STRUCTURES

ALL SENTENCE TYPES

Kanzi and Alia's overall scores are presented in Table 5; these are shown broken down by sentence type in Table 6. Overall, Kanzi was correct on 72% of all trials and 74% of the blind ones. Alia was correct on 66% of all trials and 65% of the blind ones. (Table 6 gives the number of trials for each sentence type.) The overall high performance level of both subjects provided strong evidence of their ability to comprehend most sentence types and subtypes. This comprehension ability was independent of the semantic content of any given utterance since subjects responded correctly to all sentence types and subtypes, representing a wide range of novel utterances, on their initial presentation.

PERFORMANCE BY SENTENCE TYPE

The odds that any single sentence would be responded to correctly by chance are extremely low as an error could be made in selecting the appropriate object *A*, the appropriate object *B*, the appropriate action, the appropriate location, and the appropriate recipient, all of which were represented by multiple exemplars. It was also possible to misconstrue the intended relation between the words themselves. Even in object-location sentences, if a mean of seven objects and six locations is assumed, the probability of getting any such sentence correct by chance is 2.4%. The probability of being correct on other sentence types would be less as the potential for error is higher. The possibility that, with each trial represented by different tokens, either subject would be correct on a majority of sentence types by chance approaches zero.

Whenever data consist of counts organized in contingency tables, as is

TABLE 5

Overall Proportions of Different Response Codes Obtained by Kanzi and Alia

| | Kanzi | | | | Alia | | | |
| | All Trials | | Blind Trials | | All Trials | | Blind Trials | |
Response	N	%	N	%	N	%	N	%
C	369	57	246	59	319	54	220	54
C1	11	2	10	2	20	3	18	4
C2	36	6	16	4	32	6	16	4
C3	34	5	21	5	13	2	9	2
C4	8	1	7	2	7	1	4	1
C5	9	1	7	2	0	0	0	0
Total correct	467	72	307	74	391	66	267	65
PC	153	23	87	21	124	21	84	21
OE	6	1	5	1	20	3	17	4
I	9	1	8	2	9	2	7	2
W	8	1	4	1	32	6	24	6
NR	10	2	4	1	11	2	8	2
Total wrong	186	28	108	26	196	34	140	35
Overall total	653	100	415	100	587	100	407	100

Note.—Kanzi had seven mistrials, and Alia had two mistrials. Percentages are rounded to the nearest whole number.

the case here, log-linear analyses are recommended (Bishop, Fienberg, & Holland, 1975; Fienberg, 1980; Knoke & Burke, 1980; see also Bakeman, Adamson, & Strisik, 1989; Green, 1988; Tabachnick & Fidell, 1989, chap. 7). Similar in some ways to analyses of variance, these techniques are not as familiar to most psychologists (but see Cohn & Tronick, 1987; and Stevenson, Ver Hoeve, Roach, & Leavitt, 1986), so some general comments are in order. The analysis is called asymmetric, instead of symmetric, when independent and dependent variables are distinguished as they are for the present study; in such cases, the analysis of variance analogy is particularly apt (Kennedy, 1983). For the present analyses, the dependent variable is the response categorized as correct versus not correct; this forms one dimension of a contingency table. Other variables, such as condition or sentence type, form the other dimensions. The analysis proceeds hierarchically, beginning with the most complex model and successively removing terms. Terms are identified with the interactive and main effects of the independent on the dependent variables. Each model generates expected frequencies for the cells of the contingency table; thus, the goodness of fit for each model can be assessed, usually with the log-likelihood chi-square statistic or G^2. One goal of the analysis is to find the least complex model that fits the

TABLE 6

PROPORTION OF RESPONSES TO DIFFERENT SENTENCE TYPES CODED CORRECT
FOR KANZI AND ALIA

	KANZI			ALIA		
SENTENCE TYPE	Count	% Correct	Adjusted Residual[a]	Count	% Correct	Adjusted Residual[a]
All trials:						
1A	80/126	64	−1.4	88/123	72	1.4
1B	36/49	74	.1	31/43	72	−.1
2A	56/69	81	.0	47/58	81	−.0
2B	7/21	33	−1.6	12/21	57	1.6
2C	16/18	89	.2	13/15	87	−.2
2D	61/86	71	1.5	45/75	60	−1.5
3	56/80	70	.6	41/63	65	−.6
4	10/16	63	−1.3	11/13	85	1.3
5A	64/85	75	.9	55/80	69	−.9
5B[b]	40/47	85	3.5	23/45	51	−3.5
5C[b]	27/35	77	2.2	16/31	52	−2.2
6	7/10	70	.5	6/10	60	−.5
7	7/11	64	1.5	3/10	30	−1.5
Blind trials only:						
1A	39/62	63	−1.3	47/64	73	1.3
1B	13/17	77	.4	12/17	71	−.4
2A	36/46	78	−.7	36/43	84	.7
2B	7/19	37	−1.3	12/21	57	1.3
2C	10/11	91	.0	10/11	91	.0
2D	37/49	76	1.6	31/51	61	−1.6
3	40/49	82	2.0	25/40	63	−2.0
4	8/12	67	−.9	10/12	83	.9
5A	45/58	78	.8	42/59	71	−.8
5B[b]	32/39	82	3.4	18/40	45	−3.4
5C[b]	27/35	77	2.2	16/31	52	−2.2
6	6/9	67	.5	5/9	56	−.5
7	7/9	78	1.9	3/9	33	−1.9

[a] The adjusted residuals in the table derive from an analysis of 2 × 2 frequency tables (Alia vs. Kanzi, correct or not, for each sentence type for both all and blind trials only, for a total of 52 tables). For 2 × 2 tables, adjusted residuals (a term used in the log-linear literature) are identical to the square root of the more familiar chi square; thus, for 2 × 2 tables, all four adjusted residuals are identical except for sign. Assuming independence of samples, adjusted residuals greater than 1.96 absolute should occur less than 5% of the time if the percentage correct is truly not different for Kanzi and Alia for a given sentence type.

[b] Kanzi > Alia.

observed data. Interactions and main effects are said to be significant if the terms associated with those effects are required for a model to fit. As for analysis of variance, interpretation focuses on any significant interactions, not on their component parts, because the interaction identifies significant conditional relations among the variables.

The performance of both subjects across the different sentence types is shown in Table 6. Hierarchical log-linear analyses (see Bakeman et al., 1989) were used to determine which sentence types elicited better performance from Kanzi, which did so from Alia, and whether Kanzi performed significantly better than Alia overall. The $2 \times 2 \times 11 \times 2$ contingency table included condition (blind vs. nonblind) $\times$ subject (Kanzi vs. Alia) $\times$ sentence type (11 types) $\times$ response (correct vs. not correct). All C codes were counted as "correct"; all others, including "partly correct," were counted as errors. The number of sentence types was reduced to 11: type 6 sentences were not included in this analysis because of the small N, and type 7 sentences were dropped since they represented such a variety of different kinds.

The four-way interaction terms involving condition were not significant (i.e., were not required for a fitting model); thus, we conclude that the pattern of results was essentially the same for both blind and nonblind trials (likelihood ratio of $G^2[110]$ of 7.81, $p = .640$). Removing the three-way interaction term resulted in a likelihood ratio of $G^2(31)$ of 42.62, $p = .079$, suggesting that Kanzi and Alia did perform differently. The tests of partial associations revealed a subject $\times$ sentence type $\times$ response interaction (likelihood ratio of $G^2[10]$ of 17.45, $p = .064$). However, a number of sentence types occurred only or predominantly on blind trials; consequently, differences between the subjects as a function of sentence type are best addressed with the blind data subset. Examination restricted to the blind data indicated that the three-way subject $\times$ sentence type $\times$ response term was required for a fitting model; that is, removing it resulted in an increase in the likelihood ratio of $G^2(10)$ of 24.35, $p = .006$. Examination of the adjusted residuals for all data and for the blind data subset revealed that Kanzi was more likely than Alia to do well on sentence types 5B and 5C (see Table 6). In addition, removing the subject $\times$ response term resulted in a significant increase in $G^2(1)$ of 4.15, $p = .041$; thus, Kanzi made significantly fewer incorrect responses than Alia.

In order to determine whether the trials on which the subjects engaged in a tangential activity, or those on which the experimenter repeated or reworded the sentence, might be contributing significantly to the results and causing one or both subjects to appear more competent than they actually were, all trials with a C1, C2, C3, C4, or C5 code were eliminated from the corpus, and a $2 \times 2 \times 11$ (subject $\times$ code $\times$ sentence type) analysis was rerun on the blind trials alone. Again, the subject $\times$ response terms were required for a fitting model (removing them resulted in $G^2[10]$ of 45.58, $p = .072$). Also, it was again the subject $\times$ sentence type $\times$ response interaction that was significant (likelihood ratio of $G^2[10]$ of 18.45, $p = .047$), indicating that the same pattern of results held for the data when only those trials with immediate correct responses were considered. Consequently, it is reasonable to conclude that the subjects' intervening behaviors prior to carrying out the sentence appropriately do not account for either their overall performance during this test of language comprehension or the general pattern of the results.

Although partially correct and incorrect responses were grouped together in the hierarchical log-linear analysis, both subjects generally responded correctly to at least a portion of the sentence; only rarely was either of them completely incorrect (see Table 5). Most of the time both attempted to carry out what they thought was the appropriate action with at least one correct object. Thus, rather than behaving as though they heard only key words, they behaved as though they had heard a sentence. In many cases, they carried out the correct activity with the incorrect object, suggesting that they understood the sentence structure but not all the words. The frequency with which the experimenter needed to repeat or rephrase the utterance did not differ between subjects and was minimal for both (for the frequencies with which repetitions and rephrasing occurred, see Table 5).

The error of bringing multiple objects appeared 20 times in Alia's data but only six times in Kanzi's. When sent to a location to retrieve an object, Alia often returned with two to four objects, one of which was the requested item. A few times she reported to the experimenter about her choice by saying, for example, "Mommy, I got the carrot," even though she also had a number of other things. However, on most trials, it was not possible to determine whether Alia simply enjoyed carrying many items or whether she actually forgot which item she was to retrieve. Both she and Kanzi were encouraged to bring only the requested item, and, if they brought additional items, they were usually asked to identify the one that had been the requested item. However, they were not required to return the additional items or to repeat the trial. Such occurrences were scored as object errors.

Kanzi, like Alia, was able to carry more than one item, and, on trials where multiple copies of the same item were present (such as many cans of Coke or cereal), he often brought as many exemplars of the requested item as he could carry. However, unlike Alia, he rarely made the error of bringing items that were not requested. A review of the videotapes of Alia's error trials suggested that she did not understand the words *just one* when she made an error. When the experimenter attempted to correct her error by asking her to bring "just one," Alia tended to bring all the objects, as though she thought *just one* was the name of an object (i.e., a *duston*). It appeared that, because she did not know which object was a "duston," she brought all the objects she found. In fact, the more the experimenter tried to correct Alia's tendency to bring multiple objects, the more frequently she seemed to do so.

TYPES OF ERRORS IN PERFORMANCE ON
DIFFERENT SENTENCE TYPES

Type 1

Type 1A: Put object X *in/on transportable object* Y.—Overall, both subjects evinced high levels of comprehension of this sentence type (see Table 6). Unlike some other sentence types, an important feature of type 1A requests was that the actions they required were readily reversible (i.e., it was as likely that the subjects would put object *Y* in/on object *X* as it was that they would put object *X* in/on *Y*).

One type of error that occurred for both subjects was to respond with a "typical action" rather than the one requested by the sentence. For example, Kanzi put vitamins in the bowl instead of on the shirt, while Alia cut an apple with a knife instead of putting the knife in the hat. However, the rarity of this type of error (Kanzi made it on two trials, Alia on only one) indicated that neither subject generally approached the task simply by looking for key objects on which to perform a routine action.

Other errors appeared to be due to a lack of attention to the task rather than to an inability to understand the sentence. Moments of distraction and negativism characterized the behavior of both subjects from time to time throughout the testing. For example, Kanzi ate one of the food items on four trials instead of carrying out an action with it; Alia did this five times. On a few trials both subjects played with the items instead of attempting to carry out the request, and on two trials both indicated that they did not want to do what they were asked. Both subjects also simply held one or both items on some trials and did nothing more.

The two subjects also evinced similar interpretive stances when asked to place a food that was in a closed container with some other food. For example, when Kanzi was asked to "Put the milk in the water," the milk was, by chance, left in a closed can, and the water was in a bowl. Instead of picking up the can of milk and placing it in the water, Kanzi repeatedly tried to open the milk so that he could pour it into the water. When he did not succeed in getting the milk container open, he stopped attempting to carry out the request. Alia behaved similarly when asked to "Put the peaches in the strawberries." The can of peaches was accidentally left unopened, and the strawberries were in a bowl. Alia tried repeatedly to open the can before she would execute the request. In both cases, the experimenter urged Kanzi and Alia to go ahead and place the unopened can of milk or peaches with the other food, but neither subject would do so.

Kanzi invented a unique way of complying with one of the requests. When asked to "Put some water on the carrot," he responded by tossing the carrot outdoors; since it was raining heavily at the time, his action resulted in water getting on the carrot even though he applied the water indirectly. This method of "putting water on the carrot" appeared to be deliberate on Kanzi's part. At no other time during the test did he toss food or other items outdoors. It is also noteworthy that no one could recall ever demonstrating this behavior to Kanzi as a means of putting water on any item. Moreover, at other times during the test, and when it was not raining, he readily used both the hose and the faucet at the sink as a means of obtaining water if a request required him to do so, indicating that he knew how to obtain water. The novel solution of throwing the carrot into the rain is indicative of the flexibility that characterized the behavior of both subjects throughout the test. Kanzi and Alia's "solutions" were often surprising even to those who had worked with them from infancy.

   Type 1B: Put object X *in nontransportable object* Y.—Kanzi and Alia did not differ significantly in their overall level of performance on these sentences. However, whereas Alia's performance on type 1A and 1B requests did not differ, Kanzi performed 10% better on type 1B requests, thus appearing to lend credence to Schusterman and Gisiner's (1988) contention that sentences with one transportable and one nontransportable object are simpler, as the relation to be enacted between the two objects is self-evident. However, an analysis of Kanzi's errors does not support this view because he was as likely to make an error on the item that he could pick up and carry as he was on the item that was too bulky to transport. For example, when asked to "Put the backpack on the Fourtrax," Kanzi went to the Fourtrax and sat on it without the backpack. Kanzi also revealed that "nontransportable" objects could, if needed, be treated as transportable ones. When he heard the sentence "Can you put the rest of the paint in the potty?" he put the clay—which he often confused with paint—in the potty instead. Even after the sentence was repeated, he was so certain that he had responded to it properly that he dragged the supposedly nontransportable potty over to the one-way mirror and pointed to the clay within it, to indicate to the experimenter that he had completed the request correctly. He apparently deduced that the experimenter needed a closer look in the potty to affirm that the "paint" was indeed in the potty.

   In every case but one, Alia's errors were due either to selecting the wrong nontransportable object (e.g., when asked to "Put the clay on the vacuum," she put the clay on the window sill) or to a refusal to go to the nontransportable object at all (e.g., when asked to "Put the grapes in the oven," she stood in the middle of the room and swung the grapes around instead of taking them anywhere). Since Alia was correct on 72% of the type 1B items overall, her tendency to err on nontransportable items cannot be attributed to a lack of understanding of the names of the nontransportable objects.

In general, Alia had more difficulty than Kanzi with requests that entailed traveling to another location, although she was clearly capable of doing so. It is possible that these difficulties were simply the result of the fact that she was quite young and consequently more hesitant than Kanzi to travel on her own.

Type 2

Type 2A: Give (or show) object X *to animate* A.—Giving objects to an animate was easy for both Kanzi and Alia. When errors did occur, Kanzi tended to give the wrong item to the correct person, whereas Alia tended to select the correct item but then either do nothing with it or look at the person but refuse to take it to her. Occasionally, Alia played with the items instead of responding, and on one trial she ate the item, as did Kanzi.

A few sentences in this group included the modifiers *toy* and *real*. Both subjects made errors on these sentences, although not of the same sort: Alia tended to give both the toy and the real item, while Kanzi tended to give the real item and ignore the toy item.

Type 2B: Give object X *and object* Y *to animate* A.—This sentence type proved the most difficult for Kanzi (33% correct) and the second most difficult for Alia (57% correct). Alia tended to engage in some action prior to carrying out type 2B requests more often than Kanzi (who did not do so at all). Indeed, it may have been that the extra time that Alia spent prior to carrying out this sentence was used to encode it in some way that aided the integration of both objects and the memory of the needed response.

Because both object names were spoken before the subject selected either, this sentence type required that Alia and Kanzi hold in memory two unrelated objects and perform the same action (giving or showing) on both. Each subject made the error of giving one incorrect and one correct item on one occasion. Additionally, on one occasion, each subject made the error of relating the two items in the array to each other instead of giving them to a person. Alia poured the cereal in the bowl when asked to "Show me the ball and the cereal," apparently confusing the words *ball* and *bowl*, while Kanzi dipped the lighter in the water when asked to "Give the lighter and the water." The fact that this sort of error was made only once by each subject lends additional support to the conclusion that neither was employing a strategy of listening for key words (i.e., object names) and carrying out a common or obvious action without processing the additional information inherent in the sentence structure. Had only "key-word" analysis been occurring, far more errors of this type should have appeared in responding to type 2B requests.

In order to make even more direct comparisons between sentences in which the relation was that of conjunction and those in which a particular relation was specified, half the type 2B requests utilized the same two objects that occurred in other sentences. For example, the sentence "Show me the milk and the dog" was contrasted with the sentence "Feed the dog some milk." The key object words *dog* and *milk* occurred in both sentences; however, a correct response required the subjects to integrate the information carried by the verb with the objects in different ways in each case. In the case of the conjunction, the single verb *show* applied to both objects; however, in the other case, it was necessary to apply the verb *feed* to the dog and to execute the action of moving the milk toward the dog. Both Alia and Kanzi differentiated between such sentences by showing the items in the first instance and constructing a relation between these objects in the second.

Although Kanzi often selected only one item to show, in so doing he was nonetheless still responding to the appropriate overall sentence format rather than attempting to construct a relation between two objects (i.e., putting *X* in *Y*). These data support the view that both subjects processed the sentence as a unitary relation between verb and objects rather than as key words suggesting some inherent relation between the objects. Moreover, they imply that the verb was understood to control either the relation of the objects to each other or that of an object to a recipient.

Giving only one item accounted for nearly all Kanzi's errors on type 2B requests but for only three of Alia's. On two trials, Alia gave more than two items, something that Kanzi never attempted. When Kanzi gave only one item, his errors were distributed between the first and the last items mentioned in the request, although he was more likely to give the last item mentioned. On these occasions, Kanzi understood that the verb *give* applied to both items, for all that was needed to remind him of the second item was to say "and *Y*." Kanzi would then look around, find *Y*, and hand it to the correct person.

Even though Alia did not perform significantly better than Kanzi on type 2B trials, differences in the two subjects' performances deserve special note. The syntactic structure of these sentences is simple and straightforward—the subject need only select two objects and give them to a person (usually the experimenter). The difference between the subjects' abilities to perform this activity correctly with one versus two objects was striking (for the difference between type 2A and type 2B sentences, see Table 6).

Overall, Alia selected two or more objects on 15 trials, while Kanzi selected two objects on six trials. However, these numbers fail to convey the obvious behavioral differences that could be seen in response to this request. Kanzi either processed the sentence very rapidly and gave two things quickly, or he ignored one item and gave the other. Generally, if he gave two things, he did so one at a time. Alia seemed much more deliberate, as though rehearsing the list. She typically picked up both things before orienting her attention to the recipient, then carrying both objects together to the recipient. Although no delay was artificially introduced by the experimenter, Alia's behavior suggested that she could tolerate fairly long delays before forgetting what she was to do on type 2B sentences, whereas Kanzi could not.

The simplicity of both the semantic and the syntactic components of type 2B sentences suggests that Kanzi's difficulty was perhaps due more to short-term memory limitations on the overall amount of information than to processing limitations on the information that was available to him. Indeed, it seems possible that the semantic and syntactic structure in sentences such as "Feed the doggie some milk" permitted Kanzi to go beyond the typical constraints of his short-term memory system by enabling him to process or chunk the information in a meaningful manner. By contrast, sentences such as "Give the doggie and the milk" do not engage semantic chunking strategies but rather force reliance on short-term memory alone. These data thus suggest that syntactic relations may actually make language easier for Kanzi rather than more difficult, as has been suggested by Terrace (1979).

Type 2C: (Do) action A on animate A.—Both subjects made only a few errors on type 2C sentences, and these in general appeared to be due to inattention. It is noteworthy that both made a similar interpretative error with the verb *hide*. When given the sentence "You go hide," both Kanzi and Alia went to some room or area out of the experimenter's sight. However, when asked to "Hide the toy gorilla," both subjects changed the gorilla's location (Kanzi pushed it under the fence, and Alia put it on a chair), but neither actually moved the object out of sight. They seemed to understand *hide* in the typical sense of moving out of sight when it applied to themselves, but, when it applied to the toy gorilla, they moved the pretend animate partially out of their own immediate sight, not out of that of the experimenter. Thus, the verb *hide* seemed to have one meaning when applied to themselves and another when it applied to an object that they were to act on, perhaps because they both had difficulty with assuming the experimenter's perspective.

Type 2D: (Do) action A on animate A with object X.—Interestingly, acting on a person with an object proved more difficult for both subjects than giving an object to a person. (For the comparison between type 2D and type 2A sentences, see Table 6.) All the type 2A sentences entailed the verb *give*, but the verb varied in the type 2D requests. Consequently, it might be anticipated that Kanzi and Alia's errors would center on the verbs; this, however, was not the case. Both Alia's and Kanzi's errors were distributed among all three categories: the verb, the object, and the recipient, although the recipient category had the largest number of errors.

Both subjects at times confused recipients in type 2D sentences (which they did not do in type 2A sentences); presumably, this occurred in part because the recipient class was larger in type 2D sentences, including pretend animates as well as the subjects themselves. For example, when asked, "Can you tickle me with the stick?" Alia tickled the dog instead. When Kanzi was asked to tickle Laura with the dog, he tickled the dog instead of Laura. Both Kanzi and Alia also made the error of directing activities to themselves instead of to another party. For example, when asked to "Put the hat on person X," both Alia and Kanzi put it on their own heads.

Some of the recipient errors were clearly prompted by the hesitancy of both subjects to act directly on another person with an object. This hesitancy increased when the recipient of the intended action was blinded (by holding a hand in front of the eyes) and could not give nonverbal acknowledgment when approached.

Type 3

(Do) action A on object X *(with object Y).*—The sentences in this group covered a wider variety of verbs than those in any other group and were more diverse in the types of actions required of the subjects. Both Kanzi and Alia did well on these sentences, and both subjects distributed their errors across all verbs with no particular verb—except *hide*—causing difficulty in all sentences where it occurred. As we have already noted in an earlier context, both Kanzi and Alia understood *hide* when it applied to themselves or to games of hide and seek; however, when asked to hide an object, they tended to do something with the object (such as pick it up and put it down, move it aside, play with it, etc.) but did not visually obscure it.

The remaining errors on type 3 sentences do not fall into any recognizable pattern. Instead, they seem to arise because the subjects found it difficult to respond to many of the decidedly "odd" sentences in this group. For example, "Hammer the vacuum" puzzled Kanzi, "Wash your watch" befuddled Alia, and "Bite the picture of the oil" stymied both. However, these errors should not be taken to mean that the subjects were completely unable to respond to highly novel and unusual sentences. Both correctly carried out such odd sentences as "Hammer your ball," "Knife the toothpaste," "Stab your ball with the sparklers," and "Give the sweet potato a shot."

Type 4

Announce information.—These sentences entailed announcements of impending events rather than requests. Overall, Alia made somewhat fewer errors on these trials than Kanzi, although the number of trials was too small to warrant a test of significance.

Alia often responded to the statements by vocally announcing her own intent instead of behaving in accordance with what the experimenter had announced. Since she did not do this with other sentence types, the fact that she viewed these trials as an opportunity to announce her own intentions suggests that she recognized the different pragmatic function of this sentence type. For example, when the sentence "Alia is going to chase Mommy" was uttered, Alia responded by saying, "Chase me, chase me." Although in this case she was scored as having erred because she did not follow the implications of the original statement, it is nonetheless possible that she did understand it. On other trials, such as "Nathaniel is going to chase Alia," Alia also announced to Nathaniel, "Chase me, chase me." Kanzi made no such announcements on type 4 trials, although he did so in between trials.

Alia also hesitated at times when announcements such as "Alia is going to chase Linda" were made. In this particular case, she walked past Linda and returned to say, "Chase Linda," as though to announce that she had already completed the action.

Type 5

Type 5A: Take object X *to location* Y.—All type 5 requests involved transporting an object to, or retrieving it from, a fixed location. At first, Kanzi and Alia were asked only to take an object to a location (type 5A). It was thought that this would be the easiest of the object transport requests for them because they could act on the object in front of them as soon as the sentence was completed: once they had picked up the object, they needed to remember only the name of the location. By contrast, if they were asked to retrieve an object in a distal location, they had to remember the object while traveling to that location.

Virtually all type 5A sentences employed the verb *take*. Kanzi and Alia's error patterns differed in that Kanzi's errors were more equally divided between objects and locations: on eight occasions he took the incorrect object to the correct location, while on five he selected the proper object but took it to the wrong place. Alia's errors typically consisted of taking the correct object to the wrong location; she also made three errors in which she selected both an incorrect object and an incorrect location, which Kanzi did once. Both Alia and Kanzi occasionally refused to respond or did nothing. In Kanzi's case, the sentence that elicited no response was "Take the can opener to the bedroom." The word *can* was used in a number of ways throughout this study (*can of Coke, can you, can opener*, etc.) and appeared to cause Kanzi difficulty in most instances, as he apparently had not yet resolved the different understandings of *can* that were required. On the remaining "no response" trials, it was concluded that the subjects either were not listening, did not want to carry out the request, or felt unable to do so.

Even though the locations in this category were designated "nontransportable," one of them, a portable potty, was in fact movable, although cumbersome. In all but one sentence, the word *potty* was employed as a nontransportable. In "Take the potty outdoors," however, it was suddenly treated as a transportable object, which the subjects were asked to move for the first time, something they did not generally do with the potty otherwise. Kanzi succeeded with this sentence, but Alia failed. However, she did attempt to pick up the potty, but could not do so because she was standing on it. After several attempts, she gave up, not realizing she could not move it unless she stepped off it first. The fact that Kanzi did take the potty outdoors and that Alia attempted to do so indicated that the verbal input they received via this unusual novel sentence exerted more influence over their behavior than did their previous experience with the potty. Both were able to apply at once the verb *take* to the word *potty*, an object that had always served before as a recipient and one that they did not normally transport.

Type 5B: Go to location Y *and get object* X.—Surprisingly, both subjects were able to go to a distal location, remember the object they had been asked to retrieve, and return with it. Kanzi was significantly better than Alia at doing so, although he needed to be reminded to return more often than did Alia as he was generally interested in staying to play at locations.

In the subgroup of 20 blind control trials, the item to be retrieved from location Y was also present in the array immediately in front of the subjects, requiring them to ignore the immediately available item and travel to another location for its duplicate. As noted earlier, however, these sentences were syntactically ambiguous because they could be interpreted as two sets of independent things to do: (*a*) go to a location and (*b*) get an object. The type 5B sentence structure did not clearly indicate that the item to be retrieved was to be obtained from another location.

Kanzi acted on the object in the immediate display on 50% of these trials and Alia on 25%. Kanzi required more explicit instructions to ignore the object in the immediate display and often could not be persuaded to put it down by any means other than direct intervention.

Both subjects' responses on these control trials indicated that, from their perspective, type 5B sentences were indeed ambiguous. However, neither subject invariably selected the object in the immediate array. Often their response was simply to touch the object in the immediate array and then go to retrieve the distal object. If they attempted to give the experimenter the immediate object rather than getting it from the specified location, they were asked not to do so. If they then properly retrieved the distal object, they were scored as having correctly carried out the sentence. Consequently, their overall scores were not deflated on type 5B sentences as a result of the ambiguity generated by the sentence structure.

Type 5C: Go get object X *that's in location* Y.—Both type 5B and type 5C sentences required that the subjects travel to a distal location to retrieve an object, and in both cases the requested object was also present in the array in front of them on control trials. Type 5B sentences presented the request in a linear construction that mapped the sequence of activities to be carried out, whereas type 5C sentences employed a phrasal modifier that inverted the linear sequence by mentioning the object first and the location last: "Go get object Y that's in location X." To be correct on both types, the subjects had to demonstrate an ability to process the same sort of information presented in two different formats, one that inverted the linear order and one that did not.

It could be argued that, in both types of requests, the subjects were simply responding to the verb, the location term, and the object term and that the order of these terms was irrelevant. The control trials address this issue since the embedded phrasal structure of type 5C sentences removed the semantic ambiguity inherent in type 5B sentences. The central question was whether the subjects performed better on these trials (i.e., with objects duplicated in the immediate and distal arrays) when presented with type 5B or with type 5C requests. Better performance on type 5C control trials would indicate that they processed the phrasal modifier appropriately and that the syntactic structure of type 5C sentences indeed functioned to eliminate the ambiguity inherent in type 5B control trials.

Kanzi's data provide strong support for the view that he comprehended the syntactic relation expressed in type 5C sentences. Kanzi acted on the object in the near array on only 9% of these trials, as contrasted with 50% of the type 5B control trials. (One of his two errors occurred because Kanzi looked for, but failed to see, the object in the distal location; thus, his interpretation of the sentence structure was in fact syntactically correct. His other error occurred when both the object of the modifier and its duplicate were in the array immediately in front of him. That is, in the sentence "Take the potato that's in the water outdoors," the two potatoes were side by side, but one was in a bowl of water; Kanzi took both potatoes outdoors. Since Kanzi's performance on type 1A sentences indicated that he did *not* differentiate *in* from *next to,* it seems reasonable to attribute this error to a lack of understanding of the word *in* rather than to a misreading of the syntactic structure of the sentence.)

The manner in which Kanzi responded to the type 5C sentence format was most impressive. Unlike his behavior in response to the ambiguous type 5B sentences, on hearing type 5C sentences Kanzi typically did not even glance at the array in front of him. Instead, he headed directly for the specified location, suggesting that he had deduced from the structure of the sentence itself that there was no need to search for the object in the array in front of him.

Alia's data followed a similar pattern. She was correct on 25% of the type 5B control trials and on 63% of the type 5C control trials, suggesting that the syntactic structure of type 5C sentences functioned to clarify ambiguity for her as well. Indeed, the only type 5C trial that elicited a response to the incorrect similar item from Alia was "Drink the chocolate that's hot": she drank both cups of chocolate, the cold one first. Alia appeared to relish the chocolate thoroughly (she was not often permitted to have chocolate), and her error here may well have been intentional.

Thus, both Alia and Kanzi responded appropriately to the phrasal modifier *that's* when it was used to distinguish between a distal object and one present in the immediate field of vision. However, both made an error when it was used to differentiate two objects that were both in the immediate array.

The overall performance of both subjects on type 5A, 5B, and 5C sentences, regardless of whether the object to be retrieved was present in the near array, indicated that they were able to comprehend the syntactic relations among word units, not just the units themselves. The ability to respond correctly to a set of sentences such as "Take the tomato to the microwave," "Go to the microwave and get the tomato," and "Go get the tomato that's in the microwave" demonstrated an understanding of the fact that such sentences reflect an intended relation between all words (the verb, the object, and the location). Most important was the finding that a phrasal modifier functioned to clarify the object of reference, which indicates that both subjects were capable of interpreting the syntactic device of recursion appropriately, at least within the context of type 5C sentences.

Type 6

Make pretend animate A *do action* A *on recipient* Y.—These sentences proved difficult for both subjects. They required that the subjects distinguish between agent and recipient and make the two act out different roles. Additionally, they involved an element of "pretend" not always present in other categories. For example, to "make the doggie bite the snake," one must pretend that both are animates.

It is of interest that neither subject was correct on any sentence that named a toy bug as either agent or recipient (as in "Can you make the bug bite the doggie?"). Even though both knew the word *bug* and could point out live bugs and photographs of bugs when asked, both seemed puzzled by the idea of treating a plastic bug as an animate. However, both were able to treat the toy dog, bunny, and snake as agents and recipients and to carry out some sentences correctly with these pretend "agents." Both subjects also confused the word *orang* (for *orangutan*) with *orange* on some trials.

Type 7

All other sentence types.—As noted earlier, 11 sentences that did not fit any of the other categories were grouped together into a "leftover" type. Most of these sentences required two separate actions—for example, "Open the Jello and pour it in the juice" or "Take the potato outdoors and get the apple." (Interestingly, on the latter request, both subjects took the potato outdoors, picked up the apple, and returned with both foods.)

These sentences were intended as "probes" to determine whether it would be feasible to test additional sentence types in the future. Our general impression was that the subjects might have had the potential to process sentences in which multiple actions were linked in a functional sense. For example, in order to pour the Jello into the juice, it is necessary to open it first, and this request was completed correctly by both subjects. However, sentences requiring actions that were not functionally linked from the subjects' point of view proved difficult. Kanzi did considerably better than Alia on type 7 requests (Kanzi responded correctly on seven trials, Alia on three); however, the small number of sentences and their diversity render conclusions about possible differences between the two subjects on this sentence type premature.

WORD ORDER

Although Kanzi and Alia's ability to respond to many different sentence types indicates that they are processing syntactic relations, these data do not address the issue of word order directly. To do that, it is necessary to regroup the sentences on the dimension of word order per se rather than sentence type. The data base afforded several different means of manipulating word order, some of which were meaningful (e.g., "Put the noodles in the hotdogs" vs. "Put the hotdogs in the noodles") and some not (e.g., "Wash your collar" vs. "Collar your wash"). In order to address the ability of the subjects to comprehend reversal of word order directly, we compared their performance on pairs of sentences that were presented with both possible word orderings (summary statistics are presented in Table 7). Paired instances of the three classes of word-order manipulations that occurred in the data base are presented in Table 8.

TABLE 7

COMPARISON OF KANZI AND ALIA'S PERFORMANCE ON REVERSED SENTENCES OVER THREE
SUBTYPES OF REVERSALS: SUMMARY STATISTICS

	KANZI		ALIA	
	C/N	%	*C/N*	%
Subtype A:				
Sentences	38/46	83	26/44	59
Pairs	17/23	74	8/21	38
Subtype B:				
Sentences	22/28	79	18/27	67
Pairs	8/14	57	5/13	38
Subtype C:				
Sentences	33/42	79	27/39	69
Pairs	12/21	57	7/18	39

NOTE.—*C* = number of correct responses (C, C1–C5). *N* = total number of sentences or sentence pairs given to the subject. Subtype A = verb plus word order changes, and appropriate response differs. Subtype B = word order remains constant, but appropriate response differs. Subtype C = word order changes, and appropriate response changes.

The first group includes those sentences that afforded two signals for a differential response, both word order and verb ("Could you take the pine needles outdoors?"/"Go outdoors and get the pine needles"). Consequently, the best performance would be expected on these sentences. This occurred for Kanzi but not for Alia. The second group includes those sentences in which the order of the key words remained constant but the nature of the appropriate response did not ("Take the rock outdoors"/"Go get the rock that's outdoors"). The final group reflects all sentences in which the order of the key words was reversed while maintaining the same verb ("Put the juice in the egg"/"Put the egg in the juice"; see Fig. 15).

Kanzi's performance across these three word-order manipulations did not differ significantly, nor did Alia's. However, Kanzi performed significantly better than Alia on the type A reversal (word-order manipulations in which there was a reversal of the key words with a different verb, such as *get* vs. *take*), $\chi^2(1, N = 90) = 7.12, p < .01$. Alia and Kanzi were not significantly different on type B and C reversals. Alia's difficulty with type A reversals reflected her tendency to return from various locations with more than one object.

Taken together, these sentences presented the subjects with a difficult challenge. On the one hand, some sentences required that the order of X and Y be treated as a signal about the sequence that their ensuing actions should follow. In other cases, the order of X and Y was to be ignored. Word order was to be attended to when it was the only cue or when it occurred with the verbs *get* and *take* following the command "Go. . . ." However, the

TABLE 8

COMPARISON OF KANZI AND ALIA'S PERFORMANCE ON REVERSED SENTENCES OVER THREE
SUBTYPES OF REVERSALS: SUBJECTS' PERFORMANCE ON EACH SENTENCE

A. SUBTYPE A

	Kanzi	Alia	Sentence
1	PC	C	Take the carrots outdoors.
2	C5	C	Go outdoors and find the carrot.
3	C	NG	Could you take the pine needles outdoors?
4	C	C2	Go outdoors and get the pine needles.
5	C	C	Put the sparklers in the potty.
6	PC	OE	Go to the potty and get the sparklers.
7	C	C	Take the orange outdoors.
8	C3	OE	Go outdoors and get an orange.
9	C	C	Take the umbrella [box] outdoors.
10	C	C	Go outdoors and get the umbrella [box].
11	C	C	Take the pineapple [apple] outdoors.
12	C5	W	Go outdoors and get the pineapple [apple].
13	C	C	Go to the refrigerator and get some ice.
14	C	C4	Take the ice back to the refrigerator.
15	OE	PC	Take the stick to the bedroom.
16	C5	NR	Go to the bedroom and get the stick.
17	C	C	Take the potato to the bedroom.
18	C3	C	Go to the bedroom and get the potato.
19	C	C	Take the potato outdoors.
20	C3	C	Go outdoors and get the potato.
21	C	OE	Bring the raisins to the bedroom.
22	C5	PC	Go to the bedroom and get the raisins.
23	C	C	Take the orange to the colony room [Karen's room].
24	C5	PC	Go to the colony room [Karen's room] and get the orange.
25	C	C	Take the lighter [matches] outdoors.
26	C1	NR	Go outdoors and get the lighter [matches].
27	C	W	Go to the refrigerator and get an orange.
28	C2	C	Take the orange to the refrigerator.
29	C	C	Go to the microwave [oven] and get the tomato.
30	C	W	Take the tomato to the microwave [oven].
31	C	PC	Take the tomato to the bedroom.
32	C5	PC	Go to the bedroom and get the tomato.
33	C	C	Put the raisins in the refrigerator.
34	C	C	Go to the refrigerator and get the [some] raisins.
35	C	C2	Take your collar [watch] to the bedroom.
36	C2	NR	Go to the bedroom and get the collar [watch].
37	C	PC	Go to the refrigerator and get the melon [peaches].

	Kanzi	Alia	Sentence
38	W	NG	Take the melon to the refrigerator.
39	PC	C	Take the doggie to the T-room [bathroom].
40	W	PC	Go to the T-room [bathroom] and get the doggie.
41	C	C	Take the banana outdoors.
42	C	C	Go outdoors and get the banana.
43	PC	PC	Can you make the bug bite the doggie?
44	PC	PC	Can you make the doggie chase the bug?
45	C	C	See if you can make your doggie bite your ball.
46	C	C	Can you put the ball on the doggie?

B. Subtype B

	Kanzi	Alia	Sentence
1	PC	OE	Take the rock outdoors.
2	C	C	Go get the rock that's outdoors.
3	C	C	Take the stick outdoors.
4	OE	C	Go get the stick that's outdoors.
5	C	C	Take the snake [bug] outdoors.
6	C	C	Go get the snake [bug] that's outdoors.
7	C	C	Take the banana outdoors.
8	C	C3	Go get the banana that's outdoors.
9	C	W	Take the tomato to the microwave [oven].
10	C	PC	Go get the tomato that's in the microwave [oven].
11	C	C	Put the raisins in the refrigerator.
12	C	OE	Go get the raisins that are in the refrigerator.
13	C	C	Put your collar (watch) in the refrigerator.
14	C	C	Go get your collar (watch) that's in the refrigerator.
15	C	C	Put your apple in the microwave [oven].
16	C	OE	Go get the apple that's in the microwave [oven].
17	C3	C	Put the melon [peaches] in the potty.
18	C	M	Get the melon [peaches] that's in the potty.
19	C	C2	Put the doggie in the refrigerator.
20	W	W	Go get the dog that's in the refrigerator. [Go to the refrigerator and get the dog.]
21	NR	C2	Take the can opener [fork] to the bedroom.
22	C	W	Go get the can opener [fork] that's in the bedroom.
23	C	C	Take the umbrella [box] to the colony room [Karen's room].
24	PC	OE	Go get the umbrella [box] that's in the colony room [Karen's room].

TABLE 8B (*Continued*)

	Kanzi	Alia	Sentence
25	C	C	Take the lighter [matches] outdoors.
26	C	C	Go get the lighter [matches] that's outdoors.
27	C	C	Take the doggie out of the pillow.
28	PC	PC	Hide the doggie in the pillow.

C. Subtype C

	Kanzi	Alia	Sentence
1	C	NG	Can you put some oil on your ball?
2	C	C1	Put the ball in the oil.
3	PC	C	Put the hat on your ball.
4	I	I	Put the ball on the hat.
5	C	C	Put the ball on the rock.
6	C	NG	Can you put the rock on your ball?
7	C	C3	Put the pine needles in your ball.
8	C	W	Can you put the ball on the pine needles?
9	C	C2	Put some water on the carrot.
10	C1	C2	Put the carrot in the water.
11	PC	C	Pour the milk in the cereal.
12	C	I	Pour the cereal in the milk.
13	C	PC	Pour the Coke in the lemonade.
14	C	PC	Pour the lemonade in the Coke.
15	C3	C	Pour the juice in the egg.
16	C	C	Put the egg in the juice.
17	C	C1	Put the rock in the water.
18	PC	PC	Pour the water on the rock.
19	C	C	Put the raisins in the water.
20	C2	I	Pour some water on the raisins.
21	PC	C3	Put the melon [peaches] in the tomatoes.
22	C3	NG	Put the tomatoes in the melon.
23	C	C2	Put the milk in the water.
	C2	C	Put the milk in the water.[a]
24	C	PC	Pour the Perrier water in the milk.
25	C	C	Put the tomato in the oil.
26	C	C	Put some [the] oil in the tomato.
27	I	I	Put the shoe in the raisins.
28	C2	C	Put the raisins in the shoe.
29	C	PC	Pour the juice in the Jello.
30	C	C	Open the Jello and pour it in the juice.
31	C	C	Rose/Nathaniel is gonna chase Kanzi/Alia.
32	PC	I	Kanzi/Alia is going to chase Rose/Mom.
33	C	C2	Liz/Linda is going to tickle Kanzi/Alia.
34	PC	C	Kanzi/Alia is gonna tickle Liz/Nathaniel.

TABLE 8C (*Continued*)

	Kanzi	Alia	Sentence
35	C	C	Kanzi/Alia is going to chase Liz/Nathaniel.
36	C	C	Liz/Nathaniel is going to chase Kanzi/Alia.
37	C	C	Kanzi/Alia is going to tickle Liz/Nathaniel with the bunny.
38	PC	C	Liz/Nathaniel is going to tickle Kanzi/Alia with the bunny.
39	C	PC	Make the doggie bite the snake.
40	C	C	Make the snake bite the doggie.
41	PC	PC	Hide the ball under the blanket.
42	C	C	Can you put the blanket on your ball?

NOTE.—For code definitions, see Table 3. Words in square brackets reflect changes in the sentences given to Alia since she did not know some of the words in the sentences given to Kanzi. The code "NG" indicates that the sentence was not given to Alia at all.

[a] This sentence was administered with the milk can open, instead of closed. It is counted only once for purposes of the analysis.

occurrence of the verb was not a totally reliable cue since word order was to be ignored if the same verbs were paired with the phrasal modifier *that's*.

Overall, Kanzi was correct on 71 of 88 (81%) of all sentences in which the key words were presented in both orders, while Alia was correct on 53 of 83 (64%) of these sentences. With regard to their performance on specific pairs (i.e., subjects were correct on *both orders* for a given pair), Kanzi successfully responded to 29 of 44 pairs (66%), while Alia successfully responded to 15 of 39 (38%).

It is important to note that the number of inversion errors (occasions on which the subjects performed the actions in inverse order from the request) was small (Kanzi made two inversion errors and Alia five). Consequently, even when the subjects did not carry out both sentences in a pair correctly, it was rare that their difficulties reflected a misunderstanding of the word-order cue. Semantic errors predominated. For example, when Kanzi heard "Put the melon in the tomatoes," he put the melon in the water, thus acting on the water rather than the cereal. Similarly, when Alia was asked to "Pour the lemonade in the Coke," she tried to pour the lemonade (from the can) into the bowl of lemonade. Like Kanzi, she treated the first item mentioned as the one to be moved, but placed this item in the wrong position.

A clear determination of what they failed to understand on these trials awaits future data collection, as their current errors provide only hints. For example, when asked to "Put the knife in the hat," Kanzi tried to cut the soap with the knife, while Alia tried to cut the apple with the knife. Both

Fig. 15.—This figure illustrates the array in front of Kanzi (top left) as he hears the sentence "Put the egg in the juice" (top right). It is possible for Kanzi either to put the juice in the egg, to put the egg in the juice, or to do something else entirely. Kanzi responds to this sentence by picking up the bowl containing the egg (bottom left) and tilting it until the egg falls into the juice (bottom right).

seemed compelled to use the knife to cut a small firm object in the display rather than to put it in the hat. Perhaps the idea of placing a knife in a hat is too unusual, or perhaps they enjoyed trying to cut other things. There appear to be inherent properties within some objects that caused the subjects to feel compelled to interact with them in specific ways, and the speech input from the experimenter may simply have been insufficient to override their own inclinations in such cases. Semantic errors and errors of inattention dominated the cognitive processes of both subjects at this level of language comprehension.

These data support the view that both Kanzi and Alia were sensitive to word order as well as to the semantic and syntactic cues that signaled when to ignore word order and when to attend to it. Overall, Kanzi appeared to be slightly more sensitive to word order than Alia at the time of this test, although neither was able to respond to this cue in an unfailing manner.

VII. DISCUSSION: WHY NOT GRANT SYNTACTIC COMPETENCE TO A SIBLING SPECIES?

SIMILARITIES IN KANZI AND ALIA'S PERFORMANCE

The clear outcome from the present study is that two normal individuals of different ages and different genera (*Homo* and *Pan*) were remarkably closely matched in their ability to understand spoken language. A 2-year-old human female and an 8-year-old bonobo male demonstrated that, under relatively similar rearing circumstances and virtually identical test conditions, they could comprehend both the semantics and the syntactic structure of quite unusual English sentences. The similarity between the two subjects is all the more remarkable in that, while able to comprehend sentences, neither subject was as yet a fluent speaker. The child was not fluent because she was too young, while the structure of Kanzi's laryngeal tract made it impossible for him to produce comprehensible speech. Near the completion of this test, Alia began to produce complex multiword utterances, and, across the next 6 months, her productive capacity leapt dramatically ahead of that of Kanzi, who failed to improve noticeably.

The lack of contingent reward, the novel nature of the requests, the absence of previous training to perform these specific requests, and the unique nature of each trial countermand simple explanations that depend on the conditioning of responses independently of semantic and syntactic comprehension. Both subjects clearly demonstrated a capacity to process the semantic and syntactic information in the sentences presented to them. Moreover, the manner in which they did so revealed that they did not interpret the words contained in sentences as randomly juxtaposed events, to be acted on independently. Instead, they invariably attempted to carry out a complex set of related actions that reflected their interpretation of the semantic and syntactic features of each novel utterance. Thus, for example, Kanzi's solution to "Put the water on the carrot" was to toss it out into the rain. Such innovative actions revealed a sophisticated processing of the

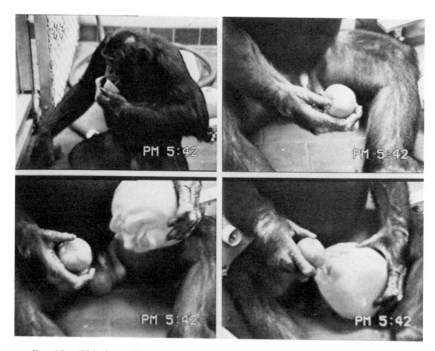

Fig. 16.—This figure illustrates Kanzi listening to the sentence "Feed your ball some tomato" (top left), selecting the tomato (top right), bringing a soft sponge ball with a "pumpkin" face embedded within it into his lap (bottom left), and then placing the tomato into the mouth on the face embedded in the ball (bottom right).

speaker's intent (in this case, to get the carrot wet) rather than a rote, unthinking solution. Even when the subjects failed, they virtually never did so in a way that would suggest that they were assigning key words randomly.

Both subjects appeared to process the experimenter's words at the sentence level. The meaning that they assigned to a word was based on its role in the sentence rather than on a dictionary-like set of referents. For example, both responded appropriately to "Give the knife to [person]" as well as to "Can you knife the sweet potatoes?" even though the word *knife* indicates an object in the first case and an action with an object in the second. It was the sentence context itself that made the difference, and this context was appropriately evaluated by both subjects.

Both subjects also responded appropriately to very unusual sentences. For example, Kanzi correctly responded to the sentence "Feed your ball some tomato" (see Fig. 16). Since in Kanzi's prior experience the word *feed* had never been juxtaposed with the word *ball,* his appropriate response can only be interpreted as indicating that he understood that the action encoded in the verb *feed* was to be directed toward the unusual recipient *ball,* regardless of whether the act appeared plausible. Kanzi also responded appropriately to the difference in sentences such as "Give the shot to Liz" and "Give Liz a shot"—by handing Liz the syringe in the first case and taking off the needle covering and touching the needle to her arm in the second case.

When the proper response to a request was not obvious from the array in front of the subjects, both proved innovative in their solutions. For example, when we asked them to "Wash the hotdogs," we assumed that, were the subjects to respond correctly, they would carry the hotdogs to the kitchen sink since that was where they had always observed food being washed. In fact, neither subject traveled to the sink; rather, each searched for closer means to wash the hotdogs. Looking around, Kanzi noticed the hose that was usually used to spray the floor and proceeded to use it for spraying water on the hotdogs, utilizing the plastic wrapping as a container for the water, even though he had not seen anyone do this before. After a moment of puzzlement, Alia selected a small sponge ball from the array and began wiping the hotdogs with it.

The ability of both subjects—and particularly the strong tendency exhibited by Kanzi—to interpret the phrasal modifier *that's* as a syntactic morpheme used to clarify which of two objects to retrieve revealed that the syntactic device of recursion was mastered for at least this sentence type. In addition, Kanzi was more likely to be correct when ambiguity was dispelled by a recursive structure. His general performance and demeanor on such trials also implied that he processed the sentence as a complete unit. For example, when asked to "Take the tomato to the microwave," Kanzi hesitated and began visually to search the items in front of him. However, when he heard "Get the tomato that's in the microwave," he did not even pause to glance at the immediate array but wheeled quickly around and proceeded to retrieve the tomato from the microwave. It is important to note that the present study was not initially designed to determine whether the subjects could process sentences that utilized a recursive structure. Rather, our tests of this capacity evolved when it became apparent that the subjects were having difficulty with an ambiguous linear structure—only then was the recursive structure introduced to resolve this ambiguity.

In addition to providing evidence for his understanding of recursion, Kanzi's data also indicate that he parsed word order appropriately in the majority of sentence reversals. Alia's data were not as strong, although she also appeared to be responding to word order. Additionally, it is important to note that, when errors were made, they tended to reflect a lack of attention or an incorrect semantic comprehension on the part of both subjects rather than difficulty in comprehending the syntax of the sentence.

Word order surely guided Kanzi's response in sentence contrasts such as "Can you put the ball on the pine needles?" and "Can you put the pine needles in your ball?" Kanzi had never encountered requests to put objects

Fɪɢ. 17.—This figure illustrates Alia listening to the sentence "Make the doggie bite the snake" (top left). Alia approaches the array and bites the doggie herself.

in balls, although he frequently opened balls. Only by listening to the sentence and decoding the word order could he have responded to both requests appropriately. Even more unusual were the opposing requests "Make the doggie bite the snake" and "Make the snake bite the doggie." In both instances, Kanzi picked up the agent first and moved the agent toward the recipient. Alia misinterpreted the agent in this sentence and bit the doggie herself (see Fig. 17). Since Kanzi's previous experience had been with real snakes and dogs, and since he had never before encountered dogs and snakes together, his ability to enact such a truly novel sentence with toy exemplars supports the view that he understood the nature of language as a representational device and that he was able to respond to important structural rules.

The range of capabilities demonstrated by these subjects becomes apparent when their performance on a given word is seen in the context of all the different sentences presented with that word. For example, the word *ball* occurred in 76 different sentences, including such different requests as "Put the leaves in your ball," "Show me the ball that's on TV," "Vacuum your ball," and "Go do ball slapping with Liz." Overall, 144 different content words, many of which were presented in ways that required syntactic parsing for a proper response (such as "Knife your ball" vs. "Put the knife in the hat"), were utilized in this study. Neither subject could have performed at the levels of correctness that we found without comprehending the basic components of syntactic relations among words in a string.

RECEPTIVE VERSUS PRODUCTIVE CAPACITIES

The abilities of Kanzi and Alia to comprehend language clearly exceeded their productive abilities to a considerable degree. The discrepancy was even greater for Kanzi than for Alia, presumably because Kanzi's output was limited to lexigrams, whereas Alia could speak. Her mean length of utterance (MLU) increased from 1.91 to 3.19 during the study period, and toward its end she was able to construct syntactically appropriate sentences such as "Monster's grabbing bunny's hand," "Mommy gonna hide the M&M's," and "The snake bit you." Maintaining his MLU at 1.15 throughout the study period, Kanzi was able to form two-symbol combinations that displayed order and to construct simple ordering rules (Greenfield & Savage-Rumbaugh, 1990). However, neither subject produced sentences with embedded phrases or employed constructions with phrasal modifiers such as *that's,* even though both evinced comprehension of such structures.

Alia and Kanzi's comprehension of novel constructions differs from that reported for dolphins (Herman, 1987) and sea lions (Schusterman & Krieger, 1986) in a number of ways. The most important is the manner in which this comprehension is acquired. Both Alia and Kanzi observed competent speaking models and began to decode the speech signal into its components as well as to assign meaning to those components on their own. By contrast, the dolphins and sea lions were taught to perform specific actions on specific objects and were rewarded with fish for so doing. The "sentences" to be comprehended were broken down into word units, and the dolphin was repeatedly rewarded for carrying out individual commands such as "peck-touch frisbee" and "tail-touch hoop" until it could perform them without error. Training was then extended to three-symbol combinations, such as "window fetch hoop" and "gate fetch frisbee." After these commands were also performed without error, test combinations that contained a minor variation, such as "peck-touch hoop" or "window fetch frisbee," were given; the dolphins were able to respond correctly about 60% of the time.

The restricted nature of the input and the training format used with dolphins make it difficult to draw meaningful comparisons between their skills and those of Kanzi and Alia. Nonetheless, it can be said that all three species apparently respond to ordering rules that indicate relations among objects, although the dolphin's ability to do so appears limited to tightly controlled training settings that permit almost no structural flexibility. However, the structural knowledge that they do exhibit is the sort of skill that an intelligent creature could build on to construct a complex language were this skill utilized to *deduce* structure and to relate structured sound units to real-world events, as Kanzi and Alia did with spoken English.

While the data indicate that Kanzi was slightly more advanced than Alia with regard to comprehension of the syntactic devices of word order and recursion, Alia was able to use her capacities for speech in ways that Kanzi could not. For example, she often attempted to repeat the sentence after she heard it, as though encoding it herself helped her store the sentence in memory for action. Also, Alia used her vocal ability to refuse to perform on some trials and to indicate her preference for a specific alteration of the request on other trials. Kanzi may have attempted similar actions as he vocalized in similar circumstances. However, the human experimenters could not decode these vocalizations as readily and did not respond to them as they did with Alia.

ARE APES WASTING THEIR INTELLIGENCE IN THE WILD?

How did Kanzi come to understand the complexities and nuances of human speech when apes generally do not? We propose that the answer is to be found in how the neural networks of a highly complex and relatively plastic brain, such as is found in the order primates (Jerison, 1985; Stephen, Bauchot, & Andy, 1970), become organized in response to recurring and complex patterns of stimulation during infancy and early development. Not only is early environmental stimulation advantageous for the development of the nervous system (Bennett, Rosenzweig, Morimoto, & Herbert, 1979), but the primate brain is also responsive to the structure and function of recurring patterns of stimulation, be those afforded by light or by motor/activity patterns (Riesen, 1982; Stell & Riesen, 1987). Also, early environmental deprivation (e.g., in the first 2 years of life) can produce long-term, probably irreversible deficits in the ape's capacity for complex learning and proficient transfer of learning (Davenport, Rogers, & Rumbaugh, 1973; Rumbaugh & Pate, 1984).

In light of these documented findings, we propose that the basic neural structures for language learning are laid down during the first year of a child's life via recurring observations and visual-auditory patterns experienced in the social contexts of communication and behavioral coordination within which the infant receives care and nurturing. Notwithstanding the fact that psychologists historically have emphasized the role of reinforcement as regards learning, we suspect that observation and perceptual learning processes are far more important to the infant for the learning of complex systems—such as a language (Hopkins & Savage-Rumbaugh, 1991; Rumbaugh et al., 1991). This perspective is compatible with arguments advanced by Mandler (1990) to the effect that the human infant's percepts can produce conceptual representations of its world. The infant is capable of perceptually parsing objects within a complex visual field well before she can manipulate those objects, a capacity held by Piaget (1954) to be requisite for the most basic form of learning (i.e., sensorimotor learning) to occur. Such perceptions can be integrated and can serve to form concepts that Mandler terms *image schemas*—even in the first year of life.

Our thesis is that, as a function of its openness/plasticity, the infant brain, be it human or ape, is uniquely responsive to structured patterns of stimulation that are focal points of life. The brain is responsive both to the patterns and to the specifics of stimulation and assumes a neural organization that is consonant to its recurring themes. Also, it defines the constancies of its constituent relations (e.g., the correlations between words and their interactive use, on the one hand, and their attendant consequences, on the other) and becomes selectively responsive to new experiences that might be incorporated so as to elaborate the emerging structure. Experiences that "fit" are keenly attended and responded to; challenges that are antithetical to the structure and function of the primary developmental format are either resisted or experienced without the accrual of any specific benefit.

We suggest that, as Kanzi grew up hearing others speak and observing the consequences/sequelae thereof, enduring changes occurred in the neurological networks of his brain that most closely approximate those that were basic to the evolution of language in humans. Such networks might serve to integrate and extend Mandler's image schemas into a developing framework for language.

We propose that human competence for language—and also Kanzi's—is a reflection of genetically defined possible modes of development that are responsive to environmental complexity. It is both the plasticity and the inherent similarity between ape and human brains that permits them to lay down the structures of complex systems, such as language, during infant development, even though the manifestation of behaviors that reflect the operations of those systems might be deferred for several months. Early environment serves not only to foster relatively specific competencies but also to preclude the possible development of other dimensions of competence, and it does so increasingly over time.

The ease with which a bonobo such as Kanzi came to understand and use a form of language not characteristic of his species suggests that the communication capacities of wild bonobos may be underestimated. Bonobos employ a wide variety of vocalizations; however, no evidence of anything like a linguistic system of bonobo communication has been suggested (de

Waal, 1987; Kano, 1980; Kuroda, 1980; Mori, 1984). Is this because a linguistic communication system is not there, or might it be that a simple "language" of sorts does exist but that we have been unable to decipher it? By what sort of criteria can we judge whether another species possesses language? While it is generally accepted that only humans possess language, there is no standard set of criteria by which it can be determined that a nonhuman lacks it. The most thoughtful analysis of the problem is still the one provided by Altmann (1967), who concludes, "Many structural properties that are universal in human language are known to occur in various species of nonhuman primates, some of which combine several of these properties. Inadequacies in the available data on social communication among nonhuman primates make it impossible to say whether any species of primate other than man combines all of these properties. Consequently, it is not yet possible to test Charles Darwin's contention . . . that the behavior of man differs from the behavior of other animals in degree, not in kind" (p. 358). This statement remains equally valid 26 years after it was made. The social communication systems of more nonhuman primates have been described in greater detail, but new functional knowledge of these systems has remained elusive. What is needed is a knowledgeable "informant."

Anthropologists face a similar problem when they look back through time to discover the emergence of patterns characteristic of human behavior. Is it possible to determine when language appeared on the scene? It surely occurred before writing, as some cultures lack a system of writing even today, but beyond this the clues to its emergence are vague. By contrast, the earliest stone tools are known to have appeared in the archaeological record some 2–3 million years before *Homo sapiens* roamed the globe. Stone tools leave a residue that language does not; thus, language could have predated the appearance of stone tools without leaving an identifiable trace of its existence.

WHEN DID LANGUAGE EVOLVE?

The widely held view that nonhuman primates lack even simple language skills has been coupled with the Chomskian position that emphasizes the complexity of formal grammar and assumes that language is distinct from other cognitive skills. The coupling of these concepts has led to wide acceptance of the proposition that language must have evolved recently, a view that has been further bolstered by a reinterpretation of the archaeological record that has led to the conclusion that language appeared only 40,000 years ago, or some 160,000 years after *Homo sapiens* came on the scene (Davidson, 1991). The evidence for this interpretation arises from a virtual explosion of the diversity of artifacts that took place 40,000 years ago, including the first documented appearance of art.

In our view, and contrary to this position, Kanzi's ability to understand complex speech and to use written symbols spontaneously suggests that present-day apes possess the capacity for a simple language system and thus that our common ancestor was capable of some sort of symbolic communication. Had Kanzi's skills been systematically shaped with rewards, his accomplishments would have little relevance in speaking to the skills of our common ancestor. However, the fact that he acquired speech comprehension and lexigram usage from exposure to input similar to that received by a child indicates that these cognitive capacities are available to bonobos to use for language or for other skills.

As it is currently employed by human adults, language may not have existed when the first *Homo sapiens* appeared; nonetheless, it is evolutionarily untenable to insist that it appeared full blown and with all the grammatical complexity that it currently manifests unless the cognitive substrate to support it was already in place. Possibly this substrate had evolved for other purposes, such as tool construction or social negotiation. Virtually all observers of nonhuman primate groups have been impressed with the complexity of their social behavior (Humphrey, 1983), and those who have watched apes repeatedly stress the similarities to human social interactions across a wide range of behaviors (Goodall, 1986). Indeed, it is puzzling that the social networks of apes can be as complex as they are without language, for similar social networks in our own species are inevitably mediated by what we call language.

It is unfortunate that the techniques available for assessing vocal communication among wild bonobos are not adequate to uncover symbolic language, if such indeed exists. Symbolic communications regarding activities not currently taking place or objects not immediately present do not lend themselves to the current stochastic coding schemes. For example, if a bonobo were to produce a vocalization that compatriots could interpret as "I am heading toward bananas," how would we decipher the meaning of the vocalization?

Even if all his compatriots understood him, their responses could vary widely. Some might accompany him, others might meet him at the banana site, or any of a number of other equally plausible possibilities might occur. Coding the compatriots' behaviors *immediately* following the vocalization would indicate nothing about their interpretation of the sound. Nor could one design a properly lagged coding system since there would be no consistent temporal relation between the announcement of the intent and the different individuals' arrival at the banana site.

Field researchers have yet to discover whether or how apes plan their daily activities and travel patterns. Yet it is unlikely that apes wander randomly around the forest hoping to come on food. It is more probable that they set out with a specific destination in mind and, in addition, that they are able to communicate that destination to others in some way. Nothing is known about how apes determine where to travel next or indeed about how far in advance they plan their travel route. Yet, being large animals who require a great deal of concentrated food, they cannot afford to expend considerable effort traveling to a location that will contain little sustenance. Their survival depends on determining when and where they will be able to find significant food resources.

Fig trees, the preferred food source among chimpanzees, are rare and do not ripen seasonally. The trees must be checked regularly, or the ripened fruit will be otherwise quickly consumed by monkeys (Ghiglieri, 1984). Arriving at a food source at precisely the right time is difficult, and any information that one could glean from other apes, monkeys, birds, or one's own memory would be of considerable help in making travel plans. All such information would yield only inferential data regarding the probable ripeness of such a tree, and it would be more helpful if the various sources could be aggregated in some manner so as to arrive at a more informed probability judgment.

Thus, the ape is faced each day with the quintessential "traveling-salesman" problem, and his solutions to the problem will depend on his memory, information received from other animals, and his ability to plan ahead. His plans may take into account nothing more than the next stop, but it is likely that they include much more. Even by the age of 5 years, Kanzi was able to specify in advance travel routes that included two and three stops. If apes in the wild are doing anything similar, it is certain that planning skills are the ones that would also serve them well should they decide to design a language system.

Regardless of whether or not apes use some simple form of symbolic communication in the wild, it is clear that they cannot produce anything like the continuous stream of highly discriminable sounds that characterizes human speech. Any communication system that may exist is necessarily limited to relatively short staccato sounds that intergrade into each other with fuzzy boundaries. Nonetheless, Kanzi's ability to understand human speech suggests that, if apes could produce human-like sounds, they might well invent and utilize a language that would be similar to our own, although probably considerably simpler.

Arguments from Tool Use

However, the currently popular evolutionary view of language—that it was a very late adaptation, occurring approximately 40,000 years ago

(Davidson, 1991)—presumes that tool use antedates language by at least 1.5 million years and that the cognitive capacities required to produce stone tools are considerably less complex than those required to develop a simple language. This view is hard to reconcile with the fact that children use language for some time before they begin to construct simple tools. Indeed, studies of the relation between tools and language have consistently looked at the emergence of tool *use* rather than tool *construction* (Bates et al., 1988) since language (both basic semantics and basic syntax) is rather well developed prior to the appearance of tool construction.

Toys involving elementary construction, such as Lego blocks, become popular with children after 3 years of age, after basic semantics and syntax are in place. Prior to this time, toys that reflect simpler schemata such as shaking, pushing, carrying, hitting, throwing, storing, stripping, opening, inserting, and extracting predominate. All these simpler schemata can be found among apes and are essential to their foraging strategies. For example, wild chimpanzees employ stones to crack nuts (Boesch, 1978). Stones used for these purposes are not modified in any manner, but they are transported for distances of several hundred meters. Because the dispersal of plant foods is predictable in space and time, it is possible to carry a rock several hundred meters, knowing that the nuts will be there waiting when one arrives. The abilities of apes to use simple tools, to plan ahead given that the environment is predictable, and to carry objects bear a remarkable similarity to the capacities of 2½-year-old children. Given the linguistic competencies of children at this age, it seems probable that early man utilized some form of language by at least 2 million years ago. Also, the fact that Kanzi displays comprehension skills that are equivalent to those of a 2½-year-old suggests that modern apes would be capable of a simple language if their vocal apparatus would but permit speech.

Ape versus Human Vocal Apparatus

Critics of ape language have often argued that, if apes could talk, they would be reported to do so in the wild (Harre & Reynolds, 1984). This perspective overlooks the fact that the vocal apparatus of the ape differs sufficiently from that of man to preclude speech. Conceivably, apes possess the cognitive capacities for language but lack the proper organ of expression. While apes are capable of a number of different sounds, their sounds grade into each other, making it difficult to determine where one sound ends and another begins (de Waal, 1988; Marler, 1976). All nonhuman primate vocalizations depend primarily on vowels. Humans alone are capable of producing phonemes with categorical boundaries such as /da/ and /ga/. The ability to produce consonants in association with vowels allows for the production of an exceedingly large number of discriminable sounds because of the phenomenon of categorical perception. Thus, any vocal language used by apes in the field would of necessity be restricted by the limited number of discriminable sounds that their oropharyngeal cavity could produce.

Of course, it is not the restructuring of the oropharyngeal cavity alone that results in speech. Along with this restructuring have also arisen the ability to control respiration and coordinate it with speech, the ability to produce voluntary sustained glottal pulses with controlled exhalation, and an increase in the degree of neurological control over fine movements of the lips and tongue. The production of each phoneme requires many muscular adjustments of the tongue, jaw, lips, soft palate, and vocal folds, in concert with the respiratory apparatus. The production of a succession of such sounds, as in the speech of modern human adults, entails motor planning of great complexity.

Nonetheless it is basically the ability to produce consonants that permits man to exploit the oral medium as a sophisticated mode of communication. Apes cannot produce consonants because the angle of articulation of their vocal-laryngeal tract prohibits velar closure (Crelin, 1987). Instances of damage to the vocal tract in human adults reveal that the ability to accomplish velopharyngeal closure is a critical dimension to the production of intelligible speech. Persons who have suffered complete loss of the tongue, half the mandible, and other oral structures can nonetheless produce speech that sounds almost normal and certainly intelligible. Yet failure of the velopharyngeal mechanism to permit closure makes speech communication virtually impossible (Perkins & Kent, 1986).

The need to balance the skull upright on the spine necessitated a rearrangement of the internal soft tissue and led to the possibility of at least partial velopharyngeal closure. Kanzi's ability to decode human sounds as well as syntactic constructions using combinations of these sounds suggests that ancestral *Homo* had developed a primitive linguistic skill that was awaiting the proper articulatory system. It seems quite probable, as Kuhl (1987) has suggested, that the articulatory system evolved to take advantage of the encoding properties already present in the mammalian auditory system. That is, the ability to produce speech was a recent evolutionary development that built on both the cognitive capacity to generate and comprehend complex ideas and the auditory capacity to perceive categorical boundaries. Once the ability to produce sounds with those acoustic properties appeared, language flowered because the other components were already in place. Early hominids could produce a greater variety of easily discriminable distinct sound units than they could form previously. The new consonants or consonant-like sounds could be used as boundaries around the vowel-like sounds that they already produced. The vowel-like sounds were thus bounded by easily discriminable units. Because of their categorical boundary properties, the consonant-like sounds were able to function as "edges" within what was previously a continuous sound system. Language was on its way.

IN CONCLUSION

Previous studies of the language capacities of apes have led to two widely accepted conclusions: (a) that they imitate their caregivers and (b) that they are not able to produce syntactically based sentences (Terrace et al., 1979). In spite of evidence that these conclusions were erroneous and premature (Greenfield & Savage-Rumbaugh, 1990, 1991; Savage-Rumbaugh, 1991; Savage-Rumbaugh et al., 1986), they have nonetheless gained wide acceptance. This has happened in part because no comparative data collected under similar conditions existed for apes and children; consequently, the ape has often been contrasted with the "idealized" child but has never been systematically compared with a real child.

Because this study focused on the comprehension of spoken English, and because Kanzi and Alia acquired this skill in similar environmental settings, they could be tested in a similar manner, permitting for the first time a systematic comparison of the language capacities of ape and child. The findings directly challenge the accepted dogma with regard to ape language capacities. Kanzi's comprehension cannot be attributed to imitation since there was nothing to imitate. The experimenter did not carry out a set of actions that Kanzi then followed. Information processing at a syntactic level was apparent throughout the data base, both in correct responses and in errors. Comprehension was evident not only for word order but for recursion as well. Additionally, the comprehension was not of an "invented language" but of spoken English, which entailed the parsing of phonemes and words as well as of sentence structure.

The fact that comprehension abilities of this level appear spontaneously in the bonobo reared in an environment similar to that encountered by a child strongly implies that apes have a heretofore unrecognized capacity for language. While it is generally assumed that bonobos exhibit no language-like communications in the field, such assumptions are based on minimal data and, in light of Kanzi's capacity, should be carefully reexamined.[2]

---

[2] The data in this *Monograph* supersede all previous preliminary reports. They reflect a more detailed scoring system and a review of all data mentioned in previous preliminary reports. Readers wishing to obtain further documentation and information about our work should contact E. Sue Savage-Rumbaugh, Language Research Center, Georgia State University, 3401 Panthersville Rd., Decatur, GA 30034.

COMPLETE CORPUS OF SENTENCES
AND CODED RESPONSES

This Appendix lists the sentences given to Kanzi and Alia, in the order in which they were presented to Kanzi. The order for Alia was roughly similar. Whenever a word in Alia's vocabulary was substituted for one of the words in the sentence presented to Kanzi, this is indicated by square brackets. During the early part of testing, as subjects were becoming acquainted with the demands of the test setting, some sentences were presented in parts. Whenever this occurred, ellipses points indicate that the subject was given an opportunity to respond to the first part of the sentence before the experimenter uttered the second part. A description of the coding criteria is given in Table 3 in the text. ("NG" indicates that a sentence has not been given to Alia.)

The first 243 trials reflect, for the most part, nonblind data, and for them just the codes and the sentences are listed. (Some blind trials did occur during this period, as both Alia and Kanzi were getting accustomed to the blind setting by the experimenter intermittently going behind the mirror.) The remaining blind (244–660) trials describe the behavior of the experimenter and the subjects in detail and give the code and, if needed, an explanation of the code. (On three trials in this group, there was inadvertent visual contact between Kanzi and the experimenter. These three trials are lumped in the nonblind data for purposes of analysis but are kept here in the order in which they were presented.)

When the description simply says, "Kanzi (or Alia) does so," it is because there is little else that can be described other than the response suggested within the sentence itself. When more explanation is given, other things occurred that, in some way, surrounded and/or interacted with the requested response. Kanzi and Alia's responses are set off by parentheses from the experimenter's utterances. Explanation of the codes applied are set off from the events by square brackets. Throughout, the experimenter is referred to as "E." Material that is unintelligible on the tapes is referred to as "U."

It should be noted that, in Kanzi's case, the experimenter is typically in a separate room, behind a metal and lexan door with a one-way lexan mirror, while uttering the sentences. This muffles and distorts the sound considerably, and the experimenter tends to speak quite loudly and repeat. Kanzi also tends to interrupt. When the experimenter repeats simply to make certain that she can be heard, this is not scored as a C2. C2 is scored only when the repetition occurs as a function of Kanzi's hesitation. When the experimenters believed that the sentence was understood but did not receive a clear response, they pressed harder for such a response than when they felt the subject either did not understand or was not willing to cooperate further.

SENTENCES AND KANZI AND ALIA'S RESPONSES

1. (C/C)[3] *Put the pine needles in the backpack.*
2. (NR/NR) *Get the hamburger [hotdog] . . . and put it in the bowl.*
3. (C/PC) *Put the backpack in the car.*
4. (PC/PC) *Put the oil in the backpack.*
5. (NR/C) *Get the flashlight . . . put it in the plastic bag.*
6. (PC/C) *Do you see the plastic bag? . . . put the rubber bands in the plastic bag.*
7. (C/NR) *Put your clay in the umbrella.*
8. (C/NG) *Get the soap and put it in the umbrella.*
9. (C/PC) *Get the paper . . . put the paper in the backpack.*
10. (C/PC) *Get the toothpaste and put it on the Fourtrax.*
11. (C/C) *Do you see the rock? . . . can you put it in the hat?*
12. (C/C2) *Get the rock . . . give it to Kelly [Nathaniel].*
13. (C/C2) *Get the peas . . . give them to Liz [Linda].*
14. (C/C) *Get the carrot . . . give it to Rose [Nathaniel].*
15. (C/C) *Get the milk bottle [cup] . . . put it in the backpack.*
16. (C/C) *Get the wipies . . . put them in the potty.*
17. (C/NG) *Get the pillow . . . put it on the vacuum.*
18. (C/C) *Put the peas on the blanket.*
19. (C/C) *Put the peas on the diaper.*
20. (PC/C) *Put the balloon . . . on the cube [chair].*
21. (PC/W) *Put the balloon . . . in the clay.*
22. (C/C) *Get the wipies . . . open the wipies . . . put the balloon in the wipies.*
23. (PC/C) *Put the ball . . . in the plastic bag.*
24. (C/C) *Put the ball on the telephone.*
25. (C/NG) *Get some clovers for Kelly.*

---

[3] In trials 1–243, the code for Kanzi is given first, followed by that for Alia.

26. (C/C) *Put the can opener [fork] on the pillow.*
27. (PC/PC) *Can you put the hat on Karen?*
28. (C/PC) *Get the phone and give it to Rose [Linda].*
29. (C/PC) *Put the rubber band on the TV tape.*
30. (C/C) *Put the rubber band on the soap.*
31. (C/C) *Put the rock on the book.*
32. (C/PC) *Get the bubbles and put them on the book.*
33. (PC/PC) *Hide the ball under the blanket.*
34. (PC/C) *Put the carrots in the backpack.*
35. (PC/NG) *Put the backpack on the Fourtrax.*
36. (C/C) *Put the apple in the umbrella [box].*
37. (PC/NG) *Get the bubbles . . . get Kelly with the bubbles.*
38. (PC/NG) *Can you ask Rose to tickle Kelly?*
39. (C/NG) *There is a new ball hiding at Sherman and Austin's play yard.*
40. (PC/NG) *There is a surprise hiding in Matata's yard.*
41. (C/PC) *Wash Kelly [Mary] . . . with a wipie.*
42. (PC/C) *Can you put the flashlight in the backpack?*
43. (C/C) *Put the mushrooms [grapes] in the potty.*
44. (NR/PC) *Do you see the tape [TV tape]? . . . can you put it in the hat?*
45. (PC/PC) *Can you get a shirt? . . . can you hide Kelly [Mary] with it?*
46. (W/NG) *Can you give the pillow to Sue?*
47. (C/PC) *Get some money . . . take it to the play yard [outside].*
48. (C/C) *Put the ball on the rock.*
49. (C/C2) *Can you put the flashlight in the potty?*
50. (C/PC) *Can you put the clay on the rock?*
51. (PC/C2) *Can you slap the hat?*
52. (C2/C3) *Can you put the money in the potty?*
53. (PC/C) *Can you put the rubber band on your foot?*
54. (C/PC) *Put the clay on the vacuum.*
55. (C/NG) *Can you tickle Sue with the umbrella?*
56. (PC/C) *Can you throw the ball?*
57. (C/C) *Can you throw the ball outdoors?*
58. (C/NG) *Can we play keep-away?*
59. (C/NG) *Can we play keep-away with some money?*
60. (PC/C) *Can you bite the stick?*
61. (C/NG) *Put some oil on Kelly.*
62. (NR/C) *Can you open the wipies?*
63. (NR/PC) *Hide the rubber band.*
64. (M/NG) *Can you hide this money?*
65. (C/C) *Can you put the rock in the cabinet?*
66. (C/OE) *Get the hammer . . . can you hide it somewhere?*
67. (PC/PC) *Can you show me the water? . . . now open it . . . pour it out!*
68. (C2/C) *Tickle Kelly [Nathaniel].*
69. (C2/NG) *Give the potato* (a photo) *to Kelly.*
70. (C2/C) *Give the sparklers to Sue [Mommy].*
71. (C2/NG) *Give Sue the bubbles.*
72. (C2/NG) *Groom Kelly.*

73. (C3/W) *Chase Kelly [Linda].*
74. (C3/OE) *Put the umbrella [box] in the backpack.*
75. (C2/C3) *Hide the ball.*
76. (C2/C) *Open the umbrella [box].*
77. (PC/C) *Put the ball on the potty.*
78. (PC/I) *Put the tomato [cookie] on the blanket.*
79. (C3/C) *Put the hammer in the backpack.*
80. (C3/C2) *Put the rubber band on the vacuum cleaner.*
81. (PC/C) *Open the clay.*
82. (PC/C) *Put the clay in the plastic bag.*
83. (PC/C) *Can you hammer the rock?*
84. (C/C2) *Can you put some clay on your ball?*
85. (PC/C) *Can you put the rubber band on the blanket?*
86. (C/C) *Can you hammer your ball?*
87. (PC/PC) *Can you put the collar [watch] on Kelly?*
88. (PC/C) *Can you put the hammer in the plastic bag?*
89. (C/C) *Can you put your collar [watch] in the backpack?*
90. (NR/C) *Can you put your shirt on?*
91. (C/NG) *Take your ball over to the vacuum cleaner.*
92. (PC/NG) *Can you bite the clay?*
93. (C/NG) *Could you take the bowl to the vacuum cleaner?*
94. (PC/C) *Can you throw your ball to Kelly [Cathy]?*
95. (C/NG) *Can you put the rock on your ball?*
96. (C2/C) *Can you take your collar [watch] outdoors?*
97. (C1/NG) *Can you put your shirt on your ball?*
98. (C3/C2) *Put your ball in your bowl.*
99. (C/C) *I want you to put some soap on your ball.*
100. (C/C) *See if you can make your doggie bite your ball.*
101. (C/C) *Put the blanket on the doggie.*
102. (PC/NG) *Can you get your ball with the umbrella?*
103. (C/NG) *Put some soap on Kelly.*
104. (C/PC) *Can you put the shirt . . . on the doggie?*
105. (PC/C) *I want you to bite the doggie.*
106. (PC/NG) *Let's put the collar on the doggie.*
107. (C/NG) *Let's put the soap in the potty.*
108. (C/NG) *Could you get a wipie out?*
109. (C/NG) *Now, could you wash your ball?*
110. (C/NG) *Can you put some oil on your ball?*
111. (C/NG) *I think we need to give the balloon to Kelly.*
112. (C3/C) *Put your hat . . . in the potty.*
113. (C/W) *Take the sparklers outdoors.*
114. (C/C) *Slap your ball.*
115. (M/C) *Put the oil on the TV.*
116. (M/C) *Put the rock . . . in the backpack.*
117. (PC/C) *Take the wipies outdoors.*
118. (PC/C) *Put your ball in the backpack.*
119. (C/C) *Can you put some toothpaste on your ball?*

120. (C/C) *Carry the rock to the bedroom.*
121. (C/NG) *Put your collar in the cabinet.*
122. (PC/C3) *Put some money in the trash.*
123. (PC/NG) *Put the blanket in the potty.*
124. (W/C) *Give your shirt to Kelly [Karen].*
125. (PC/C) *Can you put the shoe on the rock?*
126. (PC/C) *Put the sparklers on the TV.*
127. (PC/PC) *Put some toothpaste in the clay.*
128. (C2/C) *Put the dog on the vacuum.*
129. (PC/OE) *Take the rock outdoors.*
130. (C/C1) *Put the sparklers on the ball.*
131. (C2/NG) *Give me the rock.*
132. (PC/C) *Hide the dog in the backpack.*
133. (PC/NG) *Hammer the rock.*
134. (C2/C2) *Put the clay on the collar [watch].*
135. (M/NG) *Hide the ball with the hat.*
136. (C/NG) *Bite your dog.*
137. (C2/C) *Can you put the hat on your head?*
138. (PC/NG) *Can you tickle Laura with the dog?*
139. (C/NG) *Take the ball to the bedroom.*
140. (C/NG) *Go get the rock in the play yard.*
141. (C/NG) *Get the straw . . . put it in the gorilla's mouth.*
142. (PC/NG) *Can you take the backpack to the bedroom?*
143. (C2/PC) *Bite the picture of the oil.*
144. (C/I) *Get the toy gorilla . . . slap him with the can opener [fork].*
145. (C/C2) *Get the picture of the oil . . . take it to the bedroom.*
146. (PC/PC) *Get the orange juice . . . take the orange juice to the bathroom.*
147. (C/NG) *Get the gorilla . . . give him a drink of water.*
148. (PC/NG) *Hammer the vacuum.*
149. (M/NG) *Hammer the doggie.*
150. (M/PC) *Vacuum your ball.*
151. (C2/C2) *Take the doggie outdoors.*
152. (C2/NG) *Put the doggie on the cabinet.*
153. (C/PC) *Put the hat on my head.*
154. (PC/C) *Turn the vacuum on.*
155. (C/C4) *Put the doggie in the potty.*
156. (PC/C) *Take the carrots outdoors.*
157. (C/C) *Go outside and get some bark [flowers].*
158. (C5/C) *Go outdoors and find the carrot.*
159. (C/C3) *Put the mushrooms [grapes] on the TV.*
160. (C5/C) *Go to the bedroom and get the oil.*
161. (C/C2) *Take your collar [watch] to the bedroom.*
162. (C/W) *Give the doggie to Kelly [Karen].*
163. (C/PC) *Take a pillow outdoors.*
164. (C/C) *Put the oil in the potty.*
165. (C/W) *Start a fire.*
166. (C/C) *Slap the doggie.*

167. (PC/C) *Put your ball on the vacuum.*
168. (C/C) *Take the mushrooms [grapes] outdoors.*
169. (C/PC) *Give Kelly [Karen] a carrot.*
170. (C/C) *Go outdoors and get your ball.*
171. (PC/W) *Put the backpack on the potty.*
172. (W/C) *Take the paper to the bedroom.*
173. (C2/PC) *Take the potty outdoors.*
174. (C3/C) *Put some "fire" [a match] on the doggie.*
175. (I/NG) *Hide the mushrooms in your ball.*
176. (C/PC) *Can you give the collar [watch] to Kelly [Linda]?*
177. (C/C) *Take the doggie out of the pillow.*
178. (C/C) *Give the doggie some mushrooms [grapes].*
179. (C/PC) *Put a mushroom [grape] in the oil.*
180. (C/C2) *Give the lighter [pillow] to Kelly [Mommy].*
181. (C/C2) *Take the mushrooms [grapes] to the T-room [bedroom].*
182. (C/C) *Give the dog to Sue [Mommy].*
183. (W/C) *Open the T-room [bathroom].*
184. (PC/PC) *Hide the doggie in the pillow.*
185. (C/PC) *Take the doggie to the bedroom.*
186. (C/NG) *I hid a surprise in the microwave.*
187. (PC/C) *The surprise is hiding in the dishwasher [shower].*
188. (C3/PC) *Can you put the mushrooms in the microwave [oven]?*
189. (C/NG) *Could you take the pine needles outdoors?*
190. (PC/PC) *Do you see the backpack? . . . can you put it on?*
191. (C/C2) *Go outdoors and get the pine needles.*
192. (PC/C) *Give the doggie some carrots.*
193. (C/C) *Give the doggie some water.*
194. (M/PC) *Put some mushrooms [the watch] in the ice [on the toy shelf].*
195. (C/C) *Put some toothpaste on the doggie.*
196. (C/NG) *Put some hotdogs in the potty.*
197. (C/C) *Put the pine needles on the TV.*
198. (C/C) *Turn the TV on.*
199. (C/C) *Give the pine needles to Kelly [Karen].*
200. (C3/W) *Take the hat to the bedroom.*
201. (C/C2) *Put some water on the carrot.*
202. (C/C1) *Put some toothpaste on the hotdog.*
203. (C/C) *Squeeze the toothpaste.*
204. (C4/C) *Show me the stick . . . hit the dog with the stick.*
205. (C/C) *Put some hotdogs [grapes] in your ball [ice].*
206. (C3/C) *Put the mushrooms [grapes] in the cabinet.*
207. (C/PC) *Where's your stick? . . . can you tickle me with the stick?*
208. (C/NG) *Can you show me the stick? . . . can you tickle Kelly?*
209. (C/C) *Put some toothpaste in the water.*
210. (C/W) *Close the play-yard [front] door.*
211. (C2/C) *Can you throw the dog to Kelly [Nathaniel]?*
212. (PC/C) *Put the money in the mushrooms [grapes].*
213. (C3/C) *Put the hotdogs in the noodles.*

214. (C/C) *Can you put the ball on the doggie?*

215. (C2/PC) *Pour some vitamins [medicine] on the mushrooms [grapes].*

216. (C/C) *Knife your ball.*

217. (PC/PC) *Put the sparklers in the cabinet [toy shelf].*

218. (C/C) *Take the lighter [matches] outdoors.*

219. (C/C) *Put the can opener [fork] in the shoe.*

220. (PC/C2) *Put the cherries* (a photo) *on your ball.*

221. (C/NR) *Put the toothpaste on the snake picture.*

222. (OE/C) *Take the money to the bedroom.*

223. (PC/PC) *Put the ball picture in the backpack.*

224. (PC/C) *Put some soap on the carrot.*

225. (PC/PC) *Put some vitamins [medicine] on your shirt.*

226. (C/C4) *Put the telephone on the TV.*

227. (PC/NG) *Put the sparklers in the shoe.*

228. (C/C) *Put the sparklers in the potty.*

229. (C/C4) *Take the telephone outdoors.*

230. (C2/PC) *Put the shoe in the potty.*

231. (PC/C) *Put the shoe in the cabinet.*

232. (C/C) *Take the doggie to Liz [Nathaniel].*

233. (C/PC) *Give the toy gorilla a shot.*

234. (PC/C) *Put some paint on the dog.*

235. (NR/C) *Put the toy gorilla on the potty.*

236. (C/C) *Give the rock to Liz [Lisa].*

237. (C/PC) *Take the toothpaste outdoors.*

238. (PC/PC) *Hit the can opener [fork] with the rock.*

239. (PC/C) *Put the straw in the umbrella [box].*

240. (C/C) *Give the doggie the pine needles.*

241. (C/C) *Put the shot in the paint.*

242. (C/PC) *Can you pour the paint out?*

243. (C1/C) *Put the toothpaste in the paint.*

244. (C) *Can you take the paint outdoors?* (Kanzi does so.)

244A. (C) *Can you take the paint outdoors?* (Alia says, "Yes." She gets up and gets the paint. She looks in the mirror, then touches the light stand for the camera lighting.) E says, "Hot." (Alia pulls her hand back and takes the paint to the front door. Alia says something U, then points to the door handle and says, "This.") E opens the door. (Alia takes the paint outside.) [C1 was not scored here as Alia was already in the process of carrying out the sentence when she took time to do something else.]

245. (PC) *(I need your help with the rest of that paint.) Could you put the rest of that paint in the potty?* (Kanzi tosses the clay in the potty.) E says, "How about the paint, Kanzi?" (Kanzi picks up some more clay and puts it in the potty.) E says, "Thank you, that was the clay, now could you put the paint, the paint in the potty, the paint?" (Kanzi pulls the potty over to the door and points to the clay in it and makes a sound like "paint.") [PC is scored because Kanzi confused *paint* and *clay*. This is a common error for him.]

245A. (C) *Can you put the rest of the paint in the potty?* (Alia picks up the paint and heads to the potty, saying, "Here potty, here potty," stops to look in Karen's room, then puts the paint in the potty.)

246. (C) *Hide the toy gorilla, hide him.* (Kanzi tries to push the toy gorilla under the fence.) [C is scored because Kanzi generally takes *hide* to mean moving an object out of the immediate field of vision.]

246A. (C) *Hide the toy gorilla.* (Alia picks up the gorilla and hugs him, then says, "Sit here gorilla," and places him in her chair.) [C is scored because Alia has moved the gorilla out of the array and, like Kanzi did on trial 246, made him less visually evident among the set of items to be acted on.]

247. (C3) *Knife the doggie. Can you knife the doggie?* (Kanzi picks up the doggie, presses him against the wire, then kisses him.) E says, "Knife the doggie." (Kanzi slaps the doggie.) E says, "Do you see the knife?" (Kanzi ignores E and licks some food out of a pan.) E says, "Show Sue the knife." (Kanzi shows E the knife.) E says, "Yeah, can you knife the doggie?" (Kanzi does so.) [C3 is scored because E asks Kanzi to find the knife and then repeats the sentence.]

247A. (C1) *Can you knife the doggie?* (Alia says, "Yes," approaches some paper in the array, and, as she leans down to pick it up, says, "Mommy," and gives E the piece of paper. Then she says, "Knife the doggie, do that," and does so.)

248. (C) *Now go get your ball.* (Kanzi does so; the ball is not part of the array.)

248A. (C) *Go get your ball.* (Alia points to the ball, which is on the side of the room and is not part of the array; then she retrieves it.)

249. (C) *Give the lighter to Liz.* (Kanzi does so.)
249A. (C) *Give the matches to Lisa.* (Alia does so.)

250. (C) *Sit down.*
250A. (NG).

251. (C) *Put the pine needles in your ball.* (Kanzi does so.)

251A. (C3) *Put the pine needles in your ball.* (Alia goes over and looks at the hole in the basketball. She puts one hand on the ball and touches another object that looks like a golf ball. She then puts both hands back on the basketball.) E says, "See the pine needles, Alia." (Alia gets up, gets the pine needles, and takes them to E.) E says, "Put the pine needles in your ball." (Alia waves the pine needles around above her head.) E says, "Put the pine needles in your ball." (Alia says, "Put pine needles in your ball." She then takes some pine needles out of the plastic bag and puts them in the ball.) [C3 is given because E had to ask Alia first to look for the pine needles and then to put them in the ball once she had found them.]

252. (C3) *Push the knife under the door.* (Kanzi picks up the knife and touches the handle of the pan with it.) E says, "Push it under the door." (Kanzi starts to push it under the fence.) E says, "Give the knife to Sue." (Kanzi holds it out toward the mirrored surface on the door.) Sue says, "Under the door. Give it to me." (Kanzi tries to put it through the fence.) E says, "Can you put it under the door?" E says, "Here, here, can you push it under the door there," while sticking her hand out to receive the knife. [C3 is scored because E changes the phrasing from "push the knife under the door" to "give it to Sue" when Kanzi seems to understand that he is to

transfer the knife to E but not to realize that he can put things under the door. This is the first time during the test that he is requested or allowed to do so.]

252A. (OE) *Push the knife under the mirror.* (Alia picks up the knife and the shot while saying something U about the mirror. She goes over to the mirror and hits it with the knife.) E says, "Can you push the knife under the mirror?" (Alia says something U about the shot, and she hits the shot against the mirror. Then she takes both the shot and the knife and tries to push them through the mirror.) [OE is coded because Alia is trying to push two objects into the mirror. It is interesting that neither Alia nor Kanzi tries to push the object under the door. Both Alia and Kanzi understand that they are somehow to transfer the item to E through a barrier; however, only Alia tries to transfer two items.]

253. (C) *Now could you give Liz some pine needles?* (Kanzi does so.)

253A. (C) *Now can you give Linda some pine needles?* (Alia picks up the bag of pine needles and carries it over to Linda, who is sitting on the couch. While carrying the bag, Alia also tries to open it. Once at the couch, Alia slaps at the other end of the couch from Linda and looks briefly at Linda, then turns her attention back to opening the bag of pine needles as she leans on the couch. When she finally gets the bag open, Alia takes a couple of pine needles out and places them on the couch between herself and Linda and then looks at Linda. Alia continues to take the rest of the pine needles out of the bag and place them with the others on the couch, glancing at Linda briefly. She then picks up a small amount of pine needles from the pile on the couch and tosses them toward Linda, then pushes the rest of the pile toward Linda, about a foot away from Linda and still on the couch.) [C is scored because Alia's behavior is interpreted as a rather elaborate form of giving the pine needles to Linda, not a lack of comprehension.]

254. (C) *Take the telephone to Kelly.* (Kanzi does so.)

254A. (C) *Take the telephone to Nathaniel.* (Alia does so.)

255. (C) *Take the dog to Panbanisha. Take the doggie to Panbanisha.* (Kanzi does so.)

255A. (PC) *Take the dog to Lisa.* Alia picks up the dog toy and carries it across the room to Katie. She becomes interested in playing with Katie and places the toy dog to the side.) E says, "Alia, be careful." (Alia says, "OK.")

Error correction.—E says, "Alia, take the dog to Lisa." (Alia remains by Katie.) E says, "Take the dog to Lisa." (Alia takes the dog to Lisa.) [PC is scored because, unlike trial 253, Alia's actions are directed, not toward the proper recipient, but toward another party.]

256. (PC) *Cut the pine needles with the scissors.* (Kanzi picks up the pine needles, breaks some off, and eats them.) E says, "Can you use the scissors to cut the pine needles? Do you see the scissors?" (Kanzi continues to eat the pine needles.)

Error correction.—E shows Kanzi what to do, and he tries. [PC is scored because Kanzi understands *pine needles*.]

256A. (PC) *Cut the pine needles with the scissors.* (Alia cuts a leaf with the scissors.) [PC is scored because Alia understands *cut* and *scissors*.]

257. (NR) *Put the leaves in your ball.* (Kanzi picks up the scissors and tries to cut

the pine needles, still interested in this action from the last trial.) E says, "Kanzi, put the leaves in your ball." (Kanzi tries to cut the ball with the scissors.)

Error correction.—E shows Kanzi what to do. [NR is scored because Kanzi is more interested in continuing the action from the previous trial than in listening to what E is requesting on this trial.]

257A. (C) *Put the leaves in your ball.* (Alia gets the leaves while saying something like, "Put them in the ball." The leaves are clustered in a big group. Alia puts some of the leaves into the ball.)

258. (C) *Give the ball to Rose.* (Kanzi does so.)
258A. (C) *Give the ball to Lisa.* (Alia does so.)

259. (C) *Knife the toothpaste.* (Kanzi does so.)
259A. (C) *Knife the toothpaste.* (Alia does so.)

260. (C) *Give the ball a shot.* (Kanzi does so.)
260A. (PC) *Give the ball a shot.* (Alia picks up the shot and then the ball. She takes them to E and hugs her.) E says, "Alia. Alia. Thank you, but that's not what Mommy said. Listen. Give the ball a shot. Give the ball a shot." (Alia says something U.) E says, "Can you give the ball a shot?" (Alia gives the ball and shot to E.) [PC is scored because Alia understood *give, ball,* and *shot* but not the relation between the ball and the shot that is embodied in the sentence structure.]

261. (PC) *Put the lighter in the shoe.* (Kanzi puts the shot in the shoe.) [PC is scored because Kanzi understood *put* and *shoe* but not *lighter.*]

Error correction.—E says, "Put the lighter in the shoe, the lighter." (Kanzi picks up the lighter and tries to manipulate it, using the shot.) E says, "Uh huh, put the lighter in the shoe." (Kanzi continues.) E says, "Put the lighter in the shoe." (Kanzi throws down both the lighter and the shot as though they are dangerous.) E says, "Do you see the lighter?" (Kanzi throws some paper at the lighter, as though it is hot and might burn the paper.) E hands Kanzi the lighter, saying, "Take the lighter." (Kanzi does.) E says, "Now put it in the shoe." (Kanzi tosses the lighter aside as though it were dangerous. He then vocalizes an approximation of *apple*). E says, "OK, give me the lighter back and I'll put it in the shoe for you." E opens the shoe. (Kanzi tosses the lighter in the shoe.)

261A. (PC) *Put the matches in the shoes.* (Alia picks up the matchbox and tries to open it. She then gets up and goes over to E, saying, "Mommy," and something U.) E says, "Open?" E opens the matchbox and gives it back to Alia. E says, "Go back over there," and points to the mat with the objects. (Alia goes back over and sits on the mat. She drops the matchbox, and the matches fall out. She picks up the matchbox, puts it back down, and picks up some matches. She places the matches on the chair.) [PC is scored because Alia understood *matches* but not *put* or *shoes.*]

Error correction.—E says, "Alia, put the matches in the shoe." (Alia puts a match in the shoe, takes it back out, and sets it back on the chair. This is repeated with all the different matches.)

262. (C) *Put the ball in the cabinet.* (Kanzi does so.)
262A. (C2) *Put the ball on the couch.* (Alia gets up, doesn't do anything, and then says, "A pumpkin.") E says, "Alia, put the ball on the couch." (Alia picks up the ball

and drops it behind her. She mumbles something U. She picks up the ball and takes it to the couch.) [C2 is scored because Alia does nothing until E repeats the sentence.]

263. (C) *Take the shot to Krista.* (Kanzi does so.)

263A. (C) *Take the shot to Nathaniel.* (Alia does so.)

264. (C1) *Give the doggie to Rose.* (Kanzi smells the paint, then gives the dog to Rose.) [C1 is scored because it is assumed that Kanzi wanted to smell the paint, not that he misunderstood the sentence.]

264A. (C3) *Give the doggie to Linda.* (Alia looks over to Linda across the room as she slowly moves toward the objects. She then picks up the toy dog as she coyly smiles and carries the dog toward Linda and Nathaniel, who is sitting right next to Linda.) Nathaniel says, "Linda." (Alia continues toward Linda and touches the dog to Linda but then keeps hold of the dog, carrying it over her head, and spins around once and looks back at Linda.) [C3 is scored because Alia's behavior suggests that she comprehends the sentence but is simply hesitant to hand the dog to Linda and because Nathaniel says, "Linda," as she approaches him.]

Error correction.—E repeats the request, "Alia, give the doggie to Linda." (Alia then turns back to Linda, holding the dog, but not handing it to her. Linda does not show any sign of reception to Alia, and this seems to inhibit Alia from giving Linda the dog.) E says, "Give it to Linda. Put it in her lap. . . . Give it to Linda." (Alia continues to stand before Linda with the dog and looks at her but still seems hesitant about actually handing her the dog. Alia and Nathaniel then engage in a shoving match, and E verbally intervenes.) "Hurry up. Give the. . . . Nathaniel, stop it. Move over to the other chair." E then repeats the request, "Alia, give the doggie to Linda." (Alia stands by Linda but does not give her the dog. She lifts the dog slightly up to Linda while her back is turned toward Linda.) E says, "Give it to Linda, hurry up." (Alia turns slightly toward Linda and lifts the dog up slightly toward Linda but still does not clearly give it to her.) "Can you give it to Linda?" (Alia looks down at the dog as she slightly moves it toward Linda, but again she does not clearly give the dog to her.) E then comes from behind the mirror and shows Alia how to just put the dog in Linda's lap.)

265. (W) *Put the paint on the TV.* (Kanzi throws the doggie toward the blanket.) [W is scored because Kanzi did not clearly show comprehension of any part of the sentence.]

Error correction.—E says, "Put the paint on the TV." (Kanzi carries the doggie over to the television.) [Kanzi had, on trial 234, put the paint on the doggie. In this trial, he appears to be putting the doggie by the television because the doggie already has "paint" on him. In addition, during this trial, Kanzi makes a vocalization that sounds like "paint" as he is moving the dog. He makes no other vocalizations. Thus, although Kanzi is scored as wrong on this trial, it is possible that he was, in a novel way, understanding and fulfilling the request and attempting to use a vocal means of expressing this to E.]

265A. (C) *Put the paint on the TV.* (Alia does so.)

266. (NR) *Can you get your balloon out? Get your balloon out of the paint.* (Kanzi looks around as though he just does not know what to do and as though he cannot find a balloon. The balloon is *not* visible in the paint; it is completely hidden and has

been there for some time.) E says, "Get your balloon." (Kanzi still seems not to know what to do.) [NR is scored because Kanzi makes no measurable response to the sentence.]

Error correction.—E switches to another request so that Kanzi can be successful. "Well, go get your ball, get your ball." (Kanzi does so, but this is not considered part of the data base.)

266A. (C) *Get the balloon out of the paint.* (Alia does so. Her balloon is partially visible hanging out of the paint, so she does not have to determine where the balloon is and also carry out the sentence appropriately.)

267. (C) *Give the cereal to Rose.* (Kanzi takes a mouthful of the cereal as he is handing it to Rose.) [This is scored as C since it appears that Kanzi is sneaking a bit of the cereal while carrying out the sentence.)

267A. (C) *Give the cereal to Kathy.* (Alia places the cereal next to Kathy rather than actually handing it to her.) [It appears that Alia understands the sentence but is hesitant to hand the cereal to Kathy.]

268. (C) *Take the stick outdoors.* (Kanzi does so.)

268A. (C) *Take the stick outdoors.* (Alia picks up the stick and takes it to the door. She attempts to open the door, but it shuts.) E says, "Nathaniel, you can open it." Nathaniel says, "Let me open it for you," and opens the door for Alia. (Alia puts the stick outdoors.)

269. (C) *Put your ball on the hose.* (Kanzi does so.)

269A. (NG).

270. (C) *Give the cereal to Panbanisha.* (Kanzi does so.)

270A. (C3) *Give the cereal to Joshua.* (Alia picks up the cereal and starts to carry it toward E behind the mirror.) E says, "Joshua. Give the cereal to Joshua." (Alia turns around and walks slowly toward Joshua, who is sitting with Nathaniel at a table on the other side of the room. She carries the cereal to one side of Joshua. Joshua continues to play with his toys. Alia then places the box of cereal on the table to the left of the toys that Joshua is playing with, but she keeps hold of the box.) Nathaniel then points out the cereal and says to Joshua, "You have to take it, look, Josh." Josh then grabs the box of cereal from Alia. [C3 is scored because E rephrased the sentence initially and then Nathaniel told Joshua to take the cereal. Prior to that time, Alia kept hold of the cereal, and it was not clear that she was giving it to Joshua.]

271. (C) *Show Sue the ball and the cereal.* (Kanzi picks the cereal up as E starts to talk. When he hears the sentence, he grabs the ball and tries to open the door to give E the ball. He keeps the cereal in his lap but appears to be attempting to show E the ball.) [C is scored because Kanzi picks up both requested objects. Whenever either subject is asked to "show" something, they are given the benefit of the doubt if they act on it in some way that could serve to draw E's attention and if E can see this.]

271A. (PC) *Show me the ball and the cereal.* (Alia picks up the cereal, shakes it, and tries to pour it in the bowl, but it does not come out because it is in a closed plastic container. She says something U.)

272. (C) *Show Sue the doggie and the rock.* (Kanzi touches the doggie, then picks

up the rock and holds it in front of the door.) [C is scored because Kanzi picks up both requested objects.]

272A. (OE) *Show Mommy the dog and the rock.* (Alia slowly slides down from her chair toward the array of objects, looking over the array as she crawls closer to the objects. She picks up the rock with her left hand, then turns to the dog and grabs it with her right hand. She then looks at the chimp toy doll as she moves the dog to her right side, simultaneously reaching with the left hand, which still has the rock in it. She adjusts and places the rock in her right hand, then again reaches for the chimp doll with her left hand. Alia tries to carry all three objects but at the same time becomes distracted to her right, where Nathaniel is watching a video. Alia then carries all three objects to E behind the mirror. She hands E the rock first.) E says, "Oh thank you," and asks, "Is that the rock?" (Alia answers, "Uh-huh," then hands E the chimp doll.) "And what's that?" (Alia answers, "Gorilla," then hands E the dog toy.) While Alia hands E the dog, E says, "And doggie, thank you," then hugs Alia.

273. (PC) *Show Sue the toothpaste and the milk.* (Kanzi shows E the milk.)
Error correction.—E says, "And the toothpaste, what about the toothpaste?" (Kanzi does nothing.) E says, "You don't see that?" (Kanzi picks up the knife.)
273A. (C) *Show Mommy the toothpaste and the milk.* (Alia picks up the milk and then the toothpaste. She takes them back to her chair. She sits down and starts to take the cap off the toothpaste.) E comes out and says, "I guess that's good."

274. (PC) *Show Sue the carrot and the telephone.* (Kanzi picks up the telephone and holds the receiver to his ear.)
Error correction.—E says, "What about the carrot?" (Kanzi puts down the phone and picks up the carrot.)
274A. (C) *Show Mommy the carrot and the telephone.* (Alia picks up the carrot and the telephone and takes both to E.)

275. (PC) *Kanzi, show me the ball and the rubber band.* (Kanzi picks up the ball and holds it in front of the door.)
Error correction.—E says, "What about the rubber band? Do you see the rubber band too?" (Kanzi picks up the rock and tries to open the door to show the rock to E.)
275A. (OE) *Show me the ball and the rubber band.* (Alia first picks up the ball and the rubber band simultaneously, then holds the ball and the rubber band with her left hand, grabs the shot with her right hand, and tries to put the shot with the other objects in her left hand, but the shot falls onto the floor. She then picks up the rock and the shot, but this causes the ball in her left hand to fall out. Alia tries to pick up the ball, but then the other objects fall from her arms.)
Error correction.—E says, "Alia, just get the ball and the rubber band. Just the ball and the rubber band. Only the ball and the rubber band." (Alia still continues to pick up the ball, the rubber band, the shot, and the rock. She takes all the objects to E behind the mirror and hands first the ball, then the shot, then the rubber band, then the rock, to E.)

276. (PC) *Show me the milk and the doggie.* (Kanzi tries to push the doggie under the door to show him to E; then he kisses the doggie.)

Error correction.—E says, "Can you show me the milk also, the milk?" (Kanzi picks up the milk and tries to open the door to show E.)

276A. (C4) *Show me the milk and the dog.* (Alia is playing with a book.) E takes the book and tosses it back on the table. E says, "Alia turn around. Now listen. Show me the milk and the dog." (Alia gets up and gets the dog. She places the dog behind her and sets an object back up that she knocked over.) Nathaniel gets up and walks in front of the camera. E says, "Nathaniel sit down." (Alia then gets the milk and picks up the doggie. She takes them back and sits on her chair.) [C4 is scored because Alia correctly gets both objects on her own; however, E has to prevent her from engaging in other activities before she is able to do so.]

277. (PC) *Give the doggie some milk.* (Kanzi tries to push the doggie to E, as though E should give the milk to the dog.)

Error correction.—E says, "Give some milk to the doggie." (Kanzi tries to open the door, as though to give the doggie to E. When it does not open, he picks up some cereal and begins to eat it.)

277A. (C) *Listen, give the doggie some milk.* (Alia gets up, knocks over the bowl. She says, "Bowl," then picks up the milk and says, "Milk." She drops the milk, picks it back up, and pours it on the doggie.)

278. (C) *Give some milk to Rose.* (Kanzi does so.)

278A. (C) *Give some milk to Lisa.* (Alia does so.)

279. (C) *Feed the doggie some milk.* (Kanzi does so.) [Kanzi puts the milk directly in the dog's mouth in response to this sentence, in contrast with trial 277.]

279A. (C) *Feed the doggie some milk.* (Alia puts the milk carton up to the dog's mouth.) [Alia puts the milk directly in the dog's mouth in response to this sentence, in contrast with trial 277.]

280. (PC) *Give me the lighter and the water.* (Kanzi puts the lighter in the water.)

Error correction.—E holds out her hand and says, "You are supposed to give them to me." (Kanzi does.)

280A. (C1) *Give Mommy the sparkler and the water.* (Alia goes back behind where E is and gets her drink. She drinks some. She sets it down.) E puts the drink next to her and says, "Go sit down. Alia, go sit down." E takes Alia's hand and heads her in the right direction. "Go sit down. Listen." (Alia goes back and sits down.) E says, "Give Mommy the water and the sparkler." (Alia says, "More juice, Mommy.") E says, "Not yet. Give Mommy the water and the sparkler." (Alia says, "OK." She picks up the sparkler and mumbles, "Water and sparkler." She puts down the sparkler. She picks up the container with the water and says, "Ut oh, water." She puts her finger in the water. Alia says something U and takes the objects over to E.) [C1 is scored as Alia carries out the sentence properly after she drinks some juice.]

281. (C) *Give me the milk and the lighter.* (Kanzi does so.)

281A. (C) *Give me the wipies and the matches.* (Alia does so.)

282. (PC) *Put the apple in the hat.* (Kanzi puts the carrot in the hat.)

Error correction.—E says, "Apple, can you put the apple in the hat?" (Kanzi does so.)

282A. (C) *Put the apple in the hat.* (Alia picks up the apple. As she reaches for the hat, she drops the apple. She picks up the apple. She reaches toward the hat but touches the orange next to the hat. She reaches farther and pulls the hat closer to her. She then puts the apple in the hat.)

283. (C) *Put the carrot on the TV.* (Kanzi puts the carrot next to the television and makes a sound like "carrot.")

283A. (C) *Put the carrot on the TV.* (Alia picks up the carrot and walks toward the television.) The telephone rings. (Alia stops and says something U and "Get it.") E says, "Alia go ahead and put the carrot on the TV." (Alia goes to put the carrot on the television but knocks something else off the television in the process. She then drops the carrot.) E says, "OK." (Alia starts to put the carrot back up on the television.) E says, "You did it." (C is scored because the interruption and repetition were generated, not by the subject, but by the phone noise.)

284. (C) *Put your apple in the microwave.* (Kanzi takes his apple to the microwave and makes a sound like "apple.")

284A. (C) *Put the apple in the oven.* (Alia picks up the apple from the array, carries it to the oven in the kitchen, and waits as E then comes from behind the mirror to help Alia open the oven.) "Can you open it?" (Alia tries to open the main top part of the oven but cannot and says, "Too hard.") E says, "Can you open this?" (E points to the lower drawer of the oven. (Alia tries once and says, "It's too hard," but E encourages her to try. Alia then opens the drawer of the oven and places the apple inside.)

285. (PC) *Put the knife in the hat.* (Kanzi touches the knife, then the soap.) E says, "Put the knife in the hat." (Kanzi picks up the soap and puts the knife in the soap.)
Error correction.—E says, "Where's the hat?" (Kanzi puts soap on his hands, eats a tomato, then picks up the hat and uses it to wipe the soap off his hands.) E says, "Put the knife in the hat." (Kanzi puts the hat on the soap and hands the knife to E.)

285A. (PC) *Put the knife in the hat.* (Alia picks up the knife and tries to cut the apple.) E says, "Alia, put the knife in the hat." (Alia continues to hit the apple with the knife.)
Error correction.—E says, "Alia, put the knife in the hat." (Alia continues to hit the apple with the knife.) E says, "Do you see the hat?" (Alia touches the hat with the point of the knife.) E says, "Yeah, put the knife in the hat." (Alia returns to hitting her apple.) E says, "Put the knife in the hat." (Alia continues hitting the apple with the knife.) E says, "Now." (Alia continues with her apple hitting.) E comes out from behind the mirror and says, "You're going to hurt yourself. Alia, look at Mommy. Put the knife in the hat." (Alia touches the knife to the hat. She then tries to pick up the hat, but she can't seem to get under it. She looks at E.) E picks up the hat for her. (Alia takes the hat, turns it over, and puts the tip of the knife in the hat.) E says, "Yes, now put it in and leave it there. Don't play with the knife."

286. (PC) *Put the orange on your collar.* (Kanzi takes two bites of an orange sweet potato, then puts it on his collar.) E says, "Put the orange on your collar." (Kanzi tosses the orange in a bucket.)
Error correction.—E says, "On your collar." (Kanzi picks up the sweet potato, takes another bite of it, puts it in the potty, and makes a sound like "orange.")

286A. (I) *Put your orange on your watch.* (Alia picks up the tomato and the watch and looks at both, then puts the tomato down. She then rolls the orange to her so that she can set the watch on the orange.) [Alia at first appears to be attempting to determine which round food is the orange. After she looks at them, she places the watch on the orange.]

Error correction.—E continues to let Alia manipulate the objects. (Alia places the orange on top of the tomato. The orange rolls off. She picks up the tomato and sets it aside. She picks it up again and starts to pick at it.) E says, "Alia, don't do that." (Alia says something U while she continues to play with the tomato.) E says, "Alia, put your orange on your watch." (Alia puts the tomato on the watch. She picks it up and does it again. She then rolls the orange so that it is touching the watch.)

287. (C) *Kanzi, take the tomato to the colony room.* (Kanzi makes a sound like "orange"; he then takes both the tomato and the orange to the colony room.) [C is scored because it is assumed that Kanzi is announcing that he wants to take an orange and have it to eat.]

287A. (C) *Take the tomato to Karen's room.* (Alia does so.)

288. (C) *Put the monster mask on your head.* (Kanzi drops the orange that he is eating into the monster mask and then puts the mask on his head.) [C is scored as it assumed that Kanzi wants to continue eating the orange while he has the mask on, not that he misunderstands the request.)

288A. (C) *Put the monster mask on your head.* (Alia does so.)

289. (C) *Go scare Matata.* (The monster mask is on his head when this is said. Kanzi goes to the colony room door with the mask on his head but takes it off while waiting for Rose to open the door. The mask is quite hot and makes breathing difficult. Rose tells Kanzi to put it back on if he wants her to open the door. Once in the colony room, Kanzi walks by Matata's cage with the mask and vocalizes. Kanzi then begins to tease the orangs with the mask, and Rose tells him not to do so because the orangs will grab it. Kanzi takes the mask back from the orangs, puts it on again, and parades up and down in front of Matata's cage. Matata looks somewhat nervous and stares at Kanzi.) [C is scored because Kanzi goes to the correct area and, when Matata sees him, she appears scared. Kanzi teases the orangs momentarily after scaring Matata but indicates again in a few seconds, without a further reminder, that he knows what he was asked to do. Since Kanzi has never paraded up and down in front of his mother with a mask on before, it is assumed that he understood the intent of the sentence.]

289A. (C) *Go scare Nathaniel.* (Alia has the monster mask on top of her head from the previous trial. Nathaniel is inside the dinosaur tent. Alia goes to the doorway of the tent and looks at Nathaniel for a moment as she still has the monster mask on top of her head. Nathaniel leaves the tent, and Alia returns to E and says, "I scared Nathaniel.")

290. (C) *Put your collar in the refrigerator.* (Kanzi goes to the refrigerator with his collar but is hesitant to open the refrigerator on his own as Rose has not followed him and is not there to open it for him. Kanzi drops his collar on the ground right in front of the refrigerator. Kanzi calls vocally to Rose and gestures to indicate that he wants her to come and open the refrigerator.) [Kanzi is generally not allowed to

open the refrigerator on his own. C is scored as it is assumed that Kanzi does not reliably differentiate between *in, on,* and *next to* and the intent of the sentence is not to test his understanding of these prepositions.]

290A. (C) *Put your watch in the refrigerator.* (Alia picks up her watch and takes it to the refrigerator.) E opens the refrigerator for Alia. (Alia puts the watch in the refrigerator.)

291. (C) *Can you knife the hose? Can you knife the hose?* (Kanzi does so.) [This is not scored as a repeated trial since the repetition was not dependent on Kanzi waiting or hesitating. Rather, the sentence was simply said twice to attempt to make certain that Kanzi heard it, as the lab environment is very noisy. In general, when sentences were repeated rapidly and loudly and not in response to hesitancies on Kanzi's part, they were scored as Cs rather than as C2s.)

291A. (C) *Can you knife the couch?* (Alia does so.)

292. (C1) *Feed your ball some tomato. Feed your ball some tomato.* (Kanzi picks up the tomato and briefly puts it in a bowl, then takes it out, looking around for a ball as there is not one in the array. He then quickly decides to use the pumpkin ball and puts the tomato in the ball's mouth.) [C1 is scored because Kanzi briefly touches the tomato to the bowl before finding the pumpkin ball. However, he does not actually set the tomato down and leave it. Instead of appearing "intentional," the action has a momentary quality.]

292A. (PC) *Feed your ball some tomato.* (Alia says, "Feed ball. Ball [something U]." She then says, "[Something U] ball," but she does nothing.) E says, "Alia, it's the pumpkin ball." (Alia says something U about the pumpkin ball. She gets up and gets the tomato. She bangs the tomato on the pumpkin ball but does not orient the tomato toward the mouth or pay any attention to the face embedded in the ball. [PC is scored because Alia responds to *ball* and *tomato* but not to the verb *feed.* Both Alia and Kanzi had previously treated this sponge ball, with an embedded face, as a ball, and this sentence was presented to see if they were able to direct action to the ball that required revising their basic percept from the object as a "ball" to one that serves as a representation of a "face."]

293. (C) *Get the monster mask and go scare Panbanisha and Panzee.* (Kanzi makes a sound like "whuh," which is his sound for *scare,* and looks at the array, but there is no mask in the array.) E says, "Get your mask and go scare Panban and Panzee." (Kanzi says, "Whuh," while he looks around and fiddles with his ball.) E says, "Look for your mask, I know you can't see it." [The mask is about 10 feet away.] E says, "Look for it." (Kanzi gestures to E as a request for E to open the door.) E says, "It's not back here," referring to the mask. "It's out there, go look for it." (Kanzi finds the mask and goes back to the tool room with it to scare Panbanisha and Panzee, then wants to go into the middle room to scare them also; they are, however, in the tool room. Kanzi is allowed to go past E into the middle room, where he does try to scare Panbanisha and Panzee.) [This is scored as C rather than as C3 because E is not rephrasing the test sentence but is instead trying to tell Kanzi to look for the needed object elsewhere than in the array in front of him. The mask had been moved out of the array, and E did not elect to return it prior to giving the sentence.]

293A. (C) *Get your mask and go scare Lisa.* (Alia frowns and says, "I don't want to." Alia remains in her chair for a moment, then says, "Mommy, I can't put that on it," and goes to E behind the mirror. She then asks E, "Will you put that on it?" and gestures toward the array of objects.) E says, "You go get it." (Alia says, "OK," then gets the monster mask from the array of objects and carries it to E behind the mirror. E then puts the mask on top of Alia's head. Alia then goes back into the living room and walks toward Lisa. She stops in front of Katie, turns toward Katie, and giggles as she holds the mask on her head with her hands. Alia then continues to Lisa, who, when Alia approaches, gives an appropriate scared response. Alia then turns away from Lisa and runs back to the testing area.)

294. (PC) *Show me the ball and the doggie. Show me the ball and the doggie.* (Kanzi holds out his ball, then smells it.)

Error correction.—E says, "Can you show me the doggie too?" (Kanzi shows E the stuffed toy gorilla.) E says, "Look around." (Kanzi hugs and pats the toy gorilla.) E says, "Don't you see the dog?" (Kanzi pokes the toy gorilla.) E says, "Where's the dog?" (Kanzi picks up the dog.) E says, "There he is, show me the doggie." (Kanzi does so.)

294A. (PC) *Show me the ball and the doggie.* (Alia says something about the "ball" and the "doggie." She gets up and goes over to the ball and doggie. She hits the ball with her hand. She then picks up the dog and says, "Doggie." She then says something U. She puts the dog down and picks up the shot. She plays with the shot and puts it up to the doggie. She continues to play with the shot.)

295. (C) *Pour the juice on your ball.* (Kanzi starts to pour it on his big ball, then hesitates as he sees the juice will fall on the floor if he does.) E says, "Pour it on your ball, go ahead, that's right." (Kanzi looks around as though he feels very unsure about this action and then goes ahead and pours just a tiny bit.) E says, "You can pour more, it's OK." [C is scored because E is simply assuring Kanzi that his intended action, which is clear and indicates that he understands the sentence, is acceptable.]

295A. (C) *Pour the water on the ball.* (Alia says, "OK." She gets up and pours the water on the ball. She also gets it on her pants.)

296. (C) *Give the toothpaste to Rose.* (Kanzi does so.)
296A. (C) *Give the toothpaste to Linda.* (Alia does so.)

297. (C) *Show me the shot and the ball.* (Kanzi shows E the shot and looks at the ball that he is leaning on.) [C is scored because Kanzi has both items in front of E and can reasonably presume that E will see them.]

Response refinement.—E says, "Uh huh, and the ball, where's your ball? Show me your ball." (Kanzi is leaning on his ball.) E says, "Can you point to your ball?" (Kanzi stops leaning on his ball and taps it with his hand.) [This was done simply to clarify that Kanzi indeed knew where the ball was.]

297A. (C) *Alia, show me your shot and the ball.* (Alia picks up the ball and puts it behind her. She picks it up again and then picks up the shot.) [C is scored because Alia has both items in front of E and can reasonably presume that E will see them.]

Response refinement.—E waits for a clear "showing" response. (Alia hits the ball with the shot. She drops the ball and then gives the ball a shot. She sees the apple but cannot reach it. She moves closer, saying, "Apple." She gives the apple a shot.) E says, "Alia, can you show me? Show me the shot and the ball. Show me. Show me.

Alia. Alia. Show me the shot and the ball. Come here." (Alia says, "OK, coming.") E says, "Show me the shot and the ball. Show Mommy." (Alia gets up and goes over to E.) E says, "Show Mommy the shot and the ball. Show me. Show me the shot and the ball, OK? Show me. Can you show me the shot and the ball?" (Alia does so.)

298. (C) *Put the hat on Rose.* (Kanzi tosses the hat to Rose.) [C is scored because Kanzi gives the hat to Rose and it is not assumed that Kanzi understands the difference between *on* and *adjacent to.*]

298A. (C) *Put the hat on Linda.* (Alia gets the hat from the array of objects in front of her, then carries the hat toward Linda, who is sitting across the room. Alia then holds the hat high over Linda's head but still does not put the hat on Linda or toss it toward her. Alia then puts her head into the couch pillow; then, holding the hat, she climbs onto the couch behind Linda.)

Response refinement.—E waits to see if Alia will put the hat "on" Linda as opposed to next to her. (Alia watches television for a while, then brushes the hat behind Linda's head, then puts the hat on her own head.)

299. (PC) *Put it on her head.* (Kanzi puts the hat on his own head).

299A. (PC) *Put the hat on Linda. It's OK.* (Alia takes the hat off her own head and looks at Linda, who again has her back turned to Alia. Alia then puts the hat back on her own head.) [The sentences differed slightly here by mistake. However, it is clear that both Kanzi and Alia have some difficulty with a possessive term that refers to the head of another party. Also, it is generally the case that they put hats on themselves and not on other individuals.]

300. (C) *On Rose's head.* (Kanzi does so.)

300A. (PC) *Put the hat on Linda.* (Alia lifts the hat from her head and face and leaves it hanging on the back of her head, then continues to watch television.) E says, "Alia, put the hat on Linda." (Alia reaches for the hat on her head, and the hat falls onto the floor. Alia has trouble reaching for the hat from the couch, so Linda gets the hat and hands it to Alia. Alia grabs the hat quickly, then pulls it back away from Linda.) "Put the hat on Linda." (Alia lifts the hat up toward Linda's head, then at the same time moves her head under the hat so that it looks like the hat is over both Linda's and Alia's heads. She then places the hat over her own head.)

301. (PC) *Give the pineapple a shot.* (Kanzi says, "Whuh," and picks up the pineapple and takes a little nibble of it.) E says, "Give the pineapple a shot." (Kanzi picks up the hat and puts it on the pineapple.)

Error correction.—E says, "The shot, give the pineapple a shot." (Kanzi starts to pick up the shot, then stops and looks around.) E says, "Get the shot. You see the shot?" (Kanzi does not respond.) E says, "Where's the shot? Show Sue the shot." (Kanzi picks up the sparklers.) E says, "Nope." (Kanzi starts taking out a sparkler.) E says, "Nope, the shot, OK?" E then opens the door and shows Kanzi what to do.

301A. (C) *Give the apple a shot.* (Alia picks up the shot and says, "Shot." She then gives the apple a shot.)

302. (C) *Put the sparklers in the refrigerator.* (Kanzi takes the sparklers directly to the small refrigerator, where he takes them out of the package, getting ready to put them in the refrigerator.) E cannot see what Kanzi is doing but says, "In the refrigera-

tor." (Kanzi puts them in and closes the door, then brings back the rest of the package.) [This is scored as C because E's comment is made with no reference to what Kanzi is doing, E cannot see what Kanzi is doing, and the comment appears to have no effect on his behavior. Additionally, Kanzi shows no hesitation with regard to what to do in response to the sentence.]

302A. (PC) *Put the sparkler in the refrigerator.* (Alia picks up the sparkler, bangs it on the edge of the bowl, and puts the tip in the water. She then looks at and touches the tip of the sparkler. She gets up, says something U, and goes to the kitchen. Before walking into the kitchen, she stops and hits the sparkler on the floor. Alia goes over to the chair in front of the sink and hits her sparkler on the chair. She plays with the sparkler, touches the cabinet, and almost falls. She continues to play with the sparkler and then takes it over to E.)

Error correction.—E says, "Alia put the sparkler in the refrigerator." (Alia says, "OK." She goes over to the refrigerator door and takes off a magnet. The picture that was under the magnet fell to the floor along with the magnet. Alia picks up the magnet and puts it back on the refrigerator. She takes it back off and puts it in her mouth.) Meanwhile, E has come out to open the refrigerator door for Alia. E says, "Let's put the sparkler in the refrigerator. You're going around playing with other things. Come on, pull." E opens the refrigerator as Alia tries to help. (Alia knocks something out of the refrigerator.) E says, "That's OK. Don't poke yourself. Put it in. You just don't want to let go of it." (Alia puts the sparkler in the refrigerator.)

303. (C) *Give the sweet potato a shot. Give the sweet potato a shot.* (Kanzi does so.)

303A. (C1) *Give the sweet potato a shot.* (Alia picks up a knife and the shot and says, "A knife, a knife." She then hits the potato with the knife. Then she gives the potato a shot.) [C1 is scored because Alia hits the potato with the knife before carrying out the sentence appropriately.]

304. (C4) *Hide the pineapple.* (Kanzi picks the pineapple up and begins gingerly to eat it.) E says, "Hide the pineapple." (Kanzi continues to eat it.) E says, "Kanzi, you are not supposed to eat it. You are supposed to hide it. Can you hide it?" (Kanzi takes the pineapple outdoors, where it is out of immediate view.) [C4 is scored because Kanzi's eating of the pineapple had to be inhibited before he could carry out the sentence correctly.]

304A. (PC) *Hide the apple.* (Alia says, "OK." She gets the apple, moves over, puts it down, and rolls it away from her. She sings something U. She picks up the shot and puts it behind the ball. She then starts to grab the dog.)

Error correction.—E says, "Alia, hide the apple." (Alia says, "OK," but she continues to move the dog. Then she picks up another object.) E says, "Hum." (Alia continues to look at the newly picked up object.) E says, "Alia, hide the apple. Can you hide the apple? Huh?" (Alia shakes her head no.) E says, "Hide the apple." (Alia says, "OK," picks up the container of water, and says something U.) E says, "Hide the apple." (Alia picks up the apple and says something U.) E says, "Hide the apple. Can you hide the apple?" (Alia picks up the container of water and sets it down on the other side of her.) E comes out and shows Alia what to do.

305. (C) *Go wash the hotdogs, wash the hotdogs.* (Kanzi picks up the bag of hotdogs and starts opening it.) E says, "Kanzi, wash the hotdogs." Kanzi then takes the hose

and fills the plastic bag with the hotdogs in it full of water.) [C is scored here because Kanzi is not hesitating but is proceeding with his intent in a fluid motion. There was a lot of vocal noise generated by Kanzi during the request, and E is repeating the request to make certain that it is heard. This sentence was given with no water present in the array to determine how the subjects would respond to the verb *wash* with no water available. Kanzi had not previously been observed to use the hose to wash food. He typically did so in the sink.]

305A. (C1) *Wash the hot dogs.* (Alia goes over and looks in a small container in the array. There is no water there, and Alia says, "All gone." She pulls the apple near her. She then gets a sponge nerf ball and uses it to wipe off the hot dogs.) [C1 is scored because she acts on the apple before washing the hotdogs.]

306. (C) *Put some oil on Rose. Put some oil on Rose.* (Kanzi puts oil on Rose, who is sitting with her eyes covered and cannot see Kanzi at all.)

Response refinement.—E asks Kanzi again as Kanzi puts the oil on Rose while he is behind her and E cannot see that he did so, but it is clear on the tape. Kanzi puts some more oil on Rose. E still cannot see, so she asks the cameraperson, who indicates that Kanzi did do so.

306A. (PC) *Put some oil on Linda.* (Alia sits down on the mat.) E says, "On her hand." (Alia opens the oil. She sets the lid back on top but then takes it back off. She puts her finger in the oil. With a couple of tries she gets the lid back on the oil. She hits the top of the lid and then attempts to take it off again. She sets the oil down. She reaches toward the can of soap but doesn't touch it.) "Put some oil on Linda's hand." (Alia opens the oil again. She puts some on her finger and then rubs it on the can.)

Error correction.—E says, "Put some oil on Linda's hand." (Alia continues to rub oil on the side of the container.) E says, "Alia, put some oil on Linda's hand." (Alia continues to play in the oil and then closes the lid.) E says, "Put some oil on Linda's hand." (Alia says something U.) E says, "Go ahead. Can you do that? Huh? Can you go do that?" E comes out and shows Alia what to do.

307. (PC) *Take the cheese to the colony room.* (Kanzi takes the hotdogs to the colony room.)

307A. (W) *Take the cheese to Karen's room.* (Alia gets up and goes toward the cheese, then turns and picks up the apple. She says, "Apple, apple, [something U]." She holds the apple up toward the camera, then hands Nathaniel the apple.)

308. (PC) *Show me the lighter and the doggie.* (Kanzi shows the dog to Rose.)

Error correction.—E says, "Show me the lighter and the doggie." (Kanzi picks up the lighter and walks over to the couch to play with it.)

308A. (PC) *Show me the matches and the dog.* (Alia picks up the matches and takes them to E and says, "Mommy open.") E says, "No, I'm not going to open. OK." (Alia says something U to E.)

309. (C) *Give the carrot to Matata.* (Kanzi does so.)

309A. (C) *Give the carrot to Joshua.* (Alia does so.)

310. (C) *Give a banana to Kelly.* (Kanzi does so, appearing to make a sound like "Kelly" as he hands her the banana.)

310A. (C) *Give the banana to Nathaniel.* (Alia does so.)

311. (C4) *Take the orange to Panban and Panzee.* (Kanzi picks up the orange and starts to eat it.) E says, "Take the orange, you can't eat it, take it to Panban and Panzee." (Kanzi continues eating the orange.) E says, "Kanzi, you can't eat it." Rose also says, "Kanzi, stop." (Kanzi puts the orange back down on floor.) E says, "Pick it up and take it to Panban and Panzee. Carry it to Panban and Panzee. You take it to them." (Kanzi gestures toward the door where E is to indicate that he wants to go through there to take the orange to Panbanisha and Panzee, who are in the middle room.) E says, "You feel you must go through there?" (Kanzi makes a sound like "whuh, whuh.") E says, "All right," and lets Kanzi go through the door. (Kanzi goes to the middle room door and tries to shove the orange under; Rose comes and opens the door for him, and Kanzi takes the orange in to Panban and Panzee.) [C4 is scored because Kanzi has to be inhibited from eating the orange himself before he can carry out the sentence. However, his response suggests that he does comprehend the sentence.]

311A. (C) *Take the orange to Kathy and Timothy.* (Alia gets up and stands before the array of objects. It seems that she looks at the tomato in the array first, then at the orange. She picks up the orange, then the tomato, and carries both to Kathy and Timothy, who are sitting across the room. Alia hands Timothy the tomato. Timothy reaches for it and says, "That?" The tomato falls and rolls away from Timothy. Alia kicks the tomato back to Timothy as she says, "That's potato." Alia then starts to leave but turns quickly back to Kathy, carrying the orange to her and tossing it on the couch next to her.) [This is scored as C rather than OE because Alia seems to feel that she should take something to Timothy if she takes something to Kathy and she verbally reveals that she knows that the object she is taking is not an orange.]

312. (C) *Take the can opener outdoors.* (Kanzi does so, even though it is a different kind of can opener than he is accustomed to, a soda bottle opener.)

312A. (C) *Take the fork outdoors.* (Alia says, "OK," and then something U. She goes over and picks up the fork. She goes over to the front door and waits for E to come out and open it. In the meantime, she looks at her fork and says, "Mommy fork.") E opens the door. (Alia goes outside. She looks as though she is going to leave her fork on the bench, but then she sees the rock further down the bench. She goes over and touches the rock and puts the fork next to the rock.)

313. (PC) *Would you take the string to the bedroom?* (Kanzi has the string wrapped around him and is playing with his ball at the time the sentence is uttered. He starts off toward the bedroom with the string around him and with his ball. He takes the string off and proceeds to the bedroom door with the ball. Rose asks him to return.)

Error correction.—E takes the ball from Kanzi and says, "Would you take the string to the bedroom?" (Kanzi does so.)

313A. (C) *Would you take the string to the bedroom?* (Alia does so.)

314. (C3) *Put the keys in the bowl.* (Kanzi puts his hand on the keys, then pauses.) E comments, "That's right, those are the keys." (Kanzi correctly completes the sentence.)

314A. (NG).

315. (C) *Put your collar on.* (Kanzi does so.)

315A. (PC) *Put the watch on.* (Alia gets the watch and takes it to Jeannine, saying, "Mommy," and something U.) E says, "Huh? What do I do? What do I do?" (Alia continues to say something U and puts the watch in Jeannine's hand.) Jeannine waits for a second and then repeats, "What do I do? Show me. Can you do it?" Jeannine sets the watch down in front of Alia. (Alia says something U and touches the watch.) E says, "Put the watch on." (Alia says something U and gives the watch back to E.) "Where? Huh? Do you know how to put the watch on?" E finally shows Alia what to do.

316. (C3) *Put some fire on the toy gorilla.* (Kanzi picks up his ball and slaps it.) E says, "Do you see the lighter?" (Kanzi touches the shot, then the umbrella, and begins to try to open the umbrella.) E says, "That's the umbrella, we're looking for the lighter." (Kanzi picks up the lighter.) E says, "Now, put some fire on the toy gorilla." (Kanzi repeatedly pushes the lighter into the toy gorilla.) E says, "Now, can you make some fire come out?" (Kanzi holds the gorilla's head up with one hand, strikes the lighter's wheel with the other, and puts a flame under the toy gorilla's mouth.)

316A. (C3) *Put some fire on the toy gorilla.* (Alia goes over and plays with the gorilla and says something U. Then she goes over to the chair next to the computer and moves it. Next, she goes back to her original chair and leans on it.) E says, "Alia, put some fire on the toy gorilla." (Alia goes and plays with the gorilla. She says something U.) E says, "Do you know where the fire is?" (Alia says something U.) E says, "Where's the fire?" (Alia picks up the matchbox and says something U. She dumps some of the matches on the floor, and she pulls out other matches and drops them on the floor.) E says, "Can you put some on the toy gorilla?" (Alia says, "No." She continues to dump and drop the matches. When they are all out of the box, she says, "All gone." She puts down the match box, picks up the toy gorilla, and says something U. She then puts a match up to the toy gorilla's ear.)

317. (C) *Give the gorilla some toothpaste.* (Kanzi picks up the toothpaste, opens it, and puts some on the end of his finger. He then rubs it on the toy gorilla's mouth.)

317A. (C) *Give the gorilla some toothpaste.* (Alia goes over and gets the gorilla and the toothpaste. She then gets up and takes the toothpaste to E. She says, "Open.") E opens the toothpaste. (Alia takes the toothpaste and the cap back with her. She sets the cap down and puts some toothpaste on her finger. She rubs the toothpaste on the gorilla. She gets more toothpaste on her finger and does it again.)

318. (PC) *Put the raisins in the bowl.* (Kanzi picks up the raisins and looks at the bowl, but it is full of banana peels. He sort of waves the box of raisins around in the air over the bowl filled with banana peels, as though he cannot figure out where to put it. Finally, he puts it on the toy gorilla.)

Error correction.—E says, "In the bowl." (Kanzi puts them under the cushion.) E says, "In the bowl, in the bowl." (Kanzi sets them down.) E says, "With the bananas." (Kanzi takes a banana peel out of the bowl and puts it in the raisins, then another, then puts the top back on the raisins and shakes the peels and raisins up together.) E says, "Now put it all in the bowl, put it all in the bowl." (Kanzi continues to shake the container.) E says, "Put it down, in the bowl." (Kanzi holds the container to the bowl of banana peels and makes a sound like "banana.") E says, "Yes." (Kanzi opens the container and takes the banana peels out and puts them in the bowl.) E says, "Uh huh. Put the raisins in the bowl." (Kanzi makes a sound like "raisins.") E says, "That's good." (Kanzi pours the raisins in the bowl, makes a sound like "raisin.") E says, "That's right."

318A. (C) *Put the raisins in the bowl.* (Alia picks up the raisins and puts them in the bowl.)

319. (C) *Put the raisins in the refrigerator.* (Kanzi says, "Raisin," as he picks them up and looks at E and sort of gestures with the raisins. He needs to walk past E to get to the refrigerator, and he seems to be looking for permission to do so.) E says, "That's good. Put them in the refrigerator," to indicate that Kanzi should proceed. (Kanzi does so, putting them in the small refrigerator.) [During this test session, E is located behind the sliding door in the group room.]

319A. (C) *Alia, put the raisins in the refrigerator.* (Alia does so.)

320. (C) *Take your ball to the colony room.* (Kanzi does so.)
320A. (C) *Take your ball to Karen's room.* (Alia does so.)

321. (C) *Take the potato to the bedroom.* (Kanzi does so.)
321A. (C) *Take the potato to the bedroom.* (Alia does so.)

322. (C) *Give Sue the umbrella.* (Kanzi makes a sound like "uh umm.") *Give me the umbrella.* (Kanzi does so.)
322A. (C) *Give Mommy the box.* (Alia does so.)

323. (C) *Give me the money.* (Kanzi does so.)
323A. (C) *Give me the money.* (Alia does so.)

324. (PC) *Take the umbrella to the T-room.* (Kanzi takes the umbrella to the middle room.)
Error correction.—Rose says, "Kanzi, let me help you. Come here. Sue said to take the umbrella to the T-room. Can you take it to the T-room for us?" (Kanzi does so.)
324A. (OE) *Take the box to the bathroom.* (Alia picks up the box and the tomato and takes them both to the bathroom.)

325. (C1) *Give me the shot, the shot.* (Kanzi pushes the shot toward the door, but it does not go under. He then pinches the dog's nose.)
Response refinement.—E says, "Put the shot in my hand," and extends her hand under the door. (Kanzi puts the shot in her hand.)
325A. (C) *Give me the shot.* (Alia does so.)

326. (C) *Take the keys and open the play yard.* (Kanzi makes a sound like "whuh" and does so.)
326A. (PC) *Take the keys and open the bathroom.* (Alia takes the keys and goes over to the table. She stands there and plays with the keys while watching the television screen.) E says, "Alia, take the keys and open the bathroom." (She drops the keys and picks them back up. She walks to the middle of the room, stops, and shakes the keys.)
Error correction.—E says, "Take the keys and open the bathroom." (Alia walks around, playing with the keys. She goes back over and watches the television screen.)

E says, "Can you go open the bathroom? Alia. Alia. Can you open the bathroom?" (Alia continues to watch television. She drops her keys, picks them up, and Nathaniel starts to point and say something to her.) E says, "Alia, take the keys and open the bathroom. Alia, listen to Mommy. Take the keys and open the bathroom." (Alia drops her keys and says, "Mommy.") E says, "Uhh? Yes please." (Alia picks up the keys.) E says, "Go ahead." E turns off the television and then says, "Can you take the keys and open the bathroom for Mommy?" (Alia drops the keys.)

327. (C) *Put the keys in the potty.* (Kanzi does so.)
327A. (C1) *Alia, put the keys in the potty.* (Alia plays with the keys before putting them in the potty.)

328. (C4) *Take the backpack outdoors.* (Kanzi picks up the rubber bands he has been playing with and goes to the door; it is locked.) E says to Rose, "He needs some help, Rose." (Rose opens the door for Kanzi. Kanzi brings the rubber bands back in.) E asks Kanzi if he can show her the rubber bands in the array to see if he is confused about that word. (Kanzi does show her.) E repeats the sentence. (Kanzi carries the backpack directly outdoors.) [C4 is scored because the rubber bands had to be taken from Kanzi before he could carry out the sentence correctly. He indicated that he knew the word *rubber bands*, and it was therefore assumed that, had he not been occupied with them, he could have carried the sentence out properly.]
328A. (C1) *Take the backpack outdoors.* (Alia sits on the stuffed toy dog for a long time, looking at pictures. She then correctly carries out the sentence.)

329. (C) *Put the rubber band on your ball.* (Kanzi does so.)
329A. (C) *Put the rubber band on the ball.* (Alia does so.)

330. (C) *Give the lighter to Rose.* (Kanzi does so.)
330A. (C) *Give the matches to Lisa.* (Alia does so.)

331. (C) *Take the bunny picture to the bedroom.* (Kanzi does so.)
331A. (C2) *Take the bunny picture to the bedroom.* (Alia says something U as she crawls over to the bunny picture. She stops and looks at the picture intensely. She says, "Bunny. It's the bunny. It's the bunny. Linda, this is bunny.") E says, "Take the bunny picture to the bedroom." (Alia gets up and says, "Bunny, Linda." She walks to the edge of the living room and stops to look at the picture. She then continues on into the bedroom.) [C2 is scored because Alia seems to do little after talking about the photograph until E repeats the sentence.]

332. (PC) *Give the dog picture to Kelly.* (Kanzi gives the keys to Kelly.)
Error correction.—E says, "Kanzi, the dog picture, look at these things. You're lying down, sit up." (Rose helps Kanzi sit up.) E says, "You are not looking." [Rose is not blind during the error correction as Kanzi has already done the wrong thing and is being helped, although E is still behind the one-way mirror.] E says, "Give the dog picture to Kelly." (Kanzi does so.)
332A. (C) *Give the dog picture to Linda.* (Alia does so.)

333. (C) *Kanzi, take the keys and open the T-room.* (Kanzi does so.)
333A. (PC) *Take the keys and open the front door.* (Alia gets the keys and plays with them. She sits down and continues to play with the keys.) E says, "Take the keys and

open the front door." (Alia remains sitting and playing.) E says, "Alia, did you take them to the front door?" (Alia continues to play with the keys while sitting down.) E says, "Alia, take the keys and open the front door."

Error correction.—E shows Alia what to do.

334. (C4) *Wash the banana.* (Kanzi eats the banana.) E says, "He ate it, Rose." Rose says, "Kanzi," then takes the banana out of his mouth and says, "This isn't what you were supposed to do, let's listen to Sue." E says, "Kanzi, wash the banana." (Kanzi holds the banana out toward the water.) E says, "Go ahead." (Kanzi dips it in the water.)

Response refinement.—E says, "Wash it real good. (Kanzi makes a sound like "good," then puts the banana in the water and begins to peel it. Then he swishes it around in the water.)

334A. (C) *Wash the banana.* (Alia takes a paper towel and wipes the banana.)

335. (C) *Put the keys in the backpack.* (Kanzi does so.)

335A. (C2) *Put the keys in the backpack.* (Alia goes over and looks in a cup. She then picks up the rubber band and plays with it. Alia then puts the leaves in the backpack and plays with the keys.) E assumes that Alia is going to keep on playing with the items in the array unless the sentence is repeated and says, "Put your keys in the backpack." (Alia gets the keys and puts them in the backpack.)

336. (C) *Take your ball to the T-room.* (Kanzi does so.)

336A. (C) *Take your ball to the bathroom.* (Alia does so.)

337. (C) *Wash the bunny picture.* (Kanzi does so.)

337A. (C1) *Wash the bunny picture.* (Alia gets up and picks up a small towel. She then says something U and touches the doggie. She places the towel down and plays with the doggie. She picks up the towel and wipes the bunny picture.) [C1 is scored because she played with the doggie before carrying out the sentence.]

338. (C) *Brush your teeth.* (Kanzi does so.)

338A. (C) *Brush your teeth.* (Alia does so.)

339. (C) *Tickle Kelly with the keys.* (Kanzi holds the keys out toward Kelly but is hesitant to touch her with them as she is backing away from him with the camera in order to take his picture and is looking in the camera rather than at Kanzi.) [C is scored because Kanzi indicates that he understands the sentence even if he is hesitant to tickle Kelly because she is filming and moving away from him.]

339A. (C) *Tickle Nathaniel with the keys.* (Alia does so.)

340. (C) *Tickle Rose with the stick.* (Kanzi does so, although touching her only very lightly as her eyes are hidden and he does not want to be interpreted as being aggressive.)

Response refinement.—E says, "Tickle her real good. Can you make her laugh?" (Kanzi continues to poke her gently.) E says, "Tickle her tummy." (Kanzi pokes Rose's tummy gently with the stick.)

340A. (C) *Tickle Nathaniel with the stick.* (Alia does so.)

341. (C4) *Wash your collar. Wash your collar.* (Kanzi seems puzzled, picks up a stick, and begins to stir the water with it.) E says, "Kanzi, give me the stick." (Kanzi

hands the stick to E.) E says, "Now, wash your collar." (Kanzi picks up the collar and puts it in the water.) [C4 is scored because the stick has to be removed from Kanzi before he can listen to the sentence and carry it out appropriately. Since he rarely, if ever, confuses *stick* and *collar*, it is assumed that he is interested in playing in the water with the stick rather than attempting to wash to stick. Also, he does not appear to be washing the stick but rather using it playfully to stir the water.]

341A. (W) *Wash your watch.* (Alia kneels down on the floor.) E says, "Wash your watch." (Alia looks at the array of objects and picks up a small container. She picks up another small container but sets it back down. She looks off into the room.) E says, "Alia." (Alia turns her head toward E.) E says, "Wash your watch." (Alia does nothing.) [W is scored because Alia is responding and manipulating items in the array but neither acts on the "watch" nor "washes" any other object.]

342. (C2) *Eat the yogurt.* (Kanzi picks up the yogurt and opens it, looks at the top, makes a sound like "yogurt," then tries to see if he can put the top back on, but pushes it so hard that it slips off again.) E says, "Kanzi, can you eat the yogurt?" (Kanzi does.)

342A. (C2) *Eat the yogurt.* (Alia gets up and jumps up and down playfully. She then puts her mouth against the mirror in play and says something U. Then Alia picks up the yogurt. She places a bowl on the floor in front of her and picks up a spoon. She spoons the yogurt into the bowl carefully.) E says, "Alia, eat the yogurt." (Alia eats the yogurt.) [C2 was scored here because Alia was playing and had no real interest in eating the yogurt. E repeated the sentence to remind Alia that she had not yet completely carried it out.]

343. (C) *Groom Rose.* (Kanzi makes a sound like "groom" and leans over and touches Rose, hesitant to groom her because she has her eyes closed and her hands holding the headphones over her ears.) E says, "Go ahead and groom her." (Kanzi goes around and touches her back and sort of motions for her to go over to the cushions, where he likes to lay down and groom, and lays down and begins to look at a book, waiting for Rose to come.)

343A. (C) *Brush Nathaniel.* (Alia does so.)

344. (C) *Eat the raisins.* (Kanzi attempts to makes a sound like "eat," then one like "raisins," then picks up the raisins, makes food barks, and puts them in his mouth.)

344A. (PC) *Eat the raisins.* (Alia picks up the raisins and wanders over to the couch. She stops. She then goes into the kitchen and comes up behind E.) E laughs and says, "What are you doing?" The trial is terminated since E is no longer in the blind situation as Alia has approached her.

345. (C) *Groom the doggie.* (Kanzi makes a sound like "groom" as he picks up the doggie, then briefly grooms the doggie with his lips.)

345A. (C) *Brush the doggie.* (Alia does so.)

346. (C) *Bring the raisins to the bedroom.* (Kanzi does so.)

346A. (OE) *Take the raisins to the bedroom.* (Alia takes the raisins and the rock to the bedroom.)

347. (C) *Give the tomato to Rose.* (Kanzi holds it out to Rose, making a sound like

"tomato," but Rose is hiding her eyes and so does not take it. He then puts it in a hat and plays with it.) [C is scored since Kanzi has carried out the sentence short of putting the tomato on Rose's lap even though she is not looking.]

Response refinement.—E attempts to determine if Kanzi can be encouraged to place the tomato on Rose's lap or to give it to her in some way. E says, "Kanzi, go ahead and give it to her." (He stops playing with it and again hands it to Rose. She still does not take it, so he puts it in her hand.)

347A. (C) *Give the tomato to Nathaniel.* (Alia does so. Nathaniel, who is only 4, does not have his eyes closed on this trial or on other trials. It is assumed that he will not be cuing Alia and that he is too young to participate in such controls. He does, at times, intentionally help Alia, although he is asked not to do so.)

348. (C) *Eat the tomato.* (Kanzi makes a sound like "eat" and puts the tomato in his mouth.)

348A. (C) *Eat the tomato.* (Alia gets the tomato and puts it in her mouth. She tries to bite it but doesn't actually break through the skin of the tomato.)

349. (C5) *Go to the bedroom and get the raisins.* (Kanzi makes a sound like "raisin" and then picks up the raisins in the display and carries them with him, putting them in the bedroom.) E says, "You need to bring the raisins back." (Kanzi makes a sound like "raisins" and brings them back.) [C5 is scored because Kanzi acts on the item in the array in front of him rather than the one in the distal location.]

349A. (PC) *Go to the bedroom and get the raisins.* (Alia gets up, points, and says something U. She picks up a box of Jello in front of her and shakes it. She says something U. She starts to open the box.) E says, "Alia. Alia, go to the bedroom and get the raisins." (Alia touches the raisins in front of her and then returns her attention to the Jello. Alia says something U and looks at the camera. She then says something else U. She shakes the Jello box.)

Error correction.—E says, "Alia, go to the bedroom and get some raisins." (Alia picks up the raisins in front of her and throws them behind her. She picks them up again and throws them farther behind her. This is closer to E.) E says, "Okay, let Mommy show you."

350. (C) *Take the potato outdoors.* (Kanzi does so.)

350A. (C) *Take the potato outdoors.* (Alia gets up, picks up the potato while looking in the mirror, and takes it to the front door.) E opens the door for her. (Alia touches the stuffed doggie and then puts the potato down.) [C is scored because Alia is on her way with the potato when she stops to look in the mirror, and, after doing so, she continues on.]

351. (C) *Give me some raisins.* (Kanzi picks up the raisins and begins opening them to give to E while making a sound like "raisins.") Kanzi is uncertain as to how to give the raisins to E, so E says, "Can you put them under the door?" (Kanzi does so, then makes a sound like "raisin.")

351A. (C) *Give me some raisins under the mirror.* (Alia picks up the cup of raisins from the array of objects and carries them over to the mirror. She then takes one of the raisins and holds it up to the mirror, as though trying to push the raisin through the mirror. The raisin then drops on the floor. Alia picks it up and again holds it up to the mirror.) [C is scored because, even though Alia does not successfully give E raisins, she clearly understands the request.]

352. (PC) *Take the doggie to the T-room.* (Kanzi makes a sound like "whuuh," a noise he often makes for dogs, then picks up the toy dog and carries it into the bedroom and tosses it on the bed.)
Error correction.—E says, "Kanzi, to the T-room." (Kanzi again says, "Whuuh.") E says, "Take the doggie to the T-room." (Kanzi picks up the dog and takes it to the T-room.)
352A. (C) *Take the doggie to the bathroom.* (Alia gets up smiling and says something U about the doggie. She takes the doggie over to Nathaniel.) Nathaniel says something about the doggie. E says, "Nathaniel, be quiet." (Alia continues talking, saying something U, and carrying the doggie into the bathroom.) [C is scored because it is assumed that Alia wanted to visit with Nathaniel on the way to the bathroom and that this was not a mistake on her part. Since she is on her way, C1 is not coded because she is visiting, not first, but while carrying out the sentence.]

353. (PC) *Take the Jello to the T-room . . . T-room.* (Kanzi picks up the Jello, making a sound like "Jello" as he does so, and takes it to the bedroom, eating on the way.)
Error correction.—E says, "Kanzi, you have to stop eating it and put it in the T-room." (Kanzi does.)
353A. (C) *Take the Jello to the bathroom.* (Alia gets up, picks up the Jello while saying something U, and takes the Jello to the bathroom.)

354. (C3) *Go outdoors and get the potato.* (Kanzi goes outdoors and stands still, looking at something outside.) E says, "Bring me back the potato, please." Kanzi does.) [C3 is coded here because, at the time of the utterance, Kanzi does not seem to be bringing back anything and, indeed, appears to have forgotten what to do. C3 is also scored because E specifies the specific item "potato" to be brought back while Kanzi is outside.]
354A. (C) *Go outdoors and get the potato.* (Alia goes to the front door.) E opens it. (Alia says, "Thanks Mommy," and retrieves the potato.)

355. (I) *Put the raisins in the yogurt.* (Kanzi pours the yogurt into the raisins. But the yogurt just misses the edge of the bowl.) E says, "You missed." (Kanzi makes a sound like "yogurt.")
355A. (C1) *Put the raisins in the yogurt.* (Alia gets up, kneels in front of the mirror, and kisses her reflection. She then picks up the box of raisins and places it on the yogurt container.)

356. (C) *Put the rubber band on the milk.* (Kanzi does so.)
356A. (C) *Put the rubber band on the milk.* (Alia does so.)

357. (W) *Go to the T-room and get the doggie. Go to the T-room and get the doggie.* (Kanzi goes to the bedroom and gets the toy gorilla. Confusing the stuffed gorilla and the stuffed dog is a common error, although Kanzi does not confuse real dogs with gorillas.)
357A. (PC) *Go to the bathroom and get the doggie.* (Alia gets up and goes to the front door.) E opens the front door. (Alia says, "Doggie," and gets the doggie.)

358. (C3) *Go to the bedroom and get the potato. Go to the bedroom and get the potato.* (Kanzi goes to the bedroom.) E says, "Bring me the potato." (Kanzi makes a sound like "whua" and returns with the potato.) [C3 is coded here because, at the time of the utterance, Kanzi does not appear to be bringing back anything and, indeed, appears to have forgotten what to do.]

358A. (C) *Go to the bedroom and get the potato.* (Alia goes to the bedroom, stops at the crib, and says something U. She then goes and gets the potato and brings it back, saying something U.)

359. (C) *You need to open the milk.* (Kanzi makes a sound like "milk," then picks up a can of SMA (milk) and tries to bite it open. When he can't get it open, he puts a rubber band on it, then tries to bite it some more.)

Response refinement.—E says, "Maybe you could use the rock." (Kanzi says something U, then picks up the rock and starts bashing the can.) E says, "Would you like a knife?" (Kanzi says something U in reply.) E offers a knife. (Kanzi takes the knife and tries to jab a hole in the can.)

359A. (C) *Open the milk.* (Alia gets the milk and tries to get the cap off. She does not succeed, so she gets a fork and tries to get under the cap.)

360. (C) *Give the shot to Liz.* (Kanzi does so.)

Response extension.—Liz says, "Do you want a shot?" (Kanzi crouches down to position for one, so Liz gives one.)

360A. (C) *Give the shot to Kathy.* (Alia does so.)

361. (C) *Show me the real banana.* (Kanzi makes a sound like "there" and points to the banana, then attempts to make a sound like "banana.")

361A. (PC) *Show me the real apple.* (Alia picks up the toy apple, then the real apple, as she says something about "apple." She then carries both the real and the toy apples to E.) E says, "Show me the real apple." (Alia holds both apples up to E.)

362. (PC) *Show me the toy banana.* (Kanzi makes a sound like "here," picks up the real banana, and begins peeling it.)

Error correction.—E says, "The play banana." (Kanzi continues to peel the real banana.) E says, "Show me the toy banana." (Kanzi licks the banana off his fingers and continues to peel the real banana.)

362A. (C) *Show me the toy apple.* (Alia goes over to the real apple, looks at it, and then gets the toy apple. She takes the toy apple to E.)

363. (C3) *Go outdoors and get the phone. Bring me the phone.* (Kanzi goes outdoors, gets the phone receiver, and starts back with it, leaving the base caught on the lip of the outside door.) E says, "Thank you for bringing the whole thing. Bring the bottom part too." (Kanzi turns around and yanks the cord, pulling the base in over the door ledge, and then drags the whole thing to E.) [C3 is scored because E had to ask Kanzi to bring the phone cradle as he did not seem to realize that he could not just drag the phone by the receiver, although he did appear to understand the general intent of the sentence.

363A. (C2) *Go outdoors and get the phone.* (Alia goes over toward the door. She stops, turns around, and looks. She goes over the steps by the vacuum cleaner. She looks back and pauses.) E says, "Alia go outdoors and get the phone." (Alia goes and stands next to the front door.) E opens the door for her. (Alia gets the phone.)

364. (C) *Kanzi, get some water in your bowl. Get some water.* (Kanzi picks up his bowl, runs to the sink, and puts water in his bowl.) E says, "And bring it back, please." [Requests that Kanzi return with an item are not interpreted as "rephrasing of the sentence" since the original utterance does not ask Kanzi to return with the item, only to obtain it. The test setting is one in which Kanzi knows that he is supposed to return, but he often thinks of other, more interesting things to do. Thus, E often asks him to return with the item, but this does not affect the code he receives unless E renames the item.]

364A. (C) *Go get some water in your bowl.* (Alia takes her bowl into the kitchen and stands on the chair in front of the sink. E turns on the water since Alia cannot reach the faucet. Alia holds out her bowl and fills it with water.)

365. (PC) *Go to the colony room and get a banana.* (Kanzi starts to go, then pauses.) E says, "Go to the colony room and get the banana." (Kanzi touches the banana in front of him as though thinking about it, then heads off to the colony room, but as he is on his way he glances outdoors and sees a banana there, so he goes out and gets it. Rose is informed, by E, that Kanzi has gone to the wrong location. She approaches, takes the banana away, and gives it back to E.)

Error correction.—E says, "Kanzi, go to the colony room and get a banana." (Kanzi goes to the refrigerator, gets three bananas, and brings them back, then ball slaps.) E asks for a banana, then says, "Kanzi, you need to go to the colony room and get a banana." (Kanzi goes to the colony room and gets a banana, then takes it to the refrigerator, running ahead of Rose and showing her the bananas there.) [Kanzi gives the impression that he wants to eat a banana and that he does not see why he has to go to the colony room for one, although he understands the sentence. He appears to be testing the limits of what he has to do or can do in this situation.]

365A. (C) *Go to Karen's room and get a banana.* (Alia gets up and accidentally hits the orange with her foot. She stops and rolls the orange on the mat with her hand as if to make sure it is in the right spot. She then continues on and gets the banana.) [C is coded because the action on the orange appears to be the result of an unintentional kick.]

366. (C) *Kanzi, I need you to brush Liz's teeth, brush Liz's teeth. Go brush her teeth.* (Kanzi does so.) [C is coded; no restatements are made in response to confusion or hesitation on his part. They are designed to urge Kanzi to brush Liz's teeth even though he is not normally allowed to do this and may be hesitant to do so.]

366A. (NG) [It was assumed that Alia would not brush someone else's teeth because of hesitancy to do less intimate things to another party on previous trials.]

367. (PC) *Go to the potty and get the sparklers.* (Kanzi responds to this request with a sort of quizzical expression on his face.) E says, "Go look in the potty and get the sparklers." (Kanzi walks away, strolling nonchalantly, without purpose.) E says, "In the potty." (Kanzi does not see the potty in the grouproom as he is looking outdoors as he walks past it and it is in an unusual place for the test.) E says, "In here, Kanzi, look in the potty." (Kanzi walks on past the door into the other part of the group-room.) "In here." (Kanzi continues on to look in the potty in the other half of the

grouproom.) [Kanzi is confused because there are two potties in the grouproom; for some reason he ignores the closer one that objects have been placed in on previous trials and goes to the one that is further away. There are no objects in this potty, nor have there been objects in it on previous trials.]

Error correction.—E says, "Kanzi, back this way." (Kanzi looks in the other potty, which is by the video cabinet, and sees nothing.) E says something U and then, "This potty." (Kanzi picks up the potty by the video cabinet, lifts it off the floor, and carries it bipedally all the way back to E.) E says, "You didn't find any sparklers, did you? Look in the other potty." (Kanzi makes a sound like "ummm.") E says, "Right over there." (Kanzi makes a sound like "whuu" as he finally sees the other potty; he then pulls it over to him.) E says, "Get the sparklers." (Kanzi looks in and pulls out a plastic bag with something in it, probably rubber bands.) E says, "Get the sparklers." (Kanzi takes out the rubber bands, begins playing with them, and lays down on the sponge cushions.) E comes out and says, "Kanzi, come back and sit down." (Kanzi does.) E asks for the rubber band, and Kanzi gives it. E says, "Now go look in *that* potty and get the sparklers." (Kanzi does so at once.)

367A. (OE) *Go to the potty and get the sparklers.* (Alia goes to the portable potty that is located in front of the bathroom. On the potty are a sparkler and some rubber bands. Alia picks up both objects and carries them back to E, who is still behind the mirror. She hands E the sparkler first, then the rubber band.)

Error correction.—E holds up the string of rubber bands, asking, "What's this?" (Alia answers E's question, but it is not clear what she says.)

368. (C) *Give Liz a shot.* (Kanzi picks up the syringe and has the top off and has it open as he is approaching Liz. He is ready to give the shot by the time he gets over to Liz, and Liz permits him to do so.)

368A. (C) *Give Kathy a shot.* (Alia picks up the shot from the array of objects. As she heads toward Kathy, she accidentally kicks the ball that is in the array. She picks up the ball and puts it back with the array of objects, then continues to Kathy, who is sitting across the room. Alia then hands the shot to Kathy.) [This is coded C as Alia does not appear to intend to perform an action on the ball in response to the sentence.]

369. (C5) *Go to the colony room and get your ball. Go to the colony room and. . . .* (Kanzi has already turned around and is getting his big ball, which is right there behind the keyboard, before E can finish the sentence.) E says, "No, go to the colony room and get a ball." (Kanzi does so.) [C5 is scored because Kanzi acts on the object in the immediate array rather than the one in the distal array.]

369A. (PC) *Go to Karen's room and get a ball.* (Alia gets up and starts to run. She falls down. She gets back up and goes to Karen's room. She picks up a bowl, says something U, and then says, "Bowl." She puts the bowl against her face, then on her head. She holds the bowl above her head. She then takes the bowl back to E.) [Apparently, Alia thought that E said "bowl" rather than "ball."]

370. (C) *Go to the big refrigerator and get some food.* (Kanzi makes a sound like "whuu," goes to refrigerator, opens it, and begins selecting what he wants.)

Response refinement.—E says, "Bring some food back, bring it back." (Kanzi makes a sound like "good.") E says, "Whatever you want." (Kanzi makes a happy sound and selects an orange.) E says, "Get you some food." (Kanzi brings the orange back.) E says, "Is that what you got?" (Kanzi makes a sound like "good," peels the orange, and makes a sound like "orange.")

370A. (C) *Go to the refrigerator and get some food.* (Alia goes to the refrigerator and says something U while touching the refrigerator door.) E says, "I'll open it." (Alia gets out some raisins and a Coke.)

371. (C) *Go outdoors. . . .* (Kanzi interrupts.) *Go outdoors and get a banana.* (Kanzi goes to the play-yard door, looks out, and does not see any banana. Consequently, he goes to the refrigerator and gets one from there. [This is scored as C because it was an experimental oversight that there was no banana outdoors. It would have been considered a mistrial except that Kanzi indicated that he understood the sentence by going to the play yard and looking, then selecting another location where he knew a banana could be found. This sentence and others are partially repeated because Kanzi vocalizes during the sentence, making it difficult for him, or E, to hear what is being said.]

371A. (C) *Go outdoors and get the banana.* (Alia goes to the front door and says, "Mommy.") E opens the door. (Alia gets the banana.)

372. (C) *Show me the toy grapes.* (Kanzi does so.)
372A. (C) *Show me the toy grapes.* (Alia does so.)

373. (C) *Take the orange outdoors.* (Kanzi makes a sound like "orange" and takes the orange outdoors.)

373A. (C) *Take the orange outdoors.* (Alia picks up the orange and takes it to the front door.) E opens the door. (Alia sets the orange on the bench outdoors.)

374. (C) *Can you open this door by Sue? Open this door?* (Kanzi puts his hand on the edge and tries to pull it open, but it does not move.)

Response refinement.—Kanzi has already indicated that he understands the sentence but that he is hesitant to push the door hard, as on a previous trial he has been asked to stay on his side of the door. To emphasize that it is now OK to push on the door, E says, "Open it, go ahead." (Kanzi pulls harder and begins opening it.) E says, "Open it all the way." (Kanzi does.)

374A. (NG). [In Alia's case, E sat behind a one-way mirror that was not a door and could not be opened; hence, this sentence was not presented to Alia.]

375. (C) *Go to the microwave and get the shoe.* (Kanzi is interrupting E's sentence with a lot of vocalizations.) E repeats, "Go to the microwave and get the shoe." (Kanzi continues to interrupt vocally but also proceeds to the microwave. He goes to the microwave and gets the shoe out, then looks in, sees the big quart of yogurt, pulls it out, and sneaks off to the tool room to eat it.)

375A. (OE) *Go to the oven and get the shoe.* (Alia walks past the objects in front of her, among which there are no shoes, and walks to the kitchen and straight to the oven. She pats on the oven door as she waits for E, who has to come from behind the mirror, to help her open the oven door. Alia then says, "Open that.") E says, "You want me to open that?" and opens the oven. (Alia picks up all the objects from the oven—the rock, the yogurt, and the shoe—and says something U.)

Error correction.—(Alia says, "I want to get the other one shoe," and proceeds toward the open cabinet where E has stored the testing objects.) E says, "Alia, come here. I want to get rid of this behavior." (Alia continues away from E, walking past the object cabinet, looking inside the cabinet, and toward the living-room area.) E says, "Come here, Alia. Come here, Alia. Come here." (Alia then turns back toward E.) E says, "I just want the shoe. Put the other stuff back." (Alia carries all the objects back to the oven.) E says, "Just give Mommy the shoe." (Alia, with all the objects still in her arms, hands the shoe to E.) E says, "Put the other stuff back. I don't want everything." (Alia then places the rock and the yogurt back into the oven drawer.)

376. (PC) *Show me the fake orange, the toy orange.* (Kanzi picks up the real orange and puts it in a bowl.)

Error correction.—E says, "No, that's the real orange." (Kanzi says, "Whuu," and smells the orange.) E says, "Do you see the fake orange? The toy orange?" (Kanzi responds, "Umm.") E says, "Where's the toy orange?" (Kanzi leans down and sips up some liquid that was in the bowl where he had just put the orange.)

376A. (C1) *Show me the toy orange.* (Alia picks up the real orange and then puts it down and gets the toy orange. She takes it to E.) [C1 is scored because Alia acts on the real orange. She does not just look at it to determine which is which but picks it up in what could potentially be considered a "show" action.]

377. (C3) *Go outdoors and get an orange, go and get an orange, and you can eat it.* (Kanzi heads off but passes the play-yard door, going on toward the refrigerator.) E says, "Outdoors." (Kanzi changes direction and goes outdoors.) "You can eat it." (Kanzi makes a sound like "eat it," then takes a bite of the orange while sitting outside and makes a sound like "yum.") [C3 is coded because E emphasized "outdoors" and Kanzi changed his direction in response. Kanzi was told that he could eat the orange to determine whether he could process this information in addition to the request to go to a particular location. It may be that stressing "eat" caused Kanzi to go to the refrigerator.]

377A. (OE) *Go outdoors and get an orange.* (Alia first picks up the box of cereal, then turns and puts her right hand on the orange, looks back to the cereal, then to the orange. She then carries both the cereal and the orange back inside the trailer. She places the orange from outside next to the orange in the array in the trailer living room and the cereal at the end of the array.) [The sentence was modified for Alia because it is assumed that she would not want to eat the large, unpeeled orange. Thus, these sentences are not completely comparable.]

378. (PC) *Open the door and give me a shot.* (Kanzi is vocalizing while E speaks. He picks up the shot and is opening it to prepare to give a shot.) E says, "Open the door and give Sue the shot." (Kanzi gives himself a shot.) E says, "Sue, me, open the door, open the door and give me a shot." (Kanzi continues to give himself a shot.)

Error correction.—Kanzi seems hesitant to open the door and is also preoccupied with manipulating the syringe. E opens the door and repeats the sentence, and Kanzi carries it out correctly. [Kanzi has been accustomed to E giving him shots for a number of years as part of a routine medical procedure. He has not been asked to give shots to others, and, had he attempted to do so, he would have been asked not to. The phrase "give you a shot" would, in Kanzi's experience, have meant that he was about to receive a small stick from the syringe.]

378A. (C) *Give me a shot.* (Alia picked up the syringe and handed it around the edge of the mirror to E.) ["Open the door" was not part of Alia's sentence since E was not behind a door, only a mirror.]

379. (C3) *Give the shoe. . . .* (Kanzi interrupts with a vocalization.) *Give the shoe to Rose.* (Kanzi picks up the shoe and looks toward Rose, who looks away, so he veers off in a different direction.) E says, "To Rose." (Kanzi turns around and hands the shoe to Rose.) [C3 is scored because E emphasizes "to Rose" and Kanzi changes his orientation in response. However, had Rose not initially looked away when Kanzi handed her the shoe, it is likely that he would have continued to attempt to give it to her.]

379A. (C) *Give the shoe to Katie.* [Alia does so.]

380. (C) *Go to the big refrigerator. . . .* (Kanzi interrupts.) *Now listen. . . .* (Kanzi interrupts.) *To the big refrigerator and get a rock.* (Kanzi continues to vocalize loudly, drowning out E as she speaks.) *Get the rock, out of the big refrigerator.* (Kanzi goes to the refrigerator, looks in, but does not see anything, so he gesturally asks Rose to open the other side of the large double-door refrigerator. There he finds a rock and brings it back.) [C is scored because the repeated utterances are given in response to Kanzi's loud vocalizations rather than in response to his hesitating and because his behavior shows no alteration or change in response. He seems to be excited simply because he is being sent to the "big" refrigerator, where all the food is kept. However, he is not being asked to retrieve any food, just an item that is generally not in the refrigerator at all and one that Kanzi is not interested in. Consequently, E makes some effort to make certain that Kanzi actually hears the sentence.]

380A. (W) *Go to the big refrigerator and get the rock.* (Alia gets up, looks into the camera, and says something U. She then gets on her hands and knees and looks at the heating duct in the floor.) E says, "Alia, go to the big refrigerator and get the rock." (Alia gets up, saying, "OK," and something U. She stops at the toy shelf and says something U. She then touches a sticker on the toy shelf, walks away, and comes back to touch it again. She then goes to the kitchen and says something U. She continues to say something U and plays with the paneling on the wall. She then goes over to Karen's room and says, "Karen's room," as she points into the room. Alia comes out saying, "Mommy watch TV.")

Error correction.—E says, "Where'd you go?" (Alia does not respond.) E asks the cameraperson where Alia went. The cameraperson explains that Alia went to the door of Karen's room. E says, "Alia, go to the big refrigerator and get the rock." (Alia goes into the kitchen, saying something U, and sits down next to the cabinet.) E says, "Is *big* throwing you off?" (Alia does not respond.) E says, "Alia, go to the big refrigerator and get the rock." (Alia goes to the big refrigerator.) E opens the door for her. (Alia says, "Get the rock," then finds the rock in the refrigerator.)

381. (PC) *Throw the orange to Rose.* (Kanzi makes a sound like "orange" as he is picking up the orange, turns and *hands* the orange to Rose, who is only a few feet from him.) [E assumes that Kanzi understands this request but that he is not responding because Rose does not indicate that she is ready to catch the orange. However, PC is scored since there is no behavior on Kanzi's part by which to judge otherwise.]

Response refinement.—[Kanzi is familiar with the verb *throw* but often hesitates to throw things unless a person has initiated a game of catch.] E says, "Throw the orange to Rose." (Rose takes the orange from Kanzi's hand as he is getting ready to throw it since she still does not know what Kanzi has been asked to do.) E says, "Throw it." (Kanzi looks at Rose, who still has the orange.) E says, "Get it back and throw it." (Rose acts like she is going to eat it. Kanzi begins to make a lot of loud vocalizations and gestures toward the play yard.) Rose asks, "Do you want it over there?" and she points to the play yard. (Kanzi takes the orange back from Rose and walks toward the play-yard door with the orange.) E says, "Now throw it to Rose." (Kanzi keeps on going toward the play-yard door.) E says, "Throw it." (Kanzi makes a sound like "eat it," then gives an excited "waa" bonobo vocalization to indicate that he is going to do what he wants.) E says, "Throw it." (Kanzi says, "Waa," then sits down and starts to open the orange.) E says, "Throw it to Rose." (Kanzi gestures toward Rose.) Finally deciding that Kanzi is not going to throw the orange to Rose, E offers another alternative that still entails the part of the sentence that Kanzi did not respond to accurately. E offers, "You want to throw it outdoors?" (Kanzi makes loud "waa" calls but does not throw the orange anywhere.) E says, "Can you throw it?" [Rose approaches, touches the orange, and backs off, then points to the orange to indicate to Kanzi that she wants it.] E says, "Throw it. Throw to Rose." (Kanzi taps it with his knuckles.) E says, "Pick it up and throw it." (Kanzi tosses it up in the air and looks at Rose to see if she is now ready to catch it.) E says, "There you go, throw it some more." (Kanzi now tosses it to Rose, who backs off and gets ready to catch the orange. Before, she wasn't ready to catch, so Kanzi just handed her the orange instead of throwing it.)

381A. (C) *Throw the orange to Joshua.* (Alia picks up the orange, carries it toward Josh, gets Josh's attention by saying, "Josh," then throws the orange to Josh.) [Both Alia and Kanzi show a sensitivity to whether the recipient is ready to catch a thrown object; however, Alia is better at setting the stage for this to happen than is Kanzi.]

382. (C) *Throw, throw the ball to Liz.* (Kanzi gets his large red ball from behind the keyboard and tosses it toward Liz.) [The ball does not reach Liz, but a score of C is given because Kanzi's behavior indicates that he understood the sentence and was attempting to respond properly.]

Response refinement.—E says, "Throw it." (Kanzi tosses the ball further, and it bounces across the floor to Liz.)

382A. (C) *Throw the ball to Lisa.* (Alia does so.)

383. (C) *Go to the colony room . . .* (Kanzi interrupts) *. . . and get the phone. Go to the colony room and get the phone.* (Kanzi goes to the colony room and gets the phone on the wall by the colony-room door.) [C is scored because Kanzi technically does what he is asked in that he walks to the colony room, takes the receiver of the phone hanging on the wall, and starts to move away with it. The intent had been that he get an unattached phone placed in an array of objects in the colony room. Kanzi had rarely used the intercom phone attached to the wall there, and E had not thought that he might interpret the sentence referring to that phone.]

Response refinement.—[Since Kanzi did not get the specific phone that E intended, he is sent back with Rose to get the one that is in the colony room.] E asks Rose if Kanzi got the phone. (Kanzi makes a sound like "yes" even though he returns with no phone since Rose took away the receiver, returned it to the wall unit, and brought Kanzi back.) Rose explains what happened, and Kanzi is sent with Rose for the correct phone.

383A. (C) *Go to Karen's room and get the phone.* (Alia does so.)

384. (C) *Tickle Rose . . .* (Kanzi interrupts) *. . . with the phone.* (Kanzi picks up the phone and moves toward Rose, who appears hesitant since she does not know what Kanzi is going to do.) E says, "Tickle Rose with the phone." (Kanzi taps Rose very gently with phone to invite play, but she takes the phone from him instead of responding as though she is willing to play.) [C is scored because Kanzi's behavior indicates that he understands the sentence but is hesitant to carry it out since Rose does not appear prepared to be tickled. E's repetitions are designed to encourage Kanzi, even though Rose does not look as though she would appreciate being tickled with the phone at that time. While Kanzi has not been asked to tickle Rose with the phone before, he has often been asked to tickle many persons with objects in play and generally understands and responds to such requests if he wants to play with the person and if that person indicates that he or she wants to play with him.]

Response refinement.—[After Kanzi touches Rose, E continues to attempt to convince him to carry out more explicit actions for the purpose of clearly demonstrating sentence comprehension. However, this is antithetical to the normal nature of the social contract between Kanzi and Rose.] E says, "Tickle her, tickle her with the phone, take the phone and tickle her, tickle Rose, with the phone." (Kanzi picks up the base of the phone and looks at Rose.) E says, "Tickle her." (Kanzi puts the base of the phone on Rose's foot and looks at her, waiting for a response such as a smile, but receives none.) E says, "Tickle her tummy. Kanzi, take the phone and tickle Rose." (Kanzi takes the receiver from Rose's hand and looks at her, again waiting for a response.) Rose does nothing. E says, "Tickle her tummy. Tickle her with the phone." (Kanzi finally puts the phone on his tummy, then gestures with it to Rose to show Rose what he has been asked to do. Rose remains blind and in a posture that would make it difficult for Kanzi to tickle her tummy without being socially intrusive.) E says, "Yeah, you're tickling yourself, now tickle Rose's tummy." (Kanzi touches Rose on the knee with the phone and looks at her, waiting for her to raise up.) E says, "Yeah, tickle her tummy too. Go ahead, she'll let you. She'll let you." (Rose gives no indication that she will let Kanzi do so as she is still blind and maintaining a stiff posture since she does not know what has been requested of Kanzi and does not wish to guess.) E then says, "Go tickle Liz's tummy. Go tickle Liz's tummy with the phone, go tickle her tummy." (Kanzi puts the phone on Liz's knee; she laughs and is responsive to Kanzi's approach.) E says, "Yeah, tickle her tummy, tickle her tummy, tickle her tummy." (Liz smiles and looks at Kanzi, so he goes ahead and tickles her.) E says, "Yeah, that's right."

384A. (PC) *Tickle Linda with the phone.* (Alia picks up the phone from the array of objects in front of her, then carries it toward Linda and Nathaniel, who are sitting next to each other on the other side of the room. Alia takes the phone to Nathaniel and tickles him with the phone.)

Error correction.—At this point, Nathaniel says, "Tickle Linda," and gestures to Linda. Alia then takes the phone to Linda and pushes the phone into Linda's tummy in a playful manner.)

385. (C) *Take the umbrella . . . the umbrella outdoors.* (Kanzi does so.)

385A. (C) *Take the box outdoors.* (Alia does so.)

386. (C) *Kanzi, go to the refrigerator and get some melon, go get some melon.* (Kanzi heads off.) E, uncertain that Kanzi heard the last part of the sentence, says, "Get some melon." (Kanzi is already at the refrigerator looking for melon, although E is not aware of this. Kanzi looks around in the refrigerator, gets the melon out, and returns with it.) [This is scored C since E cannot see Kanzi and does not know where he is when the repetition regarding melon is made. E's comment was not made because Kanzi was hesitating or did not know what to do, and it did not cause him to alter the action in which he was engaged.]

386A. (PC) *Go to the refrigerator and get the peaches.* (Alia goes to the kitchen and picks up the doggie. She says something U and takes the doggie over and shows it to E.)

Error correction.—E says, "I see the doggie. I don't know what the doggie is doing." E takes the doggie and tosses him back on the table. (Alia goes back to the table.) E says, "Alia, leave the doggie alone. Go back to the refrigerator and get the peaches." (Alia says, "OK, bye Mommy," and goes over to the refrigerator.) E opens the refrigerator for her. (Alia says, "Here's the peaches.") E comments that those are the pears. (Alia takes the pears out of the refrigerator.) E says, "Alia, I tried to hide this one, but of course it's the one you find. It looks just like them, I'm going to give it to you."

387. (PC) *Go to the sink and get a knife.* (Kanzi takes a melon from the array and runs to the sink with it. He has previously indicated a desire to eat the melon and seems to take this sentence as a way of getting permission to do so. He gets out a bowl, rather than a knife, and proceeds to split the melon open in half with his hands and put it in the bowl.) [Kanzi at times confuses *bowl, knife,* and *spoon* as they are all "food-preparation implements." In this case, it appears that Kanzi has prepared the melon by splitting it in half with his hands as one would normally do using a knife. He has also put it in a bowl as E would do after splitting it with a knife. If Kanzi simply wanted to eat a melon, he would not normally split it in half with his hands and put it in a bowl. This type of "melon-preparation" activity is unusual for Kanzi.]

387A. (W) *Go to the sink and get a knife.* (Alia goes to the front door.) E opens the door. (Alia goes outside and looks around.)

388. (PC) *Show Rose your lip, your hurt mouth. Show her the hurt on your mouth.* (Kanzi looks down at his mouth and protrudes his lip just a bit, then glances at Rose.) [PC is scored because Kanzi does not orient toward Rose or make it reasonably possible for her to note the hurt on his lip, although he does look at her. His lip is protruded too briefly, although Kanzi probably believes that he has carried out the request appropriately and that Rose does not want to look. Showing people cuts that he has received is a common thing for Kanzi to do.]

Response refinement.—(When Rose makes no response to Kanzi, he picks up the gorilla mask and hands it to her, perhaps thinking of the relation between the mouth on the mask and his mouth.) E says, "Show her the hurt on your mouth, lip, where your mouth is hurt." (Kanzi touches Rose's knee, waiting for her to look. She does not, and he does not make the situation evident to her.) E says, "No, show her the hurt." (Kanzi points to the hurt on his leg, then one on his foot.) E asks the cam-eraperson, "Does he have a hurt on his leg, Kelly?" Kelly says, "He's got numerous hurts." E says, "Is he pointing to them?" (Kanzi makes a sound like "yes," and Kelly does not answer.) E says to Kanzi, "You are? What about your mouth, where's your mouth?" (Kanzi wiggles his lips.) E says, "That's your mouth. Go show Rose your mouth." (Kanzi picks up the toothpaste and starts to open it, perhaps thinking he will do this to his mouth.) E says, "No." (Rose comes over and takes the toothpaste away.) "Show Rose your mouth." (Rose moves away, telling Kanzi to listen to Sue.) E says, "Show her the hurt on your lip." (Kanzi puts his hand on the hurt on his lip.) E says, "Uh huh, that's your mouth . . . go show Rose." (Kanzi sucks on his hand.) E says, "Go show Rose your mouth." (Kanzi goes to the mirror by the refrigerator and begins looking at the hurt on his mouth in the mirror.) Rose is still blind and does not know what Kanzi has been asked to do. Rose says, "Kanzi," since Kanzi seems to be leaving the test setting and she does not understand why. Kanzi returns from the mirror. E tells Kanzi to sit down and announces that she is going to tell Rose what it is Kanzi should do. This is done, and Rose holds her hands out to Kanzi to indicate that he should come over. (Kanzi approaches Rose and sticks his lip out.)

388A. (NG).

389. (C2) *Give Rose a hug, go give her a hug.* (Kanzi goes to Rose and puts his face very close to her, waiting for a response from her to indicate that a more complete hug is acceptable. Rose does not respond.) E says, "Put your arms around her and give her a good hug," because E wants it to be evident that Kanzi understands the sentence. (Kanzi then holds his hand out to Rose, making a gesture that indicates some desire for contact. Rose then opens up a little, moving from her closed posture, and Kanzi moves close and puts his cheek on her. Rose finally rubs him, and he then presses his cheek closer to her. E says, "That's real nice, hug her real good." [C2 is scored because the additional phrases "put your arms around her and give her a good hug" were not intended to clarify the sentence, nor were they made because Kanzi hesitated. They were made for the purpose of getting Kanzi to behave in a way that clearly demonstrated for the camera that he knew how to give a hug, even though the recipient did not appear to be receptive to one.]

389A. (C) *Give Nathaniel a hug.* (Alia does so.) [Nathaniel, Alia's brother, is se-lected as the recipient for this sentence because Alia is likely to be hesitant to hug the other adults in the room, just as Kanzi was with Rose.]

390. (C) *Give the monster mask to Kelly.* (Kanzi does so.)
390A. (C) *Give the monster mask to Nathaniel.* (Alia does so.)

391. (C2) *Brush the doggie's teeth.* (Kanzi touches the teeth on the monster mask in a fleeting manner.) *Brush the doggie's teeth.* (Kanzi has already picked up the tooth-brush and the dog even as E starts to repeat the sentence. He orients the toothbrush properly in his hands and brushes the dog's teeth.)
391A. (C) *Brush the doggie's teeth.* (Alia does so.)

392. (PC) *Open the toothpaste.* (Kanzi picks up the Vaseline and starts to open it.) E says, "The toothpaste." (Kanzi takes the lid off the Vaseline, puts his finger in, and gets some out.) E says, "Open the toothpaste." (Kanzi puts the Vaseline on his teeth

as though it were toothpaste.) E says, "Kanzi, open the toothpaste." (Kanzi gets more Vaseline and puts it on his teeth, still acting as though he is doing the right thing.)

Error correction.—E says, "Open the toothpaste." (Kanzi puts some Vaseline on the doggie.) E says, "No, Kanzi, not the oil." (Kanzi talks to E as though he is trying to tell her something.) E says, "The toothpaste." (Kanzi gets more oil and puts it on the dog's teeth.) E says, "No." (Kanzi again gets Vaseline and puts it on the dog's teeth.) E says, "No, no, do you see the toothpaste? . . . You can't see it 'cause the umbrella's in front of it." (Kanzi puts the lid back on the oil, vocalizes to E, then picks up the bubbles and starts to open them.) E says, "No." (Kanzi stops opening the bubbles—Rose moves them out of his hand.) E says, "Open the toothpaste." (Kanzi looks more carefully, then picks up the toothpaste and the toothbrush, opens the toothpaste, and puts some on the toothbrush.)

392A. (C) *Open the toothpaste.* (Alia picks up the toothpaste and tries to open it. She cannot get it open, so she takes it to E.) E says, "You tried. She keeps . . . I screwed it off a little bit, and she keeps screwing it back on."

393. (C) *Take the umbrella to the colony room.* (Kanzi interrupts.) *Take the umbrella to the colony room.* (Kanzi puts the umbrella in his mouth, runs to the colony room, and waits for Rose to open the door. When he gets there, he wants to scare Matata with it.)

393A. (C) *Take the box to Karen's room.* (Alia picks up the box, shuts it, and takes it to Karen's room.)

394. (PC) *Kanzi, brush the teeth on the monster mask. Brush his teeth.* (Kanzi picks up the mask and puts it on his head.) E says, "Brush the teeth on the monster mask." (Kanzi picks up the toothpaste.) E says, "Uh huh." (Kanzi puts the tube of toothpaste in the monster mask as though that is a sufficient way to brush his teeth.)

Response refinement.—E says, "Brush his teeth, with your toothbrush." (Kanzi takes the top off the toothpaste, puts some toothpaste on his finger, and then puts the toothpaste on the monster mask, but on the hair, not the teeth, then on his own teeth.) E says, "Where's your toothbrush?" (Kanzi picks up the toothbrush.) "Yeah, brush his teeth." (Kanzi puts some toothpaste on the toothbrush, touches the toothbrush to the hair on the monster mask, then starts to brush his own teeth.) E says, "Don't you see his teeth?" (Kanzi continues to brush his own teeth.) E says, "The monster mask's teeth." (Kanzi then touches the toothbrush briefly to the monster mask's teeth.) "There you go, that's right, good." (Kanzi then continues brushing his own teeth.)

394. (C) *Brush the monster mask's teeth.* (Alia picks up the toothbrush, crawls over to the monster mask, and brushes its teeth.)

395. (C1) *Open the orange.* (Kanzi picks up the toothbrush and briefly touches the end of it on the apple as though he is thinking of using the toothbrush as an opening implement and is thinking with his hands.) E says, "Open the orange." (Kanzi picks up the orange and takes the peel off with his teeth.) [C1 is scored because Kanzi first acts on the apple. E's repetition is not a function of any hesitation on Kanzi's part and does not have an effect on his flow of action.]

395A. (PC) *Open the orange.* (Alia picks up the orange. She looks at it. She drops it. She picks it up again. She puts it down and starts to reach for the apple. The apple rolls away. She picks it up, drops it, picks it up, and drops it again. She then gets the knife and the petroleum jelly. She makes no clear attempt to open the orange. Perhaps she cannot figure out how to do so.)

396. (C) *Take the apple outdoors.* (Kanzi goes to the play-yard door with the apple and touches it, waiting for Rose to open it.) E comments, "That's really good." (After Rose unlocks the door, Kanzi opens it and takes the apple out.)

396A. (C) *Take the apple outdoors.* (Alia gets up, gets the apple, takes it to the front door, and waits for E to open it.) E opens the front door. (Alia takes the apple outside and places it on the bench but keeps her hands on it. Then she says, "How's that?") E says, "I don't know. OK. Very good, Alia."

397. (C) *Take the orange* . . . (Kanzi interrupts) . . . *the orange to the colony room.* (Kanzi picks up the orange, runs to the colony room, and waits for Rose to open the door.)

397A. (C) *Take the orange to Karen's room.* (Alia gets the orange. She walks part of the way and drops the orange. She picks it up and takes it to Karen's room.)

398. (C) *Go to the refrigerator and get an orange.* (Kanzi does so.)

398A. (W) *Go to the refrigerator and get an orange.* (Alia gets up and goes over to the toy shelf. She takes a game off the top shelf. She repeats, "A game," to herself several times.) E says, "Alia, go to the refrigerator and get an orange. No playing. No. No playing. Listen to Mommy. Go to the refrigerator and get an orange." (Alia says something U and tries to open the box.) E says, "Alia, no games. Put it back." (Alia rubs her eye.)

Error correction.—E says, "Go to the refrigerator and get an orange." (Alia gets up and goes to the refrigerator.) E opens the door. (Alia looks around and says something U.) E says, "OK, get down and look." (Alia gets down, looks, finds an orange, but says, "Apple.") E laughs and says, "No, that's not an apple, Alia. That's the orange. Remember Mommy asked you to get an orange? Do you see the orange? Orange."

399. (C) *Go outdoors* . . . (Kanzi interrupts) . . . *and get the umbrella. Go outdoors and get the umbrella. Go ahead. Go outdoors and get the umbrella.* (Kanzi goes to the door and points to it, waiting for Rose to unlock it. She takes quite a while, and, when it is open, he stands there and sort of looks out.) E says, "Bring it back." (Kanzi picks up the umbrella and brings it back.) [C is scored because the repetitions are a function of the noise that Kanzi is making and the general noise in the lab. E wants to be certain that Kanzi understands the sentence. When E says, "Bring it back," E has no knowledge of whether Kanzi has retrieved any item, much less the correct item. The original sentence does not specify that the item should be returned, and E is simply asking Kanzi to do so.]

399A. (C) *Go outdoors and get the box.* (Alia goes to the door.) E opens the door. (Alia gets the box and then says something about a "doggie" when looking at a dog.) E says, "Uh huh, a doggie." (Alia brings the box inside, accompanied by E.]

400. (C) *Go to the refrigerator and get some raisins.* (Kanzi says something U, goes to the refrigerator, and looks in one side and then the other until he finds the raisins, brings them back to E, and makes a sound like "raisin.")

400A. (C) *Go to the refrigerator and get the raisins.* (Alia goes to the refrigerator.) E opens the door for her. (Alia gets the raisins.)

401. (C) *Put the monster mask . . .* (Kanzi interrupts) *. . . in the refrigerator. Put it in the refrigerator.* (Kanzi does so.)

401A. (PC) *Put the monster mask in the refrigerator.* (Alia gets up, picks up the monster mask, and stops to look at it. Alia sits down and puts her hand in the monster mask's mouth. She continues to play with the monster mask. Then she turns away.)

Error correction.—E says, "Alia, put the monster mask in the refrigerator." (Alia says something U.) E says, "What?" (Alia crawls away from the monster mask and then stops and sits. She looks toward the monster mask.) E says, "Put the monster mask in the refrigerator. Yes, go ahead. Do it for Mommy. Put the monster mask in the refrigerator. Yes, please. Put the monster mask in the refrigerator, right now. Alia, put the monster mask in the refrigerator. Yes, please." (Alia lies all the way back.) E says, "Get up. Get up, please. Put the monster mask in the refrigerator." (Alia says, "No.") E says, "Yes. Do it. Do it, please. Hurry up. Alia, get up. Sit up. Sit up." (Alia crawls over to a chair. She gets up on her knees and holds onto the chair.) E says, "Alia, put the monster mask in the refrigerator. Go ahead, do it." (Alia says something U. Then she stands up.) E says, "Come on. No, don't sit down on that chair. Hurry up. Put the monster mask in the refrigerator." (By this time Alia has walked over and picked up the monster mask.) E says, "Speaking of monsters. Go ahead, do it. Put it in the refrigerator." (Alia takes the mask and puts it in the refrigerator.)

402. (C5) *Go to the colony room . . .* (Kanzi interrupts) *. . . and get the orange. Go to the colony room and get the orange.* (Kanzi touches the orange in front of him and heads off toward the colony room, stops at the refrigerator on the way, and looks in.) E says, "Go to the colony room, Kanzi, and get the orange." (Kanzi goes to the colony room and gets the orange, attempting to say "orange" as he picks it up.) [C5 is scored because Kanzi acts on the orange in the display in front of him but then carries out the sentence correctly.]

402A. (PC) *Go to Karen's room and get the orange.* (Alia gets up, says something U, and points to the orange in front of her. She picks up the orange and says something U. She takes it over and sets it on the shelf. She says something U and picks the orange back up. She carries the orange and sets it in front of the mirror and next to the toothbrush. She pats it with her hand, and it rolls away. She picks up the toothbrush and brushes the doggy's teeth, saying, "Teeth, teeth.") E comes out from behind the mirror and says, "I guess you're done." [PC is scored because Alia never attempts to take the orange anywhere.]

403. (C) *Knife the orange.* (Kanzi does so.)

403A. (C) *Knife the orange.* (Alia picks up the knife and hits the orange with it.)

404. (C) *Put your knife down.* (Kanzi does so. He is holding both the orange and the knife at the time. He keeps the orange.)

404A. (NG).

405. (C) *Put the orange down.* (Kanzi does so. He is holding only the orange at the time.)

405A. (NG).

406. (C) *Go to the refrigerator and get some bananas.* (Kanzi goes to the refrigerator and starts pulling out all the bananas.) E cannot see Kanzi but knows that Kanzi has not returned. E says, "Bring the bananas back." (Kanzi makes a sound like "bring the bananas" and does so.) [C is scored because Kanzi has gone to the refrigerator and obtained the bananas before E reminds him to bring back the specific object, bananas. Consequently, Kanzi does not use the information then provided to aid in the selection of the bananas.]

406A. (C) *Go to the refrigerator and get the banana.* (Alia goes into the kitchen and turns around to look behind her. She then turns back around and goes over to the refrigerator.) E opens the refrigerator door. (Alia takes out all three bananas.) E accompanies Alia, carrying the bananas, back to the test site.

407. (PC) *Take the potato outdoors and get the apple.* (Kanzi picks up the potato and the knife and heads toward the door. It is locked, so he waits for Rose to open it. Kanzi finally points to the lock to ask Rose to open the door as she has just stood there and not opened the door even though Kanzi was sitting by it. Rose was waiting for Kanzi to make a gesture; however, since he was cutting the potato with the knife, he did not on this occasion.) Since Kanzi has to wait a long time, E elects to remind him, saying, "Take the potato outdoors and get the apple." (Kanzi goes out and stands looking around. It is dark.) Since he seems to be hesitating and not coming back, E says, "Now bring the apple back." (Kanzi picks up the apple and brings it back but also carries the potato with him.) [PC is scored because Kanzi does not select the apple once he is outdoors until E says, "Now bring the apple back.")

407A. (PC) *Take the potato outdoors and get the apple.* (Alia gets up and gets the potato. She goes to the front door.) E opens the door. (Alia takes the potato outside, sets it on the bench, but keeps her hand on it. She then picks up the apple and the potato and brings them both inside.)

408. (C) *Take the telephone to the bedroom.* (Kanzi does so.)

408A. (C) *Take the telephone to the bedroom.* (Alia does so.)

409. (C) *Show me the toy orang.* (Kanzi does so.)

409A. (W) *Show me the toy orang.* (Alia picks up the apple and puts it in her mouth. She tries to bite it.) E says, "Alia, show me the toy orang." (Alia continues to bite on the apple. She puts the apple down, knocking over the box. She sets the box back up. She gets up and goes to the doorway of Karen's room.)

Error correction.—(Alia returns to the living room and says something U.) E says, "Alia, the toy orang." (Alia says, "All gone.") E says, "All gone? How about the toy Mari and Madu?" (Alia says something U and picks up the apple.) E says, "The toy. The Mari and Madu doll." Nathaniel says, "I'll show her." He picks it up. [Mari and Madu are proper names for the orangutans at the laboratory.]

410. (C) *Take the pineapple outdoors.* (Kanzi does so.)

410A. (C) *Take the apple outdoors.* (Alia picks up the apple and takes it to the front door.) E opens the front door. (Alia takes the apple outside and puts it on the bench.)

411. (C3) *Make the toy orang bite your ball.* (Kanzi looks around the room.) E says, "Do you see the toy orang?" (Kanzi picks up the toy orang puppet and puts it on his hand.) E says, "Make the toy orang bite your ball." (Kanzi takes the toy orang puppet off his hand, picks up the orang mask, and puts the mask's mouth on the ball.) [C3 is scored because Kanzi hesitates after looking around the room and does not look for the toy orang until specifically asked to do so. However, after this he correctly completes the sentence, even though he decides to use the mask instead of the puppet as the biting agent. This is reasonable because the puppet has no teeth while the mask does.]

411A. (PC) *Make the toy orang bite your ball.* (Alia gets up, sits down, picks up a stick, and stabs her ball with it. She then stabs the monster mask with the stick.) E says, "Alia, can you show me the toy orang?" (Alia puts down the stick, looks at the mirror, and then touches the toy orang.) E says, "Yes. Can you make it bite your ball?" (Alia says, "Ball," and then she bites the ball.) E says, "She's biting it."

412. (C) *Make the toy orang bite Rose.* (Kanzi does so.)

412A. (C3) *Make the toy orang bite Nathaniel.* (Alia falls down on the mat. She sits still for a while and then picks up the *orange*. She takes the *orange* over to Nathaniel and puts it against his arm.) E says, "Make the toy Mari Madu bite Nathaniel." (Alia gets up and puts down the juice she was drinking. She picks up the orang and makes it bite Nathaniel.)

413. (C) *Open your ball.* (Kanzi slaps his big red ball real hard, with a play face as though he is trying to smack it open.) "Open your ball." (Kanzi smacks it again harder, as if trying to open it.) [Kanzi has successfully "opened" a ball this way in the past.]

413A. (NG).

414. (C) *Bite your ball.* (Kanzi bites the ball and shakes it hard while holding the handle in his mouth.)

Response refinement.—E knows that Kanzi likes the large red ball very much and does not want to break it, although he often opens balls that he does not like very much. E says, "Kanzi, bite your ball *open*," to see if it is possible to get Kanzi to do something during the test that he really does not want to do. (Kanzi bites the ball hard, pushing his mouth down like he does when he is going to bite a ball open, but he does not execute his full force as if he does not want to ruin this ball. Then he gives the ball a good smack, like he does when trying to pop balls.) E says, "Bite, bite your ball open." (Kanzi slaps the ball, then bites the handle hard, but not clear through, then smacks the ball.) E decides to try another method and says, "Can you knife your ball?" (Kanzi puts the gorilla mask on the ball because he does not want to pop his large and favorite ball.) E says, "Can you show Sue the knife? Where's the knife?" (Kanzi picks up the knife.) E says, "Uh huh." (Kanzi pokes the knife into the cantaloupe.) E says, "You don't wanna knife your ball, do you?" (Kanzi makes a sound like "unnnn.")

414A. (C) *Bite your ball.* (Alia does so.)

415. (C) *Make the gorilla mask bite Kelly.* (Kanzi does so.)

415A. (PC) *Make the monster mask bite Nathaniel.* (Alia picks up the monster mask and carries it to Nathaniel. She holds the mask up to Nathaniel as she says something U to him and then hands the mask to him.

Error correction.—Nathaniel holds the monster mask up to Alia as he says, "You have to do it." (Alia says, "Anngh," and runs away.) Nathaniel says, "Make the monster mask bite me." Alia stops and turns back toward Nathaniel. Nathaniel repeats, "Make the monster mask bite me." Alia turns from side to side in refusal, then sits back in her chair. E asks Nathaniel to be quiet, then asks Alia, "Are you done Alia?" (Alia shakes her head first, then nods her head, changing her mind about being done.) "OK." [It appears that Alia is afraid of the monster mask and does not want it to do something bad, like biting.]

416. (OE) *Take the toy orang outdoors.* (Kanzi's foot is draped across the toy orang; consequently, when he looks at the array, he does not see it and hesitates.) E says, "Take the toy orang outdoors." (Kanzi picks up the gorilla mask and the monster mask and carries them both outdoors. Kanzi often treats the ape masks and stuffed toys as interchangeable "ape" likenesses.) [Kanzi took outdoors, not two different things, but two that he considered similar, if not identical. Consequently, this is not scored as an object error.]

416A. (W) *Take the toy orang outdoors.* (Alia picks up a blanket and drops it, then leaves.) [W is scored because Alia leaves the test setting without responding to any part of the sentence.]

Error correction.—E says, "Alia, come here. Come here." (Alia returns and picks up the blanket.) E says, "Can you take the toy orang, the orang, outdoors?" (Alia puts the ball on the orang's head.) Can you take the orang outdoors? (Alia picks up a stick and stabs the orang.)

417. (C) *Hit your ball with the stick.* (Kanzi does so.)

417A. (C4) *Hit your ball with the stick.* (Alia picks up the knife. She then grabs the petroleum jelly as if she is planning to pick it up.) E says, "Alia. Alia." (Alia stops touching the petroleum jelly and picks up the stick.) E says, "Hit your ball with the stick." (Alia touches the stick to the ball once. She then puts the stick down and continues to get the petroleum jelly.)

418. (C) *Hit the doggie with the stick.* (Kanzi does so.)

418A. (OE) *Hit the dog with the stick.* (Alia picks up the stick and the knife. She hits the dog with the knife. Then she hits the dog with the stick. She hits the dog with both the knife and the stick. Then she hits the dog with the knife and puts down the stick.)

419. (C5) *Go outdoors and get the pineapple.* (Kanzi starts to take the pineapple that is inside in the array.) E says, "Go outdoors and get the pineapple." (Kanzi does so.)

419A. (W) *Go outdoors and get the apple.* (Alia points and says something U. She gets up, and the phone rings. She goes into another room and tries to pick up the phone.) E says, "Alia, Alia no. Let's go back and sit down. Listen to Mommy. Listen to Mommy. Listen. Alia, go outdoors and get the apple." (Alia gets up, goes into a different room, and tries to get on the bed.)

Error correction.—"Alia, come here. Let Mommy show you."

420. (PC) *Take the umbrella to the T-room. Take the umbrella to the T-room.* (Kanzi takes the sparklers to the T-room.)

420A. (NR). *Take the box to Karen's room.* (Alia did not respond.)

421. (C) *Stab your ball with the sparklers.* (Kanzi takes a sparkler out of the box and puts it on the ball.)

Response refinement.—E says, "Real hard, stab it in there." (Kanzi does so.)

421A. (C) *Stab your ball with the sparkler.* (Alia does so.)

422. (OE) *Take the stick to the bedroom.* (Kanzi picks up the sparklers and the umbrella.) E says, "The stick." (Kanzi picks up the stick also and takes all three to the bedroom.)

422A. (PC) *Take the stick to the bedroom.* (Alia picks up the stick, touches it against the flashlight, and says something U. She then takes the stick to the bathroom.)

423. (PC) *Go to the T-room and get your ball.* (Kanzi starts off. While he is going, E says,) *And hit your ball with the rock.* (Kanzi goes to the T-room, gets the ball, and pauses, looking around as though he heard some sound.) E says, "Bring your ball back." (Kanzi carries the ball back and tosses it down in front of the door.) E says, "Hit your ball with the rock." (Kanzi vocalizes, then hits the ball with the rock.)

423A. (PC) *Go to the bathroom and get your ball and hit it with your rock.* (Alia picks up the rock and takes it to the bedroom, where she hits the orange with the rock.)

424. (C5) *Go to the bedroom.* (Kanzi interrupts.) *Go to the bedroom and get the stick.* (Kanzi continues to interrupt.) *Go to the bedroom and get the stick.* (Kanzi picks up the stick in front of him and carries it to the bedroom.) E says, "You need to bring the stick to Sue." (Kanzi brings back the stick that he took to the bedroom.) [C5 is scored because Kanzi acts on the object in the array in front of him rather than the one in the distal location.]

Response refinement.—E opens the door, and Kanzi is told, "Go get the stick that's in the bedroom. No, not this one, the one in there." (Kanzi does so.)

424A. (NR) *Go to the bedroom and get the stick.* (Alia says something U, indicating to E that she doesn't want to do the task.) E says, "Why?" (Alia says, "Too high.") E explains that Alia is saying "too high" and that probably means "too hard."

425. (C) *Go outdoors and get the monster mask. Go outdoors and get the monster mask.* (Kanzi does so.)

425A. (C1) *Go outdoors and get your monster mask.* (Alia gets up and goes over to the front door. She stops to pick up a balloon and hits it up in the air.) Nathaniel decides that he will open the door for Alia. (Alia takes Nathaniel's hand off the door, saying, "No, Mommy do it.") E helps Alia with the door. (Alia touches the tooth of the monster mask and pulls her hand back as if the mask is scary. She then picks up the mask, holding it out away from her body as if she doesn't want to touch it, and brings it inside.) [C1 is scored because Alia plays with the balloon before carrying out the request.]

426. (C) *Stab the pineapple with the sparklers.* (Kanzi does so.)

426A. (C) *Stab the apple.* (Alia touches the knife, then says something U about the "apple." She then hits the apple with the knife.) [Alia should have been asked, "Stab the apple with the sparklers," but was not.]

427. (C) *Go to the T-room* . . . (Kanzi interrupts) . . . *and get the pineapple. Go to the T-room and get the pineapple. Go to the T-room and get the pineapple.* (Kanzi does so.)

427A. (W) *Go to the bathroom and get the apple.* (Alia interrupts.) E says, "Alia. Alia." (Alia says something U.) E says, "Go to the bathroom and get the apple." (Alia runs to the bathroom and comes back out saying something U. She picks her coat up off the couch and says, "Coat.")

Error correction.—E says, "Alia, come here." (Alia does not listen.) "You're supposed to do what Mommy asks you, and I can tell you're not doing it on purpose." E takes Alia's hand while saying, "You come sit down and listen. OK? Now listen. Ready? Go to the bathroom and get the apple." (Alia says, "OK," goes into the bathroom, and gets the apple.)

428. (PC) *Give the water and the doggie to Rose.* (Kanzi picks up the dog and hands it to Rose.)

428A. (C) *Give the doggie and the water to Nathaniel.* (Alia does so.)

429. (C) *Give the ball and the shot to Kelly.* (Kanzi picks up the shot and the ball and hands both together in one hand to Kelly.)

429A. (W) *Give the ball and the shot to Lisa.* (Alia kneels down on the mat. She hits the mat with her hands, causing a loud slapping noise. She then picks up an apple and a container with water. She puts the container down and rolls a second apple with her hand. She then picks up the fake grapes and sets them down. She picks up the container and sets it down. The whole time she is still holding the first apple. She touches the second apple and then puts the first apple down. She rolls a styrofoam ball over toward herself. She picks up the shot and looks at it. She briefly touches the container with the water and then turns her attention back to the shot.)

Error correction.—E says, "Alia, give the ball and the shot to Lisa." (Alia briefly touches the ball, but then she picks up the container and puts the shot in it. She continues to stick the shot in and out of the container. She then goes to put the shot on the apple.) E says, "Alia, give the ball and the shot to Lisa. Can you do that?" (Alia continues to play with the objects.) E comes out.

430. (C1) *Turn the flashlight on.* (Kanzi puts a rock in his mouth, then turns on the light switch by the T-room door.) [C1 is scored because in the past the word *flashlight* has often been used to refer to any room light with Kanzi. Such multiple word usage is a function of the limited number of keys on the keyboard. And, even though the keyboard is not being used here, the history of the English usage of the word is affected by the keyboard limitations.)

430A. (PC) *Turn the flashlight on.* (Alia picks up the flashlight and puts it on the toy shelf.) [PC is scored because Alia acts on the flashlight but makes no attempt to turn it on.]

Error correction.—When E does not tell her that she has done a good job, Alia picks up the flashlight and takes it to E, saying, "Mommy, turn on flashlight.") E says, "What do you do?" (Alia says something U.) E says, "Huh? Do you know how to turn the flashlight on?" (Alia says, "Turn on.") E says, "Can you show me?" (Alia nods her head and presses the button.) E says, "Yeah, right there." [Alia apparently knew how to turn on the flashlight; however, she did not elect to do so.]

431. (C) *Hit your ball with the sugar cane.* (Kanzi does so.)

431A. (C) *Hit your ball with the sugar cane.* (Alia falls off her chair. She crawls over to the array of objects. She picks up the sugar cane and says, "Sugar cane." Then she rolls the ball so that it is right in front of her. She then says something U and picks up a long, thin object that looks like a sparkler. She holds this object in her left hand while she uses her right hand to hit the ball with the sugar cane.)

432. (C) *Can you go outdoors and get the banana?* (Kanzi interrupts.) *Go outdoors and get the banana.* (Kanzi picks up a favorite hat and carries it with him, waiting for Rose to open the door to the play yard. He sits on the potty while waiting, drops the hat, goes outdoors, looks all around, picks up the banana, and brings it back.) [C is scored because Kanzi seemed to carry the hat with him just because he was interested in it. He did not take it all the way outdoors, nor did he bring it back as he might if he had misunderstood the sentence and confused the hat with the banana.]

432A. (C2) *Go outdoors and get the banana.* (Alia says, "OK," walks to the door, knocks on it, goes to the window, looks out, and says, "[Something U] all gone." E agrees, "[Something U] is all gone." Then E repeats, "Alia, go outdoors and get the banana." Alia starts toward the door, then says, "Mommy," gestures for E to follow her, then gestures for E to open the door. Outside, she picks up the book and looks at it, puts it down, then picks up the banana, and says, "[Something U] banana.") E says, "Uh hum, take it in." (Alia says something U.) E says, "Come on," and guides Alia back inside.

433. (C2) *Go to the bedroom and get the milk.* (Kanzi has been eating some mushrooms in between trials. After listening to E, he continues eating mushrooms, then pauses.) E says, "Go to the bedroom and get the milk." (Kanzi does so.)

433A. (C) *Go to the bedroom and get the milk.* (Alia does so.)

434. (C) *Go to the microwave . . .* (Kanzi interrupts) *. . . the microwave oven and get the tomato.* (Kanzi continues to vocalize, goes to the microwave, gets both the banana and the tomato, and brings both back. He then indicates that he would like to eat the banana.)

434A. (C) *Go to the oven and get the tomato.* (Alia brings both the carrot and the tomato to E. She holds out the carrot and says, "I got the carrot.") E says, "Mmm-hmmm." (Alia says, "I going to give it for you.") E says, "What else did you get?" (Alia says, "I get green beans.") [Alia did not get green beans. C is scored because Alia carried out the sentence correctly and also announced the name of the extra object that she retrieved. The statement regarding the green beans is viewed as irrelevant for coding purposes.]

435. (PC) *Give the doggie and the mushrooms to Rose.* (Kanzi hands Rose the dog, then asks for some mushrooms.)

435A. (C) *Give the doggie and the grapes to Lisa.* (Alia does so.)

436. (OE) *Go outdoors. . . .* (Kanzi interrupts.) *Go outdoors and get the book.* (Kanzi

interrupts.) E tries to repeat the sentence but is drowned out completely by Kanzi, who is already running outdoors. (Outside, Kanzi stops and looks around.) E says, "Are you going to bring it back?" (The telephone is sitting on top of the book. Kanzi picks up both and comes back with them.) [It is doubtful that Kanzi heard the item that was requested because he was making so much noise. He probably brought back multiple items because he did not know what was requested.]

Error correction.—E says, "I want just the book. Can you show me the book?" (Kanzi does so.)

436A. (C4) *Go outdoors and get the book.* (Alia goes toward the front door but stops and takes the arm cover off the couch.) E says, "Alia." (Alia stops.) E says, "Put that back please." (Alia tries to put it back, but she puts it on sideways.) E says, "Go outdoors and get the book." (Alia says, "Coming mommy?") E says, "I guess." E fixes the arm cover. (Alia goes over to the front door.) E opens the door. (Alia goes out and opens up the book.) E says, "Take the book inside." (Alia does so.)

437. (C) *Take the doggie to the colony room.* (Kanzi does so.)

437A. (NR) *Take the doggie to Karen's room.* (Alia picks up the doggie and looks in the mirror. She sits down, says something U, and plays with the doggie.) E says, "Alia, take the doggie to Karen's room." (Alia says, "No.") E says, "Yes. Right now. Right now." (Alia continues to shake her head and say "no.") E says, "Take the doggie to Karen's room. Take the doggie to Karen's room." (Alia hits the mirror.) E says, "Hurry up." (Alia hits the mirror again.) E says, "Alia, don't hit. Take the doggie to Karen's room." (Alia continues to amuse herself with the mirror.)

438. (C) *Give the ball and the shot to Kelly.* (Kanzi does so.)

438A. (PC) *Give the dog and the shot to Lisa.* (Alia picks up the dog and a small square block and gives them to Lisa.)

439. (C) *Pour the water on the vacuum.* (Kanzi picks up the water, takes a bit into his mouth, and lets it dribble out of his mouth into a small hole in the vacuum.) E does not see that this is what he is doing and asks, "Can you pour it on the vacuum?" (Kanzi vocalizes to indicate "yes," as this is what he is doing.)

439A. (PC) *Pour the water on the strawberries.* (Alia picks up the basket of strawberries, looks at it, and holds the strawberries. She then puts the basket behind her briefly, then picks it back up.) E says, "Pour the water on the strawberries." (Alia continues to play with the strawberries.) E says, "Do you see the water? Alia, the water. Do you see the water? Do you see the water?" (Alia says something U.) E says, "Where's the water?" (Alia gets up, wanders into the kitchen.)

440. (C) *Can you open the vacuum? Can you open the vacuum cleaner?* (Kanzi unwraps the cord from around the top, then tries to pull on the catch on the edge where the vacuum cleaner comes apart if the catch is properly lifted, then tries the other catch, which is hard to operate. Then he puts his fingers in the hole in the top and tries to lift the top off, but it does not come.) [C is scored as Kanzi is clearly trying to open the vacuum in an appropriate manner even though he is not successful.]

440A. (PC) *Open the vacuum cleaner.* (Alia goes over to the vacuum. She stands there and steps on the vacuum. She presses a couple of switches on the vacuum. She gets a container with peaches in it and goes over to E.) [PC is scored because, although

Alia acts on the vacuum, none of the things that she does appear to be attempts to open it.]

441. (PC) *Put the telephone in the refrigerator.* (Kanzi picks up a rock and then goes over and looks in the vacuum.) E says, "Kanzi, put the telephone in the refrigerator." (Kanzi vocalizes and walks away with his rock.) E says, "The phone." (Kanzi takes his rock to the microwave, looks in, then takes his rock on to the little refrigerator and tosses it in there.)

Error correction.—E opens the door and tells Kanzi what to do again. Rose helps Kanzi do the correct thing.

441A. (PC) *Put the telephone in the refrigerator.* (Alia gets up and stamps her feet. She picks up the end of the telephone as if she is talking to someone. She then says something U as if she is singing.) E says, "Alia, put the telephone in the refrigerator." (Alia hits the mirror three times.) E says, "Alia, stop it. (Alia says, "OK.")

442. (C) *Do you see your ball?* (Kanzi looks at the ball.) *Pick it up.* (Kanzi does so.) *Put it in the refrigerator.* (Kanzi does so.) [E is visible during this trial.]

442A. (C2) *Alia, do you see the ball?* (Alia gets up off the chair with her arms straight in the air and says something U.) *Pick it up. Put it in the refrigerator.* (Alia spills something with her foot. She looks down, points, and says, "Ut oh.") E says, "That's all right." (Alia walks a little bit and then turns around and giggles. She then squeezes the ball a couple of times and pauses.) E says, "Put it in the refrigerator." (Alia throws the ball. She goes over and gets it and throws it again.) E says, "Alia, pick up the ball." (Alia goes over to the ball.) E says, "Pick up the ball." (Alia picks up the ball.) E says, "Put it in the refrigerator." (Alia says, "OK." Alia takes the ball to the refrigerator.) E opens the door for Alia. (Alia puts the ball in the refrigerator.) [C2 is scored here rather than C3 because the initial target sentence was broken down. Consequently, multiple repeats, also broken down, deserve a C2 score.]

443. (PC) *Take your ball to the hammock.* (Kanzi picks up the ball and goes to the other keyboard.) E says, "To the hammock." (Kanzi puts his ball in the microwave.)

Error correction.—The door is opened, and Rose shows Kanzi what to do.

443A. (PC) *Take your ball to the table.* (Alia says something U. She picks up the ball and goes over to the window. She looks out the window. She takes the ball over to the table, puts the ball on the table, and gets up on the chair so that she can put the ball on the television.)

444. (C) *Put the rock in the water.* (Kanzi does so.)

444A. (C1) *Put the rock in the water.* (Alia shakes her head yes. She picks up the container of water, says something U, and pours the water in a bowl. She then picks up the rock and puts it in the bowl.) [C1 is scored because Alia elects to pour the water in the bowl before putting the rock in the water. The original container of water was large enough for her to have placed the rock in, had she elected to do so.]

445. (C4) *Kanzi, take Rose outdoors. Kanzi, take Rose outdoors.* (Kanzi reaches up and touches Rose's hand and looks at her as though waiting for her to do something, but she does nothing.) E says, "Go ahead." (Kanzi starts to pick up the oil.) E says, "No, Kanzi. Take Rose, get her hand and take her outdoors." (Kanzi sort of gestures to Rose, and then she lets him take her hand. He holds it, leads her to the play-yard

door, and gestures to it. She opens the door, and Kanzi walks on out, expecting her to follow. Rose just stays there, but he has already taken her to the place, and she is welcome to go out if she wishes.) [C4 is scored because E has to ask Kanzi not to pick up the oil. Even though Rose does not go out to the play yard, Kanzi has taken her all the way to the small tunnel door, and it would be difficult for Kanzi to continue to lead her by the hand while going through this door.]

445A. (NR) *Take Kathy outdoors. Get her by the hand and take her outdoors.* (Alia stands up briefly, then sits back down, turns to E, and says, "I don't want to. I don't want to.") E says, "Can you take Kathy outdoors?" (Alia stays in the chair looking at E and kicks her feet.) E says, "Get her by the hand and take her outdoors. It's OK." (Alia remains seated and says, "No," and something else U as she shakes her shoulders.)

446. (PC) *Put the rock in the bowl.* (Kanzi puts the rock in the water.)

Error correction.—E says, "No, put the rock in the bowl." (Kanzi takes the rock out of the water.) E says, "Do you see the bowl?" (Kanzi picks up the knife and acts like he is going to use it to open the vaseline.) E says, "The bowl?" as Kanzi may be confusing *oil* and *bowl*. E says, "The bowl?" (Kanzi picks up another knife.) E says, "No, that's the knife. Where's the bowl?" (Kanzi again touches the knife to the oil.)

446A. (C1) *Put the rock in the bowl.* (Alia picks up the container of water in her right hand. She switches it over to her left hand and picks up the rock. She puts the rock in the bowl. She then spills the water. She says, "Ut oh, Ma. Ut oh," and points to the spilled water.) [C1 is scored because Alia picks up the container of water before she carries out the sentence.]

447. (PC) *Pour the water out on the rock. Pour the water. . . .* (Kanzi takes the rock out of the bowl and puts it in the bin, which is filled with water.) E says, "Pour the water out." (Kanzi puts the bowl in the bin of water with the rock and gets some water in the bowl.)

Error correction.—E says, "Can you pick it up? Yeah, that's right, pour some of it out on the rock." (Kanzi lifts the bowl full of water to his mouth, takes a sip, and sets it down on the floor.)

447A. (PC) *Pour the water on the rock.* (Alia gets up, goes over, and picks up the water. She sets it down next to the rock but immediately picks it back up. She says something U while she picks up her watch and puts it up against the edge of the water container. She sets the water container in the bowl and slides the bowl to the side. She then says, "What's that?" She then looks at the camera and says, "Mine, my something U. My watch.")

Error correction.—E says, "Alia. Alia. Pour the water on the rock." (Alia says, "OK." Alia slides the bowl across in front of her and says, "Hot. Hot.") E says, "Pour the water on the rock." (Alia says, "OK." Alia plays with her watch.) E says, "Do it now." (Alia says something U and continues to play with the watch. She turns around and says something like, "This is wrong, Mommy.") E says, "What?" (Alia repeats her previous statement. She then says, "Hot," and pulls the bowl closer to her.) E says, "Pour the water on the rock." (Alia pushes the bowl away from her and plays with the rock. She then pulls the bowl back toward herself and pushes it away. She resumes playing with the watch.)

448. (C3) *Take Liz to the bedroom.* (Kanzi starts to pick up knives.) E says, "Go get Liz by the hand and take her to the bedroom." (Kanzi approaches Liz bipedally with a handful of long, sharp knives, and Liz looks at him with a very wide-eyed expression. He then walks away from Liz and starts toward the bedroom.) E says, "Liz, go get Liz and take her to the bedroom." (Kanzi turns around, still holding the knives, but, dropping them down lower so that they appear less intimidating, he approaches Liz again, still bipedal, takes her hand, and leads her to the bedroom. The door is locked, and she opens it for him, and they go in the bedroom, with Kanzi still carrying the knives.) [C3 is scored because the rephrasing here clearly helps Kanzi and he reorients toward Liz in response to it. He appears to confuse the words *knives* and *Liz.*]

448A. (C) *Go get Nathaniel and take him to the bedroom.* (Alia goes to Nathaniel, taps him on the back. Nathaniel says something U. They grab each other's hands, and Alia leads Nathaniel toward the bedroom.) E then says to Nathaniel, "Follow her, just follow her." (Nathaniel and Alia let go of each other's hands as Nathaniel proceeds to follow Alia, who continues toward the bedroom.)

449. (C) *Put your ball in the water.* (Kanzi does so.)

449A. (C) *Put your ball in the water.* (Alia reaches for the ball, but it rolls out of her reach. She goes over and gets it. She pulls the dishpan closer to her and says, "Water, water." She then puts the ball in the dishpan.)

450. (C1) *Put the carrot in the water.* (Kanzi picks up a carrot, makes a sound like "carrot," takes a bite of the carrot, then puts it in the water.) [C1 is scored because Kanzi eats some of the carrot before putting it in the water.]

450A. (C2) *Put your carrot in the water.* (Alia picks the ball up out of the water, shakes it off, wipes it with her hand, shakes it again, and pauses.) E says, "Alia, put your carrot in the water." (Alia stops for a second, but then she dips her ball back in the water and starts to shake it off again. Some of the water drips onto her pants. She says, "Alia's wet." She seems to try to get the water off her pants by rubbing the sponge ball across the wet spot.) E says, "Put your carrot in the water." (Alia gets the carrot and puts the tip of it in the water.)

451. (C) *Put the milk in the water.* (Kanzi picks up a closed can of SMA [milk], looks at the water, and shakes the milk, trying to figure out how to get the milk out of the can into the water.) E says, "Put the milk, just put the whole can in the water." (Kanzi looks around for something to open the milk with.) E says, "Just put the can in, just drop the milk in the water." [C is scored because Kanzi's behavior indicates that he has understood the sentence and is trying to figure out how to open the can so that he can pour the milk in the water. E's suggestions that he just put the whole can in the water are ignored, probably because, in his experience, the cans of SMA are opened and mixed with water, never just dropped in a bowl of water. Placing a can of milk in a bowl of water seems to make no sense to Kanzi.]

451A. (C2) *Put the milk in the water.* (When this sentence is given, Alia is still interested in playing with the carrot in the water from the previous sentence. She first takes the carrot out of the water and shakes it off, then continues to put the carrot in and out of the water as though she has not heard the new sentence.) E says, "Put the milk in the water." (Alia puts the carrot down, and it rolls out of her reach.

She picks up the milk that is in a closed plastic container and says something U. She tries to open the container but is unable to do so. She tries pouring the milk, but it won't come out. She tries to open the milk again and then tries to pour it again.) E says, "Put the milk in the water." (Alia puts the container of milk close to the water but brings it back and tries to open it again.) E says, "Alia, put the whole thing, the whole milk in the water." (Alia tries to pour the milk again and then sets it down.) [C2 is scored because Alia's behavior indicates that she has understood the sentence and is trying to figure out how to open the plastic container so that she can pour the milk in the water. E's suggestions that she just put the whole container in the water are ignored, probably because, in her experience, the plastic containers of milk are opened before they are mixed with other liquids, never just dropped in a bowl of water. Placing a plastic container of milk in a bowl of water seems to make no sense to Alia.]

452. (C2) *Put the collar in the water.* (Kanzi picks up part of the collar, which is attached to a 15-foot lead, and starts to put it in the water, but the lead becomes entangled with other objects, so he gives up, breaks a carrot in half, takes a bite, and looks at the problem.) E says, "Put your collar in the water." (Kanzi figures out how to pick it up more carefully and puts it in the water.)

452A. (C1) *Put your watch in the water.* (Alia picks up the milk again and tries to pour it in the water. She puts the milk down, turns around on her hand and knees, and says, "Boo." She then picks up the watch and puts it in the water.) [Alia was still attempting to put the milk in water as a function of the instruction on the previous trial. From time to time, both she and Kanzi continued to attempt to do something they had difficulty with on previous trials.]

453. (C) *Take your ball out.* (Kanzi's ball is in the water when this sentence is uttered. Kanzi does so.)

453A. (NG).

454. (PC) *Give the big tomato to Liz.* (Kanzi picks up both the big and the little tomato and gives them to Liz.) [PC is scored because this is not a "multiple-object error" but rather a confusion between the words *big* and *little*. Kanzi consistently confuses these words throughout the test.]

454A. (PC) *Take the big tomato to Linda.* (Alia gets up and then kneels down next to the dishpan. She pulls it closer to her and plays with the water.) E says, "Alia, take the big tomato to Linda." (Alia says, "OK," then continues to play with the water.) E says, "Now." (Alia turns the dishpan around.) E says, "Eh um." (Alia picks up the small tomato and puts it in the bowl.)

Error correction.—E elects to continue to allow Alia to play with the water and the tomato, wanting to see if she will respond properly to the sentence when she has completed the activity that appears to be engaging her attention at the moment. (Alia picks up the bowl and moves it to the other side of her body. She then dumps the tomato out of the bowl and onto the floor. She slaps the bowl against the floor. She picks up the little tomato and puts it in the bowl. She dumps it out again.) E decides that Alia is not going to respond on her own and says, "Alia, can you take the big tomato to Linda?" (Alia puts down the bowl and picks up the little tomato. Alia uses the dishpan to help push herself up. It slides out from under her and splashes some water out.) E says, "Get off the water, let go of the water." (Alia lets go of the water.) E says, "Stand up without the water." (Alia takes the little tomato over to a child's table and puts it down. She hits the tomato with her hand and makes it roll.)

455. (PC) *Show me the little bitty tomato* . . . (Kanzi interrupts) . . . *the little itty bitty tomato.* (Kanzi points to the large tomato.) E says, "That's the big tomato. Show me the little tomato. Do you see the little tomato?" (Kanzi picks up the big tomato.)

455A. (C) *Show me the little tomato.* (Alia picks up the little tomato and squeezes it.) E says, "Don't squeeze it. Now do you see the big tomato?" (Alia picks up the big tomato and says, "Big.")

456. (C2) *Put the milk in the water.* (Kanzi is still poking the tomato with his thumb from trial 455 while he listens to the sentence. After the sentence, he picks up that tomato and puts it in the water.) E says, "Put the milk in the water." (Kanzi pours the milk in the water.) [This is a re-presentation of trial 451 to determine what Kanzi will do if the container of milk is open, rather than closed, when the sentence is presented. Note that Kanzi's continued interest in the item mentioned in the previous trial is very similar to Alia's behavior on trial 451. The fact that Kanzi now pours the milk directly into the water validates the interpretation of the difficulty he encountered on trial 451.]

456A. (C) *Put the milk in the water.* (The milk is in a closed plastic container that Alia cannot open. She first tries to open it but cannot. She then makes a pouring motion over the water, but nothing comes out.) E says, "Put the whole thing in the water," but Alia refuses. She continues to try to pour the milk out of the closed container after attempting to open the container. [The camera was accidentally not operating during this trial.]

457. (C3) *Wash Rose's hand.* (Kanzi very hesitantly takes a little bit of water and looks at Rose, who ignores him. He touches his finger with the water on it to Rose's hand.) Rose holds the radio in both hands stiffly as though she does not want her hands washed. Finally, she opens one hand slightly. (Kanzi seems hesitant, not knowing whether he should attempt to carry out the action more completely.) E says, "Put her hand in the water and wash it, wash it." (Kanzi gently pulls Rose's hand toward and into the bin of water as she now allows him to move her hand.)

457A. (C) *Wash Nathaniel's hand.* (Alia picks up the towel from the object array and goes to Nathaniel. Nathaniel, who has heard what E has said, has his hand out for Alia, ready to be washed. Alia uses the towel to wash Nathaniel's hand.)

458. (C) *Wash it good.* (Rose's hand is in the water when this sentence is presented. Kanzi rubs Rose's hand very briefly with his own, then says, "Sweet potato," indicating that, in his opinion, he has completed this activity and would like to eat a sweet potato.) [This sentence was presented because, even when Kanzi had placed Rose's hand in the water during the preceding trial, his attempt to "wash" it was abbreviated. E wanted to ascertain that Kanzi could respond to the verb *wash* appropriately. In this case, his response is again very perfunctory but sufficient to suggest that he comprehended the intent of the verb.]

458A. (NG).

459. (C) *Take the tomato to the bedroom.* (Kanzi picks up the tomato and points to the bedroom door, but Rose does not see him do so. He then looks at her and gestures to the bedroom, but she still does not realize what he is doing.) E says, "Tell Rose you want her to open it." (Kanzi gestures again toward the bedroom.) Rose says, "You showing me the bedroom?" Rose touches the door and looks at Kanzi. (Kanzi again gestures to the bedroom.) Rose says, "You want me to open this for you?" Kanzi touches "sweet potato" at the keyboard, and Rose comments, "You've been eating sweet potatoes," then asks, "You want me to open this?" (Kanzi again gestures to the bedroom.) Rose opens the door. (Kanzi takes the small tomato that is in his hand into the bedroom.) [C is scored because Kanzi quite clearly understands what he is to do but has difficulty conveying to Rose that she is to open the bedroom door, even though he gestures directly toward the door. He does not walk over to the door and point at it, as he often does, and Rose seems hesitant to infer the obvious from Kanzi's gesture. Kanzi's request for "sweet potatoes" is made after several clear gestures toward the door have been ignored. Kanzi appears to conclude that Rose is not going to open the door for him, so he switches topics. At this point, however, Rose again queries Kanzi about the door, and Kanzi again indicates that she should open the door. When she does, he correctly completes the request.]

459A. (PC) *Take the tomato to the bedroom.* (Alia gets up and points at the camera, saying something U. She then picks up the tomato and goes over to the table. She plays with the toys on the table and says something U.) E says, "Alia, take the tomato to the bedroom." (Alia says something U, then takes the tomato to the bathroom. She sets the tomato on the edge of the tub and says, "Uh oh," and the tomato rolls down into the tub.)

460. (C) *See the tomato that's in the water?* . . . (Kanzi interrupts.) . . . *Take the tomato to the refrigerator.* (Kanzi takes the tomato out of the water and carries it to the small refrigerator, where he puts it in and closes the door.)

460A. (W) *See the tomato that's in the water? Take it to the refrigerator.* (Alia sits on her chair for a few seconds. Then she gets up and goes over to the cabinets. She opens a cabinet and gets the bubbles.) E says, "Alia, put the bubbles back. Come here, I'll help you." (Alia puts the bubbles back.) E says, "Close the door. Come back over here." (Alia closes the door.)

Error correction.—E says, "Come here. Let me tell you again. Go sit down." (Alia goes back and sits down.) E says, "See the tomato that's in the water?" (Alia goes over to the dishpan, looks in, and says something U.) E says, "Take it to the refrigerator." (Alia goes over to Jeannine and says "Mommy" several times.) E says, "What?" (Alia says, "Come on.") E says, "Where are we going?" (Alia says, "Refrigerator.") E says, "Oh, the refrigerator." E opens the refrigerator for Alia. (One of the magnets falls off, and Alia picks it up.) E says, "Did you want me to open this?" (Alia looks inside the refrigerator and gets a tomato.)

461. (C) *Get Rose by the hand.* . . . (Kanzi interrupts.) . . . *Get Rose's hand* . . . (Kanzi extends his hand to Rose, and Rose puts her hand in his while E is trying to finish the sentence) . . . *and take her to the colony room.* (Rose rubs Kanzi's thumb and lets go of his hand.) E says, "Take Rose to the colony room." (Kanzi takes Rose's hand again, leads her to the colony room, and waits for her to open the door.) [C is scored because Kanzi appears to understand the sentence and is ready to take Rose to the

colony room when she takes her hand out of his. The repetition results from Rose's terminating the interaction rather than Kanzi's hesitancy. Rose withdrew her hand because she did not know what E had asked Kanzi to do and assumed that the requested action was completed.]

461A. (W) *Get Nathaniel by the hand and take him to Karen's room.* (Alia looks at Nathaniel, then at the array of objects in front of her. She picks up the knife with her left hand as she touches the ball, then the box of sparklers, with her right hand. She then picks up the knife with both hands, looks over to Nathaniel, turns back to the objects, hesitates, then pokes the ball with the knife and continues to push the ball along the floor with the knife.) E says, "Alia, get Nathaniel by the hand and take him to Karen's room." (Alia carries the knife over to Nathaniel and waves the knife in front of Nathaniel. She then carries the knife to the doorway of Karen's room. Nathaniel does not follow her. Alia stops and waves the knife toward Karen's room, then carries the knife into the bathroom.)

462. (C3) *Give the TV to Liz. Give the TV to Liz.* (The television is not in the array in front of Kanzi but several feet away. Kanzi walks over to the television, points to it, and looks directly at Liz. Seeing this communication directed toward her, Liz holds her hands out toward Kanzi. Kanzi hesitates, as though he is uncertain as to how to give the television to Liz. He is generally not allowed to pick up the television and carry it around for fear that he will drop and break it.) E says, "Pick it up and give it to her, Kanzi." (Kanzi does so.)

462A. (NG). [Alia was too small to pick up the television.]

463. (C5) *Go to the bedroom and get the tomato.* . . . (Kanzi interrupts, making a sound like "tomato.") . . . *Go to the bedroom and.* . . . (Kanzi picks up the tomato in front of him.) E says, "No, no, put that one down, put it down." (Kanzi vocalizes and then tosses that tomato onto the floor.) E says, "Now, go to the bedroom and get the tomato." (Kanzi goes to the bedroom and finds a small tomato by the mattress.) E says, "Did you get it?" (Kanzi responds with a vocalization that sounds like "get it.") [C5 is scored because Kanzi attends to the tomato in the immediate array and has to be asked not to do so before he carries out the sentence appropriately.]

463A. (PC) *Go to the bedroom and get the tomato.* (Alia heads toward the back rooms, stopping at the entrance to the bedroom. She does not bother to look in the bedroom but goes to the refrigerator, where she retrieves a potato.)

464. (C5) *Go to the refrigerator and get a tomato.* (Kanzi picks up the tomato in the array.) E says, "Huh un, no, put it down." (Kanzi puts it in the bin of water in front of him.) E says, "Go to the refrigerator and get a tomato." (Kanzi vocalizes right after *refrigerator,* then heads off toward the refrigerator, where he waits on the potty and gestures for Rose to open the refrigerator. It is usually open, but in this case the sliding door in front of the refrigerator is closed. Kanzi points to a bag of small tomatoes. Rose gives them to him, and he heads back to E, holding them up to his tummy and sort of slapping them as he goes. The bag breaks open, and the tomatoes spill over the floor.)

464A. (PC) *Go to the refrigerator and get a tomato.* (Alia goes to the refrigerator.) E says, "I'll open it." (Alia gets a potato and says, "Tato.") E laughs and says, "Potato. *Error correction.*—Alia, how about a tomato?" (Alia puts the potato back and looks for a tomato.) E says, "Do you see a tomato?" (Alia points to a bowl of cut-up tomatoes.)

465. (PC) *Put the melon in the tomato.* (Kanzi puts the melon in the water.)

Error correction.—E says, "Put the melon in the tomato." (Kanzi takes the melon out and puts it on top of a quart bottle that has water in it.) E says, "In the tomatoes." (Kanzi puts the melon in the tomatoes.)

465A. (C3) *Put the peaches in the tomatoes.* (Alia says, "OK." She goes over, gets a can of peaches, and tries to open it. She then goes to E and says, "Mommy open.") E says, "No, I'm not going to open it." (Alia says, "Open Mommy," as she holds the peaches out toward Jeannine.) E says, "Put the can of peaches in the tomatoes." (Alia continues to try to open the can.) "Put the can in, Alia. Don't open it. OK?" (Alia says, "OK.") E says, "Put the can of peaches in the tomatoes." (Alia says, "OK," but continues to try to open it.) E says, "Put the can of peaches in the tomatoes." (Alia says, "Mommy open it.") E says, "No, no open. Just put the can in." (Alia mumbles something U and holds the can out toward E.) E says, "No." (Alia stamps her feet.) E says, "Put the whole thing in. Go put this in the tomatoes. OK?" (Alia goes over to the tomatoes and tries to *pour* the peaches into the tomatoes. She cannot because the can is not opened. She starts picking up tomatoes.) [Alia's response here emphasizes again the accuracy of the interpretation given to her behavior on trial 451. Both she and Kanzi are unwilling to respond to a request to mix foods when one of the items is in a container that they cannot open.]

466. (C) *Tickle Rose with the sparklers.* (Kanzi picks up the sparklers and starts taking them all out of the package.) Kanzi does not hesitate and appears to be carrying out the sentence; however, E repeats, "Tickle Rose with the sparklers." (Kanzi takes something out, but it is just the plastic cover for one of the sparklers. He drops it, gets out a sparkler, touches it to Rose, and waits for some signal that it is OK to proceed. Rose ignores Kanzi, so he puts the sparkler down.) [C is scored because Kanzi's behavior indicates that he understands the sentence but is waiting for some indication that Rose also understands the sentence and is willing to participate in the two-way interaction of a tickling game.]

Response refinement.—E says, "Can you tickle her some more?" (Kanzi takes out another sparkler, again touches it to Rose, and waits for her to respond.) Rose still does not respond. E says, "Tickle her some more, tickle her some more." (Kanzi touches Rose in other places on her body with the sparkler, but still Rose does not respond.)

466A. (C) *Tickle Nathaniel with the sparkler.* (Alia does so.)

467. (I) *Pour the water on the tomatoes.* (Kanzi puts the tomato in the water. The water is in a large bin that is difficult to lift.)

Error correction.—E says, "Pour it out, on top of the tomato." (Kanzi pokes his finger in the tomato.) E says, "Pick up the bin and pour the water on the tomato." (Kanzi takes the tomato out of the water and shakes the water off of it.) E says, "Use the other water." (Kanzi licks the tomato. Rose touches his hand to remind him that he is not supposed to eat the tomato.) E says, "Use the other water, the water in the bottle. See the water in the bottle?" (Kanzi puts the tomato back in the bin of water.) E says, "Pour it on the tomato." (Kanzi picks up both the tomato and the water, one in each hand, and then drinks the water, taking it into his mouth and pouring it out of his mouth onto the tomato, as he did in trial 439.)

467A. (C) *Pour the water on the tomato.* (Alia picks up the bowl of water with her left hand and at the same time tries to pick up the bowl that has a whole tomato in it. She dumps the tomato out of the bowl, pours some of the water into the old tomato bowl and then the rest on top of the tomato. Alia then places the tomato back into its original bowl, which now has some water in it.)

468. (C) *Open the melon.* (Kanzi dips the melon in the water to wash it, as is generally done with all fruit at the lab before it is prepared. Kanzi seems interested in washing it well but is hesitating.) E says, "Open the melon." (Kanzi picks up a sparkler, takes it out of the package, and attempts to use it to open the melon. The sparkler makes a small hole in the melon.) [C is scored because washing the melon is viewed as part of the general routine that is required prior to food preparation. E's repetition is not a function of Kanzi's hesitancy but appears designed to encourage Kanzi to shorten the washing process and carry out the request. The use of a sparkler as a tool to open the melon was a novel activity on Kanzi's part, completely without precedent. It seems probable that the test sentences themselves are encouraging such novel solutions to simple everyday problems.

Response refinement.—E is somewhat surprised at Kanzi's solution as to how to open the melon and wonders why a much more direct route is not taken. Consequently, E says, "Bite it open. Bite it open." (Kanzi continues working to open the melon with the sparkler.) Observing that Kanzi seems to prefer to use a tool rather than his teeth, E inquires, "Do you need a knife?" (Kanzi makes a sound like "yes.") E says, "Would you like a knife to open the melon with?" (Kanzi attempts to say "un hmmm," then retrieves the knife from E and begins inserting it into the melon.) E says, "Open it up." (Kanzi continues to insert the knife, trying to split the melon in half.) E says, "Can you get it open?" (Kanzi continues trying to split the melon in half with the knife.) E says, "That's almost . . . pretty good." (Kanzi gets the melon almost completely sliced through with the knife, then puts it down on the floor and pulls it apart with his hands.)

468A. (C) *Open the peaches.* (Alia does so.)

469. (C3) *Put the tomatoes in the melon.* (Kanzi looks around and appears hesitant and puzzled.) E says, "Put the *tomato* in the melon." (Kanzi picks up a little tomato and puts it in the melon.) [C3 is scored because the minor rephrasing here, from the plural to the singular, may have helped Kanzi, who seemed immediately to know what to do after the sentence was rephrased. The rephrasing from plural to singular was intentional and was given in response to the puzzled expression on Kanzi's face.]

469A. (C) *Put the peaches in the strawberries.* (Alia does so.)

470. (C) *Go to the T-room and get a potato.* (Kanzi does so.)

470A. (PC) *Go to the bathroom and get the potato.* (Alia goes outdoors and gets a potato.)

471. (C) *Go to the refrigerator and get some ice.* (Kanzi makes a sound like "ice," heads off to the small refrigerator, and eats the ice from the outside of the cooler compartment.) Observing this, Rose offers to open the freezer door, which is stuck, as Kanzi appears to be trying to get ice. (Kanzi takes the ice out and brings it back.)

471A. (C) *Go to the refrigerator and get some ice.* (Alia goes to the refrigerator.) E opens the refrigerator door. (Alia retrieves the ice.)

472. (PC) *Go back to the refrigerator and get the knife.* (Kanzi goes directly to the drawer that holds the silverware, getting out a knife and a potato masher. He puts the knife in the small refrigerator, then takes it out again, then sits and eats the ice just outside the refrigerator after opening the refrigerator door for a few minutes. He then puts the ice in the refrigerator and closes the door.)

472A. (PC) *Go back to the refrigerator and get the knife.* (Alia goes to Karen's room and returns with a knife.)

473. (PC) *Go outdoors and get the milk.* (Kanzi starts to take the milk that is in the grouproom.) E says, "No, not that milk. Go outdoors and get the milk." (Kanzi goes to the refrigerator and gets a banana.)

473A. (C) *Go outdoors and get the milk.* (Alia does so.)

474. (C) *Take the ice back to the refrigerator.* (Kanzi does so.)

474A. (C4) *Take the ice back to the refrigerator.* (Alia gets up, picks up the ice, and goes into the kitchen. She stops to play with the knobs on the stove.) "Alia, you don't touch that." (Alia goes over to the refrigerator.) E opens the refrigerator door. (Alia puts the ice in the refrigerator.) [C4 is scored because Alia has to be stopped from playing with the knobs on the stove before she carries out the sentence correctly.]

475. (PC) *Go to the tool room and get a stick. Go to the tool room and get a stick. The tool room.* (Kanzi looks directly at E and gestures toward her.) E is sitting between Kanzi and the tool room, behind the blind. There is a longer route to the tool room, but Kanzi appears to be thinking about the direct route. E says, "You need to go to the tool room where you work and get a stick." (Kanzi appears to be trying to figure out how he should go to the tool room as he wants to go through the area where E is sitting behind a one-way mirror.) E, hoping that Kanzi will take the longer route, says, "You can't do that." (Kanzi stands and stares directly at the door where E is located.) E inquires, "You want to come through here? Well come on." E then explains to Rose, saying, "He wants to go this way, Rose." Rose says, "Huh?" and then takes off her headphones as she sees E open the door and that E can no longer be blind. (Once permitted to walk through the area that E is using for the blind, Kanzi goes to the window of the tool room and looks in. Rose opens the door. Kanzi enters but brings back a dish instead of a stick.)

Error correction.—E sends Kanzi back to the tool room for a stick. (Kanzi gets a knife, starts back with it, but appears to stop and reflect, puts it down, and gets a stick instead.)

475A. (W) *Go to the kitchen and get a stick.* (Prior to saying the sentence, E comes from behind the mirror and instructs Alia.) "Listen to Mommy and only do what Mommy tells you. Only get the things that Mommy tells you. OK? OK? Just what Mommy says." (Alia says, "OK.") E goes behind the mirror and says, "Go to the kitchen and get a stick." (Alia goes to the bathroom, stops at the doorway and looks inside, then turns and goes to the bedroom doorway. Then she walks back toward the living room and says, "Mom, I can't find any stick." She returns to the testing array and repeats, "I can't find any stick.")

Error correction.—(Alia knows that she has not retrieved the requested object and begins walking around the trailer looking for it. She sees it in the kitchen and says, "I find the stick. I go get it. It's in there." Alia turns back, goes into the kitchen, and retrieves the stick.)

476. (C) *Pour the milk in the bowl.* (Kanzi does so.)

476A. (C) *Pour the milk in the bowl.* (Alia does so.)

477. (C) *Put the orange in the milk.* (Kanzi does so, while making a sound like "milk.")

477A. (W) *Put the orange in the milk.* (Alia stays in her chair and does not respond.) E says, "Put the orange in the milk." (Alia picks up the bottle of Perrier water.) E says, "Alia, put the orange in the milk." (Alia drinks the Perrier water.)

Error correction.—E says, "Put the orange in the milk." (Alia starts to pick up the bottle of Perrier water.) E says, "No more water. Don't spill it. Be careful. Put the orange in the milk." (Alia looks at the orange but then picks up the ball. She says, "Ball." She then tries to pick up the bowl of milk and spills it. Alia says, "Uh oh, uh oh." She gets a sponge and tries to wipe up the milk.) E says, "Alia, can you put the orange in the milk?" (Alia says, "Uh oh.") E says, "Put the orange in the milk." (Alia says, "Uh oh, Mommy.") E says, "That's okay. Put the orange in the milk." (Alia continues to try to clean up the spill.)

478. (C) *Pour the Perrier water in the milk.* (Kanzi does so.)

478A. (PC) *Pour the Perrier water in the milk.* (Alia stays in her chair and does not respond.) E says, "Pour the Perrier water in the milk." (Alia remains seated and still does not respond.) E says, "Pour the Perrier water in the milk. Alia, pour the Perrier water in the milk." (Alia picks up the Perrier water.) E says, "Pour it in the milk. Pour it in the milk." (Alia drinks some of the water, spilling it as she does so.)

Error correction.—E says, "Pour the Perrier water in the milk." (Alia says, "Ut oh.") E says, "That's okay. Can you pour the Perrier water in the milk? Quit drinking it. That's all. Pour the Perrier water in the milk. Alia. No more drinking. Pour the Perrier water in the milk. Pour it in the milk." (Alia continues to drink the water.) E says, "No more drinking. Pour the Perrier water in the milk." (Alia just sits there.) E says, "Can you pour it in the milk? Alia, pour it in the milk. Perrier water in the milk." (Alia drinks the water.) E says, "No. No. Don't drink it. Pour the Perrier water in the milk." (Alia says something U and picks up the ball.)

479. (C3) *Pour the Perrier water in the bowl.* (Kanzi picks up the can of juice and looks as though he is going to start drinking it.) E says, "No, put that down." Rose takes the juice away. E says, "Pour the Perrier water in the bowl." (Kanzi makes sounds like "Perrier" and "water.") Kanzi picks up the Perrier bottle and takes the cap.) E says, "Pour it in the bowl." (Kanzi says, "Hmm," and pours it in the bowl.)

479A. (PC) *Pour the Perrier water in the bowl.* (Alia picks up the milk and shakes it. She then pours the milk in the bowl and says, "Look Mommy.") E says, "OK."

480. (C) *Pour the Coke in the bowl.* (Kanzi does so.)

480A. (C) *Pour the Coke in the bowl.* (Alia picks up the Coke and tries to pour it in the bowl, but she does not tilt it over far enough, and nothing comes out. She sets the Coke down and puts her finger in the opening on the can.) E says, "Alia, don't do that, you'll hurt your finger. Leave the top alone." (Alia tries to pour the Coke in the bowl again but does not succeed. She looks in a different container. She then touches the top of the Coke can.) [C is scored because Alia's behavior indicates that she understands the sentence even if she is not able to carry it out properly.]

481. (C) *Go to the bedroom and get the shot.* (Kanzi does so.)

481A. (PC) *Go to the bedroom and get the shot.* (Alia goes to the bedroom. She says something U, picks up the watch, puts it down, then picks up the shot. She picks up another object that cannot be identified from the tape and places both objects behind her back. She then puts the watch behind her back, puts the shot down, and returns with the watch.)

482. (C) *Pour the lemonade in the bowl.* (Kanzi does so.)

482A. (C) *Pour the lemonade in the bowl.* (Alia does so.)

483. (C2) *Go to the bedroom and get the collar.* (Kanzi goes to the T-room, where collars are normally located, picks up a collar, then opens the stuffed animal cabinet as he wants to play with these toys.) Rose asks Kanzi to close the cabinet and says, "Let's go back and see what Sue wants.") E says, "I need a collar that's in the bedroom." (Kanzi retrieves the collar from the bedroom.) [C2 is scored because Kanzi immediately carried out the sentence when it was repeated.]

483A. (NR) *Go to the bedroom and get the watch.* (Alia remains sitting on her chair and does not respond.) E says, "Alia, go to the bedroom and get the watch." (Alia goes to Nathaniel and says something U.) E says, "Alia." (Nathaniel says to Alia, "Go into the bedroom and get the watch.") E says to Nathaniel, "Nathaniel, you be quiet. I'll say it. Alia, come here and leave Nathaniel alone. Come here, please. Alia, leave Nathaniel alone now. Come here." (Alia laughs and goes back to E.) E says, "Now sit in your chair again. Sit down. Now listen to Mommy. OK? All right? Ready? OK. Now listen. Alia, go to the bedroom and get the watch." (Alia falls off her chair and rolls on the ground laughing.)

484. (C) *Give the doggie some yogurt.* (Kanzi does so.)

484A. (C2) *Give the doggie some yogurt.* (Alia first opens the yogurt and rubs some of it on the rug, tries to pick up the bowl of Coke, knocks the Coke can on the rug, says, "This doggie," points to the toy dog, and moves the bowl of lemonade around.) E says, "Give the doggie some yogurt." (Alia takes the top on and off the yogurt.) E says, "Give the doggie some yogurt." (Alia takes the top on and off the yogurt, says something U.) E says, "Alia, give the doggie some yogurt. Give the doggie some yogurt." (Alia says something U.) E says, "Huh?" (Alia puts the top back on the yogurt and says, "Did it, Mommy." E says, "Can you give the doggie some yogurt?" (Alia says, "Nope.") E says, "Why not?" (Alia spills more yogurt and rubs it on the rug and the chair.) E says, "Alia, give the doggie some yogurt." (Alia says, "[Something U] need spoon, Mommy. Ma, spoon.") E says, "No, just give the doggie yogurt." (Alia spills the yogurt, then dips the lid in the yogurt and uses it as a spoon, pulling the doggie to her while saying, "Come here, doggie." Then she gives the dog some yogurt using the lid.) [This is scored as C2 because Alia's difficulty seemed to be that there was no spoon in the array. Lacking a spoon for the yogurt would never have bothered Kanzi, as he prefers not to use spoons.]

485. (C1) *Go outdoors and get the lighter.* (Kanzi goes to the play-yard door and opens it himself. He goes outside, sits on a log, picks up his ball, then looks around at what is happening outside.) Rose says, "Kanzi, why don't you bring *it* to Sue?" (Kanzi puts down the ball, picks up the lighter, and brings it back.) [C1 is scored because Kanzi picks up the ball first before bringing the lighter. There is no reason to assume that Rose's request helped Kanzi since, if he thought that her use of the word *it* referred to the item in his hand, he would have returned with the ball. He apparently knew that *it* referred to the item that E had asked him to obtain.]

485A. (NR) *Go outdoors and get the matches.* (Alia goes and hides, commenting, "I'm hiding." E continues to try to get Alia to carry out this request, and Alia continues to refuse.)

486. (C) *Pour the Coke in the lemonade.* (Kanzi does so.)

486A. (PC) *Pour the Coke in the lemonade.* (Alia picks up the lemonade container and tries to toss it into the bowl of lemonade, then picks it up, looks inside it, and tries to shake out some lemonade. She puts the lemonade can down, saying, "Down." She then does the same thing with the Coke can, trying to pour it into the bowl of Coke. When it won't come out, she starts to stick her finger in the hole.) E says, "Alia, don't put your finger in there," referring to the sharp opening on the Coke can.

487. (C2) *Go to the refrigerator and get the toothbrush.* (Kanzi goes to the T-room and sort of wanders around.) Rose says, "What did Sue ask you for?" (Kanzi just pauses and does nothing.) Rose says, "Here, go listen to her again." Kanzi comes back and sits down, and Rose says to him, "We're gonna listen again. Listen to her again." E says, "Go to the refrigerator and get the toothbrush." (Kanzi goes to the little refrigerator and gets the toothbrush.)

487A. (C) *Go to the refrigerator and get the toothbrush.* (Alia does so.)

488. (C) *Pour the lemonade in the Coke.* (Kanzi does so, making a sound like "lemonade.")

488A. (PC) *Pour the lemonade in the Coke.* (Alia says, "Coke, Coke," picks up the lemonade can, and pours it in the lemonade. Then she says, "Coke," picks up the Coke can, says, "Coke," and tries to pour the Coke in the lemonade, then in the Coke, then in the lemonade, then back in the Coke. Then she looks in the Coke can.) E says, "Alia, don't put your finger in there." (Alia resumes trying to pour the Coke into the Coke.)

489. (C3) *Put a sparkler in the Coke can.* (Kanzi picks up the Coke can, looks at it, then picks up a lighter with the other hand and tries to make a fire come out.) E says, "Put a sparkler in the Coke can." (Kanzi picks up the sparklers, still holding the Coke can and the lighter, and takes out a sparkler, letting go of the Coke can. He then picks up the lighter and tries to light it, holding it in his feet and trying to turn the wheel with his finger. He repeatedly gets a flame, but not enough to ignite the sparkler. E comes out and says, "Here, I'll hold the lighter for you." (E does, and Kanzi holds the sparkler in the flame of the lighter, trying to ignite it. Once it ignites, he tosses it on the floor.) E then says, "How are you gonna put it in the Coke can?" (Kanzi takes out a second sparkler and touches it to the flame on the first sparkler to ignite the sparkler. Kanzi then watches the sparklers burn down. When

they stop, he pokes at them with the sparkler box, then tries to put a sparkler that has come out back in the box.) E says, "Now Kanzi, put a sparkler in the Coke can. (Kanzi continues to try to put a burned sparkler back in the box.) E says, "In the Coke." (Kanzi then picks up the Coke can and inserts a sparkler in it.) [C3 is scored because Kanzi executes the sentence but rephrasing was needed and appeared to help him. His initial confusion appeared to derive from a failure to understand the word *can* as a modifier of *Coke*. Kanzi appeared to think that E was asking if he *can* light the sparklers and put them in the Coke. When E recognizes this difficulty and asks Kanzi to put the sparklers in the *Coke* rather than in the *Coke can*, he responds correctly at once. E agreed to help Kanzi on this trial since he was trying to do something rather dangerous, i.e., light a sparkler. Both Kanzi and Alia were helped in such instances by E, although Kanzi needed assistance much less often than Alia. Whenever this occurs, it is noted in the transcription.]

489A. (C2) *Put a sparkler in the Coke can.* (Alia says, "Coke can, Coke, Coke, Coke," picks up the Coke can, and tries to pour out some Coke on her hand, then shakes her hand over the bowl of Coke, then tries to pour the Coke from the can into the bowl of Coke.) E says, "Put a sparkler in the Coke can." (Alia does so.)

490. (C) *Go get the . . .* (Kanzi interrupts) *. . . go get the carrot that's in the microwave.* (Kanzi goes to the microwave, makes a sound like "carrot," gets the carrot out, and brings it back.)

490A. (OE) *Go get the carrot that's in the oven.* (Alia goes to the oven and tries to open it, then says, "I can't do this." She tries again and says, "Mommy, I can't do this.") E inquires, "You need help?" (Alia says, "Yeah, I need help.") E comes from behind the mirror and opens the oven drawer. Alia gets out the soap, then the carrot, saying, "There's carrot." She then carries the carrot and the soap a few feet toward the living room but stops suddenly, turns back to the oven, and says, "Mom, close this now.") E says, "I don't need to close it." (Alia says, "Going to leave that hat," and points to the hat she left in the oven.) E says, "OK." (Alia turns back toward the living room and continues to carry the carrot and the soap there.) E says, "Bring it over here, Alia." (Alia carries the carrot and the soap to E, says, "Give Mommy the carrot, here," hands E the carrot, then repeats, "Here," hands E the soap, then starts to walk away.) E says, "Alia, point to the carrot, Alia, point to the carrot." (Alia does so.) [OE is scored because Alia brings two items and does not produce any vocal remarks about the added item, soap.]

491. (C3) *Put the toothbrush in the lemonade.* (Kanzi picks up the lemonade can, looks in it, and finds it is empty. He then puts it down and picks up the quart bottle of water as though he is thinking of making lemonade.) E says, "Put the toothbrush in the lemonade." (Kanzi picks up the lemonade can and places it upside down over the water bottle as though pouring lemonade in the water. Both containers are empty, but he appears to be playing like he is making lemonade.) E says, "You see the lemonade?" (Kanzi says, "Uh hmm.") E says, "You see the toothbrush?" "Where's the toothbrush?" Kanzi picks up the toothbrush and puts it in the quart bottle of water, which has had the imaginary lemonade poured into it.) [C3 is scored because Kanzi appears to be putting the toothbrush in the imaginary lemonade that he has "made." While this may not be the case, Kanzi frequently does hide imaginary food,

chew imaginary food, give others imaginary food, steal imaginary food, etc., so it is possible that he is pretending here, as indeed he appears to be doing.]

Response refinement.—E says, "Put it in the lemonade," meaning the empty lemonade can. (Kanzi continues to put the toothpaste in and take it out of the quart water bottle as though stirring lemonade with the toothbrush, then acts as though he is drinking lemonade from the toothbrush.) E says, "No, put it in the lemonade. No, put the toothbrush in the lemonade." (Kanzi then picks up the empty lemonade can and acts briefly as though he is again pouring it in the lemonade, then licks the empty lemonade can, then acts again like he is pouring the lemonade in the water. [On watching the tape, it appeared that Kanzi was mixing imaginary lemonade with water, then putting the toothbrush in the "lemonade" that he had made. This seemed to occur because the lemonade can itself was empty and Kanzi could not carry out the sentence as presented to him.]

491A. (C) *Put the toothbrush in the lemonade.* (Alia places the toothbrush in the empty lemonade container.)

492. (C) *Take Rose to the refrigerator and get some food. Get Rose by the hand and take her to the refrigerator.* (Kanzi touches Rose's hand with a "come" gesture and heads toward the refrigerator. He looks in for some time, picks out raisins and hands them to Rose, then opens the other side, picks out lettuce, and hands it to Rose, making a sound like "lettuce." He then picks out another food and hands it to Rose, again making a sound like "lettuce." He gestures for Rose to follow him and heads back.) [C is scored because Kanzi did not hesitate after the sentence was uttered the first time. E repeated the sentence because the lab was very noisy at the time.]

492A. (PC) *Take Joshua to the refrigerator and get some food.* (Alia goes to the refrigerator. Josh starts to follow Alia on his own but is asked to sit down. Alia ignores Josh and proceeds to the refrigerator. Alia tries to open the door but cannot and says, "I can't open this now. Open it. Ma, I can't open this.") E says, "I'll open it." (E opens the refrigerator door for Alia. Alia looks inside the refrigerator at the various foods for a while. When she finds things in the refrigerator, she asks E whether she can get them by holding the items up and saying, "This?" for each item of interest to her.) E shrugs her shoulders to encourage Alia to make her own selection. (Alia asks E if it is OK to take the Jello by holding up the box and saying, "This?")

493. (PC) *Go to the microwave.* . . . *No, let me try again.* . . . *Kanzi, get the phone and the wipies that are in the microwave.* (Kanzi goes to the play yard, stands in the doorway, and looks out as though he has heard a noise and is checking on things; then he turns, proceeds on to the microwave, gets the phone, and brings it back to E.)

493A. (C) *Get the phone and the wipies that are in the oven.* (Alia goes to the oven in the kitchen, gets only the wipies, and carries them back to the living room. Alia places the wipies with the array of objects in the living room, then returns to the oven in the kitchen, gets the phone out, and carries it back also.) [It is surprising that, on so many other trials when Alia is asked to bring only one object, she brings multiple objects and carries them all together. Now, when asked to retrieve two objects, she makes two trips, bringing only one object at a time.]

494. (C) *Open the Jello.* (Kanzi opens the Jello, then pours it on the egg in the array.) E says, "That is what I was going to ask you to do.")

494A. (C) *Open the Jello.* (Alia gets the Jello box open and then takes out the package of Jello. She tries to open the package also but is unable to do so. She tries for a long time, until E finally comes out and helps her. Then she expects to be able to eat some of it, but E does not permit her to. She becomes quite distraught, as though she expected that she would get to do so.)

495. (C) *Go get the rock that's outdoors.* (Kanzi goes to the play yard, opens the door, and looks out as though listening to something outdoors.) Rose says, "Show Sue, Kanzi." (Kanzi picks up the rock and brings it to E.) [C is scored because Rose's comment merely encourages Kanzi to return; it does not specify any item. Nor does Rose know what Kanzi has been asked to do; she assumes that he has been sent to get something.]

495A. (C) *Go get the rock that's outdoors.* (Alia goes to the front door, saying, "Get door. Get door. Get door.") E opens the door. (Alia says, "OK," and gets the rock.)

496. (C) *Go get the can opener that's in the bedroom.* (Kanzi does so.)

496A. (W) *Go get the fork that's in the bedroom.* (Alia goes toward the bedroom but stops on the way and looks in Karen's room, saying, "There's doggie, there's doggie," then something U. Then she goes in Karen's room and picks up a new doll that is part of the array there. She takes the doll halfway back, throws it on the floor, and goes to play.)

Error correction.—E returns with Alia to the array and says, "Go get the fork that's in the bedroom." (Alia does so.)

497. (C) *Can you open the juice?* (This is said while Kanzi is holding the can opener that he has just returned with from the previous trial.) Rose says, "Kanzi, listen to Sue." (Kanzi pulls the two sides of the can opener apart, as you do with this type of can opener before putting it on a can. He then begins to bang the top of the juice can with the can opener. He bangs very hard, just as he does when he is trying to bash rocks.) [C is scored as Kanzi is clearly trying to open the juice, even though his method is somewhat inept. Rose's comments only encourage him to listen; they do not redefine the sentence for him.]

Response refinement.—E says, "Hit it, hit it some more." (Kanzi sits down and opens the can opener again, as you do just before you latch it onto a can, then again bangs the top of the can with the can opener. Then he opens it again and tries to latch it onto the top edge of the can. When he cannot do this, he again bangs the top of the can. He tries again to open it and latch it onto the side of the can, but he is not successful and bangs the top of the can again. This time he succeeds in getting a small hole in the top of the can and then picks up the can and pours out some juice.)

497A. (C) *Can you open this juice?* (The juice is a box of juice that requires putting a straw in the top if it is to be opened. Alia takes the straw off the juice, then tries to get the paper off the straw. Unable to do so, she then tries to put the straw with the paper still on it into the hole on top of the juice.)

498. (W) *Go to the. . . . Go get the dog that's in the refrigerator.* (Kanzi goes to the microwave and gets the hat out, puts it on his head, and runs back.)

Error correction.—E says, "Kanzi, go get the dog that's in the refrigerator." (Kanzi goes to the microwave, looks in, then goes on to the little refrigerator, opens it up, and takes out an umbrella.) Rose says, "Kanzi, why don't you show Sue?" (Kanzi brings the umbrella back to E.) E says, "Kanzi, go get the doggie that's in the refrigerator. . . . Go get the doggie that's in the refrigerator." (Kanzi goes to the big refrigerator, opens it, and finds a ball, which he takes out. He then starts to get some food out.) Rose says, "Are you thinking about one of those? Look, I understand, go take that over." (Kanzi takes the ball to E.) E opens the door and says, "Rose, take him to the big refrigerator." Rose says, "That's where he was at. What's he need to get?" E says, "The doggie." Rose says, "Oh, OK," takes Kanzi back, asks him to get the dog, and he does.)

498A. (W) *Go to the refrigerator and get the dog.* (Alia says, "No," then, "OK," then goes to Karen's room and gets the doll.)

Error correction.—E returns with Alia to the array and says, "Go to the refrigerator and get the dog." (Alia does so.)

499. (C) *Open the Jello and pour it in the juice.* (Kanzi opens the Jello and pours it in the juice.)

499A. (C) *Open the Jello and pour it in the juice.* (Alia opens the Jello package, says something U as she gets it open, then pours it in the juice. Like Kanzi, she tries to keep on pouring until the package is empty rather than until the container with the juice in it is full.)

500. (C) *Get the lighter that's in the bedroom.* (Kanzi does so.)

500A. (C) *Get the matches that are in the bedroom.* (Alia runs into the bedroom. She looks in the playpen and says something U. She then gets the matches.)

501. (C1) *Put some oil on Rose.* (Kanzi takes a small taste of oil, then puts some on Rose.)

501A. (NG).

502. (C) *Pour the juice in the Jello.* (Kanzi does so.)

502A. (PC) *Pour the juice in the Jello.* (Alia says, "OK, juice, Jello, [something U]," then picks up the Jello and puts it to her mouth.) E says, "Don't eat it, Alia." (Alia says, "Dis, Alia," looks at the Jello, shakes it, looks at it again, then puts it down and picks up the juice, then starts to pick up the Jello again so that she can hold one container in each hand and pour. She then accidentally drops the Jello, straightens it, and sets the juice container on the Jello container.) E says, "Pour the juice in the Jello." (Alia then takes the juice and pours it into the bowl of water.)

503. (PC) *Take the telephone to the colony room.* (Kanzi goes to the colony room, taking nothing. Halfway there, he comes across an umbrella that he dropped near the refrigerator on a earlier trial, picks it up, and heads on with it in his mouth, taking it to the colony room.)

Error correction.—E says, "Kanzi, do you see the telephone?" (Kanzi says, "Whuuh.") E says, "Look at the telephone." (Kanzi picks up the receiver and holds it to his ear.) E says, "Yeah. Take it to the colony room. Would you take it to the colony room for me? Pick it up and take it to the colony room." (Kanzi licks the phone.) E says, "Uh hmmmm. . . . Kanzi, please take it to the colony room." Rose, who has taken off her headphones and is no longer blind, hangs up the receiver, shoves the phone toward Kanzi, and tells him to pick up the whole thing. Kanzi takes the phone to the colony room.

503A. (C) *Take the phone to Karen's room.* (Alia does so, then pretends to talk on it.)

504. (PC) *Pour the juice in the water.* (Kanzi pours the water in the water.)

Error correction.—E says, "Put the juice in the water." (Kanzi picks up the bowl of Jello, which is purple, just like the juice, and pours it in the bowl of water. He makes a sound like "juice" as he does so. He then tries to drink the mixture.) E says, "No, Kanzi, where's the juice?" (Kanzi picks up the can opener and begins pounding on the can of juice as though he thinks he needs to open it; perhaps this is why he did not pour it in the water.) E then says, "Pour it in the water." (Kanzi does so.)

504A. (C) *Pour the juice in the water.* (Alia does so.)

505. (C) *Get the rubber bands in the T-room.* (Kanzi goes to the T-room and points to the door. Rose opens it for him. Kanzi goes to the box of rubber bands, gets some, and returns.)

505A. (PC) *Get the rubber band that's in the bathroom.* (Alia goes to the toy shelf where a bag of rubber bands is usually found. She searches three bags but finds no rubber bands. She then gets clay and bark out and sits down to play with them. E says, "Alia, Alia, Alia, come here." (Alia says, "No.")

Error correction.—E comes out from behind the mirror and says, "Get the rubber band that's in the bathroom." (Alia does so.)

506. (C) *Take the hat to the colony room.* (Kanzi does so.)
506A. (C) *Take the hat to Karen's room.* (Alia does so.)

507. (C3) *Pour the juice in the egg.* (Kanzi picks up the bowl with the egg in it, smells it, and shakes the bowl to watch the egg wiggle.) E says, "Pour the juice in the egg." (Kanzi puts the egg down, picks up the can opener, opens it up, and tries to latch it onto the can.) E says, "It's already open, just pour it in." (Kanzi bangs on it with the can opener.) E says, "Kanzi, just pour it. Pick it up and pour it in." (Kanzi does so.)

507A. (C) *Pour the juice in the egg.* (Alia does so.)

508. (C) *Go get the lighter that's outdoors.* (Kanzi goes to the play yard, picks up the lighter, and starts flicking the lighter wheel with his thumb and looking around outside.) Rose says, "Show Sue." (Kanzi continues to try to activate the lighter.) Rose says, "Kanzi, show Sue." (Kanzi brings the lighter back.)

508A. (C) *Go get the matches that are outdoors.* (Alia does so.)

509. (C) *Take the toy gorilla to the T-room.* (Kanzi does so.)
509A. (C) *Take the toy gorilla to Karen's room.* (Alia does so.)

510. (C) *Put the egg in the juice.* (Kanzi makes a sound like "egg," then does so.)
510A. (C) *Put the egg in the juice.* (Alia does so.)

511. (NR) *Take the can opener to the bedroom.* (Kanzi just eats and does nothing.) E says, "Well, how about taking the lighter to the bedroom?" (Kanzi starts to pick up the sparklers.) E says, "No, the lighter." (Kanzi just sort of looks at the objects and does nothing.) E says, "Well, OK. Let's do something else right now." (Kanzi says, "Whuuh, whuuh, whuu.")

511A. (C2) *Take the fork to the bedroom.* (Alia picks up the fork and stabs the floor with it, rubs it in circles on the mirror, slaps the floor with it, then pretends that she is using it to eat with.) E says, "Alia, take the fork to the bedroom." (Alia says, "No.") E says, "Yes, please." (Alia hits the floor with the fork, runs the fork in circles over the plastic mat on the floor, says something U, and puts the fork on a chair.) E says, "Take the fork to the bedroom, Alia. Alia, listen to Mommy. Go do it, take the fork to the bedroom." (Alia says, "OK," then walks over to some books, fork in hand.) E says, "Right now." (Alia stands by the books doing nothing.) E says, "Take the fork to the bedroom." (Alia says something U and runs toward the bedroom.) E says, "Don't run." (Alia takes the fork to the bedroom.)

512. (C) *Take the juice to the bedroom.* (Kanzi does so, saying something that sounds like "juice" as he carries the juice to the bedroom.)

512A. (C) *Take the juice to the bedroom.* (Alia does so.)

513. (C) *Take the sparklers to the T-room.* (Kanzi does so.)

513A. (W) *Take the sparklers to Karen's room.* (Alia touches the sparklers, then picks up a bowl of Jello and takes it to the bedroom.)

514. (C) *Pour the oil in the bowl.* (Kanzi does so, saying something that sounds like "oil.")

514A. (C) *Put the oil in the bowl.* (Alia first puts oil on her finger and wipes the oil on a ball; she then wipes the oil into the bowl.) [This is not scored as doing something else first since Alia appears to be treating the word *bowl* as standing for both "ball" and "bowl."]

515. (OE) *Go get the stick that's outdoors.* (Kanzi heads outdoors, making a sound like "outdoors" as he pauses at the door to take the padlock off.) E says, "Bring it back." Rose says, "Kanzi, bring it to Sue, please." (Kanzi picks up the stick, the carrot, and the blanket and brings them all in.)

515A. (C) *Go get the stick that's outdoors.* (Alia does so.)

516. (C) *Put the ball in the oil.* (Kanzi does so.)

516A. (C1) *Put the ball in the oil.* (Alia says, "OK," then starts to pick up the tomato, but stops and picks up the ball, says something U, drops the ball, says, "Ball [something U]," retrieves the ball, says, "[Something U] go oil," and throws the ball in the oil.)

517. (PC) *Give the doggie and the cereal to Rose.* (Kanzi gives her only the cereal and then stops, without looking for anything else.)

517A. (PC) *Give the doggie and the cereal to Nathaniel.* (Alia picks up the cereal and tries to open it, but it does not open. She goes to E and says, "It open?" E says, "No, we don't open." Alia then takes it to Nathaniel, saying, "Nathaniel you," as she gives it to him. She seems to have forgotten about the dog as a result of concentrating on how to open the cereal.)

518. (C) *Pour the coffee in the bowl.* (Kanzi does so right away, but he pours so much that the bowl overflows.)

518A. (C2) *Pour the hot chocolate in the bowl.* (Alia does not respond.) There is a television playing loudly in the room. E asks that it be turned off and says, "Pour the hot chocolate in the bowl." (Alia picks up a spoon. She picks up the hot chocolate and puts the spoon down. She moves herself closer to the bowl. She rips the package and pours in the hot chocolate mix.)

519. (C) *Give the oil and the doggie to Rose.* (Kanzi picks up the dog with his right hand, transfers it to his left hand, picks up the bowl of oil, and starts to sneak a sip.) E says, "The oil and the doggie to Rose." (Kanzi makes a sound like "oil," turns, and hands the bowl of oil and the dog to Rose.) [C is scored because Kanzi does not hesitate but rather is taking a sip of the oil as he is handing it to Rose. E repeats the sentence to encourage Kanzi to go ahead.]

519A. (PC) *Give the oil and the doggie to Nathaniel.* (Alia says, "OK," picks up the dog, and carries it to Nathaniel, saying, "Here Nathaniel.")
Error correction.—Nathaniel corrects Alia by telling her that she needs to get the oil also.

520. (PC) *Put the doggie in the oil.* (Kanzi picks up the doggie and moves it aside, then puts his hand on the bowl of oil as if to pick it up, then suddenly picks up a quart container of orange drink and pours it in the oil.) E says, "Stop!" and removes the oil and the orange drink before Kanzi can drink it or play in it.
Error correction.—E starts the trial again, saying, "Kanzi, put the doggie in the oil." (Kanzi puts one hand on the oil and the other on the dog.) E says, "Kanzi, pick up the doggie and put him in the oil, put him in the bowl." (Kanzi picks up the bottle of baby oil and pours some oil into the doggie's mouth while making a sound like "oil," then, "Whuh.")

520A. (PC) *Put the doggie in the oil.* (Alia picks up the doggie, then the ball, says something U, then, "Doggie ball, doggie ball, doggie ball," then puts the ball to the doggie's mouth, saying, "There you go," then throws the ball away. E says, "Put the doggie in the oil." (Alia picks up the ball and says something U.) E says, "Alia, put the doggie in the oil." (Alia crawls away with the ball.) [Alia seems to have confused the words *ball* and *oil.*]

521. (C) *Go get the collar that's in the refrigerator. Go get the collar that's in the refrigerator.* (Kanzi goes to the refrigerator. Rose opens it for him, and he gets the collar.) E says, "Bring it back." (Kanzi looks at Rose.) Rose says, "Go show Sue." [At that point, E does not know whether Kanzi has retrieved the collar as he is out of sight. However, he has had time to do so if he understood the sentence.]

521A. (C) *Go get the watch that's in the refrigerator.* (Alia does so.)

522. (PC) *Give me Rose's cereal. Get Rose's cereal. Rose's cereal.* (Kanzi looks toward Rose.) E says, "Rose's cereal, pick it up, get her cereal, get her cereal. Kanzi, get Rose's cereal. Kanzi, Kanzi, go ahead, that's right, Kanzi, see Rose's cereal?" (Kanzi seems hesitant to take the cereal that is in Rose's lap since, when he reaches for it, she gives no indication that she is permitted to take it. Finally, Kanzi picks up a box of cereal from the array.)
Error correction.—E says, "Kanzi, Rose's cereal. No." (Kanzi continues to hold the

cereal from the array in his foot while eating a banana.) E says, "Kanzi, get Rose's cereal." (Kanzi points to Rose's hand.) E says, "Pick it up," referring to the cereal. Rose, who is blind and does not know what Kanzi has been asked to do, says, "Here's my hand. What do you want me to do?" (Kanzi touches her hand again.) E says, "Get Rose's cereal." (Kanzi hands Rose the box of cereal he has taken from the array.) E says, "Kanzi, get Rose's cereal." (Kanzi points to the box of cereal in Rose's lap.) Rose says, "This thing?" E says, "Yes," speaking to Kanzi. Rose points to the box of cereal in her lap repeatedly and looks at Kanzi with a quizzical expression on her face. E says, "Pick up, give me Rose's cereal." (Kanzi reaches for the milk in Rose's lap.) E says, "Go ahead, not the milk, the cereal. Give me Rose's cereal. Rose's cereal. The cereal that Rose has." (Kanzi picks up an item from the array and begins to eat it.) E says, "Put that down. Kanzi, can you get Rose's cereal?" (Kanzi touches the box of cereal on the cube next to Rose and looks at her for permission to have it. Rose hands Kanzi that box of cereal.) E opens the door and explains to Rose what Kanzi is to do. Rose then shows "her" cereal to Kanzi. (Kanzi looks very chagrined, as though he just does not know what to do.) [Several trials prior to the start of this trial a number of similar objects were placed in the array, in Rose's lap, and on the cube by Rose. The intent was to determine whether Kanzi showed some sensitivity to the possessive. Rose was not told that Kanzi would be asked to take something in her lap; hence, she did not understand what Kanzi was doing when he pointed to one of these objects. Kanzi was hesitant to take any object from Rose without her permission, and pointing to it was his way of asking to take it. However, Rose did not understand this. Similarly, defining a box of cereal as "Rose's" simply by physical placement did not seem to be understood either.]

522A. (PC) *Get Nathaniel's cereal.* (Alia says, "OK," picks up the cereal that is in the array, and hands it to Nathaniel, saying, "Here Nathaniel.")

523. (C) *Go get the apple that's in the microwave.* (Kanzi runs to the microwave, gets the apple out, and looks at Rose.) Rose says, "Go show Sue."

523A. (OE) *Go get the apple that's in the oven.* (Alia goes to the oven and opens the lower drawer, where she finds a ball, a box of raisins, and an apple. Alia first puts her hand on the apple but then picks up the ball and puts it on the floor. Then she decides to hold the ball as she grabs the box of raisins, then the apple, out of the oven drawer. She has trouble getting the apple out of the oven.)

Error correction.—E says, "Alia, just get the apple. Nothing else. Just the apple. Just bring me the apple." (Alia continues to try to carry the box of raisins under her chin as she holds the ball with her left hand and looks at the apple inside the oven drawer.) "Put everything else back. I just want the apple." (Alia puts the ball back into the oven but holds the box of raisins out to E and asks, "Eat this?") "Just the apple. You just bring me the apple, OK?" (Alia still holds onto the box of raisins in her right hand as she reaches for the apple in the oven with her left hand. The apple drops back into the oven. Alia turns back to E, holds out the box of raisins again, and asks something U, as if wanting the raisins to eat later.) "Listen to Mommy. Just bring the apple." (Alia repeats, "Apple," reaches into the oven drawer for the apple, but continues to hold onto the raisins with her right hand.) E says, "Just the apple. Put everything back. Just the apple." (Alia gets the apple out of the oven drawer, then holds the box of raisins out to E and asks, "This?") "Put everything else back.

I just want the apple." (Alia drops the box of raisins into the oven drawer as E repeats.) "Just bring me the apple." (Alia then carries the apple to E.)

524. (C) *Put the doggie in the refrigerator.* (Kanzi looks back and forth between the refrigerator and the dog, picks up the dog, puts it in his mouth, and heads off.) E says, "That's right, put the doggie in the refrigerator." (Kanzi puts the dog in the little refrigerator.) [C is scored because Kanzi has not hesitated at all and he is out of sight when E comments to encourage him.]

524A. (C2) *Put the doggie in the refrigerator.* (Alia picks up the dog, then becomes interested in what Nathaniel is doing, appearing to have forgotten what she was to do.) E says, "Put the doggie in the refrigerator." (Alia heads toward the kitchen, then stops to play with the dog.) E says, "Put the doggie in the refrigerator." (Alia does so.)

525. (C) *Put the tomato in the oil.* (Kanzi does so.)

525A. (C) *Put the tomato in the oil.* (Alia picks up the tomato, says, "Tomato," takes a bite of the tomato as she is putting it in the oil, and says, "Yuk.")

526. (PC) *Give the lighter and the shoe to Rose.* (Kanzi hands Rose the lighter, then points to some food in a bowl in the array that he would like to have to eat.)

526A. (C) *Give the matches and the shoe to Kathy.* (Alia does so.)

527. (C) *Take the apple to the bedroom.* (Kanzi makes a sound like "apple," looks back and forth between the bedroom and the apple, picks up the apple, and heads toward the bedroom. He waits for Rose to open the door, takes the apple into the bedroom, and puts it down on the bed.)

527A. (C) *Take the apple to the bedroom.* (Alia says, "Apple [something U], apple [something U]," then does so.)

528. (C) *Put some oil in the tomato.* (Kanzi picks up the liquid Baby Magic oil and pours it in a bowl with the tomato.)

528A. (C) *Put the oil in the tomato.* (Alia gets the petroleum jelly and opens the lid. She puts some on her finger and puts it on the tomato.)

529. (PC) *Give the apple and the hat to Rose.* (Kanzi picks up the hat and hands it to Rose. He does not look for the apple.)

529A. (C1) *Give the apple and the hat to Lisa.* (Alia picks up the umbrella, says something U, then continues to hold and look at the umbrella. She tries to take the umbrella cover off the umbrella but can't. She holds the umbrella up to Lisa and says, "That's umbrella." Alia then picks up the apple as she puts the umbrella down, then says, "Mmm hat," and gets the hat from the array. She then carries both objects to Lisa.) [C1 is scored because Alia vocally labeled the incorrect object that she picked up first. Hence, it was not assumed that she misunderstood the sentence, only that she wanted to look at the umbrella before carrying out the sentence.]

530. (PC) *Give the doggie and the milk to Rose.* (Kanzi picks up the can of milk, shakes it, and hands it to Rose. She does not take it, so he starts to shake it some more.) E says, "That's good, go ahead, thank you." (Kanzi again hands the milk to Rose, and she takes it. Kanzi does not even look for the dog.)

530A. (C) *Give the doggie and the milk to Cathy.* (Alia does so.)

531. (I) *Can you put the hat on the doggie?* (Kanzi picks up the hat with one hand and the dog with the other, then starts to smell a piece of food that is stuck to the dog's fur.) E says, "Can you put the hat on the doggie?" (Kanzi puts the dog in the hat.)

531A. (C) *Can you put the hat on the doggie?* (Alia does so.)

532. (C2) *Go get the carrot that's outdoors.* (Kanzi goes straight to the play-yard door, opens it himself, and strolls out.) E says, "Bring it back." (Kanzi sits and looks around at something that is going on outdoors.) E says, "Get the carrot that's outdoors and bring it back." (Kanzi makes "waaa" vocalizations as though something of note is happening outside.) E says, "Bring it back." (Kanzi makes more "waa" vocalizations.) Rose says, "Kanzi, listen to Sue," as Kanzi is not coming back in. (Kanzi picks up the carrot and brings it back.) [C2 is scored because Kanzi is hesitant to return and seems to do so only in response to repeated prompting from E. Additionally, the sentence is repeated so that the specific object he is to retrieve is mentioned while he is near the outdoor array of objects.]

532A. (C) *Go get the carrot that's outdoors.* (Alia does so.)

533. (PC) *Can you hit the snake with your ball?* (Kanzi moves the ball with his right hand and the snake with his left and puts the snake's mouth on the ball, then lays the snake over the ball.)

533A. (PC) *Can you hit the snake with your ball?* (Alia is afraid of the snake and refuses to respond. She refuses to pick it up, although she will pick up the ball. E tries to encourage Alia to touch the snake, but again Alia refuses. [PC is scored because Alia acts on the ball but not the snake.]

Error correction.—E substitutes *bug* for *snake* and asks, "Can you hit the bug with your ball?" (Alia picks up the bug and touches the ball.) [Had this been the initial sentence presented to Alia, it would have been scored I.]

534. (W) *Take the onions to the refrigerator.* (Immediately *before* this trial, Kanzi makes a sound like "orange drink" to ask for a large bowl of orange drink in the array. He is told that he cannot have it now and that he needs to listen. After E presents the sentence, Kanzi picks up this large bowl of orange drink and starts to walk away with it.) Rose stops him and asks, "What did Sue say?" (Kanzi makes a sound like "melon." The trial is stopped here since it is assumed that Kanzi wants the orange drink so much that he is not going to carry out the sentence even though he hears it and understands it.)

534A. (PC) *Take the pears to the refrigerator.* (Alia looks in a small container. She then picks up a chocolate bar. She then takes the small container with juice in it to the kitchen.)

Error correction.—E says, "Alia, what's this?" (Alia says, "Drink.") E says, "What kind of drink?" (Alia says something U.) E says, "I want to make a note that a lot of times when she eats pears it's in a little container like this. I don't know if she thought it was pears or not."

535. (C) *Take the snake outdoors.* (Kanzi picks up the snake, carries it directly to the play-yard door, sits by the door, and waits for Rose to open it. He helps her open it after she gets the lock off. He then stands and looks out while holding the

snake.) Rose says, "Kanzi," because he seems to be doing nothing. (Kanzi tosses the snake out.)

535A. (C) *Take the bug outdoors.* (Alia does so.)

536. (PC) *Bite the melon.* (Kanzi picks up the melon and puts it in the orange drink.) E says, "Kanzi, bite the melon." (Kanzi takes it out of the orange drink and makes a sound like "melon," then pokes it with his thumb.) E says, "Can you take a bite of the melon?" (Kanzi continues poking it.)

536A. (PC) *Bite the peaches.* (Alia bites the container.) [The tape of this trial is missing. The scoring is from E's original notes.]

537. (C) *Eat the melon.* (Kanzi takes a bite of the melon.)

537A. (C) *Eat the raisins.* (Alia picks up the container and then puts a handful of raisins in her mouth.)

538. (PC) *Put the top on the toothpaste.* (Kanzi picks up the toothpaste and squeezes some out into the shoe.) E says, "The top on the toothpaste. Do you see the top of the toothpaste?" (Kanzi squashes the tube and watches the toothpaste come out.) E says, "Put the top on the toothpaste." (Kanzi takes a bite of toothpaste.) E gives him the top and tells him again, "Put the top on the toothpaste." (Kanzi does so, holding the toothpaste in his foot and using his right hand.)

538A. (C) *Put the top on the toothpaste.* (Alia gets the toothpaste and the cap and attempts to put the top on the toothpaste, but she has difficulty.) E says, "Alia, put the top on the toothpaste." (Alia sets the top on the toothpaste.) [C is scored because Alia has not stopped attempting to put the top on. E is repeating the sentence to encourage her.]

539. (C2) *Put the chicken in the potty. Put the chicken in the potty.* (Kanzi picks up the chicken and nibbles on it, then puts it in the orange drink as he wishes to eat chicken dipped in orange-drink sauce.) E says, "Kanzi, put the chicken in the potty." (Kanzi goes over to the potty and looks in, then flushes the potty.) E says, "Put the chicken in the potty." (Kanzi picks up the chicken, smells it, and puts it in the potty.) [Kanzi wanted to eat the chicken quite badly and certainly did not want to put it in the potty. His hesitancy here appeared to result from a distaste for the request rather than an inability to understand it.]

539A. (C) *Put the ham in the potty.* (Alia goes to the potty, then whispers something U to the cameraperson, then says, "There potty," as she puts the ham on the potty.)

540. (C2) *Take the orange to the refrigerator.* (Kanzi picks up the orange and starts toward the refrigerator. For some unapparent reason, Rose assumes that Kanzi is approaching to hand the orange to her, and she holds out her hand as he walks past. Kanzi looks at her and decides that he should give it to her, so he does.) E says to Kanzi, "Go ahead and take it to the refrigerator." Rose, with the orange in her hand, says to Kanzi, "Is this what you were supposed to do?" E says, "Kanzi, take the orange to the refrigerator." (Kanzi holds out his hand as a signal to Rose to return the orange. Rose says, "OK," and gives it back. Kanzi then takes it to the refrigerator.) [C2 is scored because the repetition of the sentence results in Kanzi reorienting to the request and traveling on to the refrigerator. However, Kanzi initially showed no

hesitation and would have proceeded on to the refrigerator had Rose not misunderstood his intent and extended her hand. The rephrasing was used, not to clarify the original sentence for Kanzi, but rather to clarify the fact that he was to continue with the requested action even though Rose had taken the orange from him.]

540A. (C) *Take the orange to the refrigerator.* (Alia says, "OK," and does so, needing E's help to open the refrigerator.)

541. (C) *Take the banana outdoors.* (Kanzi makes a sound like "banana," then does so.)

541A. (C) *Take the banana outdoors.* (Alia says, "OK, banana, banana, you can eat banana," then shows the banana to the cameraperson on the way outdoors. At the door, she tries to get it open, then waits for E.) [Showing the requested item to the cameraperson was never observed in Kanzi.]

542. (C) *Put the raisins in the water.* (Kanzi takes the raisins out of the round box and puts them in a bowl of water, then makes a sound like "raisin.")

542A. (C) *Put the raisins in the water.* (Alia says, "OK," takes some of the raisins out of the container, says, "[Something U] raisins," then picks up the raisin container and smells the raisins, tastes them, drops one, says something U, picks up the raisin, then puts two raisins, one at a time, into the water. She then pours out the rest of the raisins and begins putting them in the water one or two at a time.) [Putting individual food items from a container into a liquid one or two at a time was never observed in Kanzi.]

543. (C2) *Put the raisins in the shoe.* (Kanzi places his hand on the quart water jar and pauses.) E says, "Put the raisins in the shoe." (Kanzi touches the melon and the shoe.) E says, "That's good, Kanzi, put some raisins in the shoe. Uh huh." (Kanzi takes some raisins out of the water and puts them in the shoe.)

543A. (C) *Put the raisins in the shoe.* (Alia moves the peaches around, then puts the raisins in the shoe.)

544. (C) *Take the onions outdoors.* (Kanzi picks up a bunch of green onions and walks bipedally with them toward the play-yard door. It is open, so he takes them on out.) E says, "That's good."

Response refinement.—E says, "Now leave the onions there and come back." (Kanzi picks up the onions and starts back with them as he wants to eat the onions.) E tells Kanzi to leave the onions there and that he can have some other onions when he comes back. (Kanzi hesitates, pulling off little bites of the onions.) Rose tells Kanzi to go ahead and put all of them outside. (Kanzi puts most of them outside but leaves a few inside to eat.) Rose insists that he place all of them outdoors. E says to Kanzi, "I have some in here, Kanzi, and we can eat these." (Kanzi then goes over to E and makes a sound like "onion" to request the onions that E has.)

544A. (C) *Take the onions outdoors.* (Alia says, "OK," and takes them to the door but has trouble opening it. She waits for E, then takes the onions on outside.)

545. (C3) *Put the melon in the potty.* (Kanzi stands up, puts his hand on the melon, and pauses.) E says, "Put the *melon,* the melon in the potty." (Kanzi does so.)

545A. (C) *Put the peaches in the potty.* (Alia gets the peaches and takes them to the potty. She takes out some leaves that are already in the potty.) E says, "Alia, can you put them in the potty? In. Put the peaches in. . . ." (Alia accidentally knocks the peaches in the potty.) E says, "Whoa!" (Alia takes them back out.) E says, "Go ahead, put them in. That's right." (Alia puts the leaves back in the potty.) E says, "Put the peaches in." (Alia puts the peaches in the potty.) [C is scored because Alia appears to think that the leaves must come out of the potty before the peaches go in. E's repetition is not because Alia is hesitating but simply to encourage her to continue with the requested activity.]

546. (C2) *Pour some water on the raisins.* (Kanzi picks up the quart of water, holds it for a moment near the bowl of lettuce that he has been eating, and pauses.) E says, "Kanzi, pour some water on the raisins." (Kanzi does so.)

546A. (I) *Pour the water on the raisins.* (Alia says something U. She picks up the container of raisins and dumps them out. She then puts the raisins in the water.)

Response refinement.—E allows Alia to continue to interact with the materials to see if she will correctly execute the sentence on her own. (Alia says something U and then puts the leftover raisins back into their original container. She says, "Need more water." She continues to say something U and pick up all the raisins. Then she picks up the container with the water and raisins, takes both containers over to the table, puts them down, and walks away.)

547. (C) *Go get the snake that's outdoors.* (Kanzi does so.)

547A. (C) *Get the bug that's outdoors.* (Alia goes to the front door and tries to open the door but pushes at the hinged side.) E opens the door, saying, "Watch your fingers." (Alia goes outdoors and gets the plastic bug.)

548. (PC) *Go get the umbrella that's in the colony room.* (Kanzi goes to the colony room and waits for Rose to come and open the door. Liz is in the colony with Panbanisha and Panzee, and Kanzi begins to play with the other chimps in there and is distracted.) Rose says, "Kanzi, what did Sue ask you to get?" (Kanzi gets the shoe.) Rose says, "That? OK."

Error correction.—When Kanzi returns with the shoe, E explains to Rose that he should have got the umbrella. Rose takes Kanzi back to the colony room for the umbrella.

548A. (OE) *Go get the box that's in Karen's room.* (Alia gets the box and the shoe from Karen's room.)

549. (C) *Go get the banana that's outdoors.* (Kanzi goes outdoors and looks around as there is a noise.) E says, "Bring it back." (Kanzi picks up the banana and brings it back.)

549A. (C3) *Go get the banana that's outdoors.* (Alia goes toward the front door and trips. She turns over, lies on her back, and sucks her thumb.) E says, "Go get the banana that's outdoors." (Alia just lies on the floor.) E says, "Keep going outdoors, Alia." (Alia moves her leg, and her shoe falls off.) E says, "Go get the banana that's outdoors." (Alia says something U about her shoe.) E says, "We'll fix your shoe in a minute. Go get the banana that's outdoors." (Alia says, "My shoe, Mommy, my shoe.") E comes out from the blind to fix Alia's shoe. E says, "All right, let's finish this." E picks Alia up and puts her on her feet. "Do you remember?" (Alia says, "Yeah." She goes over toward the window.) E says, "Alia, go get the banana that's outdoors." (Alia goes to the front door.) E opens it. (Alia gets the banana.)

550. (C) *Get the melon that's in the potty. Get the melon that's in the potty.* (Kanzi does so.)

550A. (M) *Go get the peaches that are in the potty.* (The peaches have fallen out of the potty, and E is not aware of this at the time the sentence is presented. Alia goes to the potty and gets leaves instead.)

551. (C) *Can you get Rose with the snake?* (Kanzi touches the snake to Rose, who pushes it away. Kanzi continues to push it toward Rose.)

551A. (PC) *Get Nathaniel with the bug.* (Alia takes the bug to Nathaniel and says, "Here Nathaniel.") [PC is scored because Alia simply handed the bug to Nathaniel rather than pretending to have the bug try to "get" Nathaniel.]

552. (PC) *Pour the milk in the cereal.* (Kanzi picks up the cereal and opens the box, then pours the cereal into a bowl of other cereal, then into a bowl of milk.)

Error correction.—E says, "That's good, put it down." (Kanzi pours the cereal into a bowl of other cereal again.) E says, "Stop." (Kanzi pours it into the bowl of milk.) E says, "Put the box down." (Kanzi continues to pour.) E says, "That's enough." (Kanzi continues to pour.) E says, "Stop." (Kanzi continues to pour.)

552A. (C) *Pour the milk in the cereal.* (Alia goes over and gets the big carton of milk. In the process, she spills the little container of milk. She says, "Ut oh," and something U. She opens the big carton of milk and then sets it down. She picks up the container of water and puts it back down. She picks up the carton of milk. She moves her foot and drags it through the spilled milk. She then moves out of the milk. She touches some of the spilled milk with her hand. She then turns her attention back to the carton of milk.) E says, "Pour the milk in the cereal." (Alia looks in the carton, shakes it, and picks up the cereal.) E comes out to try to keep Alia from spilling the milk. (Alia starts to pour the milk.) E stops Alia from pouring the milk. E says, "Alia, you're driving me crazy. Go ahead. Sit down. She was pouring it. I just wouldn't let her 'cause it was going to go on her pants." E spreads Alia's legs out so that she will not spill the milk on her pants. E says, "Look. This is the way Sue had it, so this is the way I'm going to have it." E poured some milk in the little container. E says, "Do it with that. Here. Pour the milk in the cereal." (Alia pulled the two containers closer to her.) E says, "Pour the milk in the cereal." (Alia pours the milk in the cereal.) E says, "There, good girl. That's right." [C is scored here because, in E's view, Alia attempted to pour the milk on the cereal from the start, although this is not self-evident from the tape. However, the container was too large and heavy for Alia to manipulate without spilling the milk all over the carpet. The rest of E's comments occurred in an attempt to deal with this situation. The array included both a large and a small container of milk, and Alia elected to use the large container.]

553. (C) *Can you get the snake that's in the potty?* (Kanzi does so, smelling the snake as he takes it out.)

553A. (C) *Get the bug that's in the potty.* (Alia goes to the potty and picks up the bug. She puts the bug back in the potty and goes back.)

554. (C) *Can you go scare Panban and Panzee?* (Kanzi interrupts with a "whuuh" sound as the word *scare* is mentioned.) E says, "Go scare Panban and Panzee." (Kanzi picks up a snake and looks toward the tool room, where Panban and Panzee are playing. To go directly to the tool room, Kanzi must pass through the area that has

been blocked off by the blind.) E says, "Go ahead," to indicate to Kanzi that he can go through the blocked-off area if he wishes. (Kanzi approaches the door to show E that he wants to go through the blocked-off area so that he can go directly to the tool room. He is carrying the snake. After passing through the blocked area, Kanzi goes to the room where Panban and Panzee are playing and pulls back the sheet that is blocking their window. He holds the snake up to the window.) ["Wuuh" is a sound that Kanzi makes for mildly scary things.]

554A. (C) *Go scare Kathy and Timothy with the snake.* (Alia does so.)

555. (C) *Go scare Matata with the snake.* (Kanzi says, "Whuuh," picks up the snake, and looks toward the colony room, where Matata is housed.) E says, "Go ahead." (Kanzi picks up the snake, puts it around his neck, and starts off toward the colony room. He waits by the door for Rose to open the colony-room door, goes in, and says, "Whuuh," as he pushes the snake into Matata's cage. Then he sits on the cube and watches what Matata does. Matata inspects the snake to see if it is alive. She touches its head gingerly, looks closely, pokes at it, then carries it away by the tail.) [Kanzi is not scared by the fake snake but is interested in Matata's reaction.)

555A. (C) *Go scare Joshua with the snake.* (Alia does so.) [The tape is missing, so scoring is from E's original notes.]

556. (C) *Go get the tomato that's in the microwave. . . . The tomato in the microwave.* (Kanzi goes directly to the microwave, gets the tomato, takes it out, and looks at it. Then he looks around as though thinking of running off and playing.) Rose says, "Go show Sue what you got, Kanzi." E says, "Bring it back."

556A. (PC) *Go get the tomato that's in the oven.* (Alia goes directly to the oven and pulls out the can of foamy soap. She tries to open the oven door further, but it sticks. She then reaches back into the oven drawer but does not get anything out. As she holds the soap, she says, "I just see the soap in there," gets up, and heads toward E, who is still behind the mirror. En route, Alia says, "I got the soap, Mom." When she returns, she says, "This, ha-ha."

557. (C) *Pour the cereal in the milk.* (Kanzi picks up a box of cereal, holds it with his foot, pulls the spout out, and pours it in the milk.)

557A. (I) *Pour the cereal in the milk.* (Alia says, "OK," moves the water to one side, and picks up the big carton of milk. She tries to open it. Then she tries to pour the milk in the cereal, but she holds the carton backward, and nothing comes out.)

558. (C) *Take the tomato to the microwave. Take the tomato to the microwave.* (Kanzi picks up the tomato and heads off toward the microwave.) E says, "That's right, go put it in the microwave." (Kanzi takes it to the microwave and puts it inside.) [C is scored because Kanzi does not pause or hesitate prior to the sentence repetition.]

558A. (W) *Take the tomato to the oven.* (Alia picks up the apple and then looks at another object. She drops the apple, picks up the flashlight, and tries to turn the flashlight on.) E says, "Alia, take the tomato to the oven." (Alia continues to play with the flashlight, standing up and pointing it toward the ceiling and trying to turn it on. Suddenly, she stops and says, "OK," and puts the flashlight down, but then picks up the brush and starts to brush her hair.)

Error correction.—E continues to permit Alia to engage in play with the objects as she wishes to determine whether she will respond to the sentence. (After a short time, Alia puts the brush down and picks up the tomato. She carries the tomato directly to the oven in the kitchen and places the tomato inside the open oven drawer.) [This sentence was scored wrong because Alia engaged in three different actions on three different objects prior to carrying out the request. Her subsequent behavior suggested that she indeed understood the sentence during this interval.]

559. (C) *Can you take Rose's shoe off? Rose's shoe.* (Kanzi spins around and starts to untie Rose's shoe.) E says, "Can you untie her shoe and take it off?" (Kanzi unties her shoe.) "That's right, go ahead." (Kanzi pulls Rose's shoe off.) [C is scored because Kanzi did not hesitate at any point or wait for further information from E.]

559A. (C1) *Take Nathaniel's shoe off.* (Alia says something U, crawls around, then goes over and unties Nathaniel's shoe. She continues to loosen the laces, but then she stops trying. She crawls over to a piece of paper.)

560. (C2) *Go get the shoe that's outdoors. Get the shoe that's outdoors.* (Kanzi goes to the play-yard door.) E says, "That's right." (Kanzi opens the door and stands looking out.) E says, "Now bring it back." Rose, assuming that Kanzi should get something, asks, "What are you supposed to bring Sue?" (E says, "Kanzi, get the shoe that's outdoors. Bring it back." (Kanzi vocalizes, gets the shoe, and returns.) E says, "That's right, come on," when Kanzi is seen returning with the shoe.

560A. (C) *Alia, get the shoe that's outdoors.* (Alia goes to the front door. She says, "Comin.") E says, "Uh huh," and opens the door for Alia. (Alia gets the shoe.)

561. (PC) *Can you get the orange that's in the potty?* (Kanzi looks over at the potty and sees no orange, as it has fallen down in the very bottom. He then takes an orange from the display and plops it in the potty.) E says, "Can you get the orange out that's in the potty?" (Kanzi says, "Whuu," goes over to the potty, and retrieves both oranges.)

561A. (C) *Can you get the orange that's in the potty?* (Alia says something U, then goes to the potty and retrieves the orange.)

562. (C) *Can you show me the ice water?* (Kanzi vocalizes.) *Where's the ice water?* (Kanzi vocalizes.) *Show me the ice water.* (Kanzi points to the ice water.) [C is scored since Kanzi does not hesitate. The sentence is repeated only because Kanzi keeps making noise.]

562A. (C) *Show me the ice water.* (Alia does so.)

563. (C) *Show me the hot water.* (Kanzi vocalizes.) *Can you show me the hot water?* (Kanzi makes a sound like "hot," then picks up a paint brush, points to the hot water with it, and stirs the hot water with it, not wanting to touch the hot water as it is really hot.)

563A. (PC) *Show me the hot water.* (Alia says, "OK," then picks up the bowl of cold water, says, "Hot," then stands up with it and spills it all down the front of her clothes.)

564. (C) *Can you pour the ice water in the potty? Pour the ice water in the potty.* (Kanzi picks up the bowl of ice water and heads toward the potty.) E says, "That's right." (Kanzi pours the ice water carefully into the potty.)

564A. (PC) *Pour the ice water in the potty.* (Alia picks up both cups of water—the ice water and the hot water—and carries them to the portable potty. Alia pours the hot water, then the cup of ice water, into the potty.)

565. (C) *Can you put the orange in the hot water? Can you put an orange in the hot water?* (Kanzi does so.)

565A. (C) *Put the orange in the hot water.* (Alia does so.)

566. (PC) *Can you put the other orange in the ice water? Put the other orange in the ice water.* (Kanzi puts this orange in the hot water also.)

Error correction.—E says, "Put one orange in the ice water." (Kanzi does so.)

566A. (C) *Put the other orange in the cold water.* (Alia picks up the other orange, briefly touches the bug, goes over to put the orange in the water, and steps on the side of the hot water bowl. The water spills. She puts the orange in the hot water.) [C is scored because, even though Alia stops to touch the bug, she has already begun the action of responding to the sentence.]

567. (W) *Can you get the toothpaste that's in the little refrigerator?* (Kanzi goes to the play yard, sits down, and begins to look around.) E says, "Kanzi, the toothpaste that's in the little refrigerator." (Kanzi ignores E.) E says, "Kanzi, we don't just sit outside." (Kanzi vocalizes "whuuh" many times as though there is something out there that E should see.) E says, "You come in and get the toothpaste that's in the little refrigerator." (Kanzi continues to ignore E and to sit outside.) Rose, noting that Kanzi is doing nothing, says to Kanzi, "Kanzi, listen, what were you supposed to do?" (Kanzi comes in, goes to the big refrigerator, looks all around on one side, gets nothing, and gestures to Rose to open the other side. She does, and he begins looking around in there, but gets nothing.) Rose says, "Here, come here. Let's listen to Sue again, let's listen to Sue again."

Error correction.—The sentence is repeated, and Kanzi goes to the big refrigerator again and begins looking around. When he can't find the toothpaste, he brings the hat back. He vocalizes with repeated "whuuhs" as Rose describes for E what Kanzi did. Rose then takes him to the little refrigerator, and they get the toothpaste.

567A. (NG).

568. (PC) *Put the mushrooms in the ice water.* (Kanzi puts a mushroom in the hot water.)

Error correction.—E says, "Put the mushrooms in the ice water." (Kanzi does so.)

568A. (C2) *Put the grapes in the ice water.* (Alia says, "OK." She picks up the whole bag of grapes. She almost puts it in the hot water, but she stops and puts it down. She then tries to open the bag. She holds the bag up and says, "Grapes." She puts the grapes back down and moves the plastic as though she is trying to open the bag. She picks up the bag. She sets the bag back down and looks behind her twice. She finally finds the opening to the bag and reaches in a number of times before she gets a grape. She turns around to watch Nathaniel and ignores the grapes.) E says, "Alia, put the grapes in the ice water." (Alia puts a grape in the ice water.)

569. (PC) *Put the hat on your ball.* (Kanzi picks up the shoe and plays with it next to the ball.) E says, "Put the hat on your ball." (Kanzi continues to play with the shoe.) E says, "The hat, not the shoe." (Kanzi says, "Whuuh," and continues to play

with the shoe, trying to take the laces out of it.) E says, "Put the hat, do you see the hat?" (Kanzi continues to play with the shoe and does not even look for the hat.)

Error correction.—E says, "You don't see the hat?" (Kanzi continues to play with the shoe.) E says, "Look for the hat." (Kanzi points to the hat.) E says, "That's the hat. Put the hat on your ball." (Kanzi puts the hat on the ball.)

569A. (C) *Put the hat on your ball.* (Alia says, "OK." She goes over and gets the hat. She says something about "hat and ball" and puts the hat on the ball.)

570. (PC) *Can you pour the paint in the yogurt?* . . . (Kanzi vocalizes.) . . . *Pour the paint in the yogurt.* (Kanzi says, "Whuuh," picks up the paint, and starts to pour it in the yogurt.) E says, "That's right, pour the paint in the yogurt." (Kanzi switches and pours the paint into the hot water, where there is already some paint.)

Error correction.—E says, "No, pour it in the yogurt, in the yogurt." (Kanzi points to the toothpaste.) E says, "No, Kanzi, where's the. . . ." (Kanzi points to the yogurt.) E says, "That's right." (Kanzi says, "Whuuh.") E says, "Pour the paint in the yogurt." (Kanzi pours the yogurt in the paint.)

570A. (C) *Pour the paint in the yogurt.* (Alia does so.)

571. (C) *Could you put your ball down?* (Kanzi is holding his ball when this sentence is presented. He tosses it down.)

571A. (NG).

572. (C) *Give the doggie to Karen.* (Kanzi does so.)

572A. (W) *Would you give the doggie to Karen?* (Alia says, "OK, dog [something U]," and starts to pick up the oil.) E says, "Alia, give the doggie to Karen." (Alia touches the oil, touches it again, smells it, pulls her nose back, and goes over to a one-way mirror and begins to slap it.) E says, "Give the doggie to Karen, go ahead, right now, right now, give the doggie to Karen." (Alia slaps the mirror, then picks up the rubber band.)

Error correction.—E comes out from the blind and says, "Look, Mommy wants you to give the doggie to Karen." (Alia says, "OK," and crawls away, saying, "Whoof, whoof.") E says, "Stand up, Alia. You are being a goof." (Alia goes over to the dog, then looks at E.) E says, "Give the doggie to Karen." (Alia accidentally kicks over the milk and says, "Uh oh.") E says, "That doesn't matter." E looks directly in Alia's face and says, "Let's give the doggie to Karen." (Alia looks at Karen.) E says, "You are being a goof right now. Mommy knows you can do this." (Alia takes the dog to the couch where Karen is sitting.)

573. (C) *Would you give the gorilla to Rose?* (Kanzi does so.)

573A. (C) *Would you give the gorilla to Nathaniel?* (Alia does so.)

574. (C) *Show me the snake.* (Kanzi picks up the snake from the floor, holds it in front of the door, and makes a sound like "snake.")

574A. (NG).

575. (C) *Show me the snake that's on TV.* (Kanzi immediately points to the snake on the television.)

575A. (NG).

576. (PC) *Can you give the snake a shot?* (Kanzi picks up the syringe, puts it in his mouth, removes the cover, pulls the syringe out of the casing with his mouth, and gives himself a shot in the thigh.)

Error correction.—E says, "Kanzi, give the snake a shot. Give a shot to the snake." (Kanzi puts the needle in a little bit of milk that is in a nearby bowl.) E says, "The snake." (Kanzi gives the toy gorilla a shot.) E says, "Kanzi, the snake." (Kanzi gives the toy dog a shot.) E says, "Do you see the snake?" (Kanzi grabs the dog, pulls it into his lap, and puts the needle in its mouth.) E says, "Kanzi, the snake. Can you give the snake a shot?" (Kanzi puts the needle in the dog's eye.) E says, "Look for the snake." (Kanzi gives the dog a shot in the tummy.) E says, "Kanzi, the snake. Whuh, the snake." (Kanzi says, "Whuh," and puts the needle in a small amount of milk in a nearby bowl.) E says, "Yeah, the snake, give the snake a shot." (Kanzi looks at a small place on his thumb where he accidentally pricked himself with the needle while giving the shots described above to various toy animals.) E says, "Don't you see the snake? Where's the snake?" (Kanzi rolls his ball toward himself, preparing to give it a shot.) E says, "Where's the snake?" (Kanzi gives his ball a shot, then looks again at the pricked place on his hand, then gives the ball several more shots.) E comes out of the room, hands him the snake, and asks him again to give the snake a shot. Kanzi throws the snake aside. E shows Kanzi what to do.

576A. (PC) *Give the snake a shot.* (Alia sits down by the toy snake. She picks up the toy snake and swings it around. She sets it down, picks it up, and sets it back down. She looks inside two glasses that are in front of her.) E says, "Alia, give the snake a shot." (Alia says something U and then touches the snake.)

Error correction.—E says, "OK, let me show you what I mean," and then does so.

577. (C2) *Go get some cereal and give it to Rose. Go get some cereal and give it to Rose.* (Kanzi goes to the cereal, with Rose following him, and tries to pick up all the cereal boxes that are in the bin, about eight boxes. He keeps dropping them as he tries to get all of them. Finally, he gets them all and brings them very near Rose, but then walks on past her and puts them in front of the door.) E says, "What are you supposed to do with it? Do you remember what you are supposed to do with it? What are you supposed to do with it? You're supposed to give it to Rose." (Kanzi looks at Rose while trying to open a box of cereal. He does not want to give it to Rose as he has had a disagreement with her prior to this trial and does not want to cooperate with her. She kneels down beside him, ready to take the cereal from Kanzi.) E says, "Give it to her. Hand it to her. Pick it up and give her the cereal." (Kanzi says, "Whuh," grabs up all the boxes of cereal he can, and puts them in his array.) E says, "Give it all to Rose." (He hands Rose one box of cereal.) [This was not scored as PC because Kanzi's behavior indicated that he understood he was to give the cereal to Rose but that he did not want to do so. In general, throughout the testing, from time to time Kanzi refuses to give things to Rose. This is because it is her responsibility to make certain that Kanzi does not eat things in the array that he should not have. He wants to keep all the boxes of cereal, and he is concerned that Rose may take them away. This is why he gives her just one. By contrast, see trial 579, where he is asked to get a box of cereal for Karen. Kanzi rarely, if ever, confuses Rose's name with that of anyone else.)

577A. (W) *Go get some cereal and give it to Linda.* (Alia walks through the living room past Linda and into Karen's room. She gets the hat from off the bed in the room and carries the hat back into the living room. There, by the front door, she passes a large bin full of cereal boxes. Alia looks at the cereal but continues to walk past it and carries the hat to E, who is still behind the mirror.)

578. (C) *Show me the can opener. Where is the can opener?* (Kanzi points to the television. The can opener is on the television.)

578A. (C) *Show me the fork.* (Alia picks up the fork and the spoon. She dips the spoon into a container full of cereal. Then she dips the fork in.)

Response refinement.—E says, "Alia, show me the fork." (Alia continues to dip the fork into the container.) E says, "Show me the fork." (Alia continues to play.) E says, "Show me the fork." (Alia holds up the fork.) [C was scored because Alia appeared to want to eat the cereal and apparently picked up the spoon to do so. She picked up the fork first, before doing anything else, and she did not seem to be confused between the fork and the spoon.]

579. (C) *Go get some cereal for Karen. Go get a box of cereal for Karen.* (Kanzi walks to the bin of cereal boxes and picks one up.) E says, "That's right, get just one. That's right." E speaks up here to emphasize that Kanzi should get just one box of cereal because he brought so many on trial 577. (Kanzi takes the cereal to Karen, shaking it on the way, and hands it to her as he gets there.) [C was scored because Kanzi showed no hesitation and the request that he get only a single box of cereal was not a rephrasing of the original sentence but an added specification.]

579A. (C) *Go get a box of cereal for Lisa.* (Alia does so.)

580. (C) *Make the doggie bite the snake.* (Kanzi picks up the dog and puts it on the snake, then moves it back, picks up the snake, and looks at its mouth.) E says, "Make the doggie bite the snake." (Kanzi puts the snake's mouth up to the doggie's mouth.) E says, "Yeah, that's right. Un huh. Thank you." (Kanzi opens the dog's mouth and sticks the snake's head in the dog's mouth.) E says, "Yeah, push his mouth down. Yeah, that's very good, Kanzi." (Kanzi pulls the snake back and puts it down.) [C is scored because Kanzi does not hesitate at any point and his actions appear to be directed smoothly toward carrying out the request.]

580A. (PC) *Make the doggie bite the snake.* (Alia goes over to the doggie and bites it on the head. She then pulls it closer to her and lies on top of it.)

581. (C) *Kanzi, tell Rose that you want to go outdoors.* (Kanzi turns, looks at Rose, and gestures toward the play-yard door.) Rose looks in that direction and says, "You're supposed to go over there?" (Kanzi heads toward the play-yard door, and Rose follows.) E says something U and then, "I had hoped you'd use the keyboard, but that's nice."

Response refinement.—(The potty is right in front of the play-yard door, and Kanzi stops to pee.) Rose says, "You needed to pee?" and waits for him. E says, "You have to tell her that you want to go outdoors," thinking that Rose did not understand Kanzi's gesture. (Kanzi answers with a "whuh" sound.) E says, "Un huh, you have to tell her." (Kanzi then goes to the play-yard door and gestures to the latch, then goes to the microwave to check out what food is in there. Rose sends Kanzi back to listen to E tell Kanzi what to do again. Then Rose leads him to the play-yard door.)

581A. (C3) *Alia, tell Kathy that you want to go outdoors.* (Alia remains in the chair after E makes this request and does not respond.) E says, "Can you tell Kathy that you want to go outdoors? Go tell her." (Alia gets out of her chair, goes to Kathy, and postures shyly in front of her, but she does not say anything to her. She then puts her hand on the door, looks back at Kathy, and says, "Mom, open this please." E opens the front door for Alia. Alia then tries to open the storm door but cannot and tells E, "I can't open it." E opens the storm door, and Alia goes outdoors. [C3 is scored because Alia hesitates repeatedly and E's comment spurs her to action. Although she does not vocalize, she does invite Kathy to follow her outdoors by posture and glance.]

582. (C) *Can you take the gorilla to the bedroom?* (Kanzi picks up the gorilla, goes to the bedroom, and sits and waits by the door. Rose does not approach to open the door as she does not realize that Kanzi is waiting for her to open it.) E says to Kanzi, "Rose will open it. You need to show her the door." (Kanzi points to the door, and Rose then approaches and opens it. Kanzi takes the gorilla into the bedroom.) [C is scored because Kanzi's behavior reveals that he understood the sentence. E's remarks regarding Rose were not a rephrasing of the original sentence but rather a means of telling Kanzi what he needed to let Rose know.]

582A. (C1) *Can you take the gorilla to the bedroom?* (Alia gets the gorilla and says something U. She then swings the gorilla around. She walks over to the toy shelf and throws the gorilla. She picks up the gorilla and throws it again. She picks up the gorilla, goes into the kitchen, and stops. She says, "This way," takes the gorilla into the bedroom, and throws it into the playpen.) [C is scored even though Alia throws the gorilla repeatedly since she appears to be on her way to the bedroom with the gorilla even as she is throwing it.]

583. (I) *Put the milk in the cherries. Pour the milk in the cherries.* (Kanzi pours the cherries in the milk.)

583A. (C) *Pour the milk in the cherries.* (Alia picks up the cup of milk and pours the milk into the cup of cherries.)

584. (C3) *Kanzi, go get a carrot for Rose, carrot.* (Kanzi goes to the large 50-pound bag of carrots, begins opening it, and starts taking out all the carrots.) E says, "Kanzi, can you give Rose a carrot please? Give one to Rose." (Kanzi makes a sound like "carrot" and starts breaking the carrots one at a time, apparently wanting to hear them snap.) E says, "Kanzi." (Kanzi makes a sound like "carrot.") E says, "Can you give Rose a carrot?" (Kanzi makes a sound like "carrot" and pushes several of them toward Rose with his feet.)

584A. (C) *Alia, get a carrot for Nathaniel.* (Alia gets a carrot and gives it to Nathaniel.)

585. (C) *Make the snake bite the doggie.* (Kanzi picks up the snake and then the dog. Kanzi pushes the snake's mouth down onto the dog's mouth.) E says, "Uh huh, that's real good." (Kanzi holds the snake's mouth on the doggie's mouth.)

585A. (C) *Make the snake bite the doggie.* (Alia puts the snake's mouth up to the head of the doggie. She then puts the snake's mouth up to the mouth of the dog.) E says, "She's putting it up to the doggie's mouth."

586. (C3) *Can you pour the milk in the jelly?* (Kanzi starts to but hesitates as he is reaching for the milk.) E says, "Un huh, pour the milk in the jelly." (Kanzi does so.)

586A. (I) *Can you pour the milk in the jelly?* (Alia pours the jelly in the milk.)

587. (C3) *Take Karen to the colony room.* (Kanzi turns and stares at Karen as though she should understand and get up to go with him. However, since Karen is blind, she does nothing.) E says, "Take her by the hand and take her to the colony room." (Kanzi does so.)

587A. (C) *Take Nathaniel to Karen's room.* (Alia says, "I take Nathaniel." She then goes to Nathaniel and gives him a hug. On Nathaniel's verbal suggestion, Alia takes him by the hand and starts to lead him toward the back bedrooms. About halfway there, Nathaniel gets in front of Alia and says, "Push me, Alia." Alia does so, pushing him toward the doorway of Karen's room as she says, "Nathaniel, move Karen's room.")

588. (C) *Can you put the ball on the pine needles?* (Kanzi does so.)

588A. (W) *Can you put the ball on the pine needles?* (Alia says, "Yeah," goes over to the objects, and sits down. She says something U about the ball. Alia then opens a Tupperware container and puts her hand in it.)

589. (C) *Can you put the ball on the TV?* (Kanzi holds the ball up to the front of the television.) [C is scored here as Kanzi put the ball next to the television.]

Response refinement.—E says, "Can you put it on top of the TV?" (Kanzi puts the ball on top of the television.)

589A. (PC) *Can you put the ball on the TV?* (Alia says something U as she goes over to the array of objects, picks up the egg, and says something U.) E says, "That's the egg. Put the ball on the TV." (Alia touches the ball with one hand while holding onto the egg with the other and says something U about the ball. She then looks at the egg and says, "Egg." She then gets up and takes the egg over to the television. She gets up on the chair.) E helps Alia get her positioning on the chair. (Alia puts the egg on the television.)

590. (PC) *Go get Rose a can of milk.* (Kanzi gets two cans of milk and walks deliberately away from Rose while looking at her with a challenging expression.) E says, "Kanzi, bring it back and give it to Rose." (Kanzi makes a series of sounds like "bring it back" while proceeding to stride deliberately away from Rose.) [Kanzi is still refusing to give things to Rose. However, since he walks directly away from her in this case, it is scored as PC.]

Error correction.—Rose does not realize that Kanzi is avoiding her as she does not know the sentence or that he has been asked to give the milk to her. Rose asks him to come back to E. (Kanzi goes instead to the cushions and starts to plop down and play.) As soon as Kanzi does this, Rose realizes that he cannot be responding to any sentence and says, "Kanzi, listen, that means you walk over to Sue." (Rose takes him by the shoulder and leads him back to E.) By the door she says, "Kanzi," then begins to tell E what happened. (Kanzi vocalizes repeatedly.) With both Rose and Kanzi talking loudly, E tries to talk quietly and to tell Rose what Kanzi was supposed to do. On learning that Kanzi was supposed to give her the milk, Rose says to Kanzi (with emphasis), "You mean that milk is mine?" (Kanzi immediately produces an exceptional flurry of loud "waa" vocalizations.) Rose then says to Kanzi, "You mean you were walking around with it?" (Kanzi looks reflective.) Rose says, "Can you give me that milk?" (Kanzi immediately sets off to get the milk that he left in the grouproom somewhere.) Rose says, "Come on, maybe I need that milk." (Kanzi then decides to pee.) Rose says, "You finish peeing, and then let's finish this."

590A. (PC) *Go get Linda a can of milk.* (Alia starts to pick up the bowl of milk but spills a little out. Alia then says something U about cleaning up the spill. She goes to the bathroom and gets some paper towels, then returns to the living room and uses the towels to wipe up the milk spill. E then comes from behind the mirror and helps Alia clean up the spill. E suggests using the cloth towel that's in the array to clean up the milk spill. E thinks that the spill has been cleaned up well enough and decides to repeat the trial. However, as E gets ready behind the mirror, Alia picks up the cloth towel and continues to wipe up a bit more of the milk spill.) E says, "Alia, listen." (Alia wipes one more time, then tosses the towel back into the object array. Then she inspects the area on the floor where the milk had spilled. As Alia does this, E repeats, "Go get Linda a can of milk." (Alia glances briefly at the bowl of milk, but then reaches for the cloth towel and dips the cloth towel into the milk that's in the bowl. Milk from the towel drips on the floor, so Alia uses the towel to wipe up the milk drips. Alia then finds more spilled milk underneath the bowl of milk and moves the bowl over to wipe up the milk spill with the towel. Alia continues to wipe up milk spills.) E repeats the original request, "Alia, go get Linda a can of milk." (Alia continues to hold the towel and says, "I want to do this with the towel." She dips the towel into the bowl of milk again, then puts the towel down, picks up the brush, and starts to put the brush into the bowl of milk.) E stops the trial.

591. (PC) *Can you go put the pine needles in the trash? Take the pine needles to the trash.* (Kanzi picks up the pine needles and heads off.) E says, "That's right." (Kanzi goes to the little refrigerator, opens it, and gets some ice from the ice compartment.) Rose closes up the ice compartment as Kanzi appears to be just eating ice and doing nothing with the pine needles. She says, "Where do they go, Kanzi?" (Kanzi walks over to the sofa with the pine needles and puts them under the cushions.)

Error correction.—E tells Rose where the pine needles are supposed to go. Rose takes Kanzi to the trash, and they put them in together.

591A. (C) *Can you put the pine needle in the trash?* (Alia does so.)

592. (PC) *Can you put the telephone away? Take the telephone and put it up in the video room. Uh huh.* (Kanzi picks up the phone, moves away.) E says, "In the plastic room, that's right, where it belongs. Take the telephone back where it belongs." (Kanzi goes over to the bedroom and points to the door for Rose to open it.) E says, "Kanzi, take it to the TV room. (Kanzi holds the phone and looks at it while waiting for Rose to open the door. Rose approaches with her keys. Kanzi looks up at her and points to the door to show her he wants to go in. She opens the door, and Kanzi takes the phone into the bedroom.) [The sentence is presented in a number of different ways because there is no general way of referring to this room and Kanzi is not usually allowed to go in it. Consequently, E does not anticipate that he will understand what it is that he should do and is attempting to find some appropriate way to refer to this area. Kanzi does not understand, and no further trials require Kanzi to go to this area.]

592A. (C) *Take the telephone and put it in the dinosaur tent.* (Alia picks up an open package of hot chocolate and the telephone. She throws the telephone into the tent.)

593. (I) *Put the jelly on the egg.* (Kanzi pours the egg on the bug, although he appears to be trying to pour it on the jelly. Then he takes both bowls and turns his back.) E opens the door and expresses concern that Kanzi "missed" and that the egg fell on the floor. (Kanzi begins pushing the bug around as though making it "lick up" the egg.)

593A. (PC) *Put the jelly on the egg.* (Alia gets up and goes over to the jelly. She touches it, then rubs her fingers together. She picks up the container of jelly and says something U. She goes over to the ball. She says, "In the ball, Mommy. In the ball," and puts the container of jelly in the ball.)

594. (PC) *Kanzi, go get a Coke. Go get a can of Coke and give it to Rose. The Coke that's on the table over there.* (Kanzi looks toward the table.) E says, "Uh huh. That's right." (Kanzi starts trying to get the Cokes out of the crate on the table.) E says, "Now give it to Rose." (Kanzi carries four Cokes back to E.) E says, "Would you give it to Rose, please?" (Kanzi says, "Whuh," and gives two Cokes to Rose.)

594A. (C) *Go get a Coke for Nathaniel.* (Alia does so.)

595. (C) *Can you hug the doggie? Can you give the doggie a hug?* (Kanzi does so.)

595A. (C) *Can you hug the doggie? Can you give the doggie a hug?* (Alia does so.)

596. (PC) *Can you put the hat on the bug?* (Kanzi picks up the hat, then picks up the bug and puts the bug on the ball.)

Error correction.—E says, "That's the bug on the ball." (Kanzi makes a sound like "whuh.") E says, "Can you put the hat. . . . Can you put the hat on the bug?" (Kanzi looks at the bug, puts it on the ball again, and pushes the ball down.)

596A. (PC) *Can you put the hat on the bug?* (Alia puts the hat on her head, saying, "Hat." She takes it off, plays with it, and puts it on again.) E says, "Can you put the hat on the bug?" (Alia continues to put the hat on and take it off her head.)

Error correction.—E says, "Alia, put the hat on the bug. Now." (Alia continues to play with the hat.) E says, "Put the hat on the bug. Alia, put the hat on the bug." (Alia continues to play.) E says, "Eh uhm. Alia, listen to Mommy. Alia. Put the hat on the bug." (Alia continues to put the hat on her head.) E says, "Hey you. Alia, put the hat on the bug. Can you put the hat on the bug, please? Right now. Hurry up. Put the hat on the bug. Alia." (Alia says something U and continues to play with the hat.)

597. (C) *Can you hug the ball?* (Kanzi does so.)

597A. (C) *Can you hug the ball?* (Alia does so.)

598. (PC) *Can you put the bubbles, put the bubbles on the doggie?* (Kanzi picks up a canister of clay and puts it on the dog, then picks up the dog and looks at it.)

Error correction.—E says, "Do you see the bubbles?" (Kanzi picks up the clay.) E says, "That's the clay. You're gonna. . . . Well wait. . . . Put the clay on the doggie." (Kanzi opens the clay, makes a little patty cake of it, and puts that on the dog.) [E assumes that Kanzi is confusing *clay* and *bubbles*, so she alters the sentence here in response so that Kanzi can feel successful. However, it is still scored as PC.]

598A. (PC) *Can you put the bubbles on the doggie?* (Alia says something U. She gets up and gets the bubbles and the doggie. By accident, she knocks over the egg. She picks up the egg, smells it, and attempts to place it back in its container. The egg falls back out. She picks it up, smells it, and places it back in the container. Alia then picks up the container with the egg, turns it upside down, and the egg falls out.) E says, "Alia, put the bubbles on the doggie." (Alia puts the bubbles in the empty egg container.)

Error correction.—E says, "Put the bubbles on the doggie." (Alia picks up the egg and smells it. She then puts the egg on the bubbles, which are in the container. She alternates between smelling the egg and putting it on the bubbles.) E says, "Alia, put the bubbles on the doggie." (Alia says, "OK," takes the bubbles out of the egg container, and picks up the egg. She bangs the egg against the container, then smells the egg.)

599. (I) *Put the ball on the hat.* . . . (Loud screaming from Tamuli drowns out the sentence.) . . . *Put the ball, put the ball on the hat.* (Kanzi picks up the hat and puts it on the ball.)

599A. (I) *Put the ball on the hat.* (Alia says something U and places the hat on the ball.)

600. (C) *Can you put the blanket on your ball?* (Kanzi picks up the blanket and opens it up, then puts the ball and a balloon that he is playing with in a sort of blanket nest so that the blanket is on the ball.)

600A. (C) *Can you put the blanket on your ball?* (Alia gets up, says something U, and places her blanket on her ball.)

601. (C) *Can you take the hose outdoors?* (Kanzi picks up a large coil of the hose and carries it bipedally to the door.) E says, "You can wait, Rose can open it for you." (Kanzi helps Rose open the door and then goes out, leaving the hose on the door sill.)

601A. (C) *Can you take the block outdoors?* (Alia gets the block and goes to the door.) E says, "I got it," and opens the door. (Alia goes outside and puts the block down.)

602. (PC) *Can you make the bug bite the doggie?* (Kanzi picks up the bug and puts it on the ball.) E says, "Uh huh, make the bug bite the doggie." (Kanzi puts the bug on the ball.)

Error correction.—E says, "Not the ball, the dog." (Kanzi picks the dog up and puts the ball up to the dog's mouth, then licks the dog's nose.) E says, "Where's the bug? Where's the bug?" (Kanzi picks up the bug and puts the bug on the dog, then puts the bug in the dog's mouth.)

602A. (PC) *Can you make the bug bite the doggie?* (Alia herself bites the doggie.)

603. (C2) *Can you brush Liz's hair?* (Kanzi looks at Liz, picks up the brush, and brushes his own hair.) E says, "That's your hair. Can you also brush Liz's hair? Go brush Liz's hair." (Kanzi goes over toward Liz, gets a cube, and pulls it up behind her in preparation to brush her hair. Liz loosens her hair, and Kanzi begins to brush. Even after E and Liz tell him several times that he has done a good job, he continues to brush Liz's hair as he enjoys this.) [C2 is scored because brushing his own hair is something that Kanzi does almost every time he first picks up a brush; thus, it is assumed that Kanzi did understand the sentence but elected to brush his own hair until E emphasized that he was to brush Liz's hair.]

603A. (PC) *Can you brush Linda's hair?* (After hearing E's request, Alia nods her head in agreement. Then she picks up the brush from the array in front of her and carries it toward Linda, stops short of Linda, and turns toward the big red construction toy. She slides the brush along the toy and continues to make brushing motions with the brush along the surface of the toy.) E says, "Alia, brush Linda's hair." (Alia answers, "I can't.")

Error correction.—E says, "Can you brush Linda's hair?" (Alia says something U.) E says, "What?" (Alia says, "I'm not going to say nothing.") E says, "Brush Linda's hair. Go ahead. Go ahead, you can do it." (Alia hesitates.) E says, "Do you want me to come with you?" (Alia says something U to E.) E says, "OK, I'll come with you," and walks over to Linda with Alia.) E says, "Brush Linda's hair. Go ahead. It's OK." (As Alia gets closer to Linda, Linda flips one side of her hair back toward Alia. Alia then starts to lift the brush to Linda, but stops, turns away from Linda, and says, "I don't want to.") E and Linda reassure Alia that it's OK, and E then takes the brush and brushes Linda's hair, showing Alia that Linda doesn't mind. E gives the brush back to Alia, tells her that it's her turn to do it, and again encourages Alia. Alia finally brushes Linda's hair slightly.)

604. (C) *Can you give Kelly a shot?* (Kanzi picks up the shot and holds it out toward Kelly, who moves away, so he gives himself a shot in the wrist, without removing the cover. He then offers the shot up to Kelly again, but she still moves back. Kanzi takes a bite of lettuce and offers the shot up to Kelly again, and she finally takes it.) [C is scored because Kanzi clearly attempts to give the syringe to Kelly, even though Kelly does not initially take it.]

604A. (PC) *Can you give Lisa a shot?* (Alia picks up the shot, looks up at Lisa, pokes the tent with the shot. As she pulls the shot out from the tent, the shot hits the chair behind her. Alia then turns to the chair and touches the chair with the shot a few more times. She then tries to take the red cap off the tip, then turns the shot over and tries to get the bottom cap off the shot. Still not successful, Alia goes to E behind the mirror and asks, "Can I open this, Mommy? I open it?") E says, "No, don't open it. I don't want you to open it. Do what Mommy asked you." (Alia then uses the shot to poke E.)

605. (C) *Go get the balloon that's in the microwave.* (Kanzi takes a bite of tomato out of a bag of food that he has been eating from and then goes to the microwave, gets the balloon, sits on the counter, and slaps it in his lap.)

605A. (C) *Go get the balloon that's in the oven.* (Alia goes directly to the oven in the kitchen, gets the balloon, and brings it to E.)

606. (C3) *Can you brush the doggie's hair?* (Kanzi picks up the dog, moves it out of the array, picks up the brush, and puts the brush under the dog's mouth, sort of like he is brushing it under the chin.) E is not certain that that action is "brushing" as opposed to "touching with the brush" and says, "Brush the doggie." (Kanzi continues with the same action.) [The hair on the stuffed dog is very short, and it is assumed that Kanzi uses only a minimal brushing action as there is little to brush.]

Response refinement.—E says, "Can you brush his bottom, his butt?" (Kanzi brushes his own hair, brushes under the dog's chin, then brushes his own hair again.) E says, "Can you brush his tail?" (Kanzi brushes his own hair, then brushes under the dog's chin.) E says, "Can you brush his feet?" (Kanzi holds the brush under the dog's chin.) E says, "Can you brush his tummy?" (Kanzi brushes his own hair.) E says, "Can you brush his head?" (Kanzi brushes his own arm.) E says, "Brush the doggie." (Kanzi brushes the dog's tummy, then again under his chin.) [E is suggesting different body parts to see whether Kanzi has an understanding of them and whether he will engage in a more elaborate "brushing" action.]

606A. (C) *Can you brush the doggie's hair?* (Alia does so.)

607. (C) *Can you put the blanket on the doggie?* (Kanzi does so.)
607A. (C) *Can you put the blanket on the doggie?* (Alia does so.)

608. (C) *Can you brush Rose's hair?* (Kanzi picks up the brush and looks at Rose. He is uncertain as to whether this is OK with Rose.) E says, "That's right." (Kanzi points to Rose, then touches her head and holds the brush toward it in a nonverbal request to see if it is OK with Rose.) E says, "Go ahead. That's real good, Kanzi." Rose then realizes what Kanzi wants to do and leans her head toward him, but he is still uncertain because she is wearing headphones and he doesn't know how to brush with them in her hair. (Kanzi tentatively approaches Rose's head with the brush.) Rose seems to realize what Kanzi wants to do and that the headphones may be a problem. She takes her headphones off as he tries to touch the brush to her hair. E says, "Brush it some more." (Kanzi then tries to take the tie out of her hair so that he can brush her hair.) E says, "Oh, that's very nice. Uh huh." Rose does not like him to take the tie out of her hair and will not typically let him do so, so he touches the brush to her hair in that area and then stops, waiting for her to take out the tie.]

608A. (C) *Can you brush Nathaniel's hair?* (Alia answers, "Yeah," then picks up the brush, takes it over to Nathaniel, and immediately brushes his hair. The sibling relationship between Nathaniel and Alia apparently makes it easier for Alia to negotiate interactions that entail intrusions into "personal space.")

609. (PC) *Can you make the doggie chase the bug?* (Kanzi tosses the bug at the dog, then picks up the dog and puts the bug on the dog's tummy.) E says, "Make 'em chase." (Kanzi puts the bug on the dog's tummy, then in the dog's mouth, then throws them both down to indicate that he is done.) [PC was scored because the verb was not clearly depicted in any of Kanzi's responses with the dog and the bug.]

609A. (PC) *Can you make the doggie chase the bug?* (Alia goes over and sits down by the bug. She looks at the bug and squirms. She picks up the bug and then drops it. She grabs the chimpanzee puppet with one hand, looks back at the bug, and puts her hand in the puppet. Then she picks up the toothpaste.)

610. (C) *Go get the shot that's in the microwave.* (Kanzi does so.)
610A. (OE) *Go get the shot that's in the oven.* (Alia tries to open the oven door but appears to have trouble. E opens the oven door. Alia gets all the objects out of the oven, carries them to the living room, and starts watching television.) E says, "Are you going to give them to me?" (Alia hands E the stick, then the shot, but not the pear.)

611. (PC) *Can you give the bug a shot?* (Kanzi picks up the bug.) E says, "That's right." (Kanzi holds the bug out to E.) E says, "Do you see the shot? (Kanzi holds the bug out to Kelly.)

Error correction.—E gives the bug a shot. (Kanzi holds the bug out to Kelly.) E says, "You're just gonna give the bug to Kelly, all right?" (Kanzi says, "Whuu," and hands it to Kelly.)

611A. (W) *Can you give the bug a shot?* (Alia gets the toothpaste and tries to take off the cap.) E says, "Can you give the bug a shot? Alia." (Alia looks at something across the room.) E says, "Alia." (Alia returns her attention to the toothpaste.)

612. (C) *Go get the pine needles that are in the bedroom.* (Kanzi goes to the bedroom door and waits for Rose.) E says, "That's right. Rose will open it." (As Rose approaches, Kanzi points to the door. When it is open, he strolls in, gets the pine needles, and brings them out.) Rose says to Kanzi, "Were you supposed to get the pine needles?" (Kanzi puts the pine needles in the array.)

612A. (C) *Get the pine needles that are in the bedroom.* (Alia does so.)

613. (PC) *Take the potato that's in the water outdoors.* (Kanzi takes both potatoes to the play-yard door. He gets the lock off himself, takes both potatoes outdoors, stands there, and looks around.) E says, "Yeah, leave it down and come on back. That's right." (Kanzi does so.)

613A. (NR) *Take the potato that's in the water outdoors.* (Alia goes over to the bowl of water with the potato in it and tries to pick it up. She then refuses, "Too heavy. Too heavy.") E comes out and says, "All right, I'll show you."

614. (C) *Can you put the bunny on your hand?* (Kanzi does so, making a sound like "hand," and puts his hand in the bunny's mouth, after putting the puppet on the other hand.)

614A. (C) *Can you put the chimpanzee on your hand?* (Alia gets the chimpanzee puppet and puts her hand near the opening of the puppet hole. She then rapidly moves her hands up and down on the puppet.)

Error correction.—E comes out and says, "Let me show you, Alia." [C is scored even though Alia did not place her hand in the chimpanzee puppet as she appeared to understand the sentence and the distinction between *on* and *in* is not one utilized for scoring.]

615. (C) *Can you tickle Linda with the bunny?* (Kanzi puts the bunny puppet on his hand, walks bipedally toward Linda, and touches Linda with the puppet gingerly.) [This is scored as correct since Kanzi typically initiates tickle games with a light touch and waits for a response.]

615A. (C) *Can you tickle Nathaniel with the chimpanzee?* (Alia does so.)

616. (C) *Go get the lettuce that's in the microwave.* (Kanzi gets the lettuce, then looks around and stops as he hears a noise in the colony room.) When he does not return, E says, "Now bring it back." Rose also approaches Kanzi and says, "Are you supposed to bring it to Sue? Go ahead." (Kanzi returns with the lettuce.)

616A. (OE) *Go get the lettuce that's in the oven.* (Alia goes directly to the oven in the kitchen and opens the lower drawer of the oven, where a fork, a shot, and a bag of lettuce are located. Alia first picks up the fork, then the bag of lettuce, then the shot, and carries all the objects to the living room, where she says, "Mom, I get this out oven. Mom, I get the shot out this oven. Mom, I get this. . . ." Alia then turns back to the oven and says, "I can't close this oven.") E comes out from behind the mirror and says, "You don't have to close it. That's OK. Alia, Mommy just wants the lettuce." (Alia approaches E still carrying all three objects. She extends her left hand to E—the one holding the bag of lettuce and the fork—and says, "Here.")

Error correction.—E does not take the objects. She says, "Put everything else back. Just give Mommy the lettuce." (Alia turns back toward the oven, walks a few steps, then turns back to E and holds out the shot in her right hand, asking, "This?") E says, "Put everything else back." (Alia continues to the oven.) E says, "Give Mommy the lettuce." (Alia puts the shot back into the oven, then holds out the fork to E and asks, "This?") E says, "Just the lettuce." (Alia asks, "This fork?") E says, "I don't know." E makes this reply not wanting to help Alia decide which objects should go back into the oven, wanting Alia to decide which is the lettuce and to put the other objects back. (Alia then puts the fork back into the oven and carries the lettuce to E as she says, "I got the lettuce.")

617. (C) *Make the snake bite Linda.* (Kanzi picks up the snake, approaches Linda, and holds the snake's mouth up to Linda's shin.) E says, "Ouuuh, it bit her, did it? OK."

617A. (C) *Make the snake bite Nathaniel.* (Alia gets up, touches the snake, and pulls her hands back as if scared. She then gets the snake and slowly walks toward Nathaniel as though sneaking up on him.)

618. (PC) *Give the peas and the sweet potatoes to Kelly.* (Kanzi gives the sweet potatoes to Kelly.) E says, "That's right. Give her the peas also, give her some peas."

618A. (C1) *Give the peas and the sweet potato to Linda.* (Alia eats some Jello and accidentally spills the peas while gathering up the objects.)

619. (C) *Give Linda a hug.* (Kanzi goes over to Linda and puts his cheek against her shoulder.)

619A. (C) *Give Nathaniel a hug.* (Alia says something U, then runs over and gives Nathaniel a hug.)

620. (C) *Tickle Rose with the bunny.* (Kanzi picks up the bunny puppet and holds it to Rose's knee, using the same gesture he used when asked to tickle Linda with the bunny in trial 615. Kanzi tends to touch recipients briefly and wait to see if they are willing to tickle.)

Response refinement.—However, in this case, because he has a puppet on his hand, and because Rose has no knowledge of the sentence, she assumes that Kanzi is attempting to give her the puppet, although he is clearly not handing it to her. Consequently, Rose says, "Me . . . the bunny?" takes the puppet away from Kanzi, and puts it on her hand.) E says, "Make the bunny tickle her." (Kanzi touches the bunny.) E says, "Put the bunny on your hand. Put the bunny on Kanzi's hand." (Kanzi touches Rose, sort of tickling her, as he knows that he is not permitted to grab things from Rose, and he will not do so unless he wishes to be intentionally bad.) Rose takes the puppet off her hand and hands it back to Kanzi, as he does not appear to respond to being tickled by her. E says, "Uh huh, put it on your hand and make it tickle Rose." (Kanzi puts it on his foot.) E says, "On your hand." (Kanzi continues to put it on his foot.) E says, "You want it on your foot?" (Kanzi pulls it on his foot real good.) E says, "Uh huh, now make it tickle Rose. Tickle Rose with the bunny." (Kanzi tickles her with the foot that has the bunny puppet on it.) E says, "There you go."

620A. (C) *Tickle Katie with the chimpanzee.* (Alia does so.)

621. (OE) *Go get the Coke that's in the T-room.* (Kanzi goes in, picks up the Coke, and stays in the T-room.) E says, "Bring it back, Kanzi." (Kanzi brings back the raisins and the Coke.) E says, "Kanzi, I want just the Coke." (Kanzi sets the Coke down for E.)

621A. (OE) *Go get the Coke that's in the bathroom.* (Alia goes to the bathroom and gets the Coke and the raisins.)

622. (C) *Give the knife to Kelly.* (Kanzi makes a sound like "Kelly" and hands her the knife.)

622A. (C) *Give the knife to Lisa.* (Alia does so.)

623. (C) *Can you knife the sweet potatoes?* (Kanzi does so.)

623A. (C) *Can you knife the sweet potato?* (Alia does so.)

624. (PC) *Hide the knife.* (Kanzi picks up the knife and stabs the lettuce with it, then puts the lettuce on the floor and tries to cut it. He makes a sound like "knife.") E says, "That's good, now put the knife down." (Kanzi does so.)

624A. (PC) *Hide the knife.* (Alia gets the knife and bangs it against the mirror while saying something U.) E says, "Hide the knife." (Alia says, "OK." She then walks around with the knife, saying something U. She goes in the bedroom. She looks in the trash can. She shuts the trash can and hits the knife on the lid. She says something else U and stabs the trash-can lid with the knife. She says something else U and opens the trash-can lid. She stabs into the trash can. Then she shuts the lid and resumes hitting the lid with the knife.)

Error correction.—E says, "Alia, can you hide the knife? Hide the knife." (Alia sets the knife on top of the trash-can lid.)

625. (C) *You go hide, go hide Kanzi.* (Kanzi does so.)

625A. (C) *You go hide.* (Alia goes into the bedroom and stands near the trash can.) E says, "Ah, very good. I see you." (Alia says "Boo.")

626. (C) *Drink the coffee that's hot.* (Kanzi does so very carefully.)

626A. (PC) *Drink the chocolate that's hot.* (Alia drinks one of the cups of chocolate. She then picks up the other cup of chocolate. She spills a little and wipes the spill with her hand. She then drinks the second cup.)

627. (C) *Go do ball slapping with Liz.* (Kanzi does so.)

627A. (PC) *Go do ball slapping with Nathaniel.* (Alia picks up the ball and carries it to Nathaniel. She then throws the ball at Nathaniel. Nathaniel puts his hands up in defense, and the ball drops onto the floor. Nathaniel runs to get the ball, and a game of keep-away ensues.)

628. (C) *Go get the raisins that are in the refrigerator.* (Kanzi does so, saying something that sounds like "raisin" as he takes them out.)

628A. (OE) *Get the raisins that are in the refrigerator.* (Alia runs to the refrigerator. She says, "Can't do it. Can't do it.") E opens the door for her. (Alia gets the raisins in her right hand, then looks back in the refrigerator and also gets a box of Jello.

Alia says, "I get it," while holding up the box of raisins. "I get it.") E says, "Yeah and what else?"

629. (C3) *Drink the ice coffee.* (Kanzi picks up the coffee with ice in it, pours it in a bowl, and brings it to his mouth.) E says, "Uh huh, can you take a drink?" (Kanzi drinks the coffee.)

629A. (PC) *Drink the ice chocolate.* (Alia first picks up the ice chocolate and drinks some of it, then picks up the hot chocolate and takes a small sip of that. She then drinks some more of the ice chocolate, then more of the hot chocolate.)

Error correction.—E then comes from behind the mirror and says, "Alia . . . which one's the ice chocolate?" (Alia answers, "Right here," sort of waving her hand around.) E believes that Alia has indicated the ice chocolate and says, "Then why are you drinking this one?" (E takes the cup of hot chocolate from Alia and puts it back on the floor with the other objects. Alia then continues to drink the hot chocolate.) E says, "Just wondering if you knew."

630. (C) *Go play grab with Linda.* (Kanzi goes to Linda, grabs her foot briefly, and waits to see whether she will respond in kind. Linda makes a shrugging gesture with her hands to indicate that she does not know what Kanzi has been asked to do and that she is hesitant to do anything with him, so Kanzi walks away.) [C is scored because Kanzi does attempt to initiate a game of "grab" with Linda.)

630A. (NR) *Go play grab with Linda.* (Alia refuses to do so.)

631. (C) *Liz is gonna chase Kanzi. . . .* (Kanzi interrupts.) *. . . Go tell her, go tell her to chase you.* (Kanzi goes over to Liz, touches her, and moves away. Liz interprets this as a request to chase and chases Kanzi.)

631A. (C) *Nathaniel's going to chase Alia.* (Alia goes up to Nathaniel and says, "Nathaniel, Nathaniel chase me. Got to chase me." When Nathaniel turns around to Alia, Alia turns and starts to run away from Nathaniel and into the kitchen. Nathaniel runs after Alia, who continues through the kitchen and back into the living room.)

632. (C) *Go get the noodles that are in the bedroom.* (Kanzi goes and sits by the bedroom door, waiting for Rose to open it.) E says, "Get the noodles that are in the bedroom." E repeats the sentence as Rose takes a rather long time to come open the door. (Kanzi makes a sound like "ooll," gets the noodles, and shakes them as he brings them out of the bedroom.) [C is scored here because the hesitation is a function of Rose taking a long time, not Kanzi.]

632A. (OE) *Go get the noodles that are in the bedroom.* (Alia goes directly to the bedroom, where she finds a jar of oil, noodles in a bag, and an apple lined up on the floor. Alia picks up all the objects and carries them back to the living room and to the other array of objects. She looks down at the living-room array of objects and says, "Where's the noodles?")

Error correction.—E comes out from behind the one-way mirror and says, "Alia, let's put everything back." (Alia tries to talk to E, but E insists on putting everything back since Alia had carried all the objects from the bedroom to the living room.) E says, "Let's put everything back. We're going to do this again." (E guides Alia back to the bedroom as Alia tries again to talk to E. E helps Alia put all the objects back into the bedroom, then repeats the trial.) E says, "Turn around. Now listen. Just get what Mommy tells you. Go get the noodles that are in the bedroom." (Alia says,

"OK," then runs back to the bedroom. There, she picks up the bag of noodles, carries it back to the living room and to the living-room array of objects. Alia then picks up the other bag of noodles from the living room array, holds it up to the camera, and says, "Look this." She then carries both bags of noodles back to the bedroom. En route, she slows and looks at both bags, holds up the bag of noodles she retrieved from the array and the living room, and says something U as she continues into the bedroom. She then places one bag of noodles in line with the other objects in the bedroom and carries the other bag of noodles back to the living room. Once in the living room, Alia says, "I got this one," as she holds out the bag of noodles and gestures with her other hand back toward the bedroom.)

633. (C) *Rose is going to grab Kanzi.* (Kanzi makes a sound like "grab," then looks around briefly at Rose. He sits stiffly with his back to Rose and appears to be waiting to be grabbed. Rose does nothing.) E says, "Turn around so she can grab you." (Kanzi turns part way around, touches Rose's leg, and looks at her. Then he holds his hand out to be grabbed.) Rose grabs Kanzi. [C is scored because Kanzi appeared to understand the sentence and was prepared for Rose to grab him before E encouraged him to turn around. On seeing that Rose did not know what to do, Kanzi acted in a way that clarified his expectation for Rose.]

633A. (C) *Nathaniel's going to grab Alia.* (Alia goes directly to Nathaniel and says something U to him. Nathaniel then starts to grab and tickle Alia. Alia then says, "I done." Nathaniel stops tickling Alia. Alia turns around and says, "I done grabbing.")

634. (I) *Put the shoe in the raisins.* (Kanzi picks up the raisins, opens them up, and puts them in a bowl.) E says, "OK, now put the shoe in the raisins. (Kanzi puts one tiny raisin in the shoe, then proceeds to untie the shoe.) [I is scored instead of PC because taking the raisins out of the box and putting them in a bowl is something that is often done with the raisins prior to acting on them in some other manner and probably does not reflect Kanzi's attempt to respond to the sentence.]

634A. (I) *Put the shoe in the raisins.* (Alia takes a raisin from the bowl of raisins in the array in front of her and places it in her mouth, takes it out of her mouth, then picks up the shoe in the array and puts the same raisin in the shoe. Alia then tries to get the raisin out of the shoe but seems to have trouble finding it. Alia then pauses to look across the room, apparently at the television.)

Error correction.—"Alia, put the shoe in the raisins." (Alia continues to look inside the shoe, then gets more raisins from the bowl of raisins and starts to eat them.) E says, "Don't eat them." (Alia takes the raisins out of her mouth and puts them into the shoe as she continues to watch television. When she takes her hand out of the shoe, she reaches with her other hand back inside the shoe, takes the raisin, and eats it. Her back is turned to E, so she is probably trying to sneak the raisin back into her mouth without E seeing her.)

635. (C) *Liz is going to tickle Kanzi.* (Kanzi looks toward Liz, holds his hand out to her, vocalizes "enngh," then approaches Liz, then goes over and sits down near her and holds his hand out to her. Liz stands up. Kanzi motions toward himself, then laughs, then signs *tickle*, then leans down to be tickled. Liz tickles him.)

635A. (C2) *Linda is going to tickle Alia.* (Alia slowly approaches Linda but does nothing else.) E says, "Linda is going to tickle Alia." (Alia lies down on the floor, rolls over, and looks at Lisa as if expecting to be tickled.)

636. (PC) *Kanzi is going to chase Rose.* (Kanzi looks at Rose and scoots over toward her, as though waiting for her to run away. Rose does nothing. Kanzi touches Rose. Rose gets up, and Kanzi then backs away, stops, looks at Rose, and waits for her to run. Rose doesn't, so Kanzi approaches instead.)

Error correction.—E tells Rose what is supposed to happen. Kanzi then gestures toward Rose, and she chases him.

636A. (I) *Alia is going to chase Mommy.* (Alia goes to E and says, "Mommy, chase me, chase me." E does so.) [Alia's vocal expression is the inverse of what was requested here, and she may have intended to reverse the action. However, her behavior gives no reason to conclude this. She seems to be eliciting a chase game in her typical manner and to interpret E's announcement as a general one regarding a game of chase.]

637. (C) *Go get the banana that's in the refrigerator.* (Kanzi goes to the refrigerator and gets a banana, making a sound like "ana.")

637A. (C2) *Go get the banana that's in the refrigerator.* (Alia does so.)

638. (PC) *Take the noodles outdoors.* (Kanzi walks away with his bowl of Coke, making a sound like "whuup.") E says, "Kanzi, take the noodles outdoors." (Kanzi continues to walk toward the play-yard door, saying, "Whup.") E says, "Kanzi, you have to come back here and get them. There aren't any out there." (Kanzi goes right on outdoors.) E says, "Come back." (Kanzi makes a sound like "uhhn" and vocalizes something else U.) Rose tells Kanzi to come back in as he is just sitting outside doing nothing, and she realizes that he must not be responding to a sentence.

Error correction.—E asks Kanzi to sit down and tells him to look around. (Kanzi makes a sound like "look around.") E repeats the sentence. (Kanzi carries the request out appropriately.)

638A. (C) *Take the noodles outdoors.* (Alia does so. Then she also brings the noodles back in.)

639. (C) *Take the banana to the bedroom.* (Kanzi makes a sound like "ana.") E replies, "Uh huh." (Kanzi starts to grab the banana with his foot, then picks it up with his hand and carries it bipedally to the bedroom while drinking juice.)

639A. (C) *Take the banana to the bedroom.* (Alia does so.)

640. (PC) *Go vacuum Liz.* (Kanzi goes over to the vacuum, takes the end of the hose, pulls it over, and puts it on Linda's shoe.)

Error correction.—E says, "That's pretty good, Kanzi. Can you vacuum Liz now?" (Linda giggles and laughs and looks like she is having a great time, so Kanzi continues to vacuum her.) E says, "Do it to Liz too, to Liz." (Kanzi stops vacuuming Linda and looks at Liz.) E says, "Vacuum Liz." (Kanzi briefly touches the vacuum to Liz but does not play with it as he had done with Linda.)

640A. (C) *Go vacuum Nathaniel.* (Alia goes over to the upright vacuum. She tries but is unable to get the vacuum handle into the pushing position. She continues to attempt this by stepping on the button on the front rather than the appropriate button on the side.) E steps on the appropriate button and lowers the handle to Alia.

(Alia tries to manipulate the vacuum but has great difficulty because of its weight and awkwardness.) E says, "I'll help. I'll help, OK? You tell me where to go." (With E's help, Alia directs the vacuum over to Nathaniel.) E says, "Here, I'll help." (Alia tries to run over Nathaniel's feet with the vacuum.)

641. (C) *Show me the ball that's on TV.* (Kanzi does so.)
641A. (NG).

642. (C) *Go put some soap on Liz.* (Kanzi picks up the liquid soap.) E says, "Uh huh." (Kanzi squeezes out a little, walks bipedally with it, and wipes it on Liz. He gets a big reaction out of this from Liz, so he decides to try it with Linda also to see what she does.)
642A. (C) *Go put soap on Nathaniel.* (Alia gets the can of soap and takes the lid off. She shakes it and points it toward Nathaniel. She goes over and puts the opening right up against Nathaniel's arm.)

643. (C) *Rose is gonna chase Kanzi.* (Kanzi looks at Rose.) E says, "Rose is going to chase you." (Kanzi looks at Rose, puts his bowl down, signs *chase*, points to Rose, then runs away. Rose chases Kanzi.)
643A. (C) *Nathaniel is gonna chase Alia.* (Alia looks at Nathaniel and says, "Nathaniel, chase me, chase me," then runs away from him. Nathaniel chases her.) [This sentence was inadvertently given twice as "Nathaniel" was substituted on one occasion for "Rose" and on another for "Liz." See trial 631.]

644. (C) *Put on the monster mask and scare Linda.* (Kanzi puts on the monster mask and walks bipedally toward Linda, who does not react. He then puts the monster mask in Liz's lap.) E says, "Put the monster mask on your head and scare Linda. (Kanzi puts the monster mask on his head and walks over toward Linda, who again does not react.)
644A. (PC) *Put on the monster mask and scare Linda.* (Alia says, "Don wanna [something U]," then goes over to her toy shelf and says, "That, see this hat.") E says, "OK." (Alia puts on the hat and looks at Linda, then covers her face with the hat, then puts the hat on her head and walks back to E.)
Error correction.—E says, "What are you doing?" (Alia says something U.) E says, "Well, do it." (Alia looks at E.) E says, "Alia, go back. Listen, can you put on the monster mask and scare Linda?" (Alia says, "[Something U] not.") E says, "It's OK." (Alia says, "I want this hat," and puts the hat on her head, then says, "Mommy, I wanna wear this hat.") E says, "OK."

645. (C) *I want Kanzi to grab Rose.* (Kanzi turns around and grabs Rose on the leg, then walks away.)
Response refinement.—E says, "Grab her some more." (Kanzi grabs Rose again.) E says, "That's right, go ahead." (Kanzi grabs her again.) E says, "Grab her again." (Kanzi grabs her foot.) E says, "Grab her good." (Kanzi continues grabbing her foot, then stops.) E says, "Can you grab her foot?" (Kanzi grabs her foot and pulls hard on it.) E says, "Can you grab her hand? Grab her hand." (Kanzi continues to grab her foot, then grabs the other foot.) E says, "Can you grab her hair?" (Kanzi grabs

her foot.) E says, "Can you grab her tummy?" (Kanzi continues to grab her foot.) Rose says, "Where are you supposed to grab me?"

645A. (C) *I want Alia to grab Joshua.* (Alia does so.)

646. (C) *Kanzi, take the mushrooms to Matata.* (Kanzi picks up the mushrooms quickly and heads off toward the colony room. He pauses at the colony-room door, waiting for Rose to open it. When Rose gets there, he opens the door, takes the mushrooms into the colony room, and shoves them under the door of Matata's cage.)

646A. (C) *Take the grapes to Katie.* (Alia does so.)

647. (PC) *Show me the snake that's on the floor.* (Kanzi immediately points to the television without even looking at the array on the floor. The television is on top of the keyboard.) [There is a snake on the television.]

Error correction.—E says, "Where's the snake that's on the floor?" (Kanzi again points to the television.) E says, "The one on the floor. The snake on the floor. Look around. Look, the snake on the floor." (Kanzi finally sees the one on the floor. He pulls it over and bangs it with the back of his hand.)

647A. (NG).

648. (C) *Kanzi is going to chase Liz.* (Kanzi looks around but stays seated.) E says, "Kanzi is going to chase Liz." (Kanzi goes over to Liz, taps her on the leg, and moves away. She gets up and chases him.)

648A. (C) *Alia is going to chase Linda.* (Alia gets up from her chair, takes a few steps toward Linda, then stops, it seems, to watch television for a moment. She then looks over to Linda, walks two steps toward her, but then switches directions to the right and goes behind Linda and toward the kitchen. Linda and Nathaniel remain seated as Alia continues to walk into the kitchen. There, Alia says to E, "Mommy, I chase Linda. I chasing Linda.") E says, "Oh. Did you?" (Alia answers, "Yeah," although she never did chase after Linda, perhaps thinking that somehow Linda would follow her into the kitchen to chase.) [C is scored because she is attending to Linda but does not quite know how to get Linda to run away. She seems to be attempting to initiate some sort of interaction with Linda from a distance that would be appropriate to chasing, and, by self-report, she views her behavior as sufficient to have carried out the request.]

649. (C) *Go get the melon that's in the T-room.* (Kanzi stands up, makes a sound like "uh huh.") E says, "And bring it back to Sue." (Kanzi does so.)

649A. (C) *Get the peaches that are in the bathroom.* (Alia says, "OK," and does so.)

650. (C) *Linda is going to grab Kanzi.* (Kanzi walks over to Linda, looks at her, and sort of offers his side in an inviting grab posture. Linda reaches out and grabs his leg.)

650A. (C) *Linda is going to grab Alia.* (Alia goes to Linda and smiles and stays back as though anticipating that she will be grabbed.)

651. (C) *Kanzi is going to tickle Liz with the bunny.* (Kanzi picks up the bunny puppet, puts it on his hand, walks over to Liz, and begins tickling her leg. He also tickles Linda.) E says, "Just Liz." (Kanzi returns to tickling Liz.) E says, "You can

come back now." (Kanzi returns and makes a sound like "ana" as he picks up a piece of banana.)

651A. (C) *Alia is going to tickle Nathaniel with the bunny.* (Alia does so.)

652. (PC) *Linda is going to chase Kanzi.* (Kanzi goes to Linda and walks around her looking at her, watching for her to get up and chase him. She does nothing, so he walks on over to Liz and around her. Liz interprets this as a request to chase, which she does.)

652A. (PC) *Lisa is going to chase Alia.* (Alia smiles, gets up from her chair, and seems to look in the direction of Lisa. Alia then goes to the dinosaur tent and lies down inside the tent. She rolls over and seems to look again at Lisa and smiles. Then she gets out of the tent, walks past the testing mirror, through the kitchen, and back into the living room. Alia then climbs on the red construction toy, glancing back at Lisa once. Alia continues to play on the construction toy, then starts to talk to Katie and leans the construction toy toward her.) E says, "Alia, don't." (E comes from behind the mirror and gets Alia off the construction toy.) E says, "OK, we'll do the next one."

653. (C1) *Use the toothbrush and brush Liz's teeth.* (Kanzi looks around, grabs the toothbrush, and walks over to Liz. Liz opens her mouth when she sees the toothbrush coming, and Kanzi puts the toothbrush in and gently brushes once, then goes over and brushes Linda's teeth, as Linda is also waiting with her mouth open.)

653A. (PC) *Use the toothbrush and brush Linda's teeth.* (Alia picks up the toothbrush and carries it past Linda and toward the bathroom. She stops short of the bathroom and heads back into the living room, saying something U about brushing, then, "I want a toothpaste. Mommy, I need the toothpaste." Alia continues to E, "Mommy, I have no toothpaste.") Linda says, "I don't think you need toothpaste." E comes out from behind the mirror and says, "We don't have toothpaste. Don't use the toothpaste. Yeah, it's at home. Just brush Linda's teeth." (E goes back behind the mirror. Alia now has the toothbrush in her own mouth. She takes the toothbrush out of her mouth as she walks toward Linda. Alia stands facing Linda, then puts the toothbrush back in her own mouth and brushes her own teeth as she turns and watches television. Alia takes the toothbrush out of her mouth, looks back at Linda, and extends the toothbrush out to Linda at Linda's chest level. Linda takes the toothbrush from Alia. Alia then quickly turns away and goes to E behind the mirror.)

654. (C) *Drink the ice juice.* (Kanzi walks over to the array, picks up a straw, removes the paper wrapper, inserts the straw in the ice juice, and drinks it.)

654A. (PC) *Drink the ice juice.* (Alia first picks up the bowl of plain juice and takes a small sip, then puts it down. She then picks up the bowl of juice that has ice in it and proceeds to drink the entire amount, announcing, "All gone." She then turns toward E behind the mirror and holds the cup out to E as she says, "I drink it up.")

655. (PC) *Kanzi is gonna tickle Liz.* (Kanzi goes over to Liz and touches her briefly on the leg with his index finger, then backs away. Liz reaches her hand out to him and starts to tickle his neck. He gets down on the floor in a tickle posture.) [Kanzi

appeared to be initiating a "tickle" interaction with Liz, but the direction of the interaction was not clear.]

655A. (C) *Alia is going to tickle Nathaniel.* (Alia does so.)

656. (C) *Can you give the butter to Rose?* (Kanzi does so.)

656A. (C) *Can you give the butter to Nathaniel?* (Alia does so.)

657. (PC) *Drink the hot juice.* . . . (Someone has the external jack on her radio turned up right then, and music blares out while E is speaking.) . . . *Drink the hot juice.* (Kanzi goes over to the array, picks up the same straw used earlier to drink the ice juice, and inserts it into the warm orange juice. After drinking the warm orange juice, Kanzi takes the straw out of the orange drink and puts it into the iced grape juice.) E says, "Kanzi, the juice that's hot." (Kanzi makes a sound like "drink," then a sound like "hot.") E says, "Drink the juice that's hot." (Kanzi puts the straw in the hot grape juice and drinks it.)

657A. (PC) *Drink the hot juice.* (Alia picks up the ice juice and drinks from this cup for a while but, before finishing it, puts it down and picks up the other cup of juice. After taking a sip from the second cup of juice, Alia drops that cup, spills the juice, and stops drinking any more juice.)

658. (PC) *Can you make the bunny eat the sweet potato?* (Kanzi continues to drink his juice.) E says, "You wanna try again? Kanzi, make the bunny eat some sweet potato." (Kanzi goes over and looks at the television as though he is waiting for the bunny to appear and do something. He had been watching scenes of the bunny on television earlier that afternoon.) E says, "Give the bunny some sweet potato." (Kanzi picks up his bowl of partially eaten sweet potato and holds it out to E, then to the television, where he had seen the bunny.) [Kanzi seems to be trying to give the bunny on the television some sweet potato, except that the bunny is no longer on the television. Once Kanzi decides that E is talking about the bunny that was on the television, it is very difficult to focus his attention on the array or to get him to search for the bunny puppet.]

Error correction.—E says, "Do you see the bunny? Where's the bunny?" E is referring to the bunny puppet. (Kanzi answers E's query by pointing to the television and making a sound like "bunny.") E says, "I know he's not on TV." (The bunny is not on the screen now, and Kanzi is looking and waiting for him to appear there. Kanzi sits down, puts the potatoes down, and gestures to the bedroom. He wants to go in there and play as that is what he does at the end of each test session, and he is feeling done.) E says, "You wanna go in there and look for the bunny? Well, can you do what I. . . . (Kanzi makes a sound like "waah, waah, waah, waah.") E asks, "Where's the sweet potato? Find the sweet potato. Look for the sweet potato, please." Rose says, "Kanzi." (Kanzi goes to the display, picks up a sweet potato, and hands it to Rose, who ignores this.) E says, "Now give it to the bunny." (Kanzi says, "Whuh," and holds the sweet potato up to the television, making a sound like "there.") E says, "Put it down." (Kanzi then holds it up to the television again.) E comes out from behind the mirror. Rose says, "Kanzi, do you see a bunny any place?" (Kanzi points to the television.) Rose says, "You know what we're talking about . . . the toy bunny." Rose taps Kanzi on the head to get his attention. (Kanzi then picks up the bunny puppet, puts it on his hand, and holds the hand with the puppet on it up to the television.) E asks Kanzi if the bunny can bite the sweet potato and hands Kanzi the sweet potato. (Kanzi puts the sweet potato inside the hand puppet. This is reminiscent of his placing the toothpaste inside the monster mask on trial 394 when asked if he could brush the monster mask's teeth.)

658A. (C) *Can you make the bunny eat the sweet potato?* (Alia says, "Yes," says something else U, then picks up the sweet potato and says something U. Alia picks up the toy bunny and says, "Mr. Bunny want something to eat?" She then puts the sweet potato up to the bunny's mouth.)

659. (C) *Tickle Liz with the umbrella.* (Kanzi starts to turn around, then looks back at the display as though he realizes he needs to take something with him. He returns to grab the umbrella.) Meanwhile, E says, "Tickle Liz with the umbrella." (Kanzi picks up the umbrella, walks bipedally to Liz, touches her with the umbrella, then also touches Linda with the umbrella.) E says, "Not Linda, just Liz." (Kanzi returns to tickling Liz.)

659A. (C) *Tickle Nathaniel with the umbrella.* (Alia picks up the umbrella and gently touches Nathaniel once with the umbrella, then turns away and appears interested in opening the umbrella.)

660. (PC) *Liz is gonna tickle Kanzi with the bunny.* (Kanzi stands up and lifts the toy gorilla up briefly. It is laying on top of his keyboard.) E says, "Give Liz the bunny so she can tickle you." (Kanzi takes the toy gorilla to Liz and drops it on the floor in front of her with a play face. Liz picks it up and begins to tickle Kanzi.)

660A. (C) *Nathaniel's going to tickle Alia with the bunny.* (Alia stands up from her chair and goes to Nathaniel as she says, "Nathaniel, tickle me . . . with the bunny." Nathaniel turns to look at the television and does not respond to Alia. Alia says something U to Nathaniel about tickling her with the bunny. Nathaniel seems to ignore Alia and continues to watch the television. Alia then leaves Nathaniel and picks up the toy that Linda is playing with. Linda directs Alia back to the testing area, saying, "I think you need to finish what you're doing over there," and does not let Alia have the toy. Alia walks back to the array of objects as Linda adds, "Mommy didn't say you were done." Alia then picks up the toy bunny and carries it to Nathaniel. She hands the bunny to Nathaniel and says, "Nathaniel." Nathaniel then tickles Alia with the bunny.)

REFERENCES

Ainsworth, M. D. S. (1973). The development of infant-mother attachment. In B. M. Caldwell & H. N. Ricciuti (Eds.), *Reviews of child development research* (Vol. **3**). Chicago: University of Chicago Press.

Ainsworth, M. D. S. (1979). Attachment as related to mother-infant interaction. In J. S. Rosenblatt, R. A. Hinde, D. Beer, & M. Busnel (Eds.), *Advances in the study of behavior* (Vol. **9**). New York: Academic.

Altmann, S. A. (1967). The structure of primate social communication. In S. A. Altmann (Ed.), *Social communication among primates*. Chicago: University of Chicago Press.

Andrews, P., & Martin, L. (1987). Cladistic relationships of extant and fossil hominoids. *Journal of Human Evolution,* **16,** 101–108.

Asano, T., Kojima, T., Matsuzawa, T., Kubota, K., & Murofushi, K. (1982). Object and color naming in chimpanzees. (*Pan troglodytes*). *Proceedings of the Japan Academy,* **58B,** 118–122.

Bakeman, R., Adamson, L., & Strisik, P. (1989). Lags and logs: Statistical approaches to interaction. In M. H. Bornstein & J. Bruner (Eds.), *Interaction in human development*. Hillsdale, NJ: Erlbaum.

Bates, E., Benigni, L., Bretherton, I., Camaioni, L., & Volterra, V. (1979). *The emergence of symbols: Cognition and communication in infancy*. New York: Academic.

Bates, E., Bretherton, I., & Snyder, L. (1988). *From first words to grammar: Individual differences and dissociable mechanisms*. Cambridge: Cambridge University Press.

Bates, E., MacWhinney, B., Caselli, C., Devescovi, A., Natale, F., & Venza, V. (1984). A cross-linguistic study of the development of sentence interpretation strategies. *Child Development,* **55,** 341–354.

Bates, E., Thal, D., & Marchman, V. (1991). Symbols and syntax: A Darwinian approach to language development. In N. A. Krasnegor, D. M. Rumbaugh, R. L. Schiefelbusch, & M. Studdert-Kennedy (Eds.), *Biological and behavioral determinants of language development*. Hillsdale, NJ: Erlbaum.

Bayley, N. (1969). *The Bayley scales of infant development*. New York: Psychological Corp.

Benedict, H. (1979). Early lexical development: Comprehension and production. *Journal of Child Language,* **6,** 183–200.

Bennett, E. L., Rosenzweig, M. R., Morimoto, H., & Herbert, M. (1979). Maze training alters brain weights and cortical RNA/DNA ratios. *Behavioral and Neural Biology,* **26,** 1–22.

Bever, T. G. (1970). The cognitive basis for linguistic structures. In J. R. Hayes (Ed.), *Cognition and the development of language*. New York: Wiley.

Bishop, M. J., & Friday, A. E. (1986). Molecular sequences and hominoid phylogeny. In

B. Wood, L. Martin, & P. Andrews (Eds.), *Major topics in human evolution*. Cambridge: Cambridge University Press.

Bishop, Y. M. M., Fienberg, S. R., & Holland, P. W. (1975). *Discrete multivariate analysis: Theory and practice*. Cambridge, MA: MIT Press.

Bloom, L. M. (1973). *One word at a time: The use of single word utterances before syntax*. The Hague: Mouton.

Bloom, L. M. (1978). Language development and language disorders. New York: Wiley.

Boesch, C. (1978). Nouvelles observations sur les chimpanzes de la Foret de Tai (Côte d'Ivoire). *La Terre et la Vie*, **32**, 195–201.

Brown, R. (1973). *A first language: The early stages*. Cambridge, MA: Harvard University Press.

Brown, R., & Hanlon, C. (1970). Derivational complexity and the order of acquisition in child speech. In R. Brown (Ed.), *Psycholinguistics*. New York: Free Press.

Bruner, J. (1973). The organization of early skilled action. *Child Development*, **44**, 1–11.

Bruner, J. (1983). *Child's talk: Learning to use language*. New York: Norton.

Calvin, W. H., & Ojemann, G. A. (1980). *Inside the brain*. New York: New American Library.

Chapman, R. S., & Kohn, L. L. (1978). Comprehension strategies in two and three year olds: Animate agents or probable events? *Journal of Speech and Hearing Research*, **21**, 746–761.

Chapman, R. S., & Miller, J. F. (1975). Word order in early two and three word utterances: Does production precede comprehension? *Journal of Speech and Hearing Research*, **18**, 355–371.

Chomsky, N. (1988). *Language and problems of knowledge: The Managua*. Cambridge, MA: MIT Press.

Cocking, R. R., & McHale, S. (1981). A comparative study of the use of pictures and objects in assessing children's receptive and productive language. *Journal of Child Language*, **8**, 1–13.

Cohn, J. F., & Tronick, E. Z. (1987). Mother-infant face-to-face interaction: The sequence of dyadic states at 3, 6, and 9 months. *Developmental Psychology*, **23**, 68–77.

Crelin, E. S. (1987). *The human vocal tract: Anatomy, function, development and evolution*. New York: Vantage.

Cuvo, A. J., & Riva, M. T. (1980). Generalization and transfer between comprehension and production: A comparison of retarded and nonretarded persons. *Journal of Applied Behavior Analysis*, **13**, 315–331.

Davenport, R. K., Rogers, C. W., & Rumbaugh, D. M. (1973). Long-term cognitive deficits in chimpanzees associated with early impoverished rearing. *Developmental Psychology*, **9**, 343–347.

Davidson, I. (1991). The archaeology of language origins: A review. *Antiquity*, **48**, 63–65.

Demetras, M., Post, K., & Snow, D. (1986). Feedback to first language learners: The role of repetitions and clarification questions. *Journal of Child Language*, **13**, 275–292.

de Villiers, J. G., & de Villiers, P. A. (1973). Development of the use of word order in comprehension. *Journal of Psycholinguistic Research*, **2**, 331–342.

de Waal, F. B. M. (1987). Tension regulation and nonreproductive function of sex in captive bonobos (*Pan paniscus*). *National Geographic Research*, **3**, 318–335.

de Waal, F. B. M. (1988). The communicative repertoire of captive bonobos (*Pan paniscus*), compared to that of chimpanzees. *Behavior*, **106**, 183–251.

Falk, D. (1983). Cerebral cortices of East African early hominids. *Science*, **221**, 1072–1074.

Fienberg, S. E. (1980). *The analysis of cross-classified categorical data* (2d ed.). Cambridge, MA: MIT Press.

Fodor, J. (1983). *The modularity of mind*. Cambridge, MA: MIT Press.

Fouts, R. S. (1973). Acquisition and testing of gestural signs in four young chimpanzees. *Science*, **180**, 978–980.

Fouts, R. S. (1975). Communication with chimpanzees. In G. Jurth & I. Eibl-Eibesfeldt (Eds.), *Hominisation und Verhalten*. Stuttgart: Gustav Fischer.

Fouts, R. S., & Fouts, D. H. (1989). Loulis in conversation with cross-fostered chimpanzees. In R. A. Gardner, B. T. Gardner, & T. E. Van Cantfort (Eds.), *Teaching sign language to chimpanzees*. Albany: State University of New York Press.

Fouts, R. S., Fouts, D. H., & Schoenfeld, D. (1984). Sign language conversational interaction between chimpanzees. *Sign Language Studies*, **42**, 1–12.

Fouts, R. S., Fouts, D. H., & Van Cantfort, T. E. (1989). The infant Loulis learns signs from cross-fostered chimpanzees. In R. A. Gardner, B. T. Gardner, & T. E. Van Cantfort (Eds.), *Teaching sign language to chimpanzees*. Albany: State University of New York Press.

Fraser, C., Bellugi, U., & Brown, R. (1963). Control of grammar in imitation, production, and comprehension. *Journal of Verbal Learning and Verbal Behavior*, **2**, 121–135.

Furness, W. (1916). Observations on the mentality of chimpanzees and orangutans. *Proceedings of the American Philosophical Society*, **45**, 281–290.

Gardner, B. T., & Gardner, R. A. (1971). Two-way communication with an infant chimpanzee. In A. M. Schrier & F. Stollnitz (Eds.), *Behavior of nonhuman primates* (Vol. **4**). New York: Academic.

Gardner, R. A., Gardner, B. T., & Van Cantfort, T. E. (Eds.). (1989). *Teaching sign language to chimpanzees*. Albany: State University of New York Press.

Gauker, C. (1990). How to learn language like a chimpanzee. *Philosophical Psychology*, **3**, 31–53.

Ghiglieri, M. P. (1984). *The chimpanzees of Kibale Forest: A field study of ecology and social structure*. New York: Columbia University Press.

Gibson, D., & Ingram, D. (1983). The onset of comprehension and production in a language delayed child. *Applied Psycholinguistics*, **4**, 359–375.

Gleason, J. G. (1989). *The development of language*. Columbus, OH: Merrill.

Goldin-Meadow, S., Seligman, M. E. P., & Gelman, R. (1976). Language in the two-year-old. *Cognition*, **4**, 189–202.

Golinkoff, R. M. (1991, May). *Principles in language acquisition: Advance or retreat*. Paper presented at the twenty-fourth annual Gatlinburg Conference on Research and Theory in Mental Retardation and Developmental Disabilities, Miami.

Golinkoff, R. M., Hirsh-Pasek, K., Cauley, K. M., & Gordon, L. (1987). The eyes have it: Lexical and syntactic comprehension in a new paradigm. *Journal of Child Language*, **14**, 23–45.

Goodall, J. (1986). *The chimpanzees of Gombe: Patterns of behavior*. Cambridge, MA: Belknap.

Green, J. A. (1988). Loglinear analysis of cross-classified data: Applications in developmental research. *Child Development*, **59**, 1–25.

Greenfield, P. M., & Savage-Rumbaugh, E. S. (1984). Perceived variability and symbol use: A common language-cognition interface in children and chimpanzees (*Pan troglodytes*). *Journal of Comparative Psychology*, **98**, 201–218.

Greenfield, P. M., & Savage-Rumbaugh, E. S. (1990). Grammatical combination in *Pan paniscus:* Processes of learning and invention in the evolution and development of language. In S. Parker & K. Gibson (Eds.), *Comparative developmental psychology of language and intelligence in primates*. Cambridge: Cambridge University Press.

Greenfield, P. M., & Savage-Rumbaugh, E. S. (1991). Imitation, grammatical development and the invention of a protogrammar by an ape. In N. A. Krasnegor, D. M. Rumbaugh, R. L. Schiefelbusch, & M. Studdert-Kennedy (Eds.), *Biological and behavioral determinants of language development*. Hillsdale, NJ: Erlbaum.

Greenfield, P. M., & Smith, J. H. (1976). *The structure of communication in early language development.* New York: Academic.

Greenough, W. T., Black, J. E., & Wallace, C. S. (1987). Experience and brain development. *Child Development,* **58,** 539—559.

Guess, D., & Baer, D. M. (1973). An analysis of individual differences in generalization between receptive and productive language in retarded children. *Journal of Applied Behavior Analysis,* **6,** 311–329.

Hakuta, K. (1982). Interaction between particles and word order in the comprehension of simple sentences in Japanese children. *Developmental Psychology,* **18,** 62–76.

Harre, R., & Reynolds, V. (1984). *The meaning of primate signals.* Cambridge: Cambridge University Press.

Harris, J. W. K. (1983). Cultural beginnings: Plio-Pleistocene archaeological occurrences from the Afar, Ethiopia. *African Archaeological Review,* **1,** 3–31.

Hayes, C. (1951). *The age in our house.* New York: Harper Bros.

Hayes, K. J., & Hayes, C. (1950). *Vocalization and speech in chimpanzees* [16-mm sound film]. State College, PA: Psychological Cinema Register.

Hayes, K. J., & Hayes, C. (1951). The intellectual development of a home-raised chimpanzee. *Proceedings of the American Philosophical Society,* **95,** 105–109.

Hayes, K. J., & Hayes, C. (1952a). Imitation in a home-raised chimpanzee. *Journal of Comparative and Physiological Psychology,* **45,** 450–459.

Hayes, K. J., & Hayes, C. (1952b). *Imitation in a home-raised chimpanzee* [16-mm silent film]. State College, PA: Psychological Cinema Register.

Hayes, K. J., & Hayes, C. (1953a). *The mechanical interest and ability of a home-raised chimpanzee* [16-mm silent film]. State College, PA: Psychological Cinema Register.

Hayes, K. J., & Hayes, C. (1953b). Picture perception in a home-raised chimpanzee. *Journal of Comparative and Physiological Psychology,* **46,** 470–474.

Hayes, K. J., & Hayes, C. (1954). The cultural capacity of chimpanzee. *Human Biology,* **26,** 288–303.

Hayes, K. J., & Nissen, C. (1971). Higher mental functions of a home-raised chimpanzee. In A. M. Schrier & F. Stollnitz (Eds.), *Behavior of nonhuman primates: Modern research trends.* New York: Academic.

Hayes, K. J., Thompson, R., & Hayes, C. (1953a). Concurrent discrimination learning set in chimpanzees. *Journal of Comparative and Physiological Psychology,* **46,** 105–107.

Hayes, K. J., Thompson, R., & Hayes, C. (1953b). Discrimination learning set in chimpanzees. *Journal of Comparative and Physiological Psychology,* **46,** 99–104.

Herman, L. (1987). Receptive competencies of language-trained animals. In J. S. Rosenblatt, C. Beer, M. C. Busnel, & P. J. B. Slater (Eds.), *Advances in the study of behavior* (Vol. **17**). Petaluma, CA: Academic.

Hirsh-Pasek, K., & Golinkoff, R. M. (1991). Language comprehension: A new look at some old themes. In N. A. Krasnegor, D. M. Rumbaugh, R. L. Schiefelbusch, & M. Studdert-Kennedy (Eds.), *Biological and behavioral determinants of language development.* Hillsdale, NJ: Erlbaum.

Hirsh-Pasek, K., Treiman, R., & Schneiderman, M. (1984). Brown and Hanlon revisited: Mothers' sensitivity to ungrammatical forms. *Journal of Child Language,* **11,** 81–88.

Hopkins, W. J., & Savage-Rumbaugh, E. S. (1991). Vocal communication as a function of differential rearing experiences in *Pan paniscus:* A preliminary report. *International Journal of Primatology,* **12,** 559–583.

Humphrey, N. K. (1983). *Consciousness regained.* Oxford: Oxford University Press.

Huttenlocher, J. (1974). The origins of language comprehension. In R. L. Solso (Ed.), *Theories of cognitive psychology.* Hillsdale, NJ: Erlbaum.

Jerison, H. J. (1985). On the evolution of mind. In D. A. Oakley (Ed.), *Brain and mind*. London and New York: Methuen.

Kano, T. (1980). Social behavior of wild pygmy chimpanzees (*Pan paniscus*) of Wamba: A preliminary report. *Journal of Human Evolution, 9*, 243–260.

Kano, T. (1982). The social group of pygmy chimpanzees (*Pan paniscus*) of Wamba. *Primates, 23*, 171–188.

Kellogg, W. N., & Kellogg, L. A. (1933). *The ape and the child*. New York: McGraw-Hill.

Kennedy, J. J. (1983). *Analyzing qualitative data: Introductory log-linear analysis for behavioral research*. New York: Praeger.

Klix, F. (1982). On the evolution of cognitive processes and performances. In D. R. Griffin (Ed.), *Animal mind—human mind*. New York: Springer.

Knoke, D., & Burke, P. J. (1980). *Log-linear models*. Newbury Park, CA: Sage.

Kuhl, P. K. (1987). Perception of speech and sound in early infancy. In P. Salapatek & L. Cohen (Eds.), *Handbook of infant perception: Vol. 2. From perception to cognition*. Orlando, FL: Academic.

Kuhl, P. K., & Miller, J. D. (1975). Speech perception by the chinchilla: Voiced-voiceless distinction in alveolar plosive consonants. *Science, 90*, 69–72.

Kuhl, P. K., & Miller, J. D. (1978). Speech perception by the chinchilla: Identification functions for synthetic VOT stimuli. *Journal of the Acoustical Society of America, 63*, 905–917.

Kuhl, P. K., & Padden, D. M. (1982). Enhanced discriminability at the phonetic boundaries for the voicing feature in macaques. *Perception and Psychophysics, 32*, 542–550.

Kuhl, P. K., & Padden, D. M. (1983). Enhanced discriminability at the phonetic boundaries for the voicing feature in macaques. *Perception and Psychophysics, 32*, 542–550.

Kuroda, S. (1980). Social behavior of the pygmy chimpanzees. *Primates, 21*, 181–197.

Kuroda, S. (1984). Interaction over food among pygmy chimpanzees. In R. L. Susman (Ed.), *The pygmy chimpanzee*. New York: Plenum.

Lamb, M. E. (1981a). Developing trust and perceived effectance in infancy. In L. P. Lipsitt (Ed.), *Advances in infancy research* (Vol. 1). Norwood, NJ: Albex.

Lamb, M. E. (1981b). The development of social expectations in the first year of life. In M. E. Lamb & L. R. Sherrod (Eds.), *Infant social cognition: Empirical and theoretical considerations*. Hillsdale, NJ: Erlbaum.

Le Gros Clark, W. E. (1978). *The fossil evidence for human evolution*. Chicago: University of Chicago Press.

Lempert, H. (1978). Extra syntactic factors affecting passive sentence comprehension by young children. *Child Development, 49*, 694–699.

Lieberman, P. (1968). Primate vocalizations and human linguistic ability. *Journal of the Acoustical Society of America, 44*, 1157–1164.

Lieberman, P. (1975). *On the origins of language*. New York: Macmillan.

Lock, A. (1980). *The guided reinvention of language*. London: Academic.

Lock, A. (1991). The role of social interaction in early language development. In N. A. Krasnegor, D. M. Rumbaugh, R. L. Schiefelbusch, & M. Studdert-Kennedy (Eds.), *Biological and behavioral determinants of language development*. Hillsdale, NJ: Erlbaum.

Lovell, K., & Dixon, E. M. (1967). The growth of the control of grammar in imitation, comprehension, and production. *Journal of Child Psychology and Psychiatry, 8*, 31–39.

McNeil, D. (1970). *The acquisition of language: The study of developmental psycholinguistics*. New York: Harper & Row.

Macphail, E. M. (1982). *Brain and intelligence in vertebrates* (Life Sciences Research Report). Oxford: Clarendon.

Macphail, E. M. (1985). Vertebrate intelligence: The null hypothesis. In L. Weiskrantz

(Ed.), *Animal intelligence: Proceedings of a Royal Society discussion meeting.* Oxford: Clarendon.

Mandler, J. M. (1990). A new perspective on cognitive development in infancy. *American Scientist,* **78,** 236–243.

Marler, P. (1976). Social organization, communication and graded signals: The chimpanzee and the gorilla. In P. P. G. Bateson & R. A. Hinde (Eds.), *Growing points in ethology.* New York: Cambridge University Press.

Matsuzawa, T. (1985a). Color naming and classification in a chimpanzee (*Pan troglodytes*). *Journal of Human Evolution,* **14,** 283–291.

Matsuzawa, T. (1985b). Use of numbers by a chimpanzee. *Nature,* **315,** 57–59.

Matsuzawa, T. (1989). Spontaneous pattern construction in a chimpanzee. In P. Heltne & L. A. Marquardt (Eds.), *Understanding chimpanzees.* Cambridge, MA: Harvard University Press.

Matsuzawa, T., Asano, T., Kubota, K., & Murofushi, K. (1986). Acquisition and generalization of numerical labeling by a chimpanzee. In D. Taub & F. King (Eds.), *Current perspectives in primate social dynamics.* New York: Van Nostrand Reinhold.

Miles, L. H. (1983). Apes and language: The search for communicative competence. In J. de Luce & H. T. Wilder (Eds.), *Language in primates: Perspectives and implications.* New York: Springer.

Morgan, J. L. (1986). *From simple input to complex grammar.* Cambridge, MA: MIT Press.

Mori, A. (1984). An ethological study of pygmy chimpanzees in Wamba, Zaire: A comparison with chimpanzees. *Primates,* **2,** 255–278.

Nelson, K. (1985). *Making sense: The acquisition of shared meaning.* New York: Academic.

Nelson, K. (1986). *Event knowledge: Structure and function in development.* Hillsdale, NJ: Erlbaum.

Oviatt, S. L. (1980). The emerging ability to comprehend language: An experimental approach. *Child Development,* **51,** 97–106.

Pate, J. L., & Rumbaugh, D. M. (1983). The language-like behavior of Lana chimpanzee: Is it merely discrimination and paired-associate learning? *Animal Learning and Behavior,* **11,** 134–138.

Patterson, F. G. (1978). The gestures of a gorilla: Language acquisition in another pongid. *Brain and Language,* **5,** 72–97.

Penner, S. (1987). Parental responses to grammatical and ungrammatical child utterances. *Child Development,* **58,** 376–384.

Perkins, W. H., & Kent, R. D. (1986). *Functional anatomy of speech, language, and hearing.* San Diego: College Hill.

Peters, A. (1983). *The units of language acquisition.* Cambridge: Cambridge University Press.

Piaget, J. (1954). *The construction of reality in the child* (M. Cook, Trans.). New York: Basic.

Pinker, S. (1981). A theory of the acquisition of lexical-interpretive grammars. In J. Bresnan (Ed.), *The mental representation of grammatical relations.* Cambridge, MA: MIT Press.

Pinker, S. (1984). *Language, learnability and language development.* Cambridge, MA: Harvard University Press.

Pinker, S. (1987a). The bootstrapping problem in language acquisition. In B. MacWhinney (Ed.), *Mechanisms of language learning.* Hillsdale, NJ: Erlbaum.

Pinker, S. (1987b). Formal models of language learning. *Cognition,* **7,** 217–283.

Premack, D. (1971). On the assessment of language competence in the chimpanzee. In A. M. Schrier & F. Stollnitz (Eds.), *Behavior of nonhuman primates* (Vol. **4**). New York: Academic.

Quine, W. V. (1960). *Word and object.* Cambridge, MA: MIT Press.

Rice, M. L. (1980). *Cognition to language: Categories, word meanings, and training.* Baltimore: University Park Press.

Rice, M. L., Buhr, J., & Nemeth, M. (1990). Fast mapping word learning abilities of language delayed preschoolers. *Journal of Speech and Hearing Disorders, 55,* 33–42.

Rice, M. L., & Woodsmall, L. (1988). Lessons from television: Children's word learning when viewing. *Child Development, 59,* 420–429.

Riesen, A. H. (1982). Effects of environments on development in sensory systems. In W. D. Neff (Ed.), *Contributions to sensory physiology* (Vol. 6). New York: Academic.

Roberts, K. (1983). Comprehension and production of word order in Stage I. *Child Development, 54,* 443–449.

Romski, M. A., & Sevcik, R. A. (1991). Patterns of language learning by instruction: Evidence from nonspeaking persons with mental retardation. In N. A. Krasnegor, D. M. Rumbaugh, R. L. Schiefelbusch, & M. Studdert-Kennedy (Eds.), *Biological and behavioral determinants of language development.* Hillsdale, NJ: Erlbaum.

Romski, M. A., Sevcik, R. A., & Pate, J. L. (1988). The establishment of symbolic communication in persons with mental retardation. *Journal of Speech and Hearing Disorders, 53,* 94–107.

Rumbaugh, D. M. (1977). *Language learning by a chimpanzee.* New York: Academic.

Rumbaugh, D. M. (1981). Who feeds Clever Hans? In T. A. Sebeok & R. Rosenthal (Eds.), *The Clever Hans phenomenon: Communication with horses, whales, apes, and people. Annals of the New York Academy of Sciences, 364,* 26–34.

Rumbaugh, D. M., Gill, T. V., & von Glasersfeld, E. C. (1973). Reading and sentence completion by a chimpanzee *(Pan). Science, 182,* 731–733.

Rumbaugh, D. M., Hopkins, W. D., Washburn, D. A., & Savage-Rumbaugh, E. S. (1991). Comparative perspectives of brain, cognition, and language. In N. A. Krasnegor, D. M. Rumbaugh, R. L. Schiefelbusch, & M. Studdert-Kennedy (Eds.), *Biological and behavioral determinants of language development.* Hillsdale, NJ: Erlbaum.

Rumbaugh, D. M., & Pate, J. L. (1984). The evolution of primate cognition: A comparative perspective. In H. L. Roitblat, T. G. Bever, & H. S. Terrace (Eds.), *Animal cognition.* Hillsdale, NJ: Erlbaum.

Rumbaugh, D. M., & Savage-Rumbaugh, E. S. (1980, Winter). A response to Herbert Terrace's article "Linguistic apes: What are they saying?" *New York University Education Quarterly,* p. 33.

Rumbaugh, D. M., von Glasersfeld, E., Warner, H., Pisani, P. P., Gill, T. V., Brown, J. V., & Bell, C. L. (1973). A computer-controlled language training system for investigating the language skills of young apes. *Behavioral Research Methods and Instrumentation, 5,* 385–392.

Sachs, J., & Truswell, L. (1978). Comprehension of two-word instructions by children in the one-word stage. *Journal of Child Language, 5,* 17–24.

Sarich, V. M. (1983). Retrospective on hominoid macromolecular systematics. In R. L. Ciochon & R. S. Corruccini (Eds.), *New interpretations of ape and human ancestry.* New York: Plenum.

Sarich, V. M. (1984). Pygmy chimpanzee systematics: A molecular perspective. In R. L. Susman (Ed.), *The pygmy chimpanzee: Evolutionary biology and behavior.* New York: Plenum.

Savage, E. S., & Bakeman, R. (1978). Sexual morphology and behavior in *Pan paniscus.* In *Proceedings of the Sixth International Congress of Primatology, Contemporary Psychology.* Basel: Karger.

Savage, E. S., Wilkerson, B. J., & Bakeman, R. (1977). Spontaneous gestural communication among conspecifics in the pygmy chimpanzee *(Pan paniscus).* In G. H. Bourne (Ed.), *Progress in ape research.* New York: Academic.

Savage-Rumbaugh, E. S. (1979). Symbolic communication—its origins and early development in the chimpanzee. *New Directions for Child Development, 3,* 1–15.

Savage-Rumbaugh, E. S. (1981). Can apes use symbols to represent their world? In T. A. Sebeok & R. Rosenthal (Eds.), *The Clever Hans phenomenon: Communication with horses, whales, apes, and people. Annals of the New York Academy of Sciences,* **364,** 35–59.

Savage-Rumbaugh, E. S. (1982). A pragmatic approach to chimpanzee language studies. In H. E. Fitzgerald, J. A. Mullins, & P. Gage (Eds.), *Child nurturance* (Vol. **3**). New York: Plenum.

Savage-Rumbaugh, E. S. (1984a). Acquisition of functional symbol use in apes and children. In H. L. Roitblat, T. G. Bever, & H. S. Terrace (Eds.), *Animal cognition.* Hillsdale, NJ: Erlbaum.

Savage-Rumbaugh, E. S. (1984b). *Pan paniscus* and *Pan troglodytes:* Contrasts in preverbal communicative competence. In R. Susman (Ed.), *The pygmy chimpanzee: Evolutionary biology and behavior.* New York: Plenum.

Savage-Rumbaugh, E. S. (1984c). Verbal behavior at a procedural level in the chimpanzee. *Journal of the Experimental Analysis of Behavior,* **41,** 223–250.

Savage-Rumbaugh, E. S. (1986). *Ape language: From conditioned response to symbol.* New York: Columbia University Press.

Savage-Rumbaugh, E. S. (1987). Communication, symbolic communication, and language: Reply to Seidenberg and Petitto. *Journal of Experimental Psychology: General,* **116,** 288–292.

Savage-Rumbaugh, E. S. (1988). A new look at ape language: Comprehension of vocal speech and syntax. In D. Leger (Ed.), *Comparative perspectives in modern psychology* (Nebraska Symposium on Motivation, Vol. **35**). Lincoln: University of Nebraska Press.

Savage-Rumbaugh, E. S. (1990). Language acquisition in a nonhuman species: Implications for the innateness debate. *Developmental Psychobiology,* **23,** 599–620.

Savage-Rumbaugh, E. S. (1991). Language learning in the bonobo: How and why they learn. In N. A. Krasnegor, D. M. Rumbaugh, R. L. Schiefelbusch, & M. Studdert-Kennedy (Eds.), *Biological and behavioral determinants of language development.* Hillsdale, NJ: Erlbaum.

Savage-Rumbaugh, E. S., & Brakke, K. (1990). Animal language: Methodological and interpretive issues. In M. Bekoff & D. Jamieson (Eds.), *Interpretation and explanation in the study of animal behavior: Vol. 1. Interpretation, intentionality and communication.* Boulder, CO: Westview.

Savage-Rumbaugh, E. S., Brakke, K., & Hutchins, S. (1992). Linguistic development: Contrasts between co-reared *Pan troglodytes* and *Pan paniscus.* In T. Nishida (Ed.), *Proceedings of the 13th International Congress of Primatology.* Tokyo: University of Tokyo Press.

Savage-Rumbaugh, E. S., McDonald, K., Sevcik, R. A., Hopkins, W. D., & Rubert, E. (1986). Spontaneous symbol acquisition and communicative use by pygmy chimpanzees *(Pan paniscus). Journal of Experimental Psychology: General,* **115,** 211–235.

Savage-Rumbaugh, E. S., Pate, J. L., Lawson, J., Smith, S. T., & Rosenbaum, S. (1983). Can a chimpanzee make a statement? *Journal of Experimental Psychology: General,* **112,** 457–492.

Savage-Rumbaugh, E. S., Romski, M. A., Hopkins, W. D., & Sevcik, R. A. (1989). Symbol acquisition and use by *Pan troglodytes, Pan paniscus,* and *Homo sapiens.* In P. G. Heltne & L. A. Marquardt (Eds.), *Understanding chimpanzees.* Cambridge, MA: Harvard University Press.

Savage-Rumbaugh, E. S., Romski, M. A., Sevcik, R. A., & Pate, J. L. (1983). Assessing symbol usage versus symbol competency. *Journal of Experimental Psychology: General,* **112,** 508–512.

Savage-Rumbaugh, E. S., & Rumbaugh, D. M. (1978). Symbolization, language and chimpanzees: A theoretical reevaluation based on initial language acquisition processes in four young *Pan troglodytes*. *Brain and Language,* **6,** 265–300.

Savage-Rumbaugh, E. S., & Rumbaugh, D. M. (1979). Chimpanzee problem comprehension: Insufficient evidence. *Science,* **206,** 1201–1202.

Savage-Rumbaugh, E. S., & Rumbaugh, D. M. (1982). Ape language is alive and well. *Anthropos,* **77,** 568–573.

Savage-Rumbaugh, E. S., Rumbaugh, D. M., & Boysen, S. (1978a). Linguistically mediated tool use and exchange by chimpanzees (*Pan troglodytes*). *Brain and Behavioral Sciences,* **4,** 539–554.

Savage-Rumbaugh, E. S., Rumbaugh, D. M., & Boysen, S. (1978b). Symbolic communication between two chimpanzees (*Pan troglodytes*). *Science,* **201,** 641–644.

Savage-Rumbaugh, E. S., Rumbaugh, D. M., & Boysen, S. (1980). Do apes use language? *American Scientist,* **68,** 49–61.

Savage-Rumbaugh, E. S., Rumbaugh, D. M., & McDonald, K. (1985). Language learning in two species of apes. *Neurosciences and Biobehavioral Reviews,* **9,** 653–665.

Savage-Rumbaugh, E. S., & Sevcik, R. A. (1984). Levels of communicative competency in the chimpanzee: Pre-representational and representational. In G. Greenberg & E. Tobach (Eds.), *Behavioral evolution and integrative levels.* Hillsdale, NJ: Erlbaum.

Savage-Rumbaugh, E. S., Sevcik, R. A., Brakke, K. E., Rumbaugh, D. M., & Greenfield, P. (1990). Symbols: Their communicative use, comprehension, and combination by bonobos (*Pan paniscus*). In C. Rovee-Collier & L. P. Lipsett (Eds.), *Advances in infancy research* (Vol. **6**). Norwood, NJ: Ablex.

Savage-Rumbaugh, E. S., Sevcik, R. A., Rumbaugh, D. M., & Rubert, E. (1985). The capacity of animals to acquire language: Do species differences have anything to say to us? *Philosophical Transactions of the Royal Society of London,* **308,** 177–185.

Savage-Rumbaugh, E. S., & Wilkerson, B. J. (1978). Socio-sexual behavior in *Pan paniscus* and *Pan troglodytes:* A comparative study. *Journal of Human Evolution,* **7,** 327–344.

Schank, R. C., & Abelson, R. P. (1977). *Scripts, plans, goals and understanding.* Hillsdale, NJ: Erlbaum.

Schusterman, R. L., & Gisiner, R. (1988). Artificial language comprehension in dolphins and sea lions: The essential cognitive skills. *Psychological Record,* **34,** 311–348.

Schusterman, R. L., & Krieger, K. (1986). Artificial language comprehension and size transposition by a California sea lion (*Zalophus californianus*). *Journal of Comparative Psychology,* **100,** 348–355.

Sebeok, T. A., & Umiker-Sebeok, J. (1980). *Speaking of apes: A critical anthology of two-way communication with man.* New York: Plenum.

Seidenberg, M. S., & Pettito, L. A. (1979). Signing behavior in apes: A critical review. *Cognition,* **7,** 177–215.

Seidenberg, M. S., & Pettito, L. A. (1987). Communication, symbolic communication, and language: Comment on Savage-Rumbaugh, McDonald, Sevcik, Hopkins, and Rubert (1986). *Journal of Experimental Psychology: General,* **116,** 279–287.

Shipley, E. G., Smith, C. S., & Gleitman, L. R. (1969). A study in the acquisition of language: Free responses to commands. *Language,* **45,** 322–342.

Sibley, C. G., & Ahlquist, J. E. (1984). The phylogeny of hominoid primates as indicated by DNA-DNA hybridization. *Journal of Molecular Evolution,* **20,** 2–15.

Sibley, C. G., & Ahlquist, J. E. (1987). DNA hybridization evidence of hominoid phylogeny: Results from an expanded data set. *Journal of Molecular Evolution,* **26,** 99–121.

Sinclair, H., & Bronckart, J. (1972). SVO—a linguistic universal? A study in developmental psycholinguistics. *Journal of Experimental Child Psychology,* **14,** 329–348.

Slobin, D., & Bever, T. (1982). A cross-linguistic study of sentence comprehension. *Cognition,* **12,** 229–265.

Snowdon, C. T. (1988). A comparative approach to vocal communication. In D. Leger (Ed.), *Comparative perspectives in modern psychology* (Nebraska Symposium on Motivation, Vol. **35**). Lincoln: University of Nebraska Press.

Snowdon, C. T. (1990, March). Language parallels in animal communication: The emperor's new clothes. In K. Gibson & T. Ingold (Chairs), *Tools, language, and intelligence: Evolutionary implications.* Symposium conducted at the meeting of the Wenner-Gren Foundation for Anthropological Research, Cascais, Portugal.

Snyder, L. S., Bates, E., & Bretherton, I. (1981). Content and context in early lexical development. *Journal of Child Language,* **8,** 565–682.

Stell, M., & Riesen, A. (1987). Effects of early environments on motor cortex neuroanatomical changes following somatosensory experience: Effects of Layer III pyramidal cells in monkey cortex. *Behavioral Neuroscience,* **101,** 341–346.

Stephen, H., Bauchot, R., & Andy, O. J. (1970). Data on size of the brain and of various brain parts in insectivores and primates. In C. R. Noback & W. Montagna (Eds.), *The primate brain.* New York: Appleton-Century-Crofts.

Stern, D. N., Beebe, B., Jaffe, J., & Bennett, S. L. (1977). The infant's stimulus world during social interaction: A study of caregiver behaviours with particular reference to repetition and timing. In H. R. Schaffer (Ed.), *Studies in mother-infant interaction.* London: Academic.

Stevenson, M. B., Ver Hoeve, J. N., Roach, M. A., & Leavitt, L. A. (1986). The beginning of conversation: Early patterns of mother-infant vocal responsiveness. *Infant Behavior and Development,* **9,** 423–440.

Straub, R. O., Seidenberg, M. S., Bever, T. G., & Terrace, H. S. (1979). Serial learning in the pigeon. *Journal of the Experimental Analysis of Behavior,* **32,** 137–148.

Straub, R. O., & Terrace, H. S. (1981). Generalization of serial learning in the pigeon. *Animal Learning and Behavior,* **9,** 454–486.

Strohner, H., & Nelson, K. (1974). The young child's development of sentence comprehension: Influences of event probability, nonverbal context, syntactic form, and strategies. *Child Development,* **45,** 567–576.

Sugarman, S. (1983). Why talk? Comment on Savage-Rumbaugh et al. *Journal of Experimental Psychology: General,* **112,** 493–497.

Tabachnick, B. G., & Fidell, L. S. (1989). *Using multivariate statistics.* New York: Harper & Row.

Terrace, H. S. (1979). *Nim.* New York: Knopf.

Terrace, H. S., Pettito, L. A., Sanders, R. J., & Bever, T. G. (1979). Can an ape create a sentence? *Science,* **206,** 891–900.

Terrace, H. S., Straub, R. O., Bever, T. G., & Seidenberg, M. S. (1977). Representation of a sequence by a pigeon. *Bulletin of the Psychonomic Society,* **10,** 269.

Thompson, C. R., & Church, R. M. (1980). An explanation of the language of a chimpanzee. *Science,* **208,** 313–314.

Waters, R. S., & Wilson, W. A., Jr. (1976). Speech perception by rhesus monkeys: The voice distinction in synthesized labial and velar stop consonants. *Perception and Psychophysics,* **19,** 285–289.

Whitehurst, G. J., & Valdez-Menchaca, M. C. (1988). What is the role of reinforcement in early language acquisition? *Child Development,* **59,** 430–440.

Yerkes, R., & Learned, B. W. (1925). *Chimpanzee intelligence and its vocal expressions.* Baltimore: Williams & Wilkins.

ACKNOWLEDGMENTS

The research described in this *Monograph* and its preparation were supported by National Institutes of Health (NIH) grant NICHD-06016, which supports the Language Research Center of Georgia State University. This research was conducted at the Language Research Center, College of Arts and Sciences, Georgia State University. The research was supported in part by NIH grant RR-00165 to the Yerkes Center of Emory University.

Special appreciation is extended to Kelly McDonald and to Elizabeth Rubert, without whose assistance this work would never have been possible. They participated in all phases of rearing and testing Kanzi, and it was through their conscientious effort and care that he came to understand the English language. The efforts of Linda Gilmore in coding and preliminary data analysis are also much appreciated, as is the help in tape transcription provided by Lisa Conger, Shane Keating, and Linda McGarrah.

Thanks are also extended to Mike Tomasello for many helpful comments during various drafts of the manuscript and to Lois Bloom and Roberta Golinkoff for advice during the initial phases of data analysis.

Much gratitude is owed to Roger Bakeman, who introduced Sue Savage-Rumbaugh to the intricacies of log-linear analysis and patiently helped her apply it to this data set. However, any errors are of course the authors'.

Finally, a great debt is owed to the three reviewers for their insightful and instructive critiques. Because of their effort, this *Monograph* is a much better one.

COMMENTARY

COMPREHENSION AND PRODUCTION IN
EARLY LANGUAGE DEVELOPMENT

Elizabeth Bates

Savage-Rumbaugh and her colleagues have provided us with yet another ground-breaking investigation into the linguistic abilities (or "quasi-linguistic abilities"—see below) of our nearest phylogenetic neighbor, the chimpanzee. Their *Monograph* begins with some brief but useful reviews of the primate language literature and the literature on early comprehension and production of language in human children. The authors document the peculiar bias toward production and the relative neglect of comprehension that have characterized the child language literature, and they ask a perfectly reasonable question: If we want to understand what an organism *knows* about language, is comprehension not a better place to start? And, if we want to compare knowledge of language in two related species, how can we draw any firm conclusions if our work is based exclusively on what the animal can produce?

With this foundation, Savage-Rumbaugh et al. go on to present (in exquisite methodological and empirical detail) a longitudinal study comparing the development of word and sentence comprehension in a human child (Alia) and a bonobo (Kanzi), raised and tested in settings that are as comparable as ethics and common sense will allow. In contrast with many previous studies of primate language, blind testing procedures are used to ensure against the kind of cuing that proved to be responsible for the supposed linguistic and arithmetic comprehension of the infamous horse Clever Hans. In all honesty, I cannot think of anything else that the authors could have done to convince their audience that this is a fair test of the hypothesis that apes are capable of at least some language comprehension, at both the lexical and the structural levels.

I, for one, am convinced. Indeed, it seems fair to conclude from this work that the bonobo (or at least one bonobo) is capable of language comprehension that approximates (in level if not detail) the abilities of a human 2-year-old on the threshold of full-blown sentence processing. I will therefore devote my comments to the implications of this important and startling result, with particular emphasis on the relation between comprehension and production in human children.

Humans I:
Why Is There So Little Research on Comprehension?

I agree wholeheartedly with Savage-Rumbaugh et al. that our field has neglected the early stages of language comprehension in human children. With very few exceptions (most of them listed in their review), most of what we know about the first stages of language development is based on the child's stumbling efforts to produce and reproduce meaningful speech. The authors put their fingers on the main reason why comprehension receives so little attention: it is notoriously difficult to study in this age range. Behavioral methods all require the child to pay attention, follow instructions, and carry out some kind of task set up by the adult—whether it is pointing at a picture, choosing an object from an array, looking back and forth at slides, or carrying out a series of commands. Children under the age of 2 years are often (very often) unwilling to cooperate in a study of this kind. Hence, the proportion of false negatives is unacceptably high.

As a direct result of this compliance issue, the internal reliability of comprehension tests tends to be unacceptably low. In several previous studies (e.g., Bates, Benigni, Bretherton, Camaioni, & Volterra, 1979; Bates, Bretherton, & Snyder, 1988), my colleagues and I have examined the correlations *between* alternative tests of comprehension at 10, 13, 20, and 28 months of age (e.g., a multiple-choice test using real objects, a picture-pointing task, and a task in which children are asked to follow simple commands). We have also looked at test-retest and split-half correlations *within* several of our laboratory measures. Results so far have been very discouraging. By 28 months of age, it is possible to administer structured tests like the Peabody Picture Vocabulary Test to normally developing children (Dunn & Dunn, 1981). We can also obtain systematic and reliable data from 2-year-old children using experimental measures of sentence comprehension (e.g., Bates et al., 1984). Before that age, however, comprehension tasks are highly unreliable. At 13 months, correlations among laboratory measures of word comprehension hover in the .10–.50 range (compared with correlations between .50 and .75 for laboratory measures of word production). By 20 months of age, internal correlations for production have gone up still further, but reliability coefficients for laboratory measures of comprehension are still very low (in the nonsignificant .18–.28 range for many tasks).[1] Spearman's law states that no measure can correlate with another measure at a level higher than it correlates with itself. Hence, if we try to examine the cognitive, social, or neurological predictors of language comprehension in this age range, the unreliability of our comprehension measures sets an absolute ceiling on the power and reliability of any results that we might hope to obtain. This reliability problem extends beyond studies using the correlational method. Developmental researchers sometimes forget that traditional experimental designs (e.g., age × experimental condition) are also limited by the internal reliability of the dependent variable. If we use a behavioral measure of comprehension as an outcome variable in a study of this kind (e.g., a study comparing novel-word learning under different conditions), it will be difficult to obtain reliable between-group results with a dependent variable that barely correlates with itself.

In short, if we compare comprehension (based on what we tell the child to do) with production (based on what the child chooses to do, of her own free will), we run the risk of underestimating the former and overestimating the latter. To be sure, some progress has been made in the assessment of early language comprehension. Three methods come to mind: (1) improved uses of parental report to tap into "language comprehension in the wild"; (2) new preferential-looking paradigms that minimize behavioral demands on the child; and (3) event-related brain potentials recorded while children are listening to linguistic stimuli. Each of these techniques has some real advantages over traditional methods of laboratory testing, but each has some serious disadvantages that make them unsuitable for a study of the kind that Savage-Rumbaugh and her colleagues have presented here. Let us consider each of these innovations in turn.

Parental Report

We have known for some time that parental diaries are the best way to measure emerging language abilities in the first 2 years of life (Darwin, 1971; Dromi, 1987; Leopold, 1949; Stern, 1965). After all, parents are with the child in many different situations, including all those highly predictable routine settings that are the birthplace of early words (e.g., feeding, bathing, going to bed—see Chap. III in this *Monograph*). Typically, a child who is capable of producing 20–40 words will show no more than five of these words to an itinerant researcher visiting the home for 2 hours with a camera crew. When the same child is brought into an unfamiliar laboratory setting, our estimates of language production may be even lower. For example, we

---

[1] Internal reliabilities tend to be substantially higher for parental report measures of comprehension—but, as we shall see shortly, parental report has limitations of its own.

combined parental report with laboratory and home observations in our longitudinal study of 27 infants, from 10 to 28 months of age (Bates et al., 1988). According to detailed interviews with the parents (a predecessor to our current parental report scale—see below), these children had an average expressive vocabulary of 12 words at 13 months of age, with a range from 0 to 45. By contrast, we observed an average of only 1.69 distinct words in a 2-hour combination of laboratory and home testing at the same age level, with a range from 0 to 9. In the same interview, parents reported an average receptive vocabulary of 48 words, with a range from 17 to 97. By contrast, performance for the group as a whole was barely above chance in a three-way multiple-choice test for the comprehension of familiar object names. To be sure, these different sources of information were significantly correlated, in relatively specific patterns (i.e., parental reports of comprehension with comprehension testing; parental reports of production with observations of production). But it should be clear that parental report offers a much broader view of early words. As we have pointed out (see Bates et al., 1988), parental report yields information about what the child knows how to do, while observations give us a robust estimate of what the same child is willing to do in a short period of time.

Of course, one might argue that parental reports reflect wishful thinking, compared with foolproof laboratory evidence. That is, we can trust positive findings in the laboratory (e.g., the child really did say *tiger*) more than we can trust parental report (e.g., Mom thinks that the child can say *tiger*). However, we were surprised to find that our 13-month parental report measures were much better long-term predictors of language performance in the laboratory! For example, parental reports of comprehension at 13 months were significantly related to performance on the Peabody Picture Vocabulary Test at 28 months of age (.56, $p < .01$); by contrast, our 13-month laboratory measure of word comprehension bore no significant relation to any of our later comprehension tests. In fact, this finding follows in a straightforward fashion from Spearman's law, that is, from the fact that parental reports of early language have higher internal reliability than corresponding laboratory measures.

As a result of this study (and others that yield similar results), we joined efforts with a large group of developmental researchers in the United States and Europe, trying to find a valid and reliable way to bottle the diary study for mass production. This effort has resulted in a product called the MacArthur Communicative Development Inventories (CDI; Fenson et al., in press). The CDI contains two overlapping instruments: the Words and Gesture Scale (for normal infants from 8 to 16 months of age, or their developmental equivalent in retarded populations) and the Words and Grammar Scale (for toddlers between 16 and 30 months, or their developmental equivalent in retarded populations). The Words and Gesture Scale taps into word comprehension and production through a 396-word checklist (derived by trial and error through several successive studies, with parents adding new words on every round). There is also a 67-item checklist for different aspects of communicative and symbolic gesture. The Words and Sentences Scale includes a 680-item checklist for the evaluation of word production, followed by a series of checklists that measure aspects of early grammar. The CDI has now been normed with a sample of more than 1,800 healthy children between 8 and 30 months of age, and numerous studies are now available demonstrating the reliability and validity of the various subscales. For example, Dale and his colleagues have shown that the grammatical complexity subscales correlate with laboratory measures of grammar (including mean length of utterance and a standard index of syntactic complexity), with coefficients ranging from .60 to .86 depending on the age of the sample and the outcome measure in question (Dale, 1991; Dale & Bates, in preparation; Dale, Bates, Reznick, & Morisset, 1989). In short, these measures work very well for the global assessment of lexical, gestural, and grammatical ability before 30 months of age. The success of these measures reflects three rules that we had to learn the hard way: (1) ask only about current behaviors (retrospective reports of language development have proved unreliable); (2) ask only about newly emerging behaviors (i.e., aspects of language and communication that are still so new that parents can keep track); and (3) rely on recognition memory instead of recall, avoiding any need for parents to make complicated inferences that they are not trained to carry out (hence the reliance on checklists instead of "fill in the blank").

At this point, we are convinced that parental report is the best way to obtain a global estimate of language comprehension for children in the first and second years of life. In particular, parental report permits us to circumvent the problem of internal reliability in behavioral measures of comprehension. At the same time, the CDI has serious limitations, all of which are relevant to the Savage-Rumbaugh et al. study. First, the parents of normally developing children can keep track of word comprehension only up to about 16 months of age. After that point, they throw up their hands and say, "I don't know, she seems to understand just about everything." Second, parental report can tell us only about comprehension in context, where the child has many additional sources of information available to support comprehension of words (e.g., parental gestures and tone of voice; familiar objects and events). We have no way of knowing how well the same child would perform out of context, in a blind testing situation. Third, because it seems to be all but impossible for parents to keep track of comprehension after 16 months, we cannot use this method to assess the emergence of receptive grammar. And there is, of course, a fourth limitation that is particularly important for researchers interested in the symbolic abilities of nonhuman primates: many readers are still very skeptical of parental report, and any benefit of the doubt that they might be willing to lend in a study of human beings would be denied to researchers working with another species.

Preferential Looking

As Savage-Rumbaugh et al. point out in their review of the child comprehension literature, Golinkoff and Hirsh-Pasek have had considerable success in the use of a preferential-looking measure to assess early comprehension of grammar (Golinkoff, Hirsh-Pasek, Cauley, & Gordon, 1987; Hirsh-Pasek & Golinkoff, 1991).[2] Like the research team who developed the CDI to "bottle" parental report, these two researchers have spent many years perfecting the preferential-looking paradigm, holding many of the usual disadvantages of that measure to an absolute minimum. Problems of wandering attention have been minimized by monitoring the child's eye movements carefully and presenting stimuli only when it is clear that the child is attending to the display. To ensure attention to the two screens and the linguistic stimuli that are emitted from a central speaker, they have developed a kind of "sound and light show" that precedes each language trial. Children are briefly familiarized with both the visual display and the relevant sounds before the crucial trials, that is, the trials in which measures are taken of preferential looking to the picture that "matches" the input sentence (e.g., "Big Bird is hugging Cookie Monster!" presented simultaneously with two scenes, one of Big Bird hugging the Monster, another with the Monster hugging Big Bird). Various steps are also taken to eliminate any possibility of unconscious cuing by the parent (e.g., parents wear earphones that play music to mask verbal input to the child, and they are unable to see the screen even though the child is sitting on the parent's lap with a perfect view). Thanks to all these hard-won precautions, Golinkoff, Hirsh-Pasek, and their colleagues have been able to demonstrate that several aspects of phrase and sentence comprehension precede production of the same forms, by several weeks or months. In my view, this work has decisively settled an old controversy (noted by Savage-Rumbaugh et al. in their review) on the relative timing of comprehension and production at the sentence level.

Although these improved preferential-looking methods have provided important new evidence concerning the average onset time for receptive

---

[2] A number of investigators have used this technique successfully to assess comprehension of single words. At the word level, it is also possible to obtain many more trials for individual subjects. For some pertinent examples and a review of past work, see Reznick (1990).

grammar in healthy human children, they too have serious limitations. First, the preferential-looking method rests on a critical assumption: that the child will look longer at a visual stimulus that "matches" the auditory input. The fact that Golinkoff and Hirsh-Pasek have obtained good results so far suggests that this assumption is valid—at least for a significant majority of the children in each study. However, it is worth pointing out that there is a large literature on preferential looking in children under 6 months of age that makes exactly the opposite assumption: children will look longer at novel or surprising stimuli that do not match their expectations (Spelke, Breinlinger, Macomber, & Jacobson, 1992). If both tendencies are present in individual children, we have to worry about the meaning of null results (i.e., those stimuli or those age groups that do not produce preferential looking at the "match").

Second, although this method works well for group studies, it has proved impossible (at least so far) to adapt the preferential-looking technique for use with individual children (Golinkoff, personal communication, June 1989). In the experiments that they have conducted to date, Golinkoff and Hirsh-Pasek can obtain no more than four to six crucial target trials for any linguistic contrast. Although the results are quite reliable at the group level, the predicted pattern (i.e., preferential looking at the pictures that match the language input) is typically displayed by only two-thirds of the children, with looking biases that average around 66% for individual subjects. It should be clear why this kind of hit rate would be unacceptable for individual case studies. To research significance by a binomial test in a two-choice situation with six trials, an individual child must perform perfectly on six of six trials. Yet the base-rate performance observed in these studies averages four trials out of six—despite all the authors' heroic efforts. If the number of trials could be extended through multiple sessions with the same child, this limit could be overcome. However, this would provide us with information about only a few linguistic contrasts, leaving us with little information about the rest of language comprehension.

These two problems probably suffice to explain why Savage-Rumbaugh and her colleagues have avoided preferential looking in favor of traditional behavioral measures (where the probability of getting the right answer by chance is considerably smaller). But there is another reason as well: preferential looking works best with docile children who are willing to sit on the parent's lap for at least 15 min, looking at pictures. From the authors' description (and my own observations as a visitor in their laboratory many years ago), chimpanzees are considerably less cooperative that many human children with attention deficit disorders. Barring heavy use of sedatives, I doubt that the preferential-looking measure would prove reliable for the healthy, active, mobile chimpanzee—which brings me to the next point.

Event-related Brain Potentials (ERPs)

In the last few years, two laboratories have begun to apply electrophysiological techniques to the study of early language comprehension (Mills, Coffey, & Neville, in press-a, in press-b; Molfese, 1990). Electric potentials are measured at the scalp, from infants and children who are wearing a special "hat." Behavioral demands on the children are relatively minimal: they need to cooperate by keeping the hat in place, and they must attend to a series of auditory stimuli played over speakers (holding relatively still while each stimulus is played). Nothing else is required. These techniques have at least four advantages over the preferential-looking technique. (1) Although both measures require the child to pay attention to linguistic stimuli, electrophysiological measures make no assumptions about direction of preference (i.e., the assumption that children prefer to look at a "match"). (2) The preferential-looking method usually requires a complex coordination of visual and auditory stimuli, in contrast with ERP studies where auditory stimuli alone are sufficient. (3) Because the presentation of stimuli is so straightforward in ERP studies, most individual children can handle a relatively large number of trials. (4) Whereas preferential looking provides only a single, relatively unstable dependent variable (percentage of time looking at the "matching" display), ERP studies elicit a complex, multidimensional dependent variable, with variations in timing, amplitude, polarity, and scalp distribution. Because of the complex and multidimensional nature of the ERP, it is possible (at least in principle) for electrophysiological researchers to detect fine-grained discriminations among linguistic stimuli and/or the characteristics of individual subjects.

One of the most important ERP studies of early language comprehension is a recent paper by Mills et al. (in press-a), who examined the ERPs associated with familiar versus unfamiliar words in infants between 13 and 20 months of age. Among other things, these authors have discovered a particular component of the ERP that distinguishes between the two word types. This "comprehension wave" is present in children whose parents report relatively high levels of comprehension; it is absent in children whose parents report relatively little evidence for word comprehension. The topological distribution of this component changes with development, from a bilateral distribution that is larger over posterior regions of the brain to a distribution that is more prominent over the left frontal cortex. Most important for our purposes here, there are differences in the shape and distribution of the "comprehension wave" in children who are also able to produce those words. In other words, the ERP can be used to distinguish between "comprehenders" and "producers" during the first 2 years of life, suggesting that different brain systems are involved in these two aspects of early language—a difference that can be detected in a "pure" comprehension task, with no overt motor response.

The Mills et al. paper raises an obvious question for Savage-Rumbaugh et al. Given the similarities that have been observed in the comprehension abilities of child and chimpanzee, would we also expect similar patterns of brain activity in response to known and unknown words? On the other hand, in view of the fact that Alia goes on to achieve much higher levels of word and sentence production than Kanzi has displayed so far, would we find telltale differences in the brain waves associated with known and unknown words, differences that predict their later differentiation in language output? I would love to know the answer to this question—but I suspect that it will be long in coming. It has taken Molfese, Neville, Mills, and their colleagues many years to develop the normative information required for the interpretation of brain waves in human infants and children. When this technique is applied to another species, with a very different brain, all this norming and validation would have to begin from scratch. At the end of this process, it would be difficult to say whether we are seeing the "same" brain waves in response to the "same" linguistic stimuli. I also suspect that the compliance problems associated with preferential-looking studies would also plague electrophysiological research with chimpanzees. Mills et al. have used every trick in the book to obtain cooperation from their human subjects—yet it is still the case that many children absolutely refuse to wear the hat or will not sit still long enough to permit collection of passive ERPs without motor artifacts. I sometimes wonder whether we are working toward a rich theory of language comprehension in the docile child—a theory that may not extend to their more rambunctious peers. Obviously, the same problem is multiplied a hundredfold when the technique is applied to chimpanzees.

I have reviewed these three techniques for two reasons: to amplify the review of human language comprehension presented by the authors of this *Monograph* and to prepare the way for some of the additional findings that I will review below, on the dissociation between comprehension and production in the first 2 years of life. I have not reviewed these techniques to suggest that Savage-Rumbaugh et al. could have done a better job. Indeed, I am persuaded that the behavioral techniques applied in this study are exactly right for the questions that they ask. They have compensated for the notorious problems of reliability and compliance by collecting a very large sample, under blind testing conditions, with careful training to maximize attention and minimize extraneous sources of misunderstanding. Detailed information is provided on the conditions that surround every success and every failure. The only imperfections that I can detect in this study are those imposed by an imperfect reality.

Humans II:
Why Do Comprehension and Production Come Apart?

In this section, I review four new findings on the relation between comprehension and production in human children and then explore the implications of these findings for the comparison of apes and children.

Dissociations between Comprehension and Production in Normal Children

For many years, parents and psycholinguists have known about children who appear to understand far more than they are able or willing to say (Bates et al., 1988; Benedict, 1979; Goldin-Meadow, Seligman, & Gelman, 1976; Snyder, Bates, & Bretherton, 1981). The prevalence of this pattern in normal children has now been established on a large scale in the MacArthur CDI norming study (Fenson et al., in press; see also Thal, Fenson, & Bates, in preparation). Figure C1 illustrates the relation between receptive and expressive vocabularies in a cross-sectional sample of 659 children whose parents filled out the Word and Gestures Scale of the CDI when their children were between 8 and 16 months of age. The overall correlation between comprehension and production in this sample was .65 (.45 when age is partialed out). This is actually somewhat higher than the coefficients reported in some of our other studies (e.g., Snyder et al., 1981). Nevertheless, we can see from Figure C1 that a significant number of children are producing very little meaningful speech despite receptive vocabularies of 150 words or more. As Bates et al. (1988) have shown, this pattern of dissociation also tends to be a stable characteristic of individual children between 13 and 28 months of age, starting at the single-word level and continuing into the early stages of grammar. The reasons for this robust dissociation are still unclear, but a possible explanation has begun to emerge from studies of abnormal populations.

Dissociations between Comprehension and Production in Late Talkers

Specific language impairment (SLI) is, by definition, a syndrome in which children fall at least 1 standard deviation below the mean on a criterial language measure, in the absence of any frank evidence for mental retardation or neurological disorders that might account for the delay (Miller, 1991; Tallal, 1988). Most clinicians are unwilling to make a diagnosis of SLI before the child is 3–4 years of age. The term *late talkers* is reserved for children who fall far below the mean on measures of expressive language before the 3-year point. For example, Thal and her colleagues define late

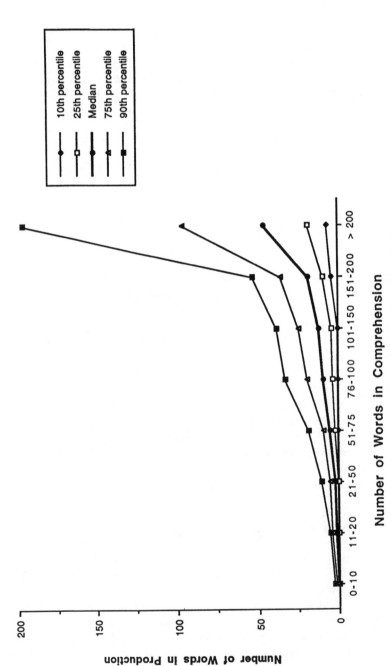

Number of Words in Comprehension

FIG. C1.—Production by comprehension level

Legend:
- 10th percentile
- 25th percentile
- Median
- 75th percentile
- 90th percentile

Y-axis: Number of Words in Production (0, 50, 100, 150, 200)

X-axis categories: 0-10, 11-20, 21-50, 51-75, 76-100, 101-150, 151-200, > 200 talkers as children with expressive vocabulary scores in the bottom tenth percentile on the CDI Words and Sentences Scale between 18 and 28 months of age. Although this is an intentionally "preclinical" label, several recent studies have shown that approximately 40% of the late-talker population goes on to qualify for a diagnosis of SLI (Rescorla & Schwartz, 1990; Thal, 1991; Thal, Tobias, & Morrison, 1991; Whitehurst, Fischell, Arnold, & Lonigan, 1992).

Late talkers are defined by their delays in language production. As Thal and her colleagues have shown, there is enormous variability in receptive language skills within the late-talker group, ranging from children who are equally delayed in comprehension and production to children who are indistinguishable from their chronologically matched controls on measures of comprehension despite severe delays in language output. In other words, a subset of the late-talker population presents with an extreme variant of the comprehension/production dissociation described above. A follow-up study of 10 late talkers by Thal, Tobias, and Morrison (1991) suggests that comprehension is an excellent predictor of recovery from expressive language delays. That is, children who are building their receptive knowledge of language on a normal schedule have a much better chance of catching up with their age-mates across the board in the next 6–12 months. What the child *knows* is ultimately a better predictor of language ability than what she actually *does* between 18 and 28 months of age. Although we cannot generalize instantly from language-delayed children to the chimpanzee, I believe that this finding is relevant to the work that Savage-Rumbaugh et al. have presented here. It underscores the importance of cross-species comparisons based on levels of language comprehension to supplement the usual comparisons based on language production. This is particularly true in the developmental range that Savage-Rumbaugh et al. have explored in the present study.

Cognitive Correlates of Comprehension versus Production

In the last 20 years, a host of studies has appeared examining the nonlinguistic correlates of early language development (for reviews, see Bates & Thal, 1991; Bates, Thal, & Janowsky, 1992; and Bates, Thal, & Marchman, 1991). Many of these studies were initially inspired by Piaget's theory of the passage from sensorimotor to symbolic cognition in the first 3 years of life (e.g., Piaget, 1962), and researchers began with the expectation that language milestones would follow across-the-board changes in many different cognitive domains. That is not at all how things turned out. Instead, most researchers in this field have arrived at a consensus: specific linguistic skills are associated with specific abilities outside language, in a many-to-many relation that is quite different from the one-to-one stage shifts predicted by orthodox Piagetian theory. Bates et al. (1979) refer to this as the *local homology model;* Fischer and his colleagues describe similar results under the term *skill theory* (Fischer, 1980); Gopnik and Meltzoff (1986) refer to the same conclusions as *the specificity hypothesis.* Although details differ, the basic underlying intuition is the same in most modern studies of language and cognitive development during the infant and preschool years. For example, we now know that the onset of word comprehension between 8 and 10 months of age is correlated with a host of changes inside and outside language proper: imitation of novel models, gestural routines (e.g., "bye-bye") and other communicative gestures (e.g., giving, showing, and pointing), changes in the ability to recognize a category shift in a passive categorization task, a decline in the ability to recognize phonetic distinctions that are not in the child's native language, and advances in causal analysis and the ability to use tools. Around 12–13 months of age, the onset of naming in the vocal modality (e.g., pointing and saying, "Doggie!") is accompanied by a much more specific set of changes outside language, in particular, the use of conventional gestures to recognize or "name" familiar objects (e.g., putting a telephone receiver to the ear, touching a shoe to the foot, or touching a comb briefly to the top of the head). Between 16 and 20 months, two dramatic changes take place within expressive language: a rapid acceleration in the rate of language development and the onset of multiword speech. These two changes are correlated with several developments outside the boundaries of language, including reorganizations in symbolic play (in particular, a shift from "one-gesture" to "two-gesture" sequences in doll play), changes in active categorization tasks (e.g., successive touching of all the objects in one category, followed by successive touching of objects in a different category), and a shift in the kind of planning that a child displays in block construction. Some researchers have also reported a correlation between the "grammar burst" that usually takes place between 20 and 30 months of age and a marked increase in the use of conventionally ordered scripts in doll play (e.g., giving a teddy bear a bath, with each action occurring in the right order).

All these correlational studies involve children who are developing on a normal schedule. What happens when components of language fall out of synchrony? In particular, who gets custody of the cognitive correlates when comprehension and production come apart? So far, our studies of normal children and late talkers yield one very clear conclusion: *in almost every case,* the child's level of performance in nonverbal cognitive tasks is best predicted by her current level of language comprehension. In other words, cognitive measures are tied most closely to what the child knows about language. Expressive deficits may reflect impairments or delays in some more peripheral aspect of language processing—which brings me to the next point.

Comprehension and Production in Children with Early Focal Brain Injury

We have known for some time that children can recover from brain injuries that would result in irreversible damage in an adult (e.g., Hecaen, 1976; Woods & Teuber, 1978). This does not mean, however, that the brain is totally plastic and equipotential for language or any other cognitive function (Bates et al., 1992; Satz, Strauss, & Whitaker, 1990; Stiles & Thal, in press; Thal et al., 1991). Children with early focal brain injury do display initial problems with language, spatial cognition, affect, and attention—that is, with those behavioral domains that are mediated by specific brain regions in the adult. This suggests that there are indeed some initial biases in the human brain. Under normal circumstances, these initial biases lead to the familiar patterns of brain organization that are described in the neuropsychological literature for adults. However, when these "default" conditions do not apply, the infant brain can find alternative neural and/or behavioral solutions, resulting in unusual forms of brain organization that are not usually seen in normal or brain-damaged adults. This seems to be particularly true for language; indeed, most children with early unilateral brain lesions go on to achieve levels of language performance that are indistinguishable from normal on almost every measure (Aram, Holland, Locke, Plante, & Tomblin, 1992; Vargha-Khadem, Isaacs, Papaleloudi, Polkey, & Wilson, 1991; Vargha-Khadem, Isaacs, Van Der Werf, Robb, & Wilson, 1991).

This evidence for the plasticity of language in the human brain is of considerable interest in its own right. However, I want to focus here on those initial biases that have been found in the first years of language learning—with special reference to the brain regions associated with deficits in language comprehension and production. In mature right-handed adults, lesions to anterior (pre-Rolandic) and posterior (retro-Rolandic) areas of the left cerebral cortex tend to result in qualitatively different forms of language breakdown: anterior lesions are associated with nonfluent speech with relatively preserved comprehension at the clinical level (i.e., Broca's aphasia), and posterior lesions are associated with fluent but empty speech, marked by word-finding deficits, substitution errors, and mild to severe impairments in comprehension (i.e., Wernicke's aphasia). If the initial delays observed in infants with focal brain injury follow the adult pattern, then we should expect the following patterns in early language development: more severe deficits in expressive language following left anterior injury (i.e., the Broca hypothesis) and more severe deficits in receptive language following left posterior injury (i.e., the Wernicke hypothesis).

In fact, both these hypotheses have been overturned in our recent prospective studies of language development in children with unilateral brain lesions acquired prelinguistically, that is, before 6 months of age (Marchman, Miller, & Bates, 1991; Thal et al., 1991). First, results suggest that *all* children with early focal brain injury are at risk for language delay in the early stages, regardless of size, side, or site of lesion. Second, children with lesions extending into the left posterior cortex display more severe and persistent delays in expressive (but not receptive) language across this period—directly contradicting both the Broca and the Wernicke hypotheses. Third, receptive deficits were actually more common in children with right-hemisphere damage—direct evidence against the Wernicke hypothesis. These patterns do not occur in our studies of older children with the same etiology; indeed, most of our older children are performing within the normal range. We tentatively suggest that the most intense period of recovery from language delay takes place between 1 and 5 years of age. Furthermore, the regions that mediate language acquisition in the first years of life are not necessarily the same regions that mediate processing and maintenance of language in the adult.

These results for language contrast markedly with our studies of spatial cognitive development in the same population (Stiles & Nass, 1991; Stiles & Thal, in press; Stiles-Davis, 1988). In fact, spatial cognitive deficits (although subtle and less persistent) do bear a systematic relation to the brain-behavior correlations observed in adults. In line with recent studies of visual analysis in brain-damaged adults, left hemisphere (LH) injuries in 3–12-year-old children result in an *analytic deficit* (i.e., problems with the extraction of "local" perceptual details within a complex visual pattern), and right hemisphere (RH) injuries in the same age range result in an *integrative deficit* (where details are intact but the global configuration is impaired). This suggests that plasticity for language may be greater than plasticity observed with phylogenetically older cognitive systems.

We have proposed two working hypotheses to unify some of our findings for early language and spatial cognition. They are worth reproducing here because they may be relevant to the comprehension/production disparities observed in other species.

1. *Comprehension as sensory integration.*—In research on language breakdown in adults, RH lesions do have some effect on complex aspects of discourse processing, for example, the ability to tell a coherent story or understand the point of a joke (Brownell, Potter, Bihrle, & Gardner, 1986; Gardner, Brownell, Wapner, & Michelow, 1983). However, RH lesions typically do not lead to deficits in the comprehension of individual words. Yet our infant work suggests that RH lesions are sometimes associated with

delays in word comprehension. Why should this be the case? To understand this paradox, we have to remember that 1-year-old infants are learning to comprehend words for the first time. For adults, comprehension of familiar words is an automatic process, one that takes place without awareness and with very little effort. By contrast, 1-year-old infants are still in the process of "cracking the code." For these children, word comprehension may be viewed as a form of multimodal problem solving, requiring the integration of many different sources of information, including gesture, facial expressions, tone of voice, and a host of situational cues (e.g., we are having breakfast now). The adult literature on spatial cognitive deficits suggests that the right hemisphere plays a particularly important role in the integration of sensory information. Stiles's research suggests that the same right-hemisphere bias is operating in early childhood. We propose that sensory integration also plays a particularly important role in the first stages of language comprehension, when children have to use many different sources of information to figure out what words mean. If it is the case that right-hemisphere tissue plays a privileged role (although not an exclusive role) in sensory integration, then we might expect a correlation between right-hemisphere damage and delays in the initial stages of language comprehension.

2. *The local detail hypothesis.*—On the basis of a large body of neuropsychological research with adults and children, we propose that the sensory regions of the left posterior cortex are particularly important for the extraction of sensory detail. Furthermore, this regional specialization for "local detail" holds for both visual and auditory stimuli. Now, why should a deficit in sensory detail affect production more than comprehension? At first glance, this appears to be a contradiction because we have always assumed that comprehension is a product of sensory processing while production relies more on motor factors. For adults who have already acquired their language, this may be true. However, we should remember that children between 0 and 2 years of age are learning to produce their language for the first time. Among other things, this means that they must extract enough perceptual detail from the linguistic signal to support construction of motor templates for production. Our point is really a very simple one: perception for production requires more sensory detail than perception for understanding.

Let me offer one simple example to illustrate this point. Imagine a 14-month-old infant sitting in her stroller at the zoo. Daddy rolls the child in front of a cage that contains huge, long-necked creatures munching away at the lower boughs of a tree. Daddy points to these surprising creatures and says, "Cindy, look at the giraffes!" How much acoustic detail does the child need to remember or to learn the word *giraffe* in this situation? In fact, she may get by with nothing more than a salient piece of the word (e.g., something like "uh-RA"). However, the situation changes when Cindy goes home to Mom and tries to tell her about her day, reproducing "uh-RA" in a vain effort to talk about that animal with a long neck. A reproduction like "uh-Raff" might be sufficient to do the job (particularly in view of the fact that Mommy knows her child has just returned from the zoo). But "uh-RA" is not sufficient. Back to the drawing board.

Of course, we could equate the sensory demands on comprehension and production by presenting words in isolation, with no context of any kind. Under these conditions, any differences that we observed between comprehension and production could be blamed on motor demands (the usual suspect in cases of expressive language delay). However, this kind of disembodied speech is rare in the first stages of language learning, and there is no reason to believe that it plays a serious role in the learning process. We agree with Savage-Rumbaugh and her colleagues on the role of familiar routines and contextual support in early language learning. Under these conditions (i.e., "language in the wild"), comprehension and production differ markedly in their reliance on perceptual versus contextual information. This means, in turn, that there may be proportional differences in the contribution of brain regions that specialize in perceptual analysis (i.e., extraction of sensory detail) and contextual analysis (i.e., integration of information across and within modalities).

In our work with human children, we have proposed that different forms of language delay may result from differential patterns of brain maturation and/or from subtle deficits at some level of neural computation (i.e., fast vs. slow, detail oriented vs. integrative units). Notice that we have not invoked *any* domain-specific language organs to account for these differential patterns of language breakdown. At the same time, we disavow old-fashioned "general cognition" accounts for language delay. There is no such thing as "vanilla cognition." The human brain is a complex and highly plastic computational organ. There are variations in computational style and computational power from one region to another, from one layer to another within a single region, and from cell to cell. Small quantitative variations in computing power (local or distributed) can have important effects on the nature of learning and the way in which problems are ultimately solved. Yet none of this requires us to presuppose a rigid, content-specific, and highly specialized blueprint for language or any other aspect of cognition (for a more detailed version of this argument, see Churchland & Sejnowski, 1992). Instead, there may be very indirect routes to "default" brain organization in children and adults, and many alternative routes are possible when default conditions do not hold.

What are the implications of this view for children and chimpanzees? Savage-Rumbaugh and her colleagues have shown that chimpanzees are capable of *some* symbolic ability (although not as much as Alia shows by the end of the study) and *some* grammatical ability (although not enough to support full-fledged parsing of a complex sentence). Furthermore, the chimpanzee's level of language ability appears to be better in comprehension than it is in production. Within comprehension, there are subtle differences between child and chimpanzee in item difficulty. For example, Alia performs better with phrasal compounds (e.g., "Get the ball and the banana"), whereas Kanzi has an edge on items with recursion. In my view, this complex pattern of quantitative and qualitative variation between species cannot be explained by postulating a language organ that is present in Alia but absent in Kanzi.

I think that it is time for us to abandon the idea that our brain is organized around content-specific faculties (for language, music, faces, etc.). Is the chimpanzee brain different from the human brain? Of course it is. Without question, these differences are responsible for the presence of full-fledged language in humans and the absence of anything but "quasi language" and "weak symbolic capacity" and "rudiments of grammar" in the chimpanzee. However, I believe that these differences are due to the computational properties of neural systems that *indirectly* support language learning and language use in human beings. As we have seen, the areas that support language learning are not the same as the areas that support maintenance and use of fluent language in a mature adult. Furthermore, studies of brain activity during language processing in the adult suggest that many different regions are active when language is in use, with different patterns of activation depending on the task (e.g., word comprehension, covert word production, categorization of words in a novel task, categorization of words in a familiar task, translation from one language to another, judgments of grammaticality, studies of priming between word pairs—for reviews, see Damasio, 1989; Kutas & Kluender, 1991; and Petersen, Fiez, & Corbetta, 1992). In other words, even within the human species, we find little evidence for a circumscribed language organ. The whole brain participates in language, although the pattern of participation that we see varies, depending on the task at hand, and some regions are clearly more important than others.

In a species with a quantitatively and qualitatively different brain, we should not be at all surprised to find quantitative and qualitative variations in language ability. Savage-Rumbaugh et al. have provided evidence for both. They are cautious, even scrupulous in their efforts to specify where the species differ and where they overlap. In my view, this is a model for comparative research in cognitive neuroscience. The twenty-first century is upon us. It is time to abandon phrenology and faculty psychology in favor of dynamic, quantitative models of brain and behavior. Savage-Rumbaugh and her colleagues have encountered opposition and skepticism for many years because their readers (being human beings) are loath to abandon the idea that we are "special," separate, qualitatively different, and unquestionably better than the humble chimpanzee. Of course their opponents are right in one respect: humans are certainly better at language! But *better* is a relative term. The Berlin Wall is down, and so is the wall that separates man from chimpanzee. We are going to have to learn to live with relative differences and permeable borders. It will be hard, but I believe that the world will be the better for it.

References

Aram, D., Holland, A., Locke, J. L., Plante, E., & Tomblin, J. B. (1992, November). *The biological basis of developmental language disorders.* Miniseminar presented at the annual meeting of the American Speech-Language-Hearing Association, San Antonio.

Bates, E., Benigni, L., Bretherton, I., Camaioni, L., & Volterra, V. (1979). *The emergence of symbols: Cognition and communication in infancy.* New York: Academic.

Bates, E., Bretherton, I., & Snyder, L. (1988). *From first words to grammar: Individual differences and dissociable mechanisms.* New York: Cambridge University Press.

Bates, E., MacWhinney, B., Caselli, C. M., Devescovi, A., Natale, F., & Venza, V. (1984). A cross-linguistic study of the development of sentence interpretation strategies. *Child Development*, **55**, 341–354.

Bates, E., & Thal, D. (1991). Associations and dissociations in child language development. In J. Miller (Ed.), *Research on child language disorders: A decade of progress.* Austin, TX: PRO-ED.

Bates, E., Thal, D., & Janowsky, J. (1992). Early language development and its neural correlates. In I. Rapin & S. Segalowitz (Eds.), *Handbook of neuropsychology: Vol. 7. Child neuropsychology.* Amsterdam: Elsevier.

Bates, E., Thal, D., & Marchman, V. (1991). Symbols and syntax: A Darwinian approach to language development. In N. Krasnegor, D. Rumbaugh, R. Schiefelbusch, & M. Studdert-Kennedy (Eds.), *Biological and behavioral determinants of language development.* Hillsdale, NJ: Erlbaum.

Benedict, H. (1979). Early lexical development: Comprehension and production. *Journal of Child Language*, **6**, 183–200.

Brownell, H. H., Potter, H. H., Bihrle, A. M., & Gardner, H. (1986). Inference deficits in right-brain-damaged patients. *Brain and Language*, **27**, 310–312.

Churchland, P., & Sejnowski, T. (1992). *The net effect.* Cambridge, MA: MIT Press/Bradford.

Dale, P. S. (1991). The validity of a parent report measure of vocabulary and syntax at 24 months. *Journal of Speech and Hearing Sciences*, **34**, 565–571.

Dale, P., & Bates, E. (in preparation). *The relation between lexical and grammatical development from 16 to 30 months.*

Dale, P., Bates, E., Reznick, S., & Morisset, C. (1989). The validity of a parent report instrument of child language at 20 months. *Journal of Child Language*, **16**, 239–249.

Damasio, A. (1989). Time-locked multiregional retroactivation: A systems-level proposal for the neural substrates of recall and recognition. *Cognition*, **33**, 25–62.

Darwin, C. (1971). A biographical sketch of an infant. In A. Bar-Adon (Ed.), *Child language: A book of readings.* Englewood Cliffs, NJ: Prentice-Hall. (Reprinted from *Mind*, 1877, **2**[285], 292–294)

Dromi, E. (1987). *Early lexical development.* New York: Cambridge University Press.

Dunn, L., & Dunn, R. (1981). *Peabody Picture Vocabulary Test—Revised.*

Fenson, L., Dale, P., Reznick, J. S., Thal, D., Bates, E., Hartung, J., Pethick, S., & Reilly, J. (in press). *The MacArthur Communicative Development Inventories: User's guide and technical manual.* San Diego: Singular.

Fischer, K. (1980). A theory of cognitive development: The control and construction of hierarchies of skills. *Psychological Review,* **87**(6), 477–531.

Gardner, H., Brownell, H. H., Wapner, W., & Michelow, D. (1983). Missing the point: The role of the right hemisphere in the processing of complex linguistic materials. In E. Perceman (Ed.), *Cognitive processing in the right hemisphere.* New York: Academic.

Goldin-Meadow, S., Seligman, M. E. P., & Gelman, R. (1976). Language in the two-year-old. *Cognition,* **4**, 189–202.

Golinkoff, R. M., Hirsh-Pasek, K., Cauley, K. M., & Gordon, L. (1987). The eyes have it: Lexical and syntactic comprehension in a new paradigm. *Journal of Child Language,* **14**, 23–45.

Gopnik, A., & Meltzoff, A. (1986). Relations between semantic and cognitive development in the one-word stage—the specificity hypothesis. *Child Development,* **57**, 1040–1053.

Hecaen, H. (1976). Acquired aphasia in children and the ontogenesis of hemispheric functional specialization. *Brain and Language,* **3**, 114–134.

Hirsh-Pasek, K., & Golinkoff, R. M. (1991). Language comprehension: A new look at some old themes. In N. Krasnegor, D. Rumbaugh, R. Schiefelbusch, & M. Studdert-Kennedy (Eds.), *Biological and behavioral determinants of language development.* Hillsdale, NJ: Erlbaum.

Kutas, M., & Kluender, R. (1991). What is who violating? A reconsideration of linguistic violations in light of event-related potentials. *Center for Research in Language Newsletter* (University of California, San Diego), **6**(1).

Leopold, W. F. (1949). *Speech development of a bilingual child: A linguist's record.* Evanston, IL: Northwestern University Press.

Marchman, V., Miller, R., & Bates, E. (1991). Babble and first words in children with focal brain injury. *Applied Psycholinguistics,* **12**, 1–22.

Miller, J. (1991). Research on language disorders in children: A progress report. In J. Miller (Ed.), *Research on child language disorders: A decade of progress.* Austin, TX: PRO-ED.

Mills, D., Coffey, S., & Neville, H. (in press-a). Changes in cerebral organization in infancy during primary language acquisition. In G. Dawson & K. Fischer (Eds.), *Human behavior and the developing brain.* New York: Guilford.

Mills, D., Coffey, S., & Neville, H. (in press-b). Language acquisition and cerebral specialization in 20-month-old children. *Journal of Cognitive Neuroscience.*

Molfese, D. (1990). Auditory evoked responses recorded from 16-month-old human infants to words they did and did not know. *Brain and Language,* **38**, 345–363.

Petersen, S. E., Fiez, J. A., & Corbetta, M. (1992). Neuroimaging. *Current Opinion in Neurobiology,* **2**, 217–222.

Piaget, J. (1962). *Play, dreams and imitation.* New York: Norton.

Rescorla, L., & Schwartz, E. (1990). Outcome of toddlers with specific expressive language delay. *Applied Psycholinguistics,* **11**, 393–408.

Reznick, J. S. (1990). Visual preference as a test of infant word comprehension. *Applied Psycholinguistics,* **11**, 145–165.

Satz, P., Strauss, E., & Whitaker, H. (1990). The ontogeny of hemispheric specialization: Some old hypotheses revisited. *Brain and Language,* **38**(4), 596–614.

Snyder, L., Bates, E., & Bretherton, I. (1981). Content and context in early lexical development. *Journal of Child Language,* **8**, 565–582.

Spelke, E. S., Breinlinger, K., Macomber, J., & Jacobson, K. (1992). Origins of knowledge. *Psychological Review,* **99**, 605–632.

Stern, C. (1965). *Die Kindersprache: Eine psychologische und sprachtheoretische Untersuchung [von] Clara und William Stern* [Child language: A psychological and linguistic study]. Darmstadt: Wissenschaftliche. (Unrevised reprographic reproduction of new 4th ed., Leipzig, 1928)

Stiles, J., & Nass, R. (1991). Spatial grouping activity in young children with congenital right- or left-hemisphere brain injury. *Brain and Cognition, 15,* 201–222.

Stiles, J., & Thal, D. (in press). Linguistic and spatial cognitive development following early focal brain injury: Patterns of deficit and recovery. In M. Johnson (Ed.), *Brain development and cognition: A reader.* Oxford: Blackwell.

Stiles-Davis, J. (1988). Spatial dysfunctions in young children with right cerebral hemisphere injury. In J. Stiles-Davis, M. Kritchevsky, & U. Bellugi (Eds.), *Spatial cognition: Brain bases and development.* Hillsdale, NJ: Erlbaum.

Tallal, P. (1988). Developmental language disorders. In J. Kavanagh & T. Truss (Eds.), *Learning disabilities: Proceedings of the National Conference.* Parkton, MA: York.

Thal, D. (1991). Language and cognition in late-talking toddlers. *Topics in Language Disorders, 11,* 33–42.

Thal, D., Fenson, L., & Bates, E. (in preparation). *Variations in rate of language development.*

Thal, D., Marchman, V., Stiles, J., Aram, D., Trauner, D., Nass, R., & Bates, E. (1991). Early lexical development in children with focal brain injury. *Brain and Language, 40,* 491–527.

Thal, D., Tobias, S., & Morrison, D. (1991). Language and gesture in late talkers: A one-year follow-up. *Journal of Speech and Hearing Research, 34*(3), 604–612.

Vargha-Khadem, F., Isaacs, E. B., Papaleloudi, H., Polkey, C. E., & Wilson, J. (1991). Development of language in 6 hemispherectomized patients. *Brain, 114,* 473–495.

Vargha-Khadem, F., Isaacs, E., Van Der Werf, S., Robb, S., & Wilson, J. (1991). Development of intelligence and memory in children with hemiplegic cerebral palsy. *Brain, 115,* 315–329.

Whitehurst, G., Fischell, J., Arnold, D., & Lonigan, C. (1992). Evaluating outcomes with children with expressive language delay. In S. Warren & J. Reichle (Eds.), *Causes and effects in communication and language intervention.* Baltimore: Brookes.

Woods, B., & Teuber, H. (1978). Changing patterns of childhood aphasia. *Annals of Neurology, 3,* 273–280.

HOW DOES EVOLUTION DESIGN
A BRAIN CAPABLE OF LEARNING LANGUAGE?

E. Sue Savage-Rumbaugh

Cross-Validation through Alternative Measures of Comprehension

In an insightful and far-ranging Commentary, Elizabeth Bates provides us with a clear explanation of the methods presently available for the assessment of linguistic comprehension in young children. Will some of these methods be applied to apes in the future to validate the results reported here?

Certainly "parental report" (or, in this case, "experimenter's report") can and should be applied; however, it must be accompanied by other measures to avoid being viewed as "anecdotal." Measures of glance will be problematic, for the reasons that Bates offers. We have conducted pilot studies of this procedure with Kanzi and found that he tends to look at the scenes that interest him and to ignore others, regardless of the auditory stimulus. However, if asked, he can nonetheless point to a specific video image. Consequently, we are developing an alternative procedure, one that requires the use of a joystick to signal which of four moving images (presented on a single screen) matches the auditory stimulus. Pilot work has also been done with evoked potentials, and the problems that Bates mentions do indeed cloud data interpretation. In addition, we found that strong artifacts were created by even the smallest movements in the large jaw muscles that cover the skull in apes. Currently, we are investigating the feasibility of utilizing SPECT images to contrast the performance of apes on linguistic and nonlinguistic tasks.[1] It is hoped that these and other measures, includ-

[1] For an explanation of SPECT scans, see n. 2 below.

ing those of nonlinguistic skills, will continue to provide an increasingly sophisticated understanding of the behavioral and neurological relation between man and ape as regards complex cognitive processes.

Productive versus Receptive Skills: Why Do Differences Exist?

With regard to the discrepancy between Kanzi's productive and receptive language skills, Bates observes that many normal children, particularly "late talkers," manifest a similar discrepancy. She attributes this to the different roles that the two hemispheres play in the development of language competency, roles that incidentally appear to be quite different from those they play in adult language use. According to Bates, during development, the right hemisphere mediates holistic-integrative processes and the left hemisphere analytic-sequential processes. Because comprehension requires the integration of a great deal of divergent information, it is initially right-hemisphere dependent. Speech production requires quite a different set of skills, those of attention to the sequential detail of motor movement entailed in speech production, an activity Bates terms *analytic*.

We suggest that the productive-receptive discrepancy itself results from a more basic dichotomy, one that characterizes many activities in addition to language. Whether an organism is engaged in language, imitation, problem solving, etc., its brain must cope with inherently different neurological requirements while integrating and storing environmental information than when selecting and executing a course of action. When the brain directs the occurrence of "behavior," it must orchestrate and program the motoric actions, be such actions movements of the tongue and respiratory muscles, arms, legs, etc. Much of the integration and synthesis of information done by the brain results in no overt behavior at all, however. This was certainly the case as Kanzi came to understand language. When increases in language understanding occurred, there was no overt behavior to signal what was happening. Only as Kanzi was asked to execute explicit motoric actions in response to specific requests did it become apparent that a great deal of synthetic conceptual activity had taken place.

How would evolution design a nervous system that could readily switch back and forth between two such divergent ways of responding? To begin to answer this question, it is important to consider the kinds of information that the genome can reliably provide to allow an organism to survive in its environment. All vertebrate organisms need to take in environmental information through a number of sensory organs and to integrate the information provided by these different organs. Thus, somehow the central nervous system needs to become connected to the sense organs in a manner that permits the brain to determine which organ is sending a signal and to execute some control over the receptive capacities of that sensory organ (e.g., to focus the eyes on a particular object). The brain will also need to be able to control other parts of the body, such as the stomach, the legs, and the trunk, and to orchestrate movements of appendages in such a manner that fleeing, eating, copulation, etc. are all possible. As all organisms of a given species sense, move, and ingest food in a manner that is much the same across individuals and across repeated executions of such actions, the genome can afford to design a brain that prewires itself to do many of these things in a specific fashion. We tend to consider such actions "innate" and to construct "ethograms" or lists of the "species typical behaviors" that the brain appears able to generate in relatively the same manner in all members of the species.

However, there are many things that all members of a given species do not do in the same manner. Generally speaking, as mammalian brains increase in size, there is a concomitant increase in the number of things that individuals of the same species do differently. Some of these things overlap in part with innate behaviors, suggesting that some action patterns are only partially prewired, others completely novel. We tend to refer to these behaviors as "learned." However, if we consider the case of our own species, it is quite clear that many of the things we learn are not immediately reflected in overt behavior at all, if ever, just as Kanzi's mastery of language was typically not reflected in overt behavior.

Other things we come to be able to do, such as learning to ride a bike or to pronounce words properly, do require the orchestration of complex motoric actions that are manifest quite overtly. Acquisition of such skills depends heavily on practice and complex sensory feedback systems. Thus, the dichotomy posed here is not to be interpreted as one of *learned* versus *innate* behaviors; rather, it is between the processing and synthesizing of information (such activities may be reflected in behavior only indirectly, if at all) and the active processes that guide the gathering of sensory information and produce observable complex learned patterns of behavior such as language or other skilled activities as well as species typical behaviors. It is proposed that, because these interdependent processes make very different demands on nervous systems, evolution has had to evolve different processing mechanisms to handle the special requirements of these different modes of environmental response. In order to guide moment-by-moment behavior, operate a complex muscular and perceptual system, make rapid decisions, etc., evolution needed an active nervous system. In order to remember experiences over time, to compare, evaluate, and synthesize images, odors, feelings, etc. over time, and to use the compilation of such information to direct the active, ongoing behavior of the organism, evolution needed a nervous system that could process information that would perhaps never be utilized.

Whenever possible, nature is inclined to prewire nervous systems to know what they need to do and to be able to do it with minimal environmental information. For example, the manner in which bees locate and transmit information about nectar reserves depends on the location of the sun relative to the nest (Frisch, 1967). This system requires that the bee take in minimal environmental information in order to plot a novel travel path. Imagine how much more information would need to be processed if the bee who had visited a productive site had to return and explain to the nestmates just how the flower looked and smelled, what it was next to, and all the pertinent landmarks between the nest and the flower so that a forager bee who had not previously visited the flower could find it without getting lost.

Simple systems do not, however, generate a variety of situationally appropriate novel behaviors. Mammalian organisms will inevitably encounter many novel situations that demand behaviors that reflect previous experiences of that particular animal or observations that animal has made of others. For these creatures, nature has designed brains that have the ability to identify such situations and decide which behaviors, if any, to produce.

But how is the genome to build an organism that is capable of doing things not laid down in its wiring diagram? How can it guide behaviors designed, for example, to construct a stone tool, made according to another's plan and for a purpose far distant in time and space from the action of construction? For behaviors that were "needed" but could not be prewired, evolution had to develop a mechanism that would permit the integration of environmental information with the preplanned neural wiring in flexible ways. One way of doing this is to permit the wiring of the brain to depend on environmental input from the sensory organs to guide the organization of cortical cells (Killackey, 1990). Areas of the brain that are normally destined to receive input from the visual system can spontaneously reprogram themselves to receive input from other systems if the sensory organ they are supposed to serve is removed or incapacitated. Indeed, a sensory organ that is not normally present, such as a third eye, can be added to a developing frog embryo. This additional eye will send neuronal projections into the appropriate area of the brain, where they will compete for space with projections from the other eyes, and the brain will form a retinotopic map that permits the added eye to function (Constantine-Paton & Law, 1982).

It is, however, self-evident that the genome must exert some limits on the nature of wiring plasticity; otherwise, the organism could end up without the ability to control its own body adequately. After all, the peripheral nervous system must innervate certain structures, and the central nervous system must know how to connect with the neurons that lead to those structures. If this were not so, we could will to move our hand, only to find our feet wiggling.

Thus, the kind of plasticity that resides in the flexible wiring of the developing brain cannot account for how it is that different individuals become exquisitely skilled in completely different ways. How, for example, can an ape readily learn language when other members of its species have never done so? How is it that one person can become extremely proficient at navigating without a compass while another would be easily lost in the woods yet can effortlessly locate an error in the complex sequence of symbols of a computer program? Certainly these skills are learned, yet the simple truth remains that, for most experiences that are conceptual in nature, rather than sensory or motoric, we have not succeeded in localizing neuronal structures that guide such activities. Certainly techniques such as PET imaging indicate that various locations within the brain take up glucose differentially as we engage in different activities, but they do not tell us how a region of the brain "processes a story," in the sense that stimulation of individual neurons tells us how the primary visual system extracts information from the retinal image. Indeed, PET images do not actually localize a skill; they only show us that certain types of tasks produce higher uptakes of glucose in some brain regions than others (Dudai, 1989). Even PET images of "resting" brains show "hot spots." Are we to conclude that the person is "thinking about resting"?[2]

Thus, we are in the curious position of knowing a great deal about how the brain moves the hand or translates the photoelectric messages transduced by the retina, but almost nothing about how we develop even a simple concept, such as the fact that all monkeys have tails while apes do not. We know even less about how it is that we can observe a complex set of events and at some future time translate a portion of what we observed to enable us to do things we have never done before. Such skills, termed *observational learning* or *imitation*, cannot rely on traditionally defined brain areas,

---

[2] PET scans are visual images of blood flow in the brain. They are produced by the injection of a radioactive isotope into the blood while a person is performing a mental task. The areas of the brain with a higher degree of metabolic activity take up more blood and consequently more of the radioactive isotope. The gamma rays given off by the radioactive isotope are measured by sensitive detectors placed around the subject's head. With the aide of a computer, this information is summed and overlayed over an image of the subject's brain and color coded in accordance with the degree of activity recorded in different brain regions. SPECT scans are similar in principle but detect radioactive substances that are taken up more slowly and remain in the brain somewhat longer; consequently their temporal resolution is less than that provided by a PET scan. Nonetheless, they are preferable for animal studies because they permit the animal to be anesthetized immediately after performing a task and then scanned. By contrast, PET scans require an awake and virtually immobile subject in a head restraint.

such as those that promote language, planning, etc. Although we typically do not look for "imitation centers" in the brain, if one observes children for long, it becomes quite clear that this capacity is fundamental to most other "higher cognitive processes."

Apes, as are we, are adept in their ability to observe and incorporate information. Recently, we have demonstrated that, under appropriate rearing conditions, apes can observe and imitate novel actions on objects (Tomasello, Savage-Rumbaugh, & Kruger, in press); however, the movement skills of apes, when compared to children, appear unpracticed and uncoordinated. Surprisingly, even though the motoric component of most imitated novel tasks leaves something to be desired on the part of the apes, it is nonetheless apes, rather than children, who are most able to handle lengthy delays and still imitate the modeled behavior.

Synaptic versus Volume Transmission within the Brain

Ever since the work of early neuroanatomists such as Cajal, it has been assumed that all information transmitted in the brain is conducted by the buildup and release of electrical potentials within individual neurons. This is called the *standard* model of brain function, and it relies completely on connections formed between neurons. It has recently been shown, however, that information transmissions can occur in the extracellular space as well (Agnati, Bjelke, & Fuxe, 1992). Like standard neuronal transmission, extracellular transmission is accomplished through neuropeptides found in the terminal butons of neurons. However, these neuropeptides are diffused into the extracellular space rather than being discharged at the synaptic cleft. Unlike synaptic transmission, which is rapid, volume transmission is slow because it depends on diffusion. Additionally, the terminals that engage in dispersion of neuropeptides into the extracellular space and the receptors that bind to those neuropeptides are frequently *not* adjacent to one another. Moreover, additional enzymes may be released to alter the neuropeptides as they diffuse through the extracellular space. It appears that the volume transmission system is designed to communicate information in a rather global fashion.

Synaptic transmission, by contrast, is designed to arrange and orchestrate complex sequences of motor actions that must be carried out in a specific way. Because synaptic transmission is rapid, local, specific, and sequential, it is the ideal system to guide a limb or a tongue through a complex programmed pattern of coordinated movements such as those required by speech production. Because the human organism is prewired to produce fine motor movements of the tongue and to coordinate these movements with those of the respiratory system, learning "language" can tap into a motor system that permits the ready integration of the motor skills needed to produce speech. All members of the human community produce speech in essentially the same way—through extensive control of the respiratory and vocal-laryngeal system. While this system needs to be fine-tuned through action, there is no need for any individual human to watch another "talk" in order to operate this system. Even children who are born deaf and blind begin to babble in a manner that apes cannot accomplish even if they try to do so. In this sense, we do appear to be "prewired" for language.

However, the skills required to understand language, as well as those required to determine which words to speak and when, are vastly different from those needed to produce audible sounds. These skills cannot be pre-wired because they depend on the ability to interpret and integrate vast amounts of information, which differs on each occasion and for each individual. While all humans speak, we speak very different languages, and even the same individual uses words and sentences in very different ways. The human brain can be prewired to transduce sound, but it cannot be prewired to know that, when John utters a sequence of phonemes before he gets in the car, he is going to visit a friend one time, to get a new tire another time, and to buy food still another time. This information can be gained only through the integration of a multitude of previous experiences with the present sensory input. Even though it is not prewired to produce speech, Kanzi's brain is nonetheless capable of the vast informational integration necessary to understand such sentences.

Because it is slow, diffuse, and holistic, volume transmission may be more suited to handle the integration of information that differs greatly from one time to the next with little overlap. Moreover, because the integration of new information often requires no immediate overt behavior on the part of the organism, rapid learning is not essential. Language and other similarly complex cognitive tasks seem to benefit far more from distributed than massed practice. Were synaptic connections simply being strengthened through excitation, it would seem that, the more concentrated the practice, the greater the overall probability of strengthening synaptic connections.

Volume transmission, however, could not be speeded up through massed practice, although repeated intermittent practice could potentially result in the release of a large number of neuropeptides into the extracellular space. Since we currently do not know how, or even whether, these neuropeptides interface with environmental events, we can only speculate as to what sort of temporal framework might be optimal within such an information-transmission system.

While massed repetition has little effect on declarative memory or the integration of new information, it does aid in the improvement of motor skills such as playing the piano, typing, driving, etc. This observation suggests that procedural learning that requires the orchestration of complex, finely tuned motor sequences that are at least partially repetitive is the likely product of strengthened synaptic connections.

The standard model of neuronal transmission has guided all previous attempts of comparative psychologists to understand the evolution of intelligent behavior. In attempts to relate neural structure to behavior, scientists have attempted to locate the precise neural structures that give rise to various behaviors (including language), lesioning the brain and noting which activities are impaired as a result. Although lesions often result in rather specific impairments and consequently appear to support, at least in part, the standard synaptic model, it is important to note here that lesions affect extracellular space and consequently volume transmission as well as synaptic transmission.

Early attempts to locate language in Broca's and Wernicke's areas as regions that are found only in humans have given way to more recent attempts to locate language in the wiring of the brain rather than specific structures (Greenfield, 1991) as well as to attempts to track language through the brain as it develops (as Bates notes). Since no current consensus exists regarding the manner in which the brain's wiring results in language, this percept is attractive to all who believe that something as complex as language can be accounted for only by qualitative structural differences between the brains of apes and humans.

While it has, for over 100 years, proved extremely difficult to locate the structure that Chomsky dubbed "the language organ," there does exist a very simple and consistent relation between brain size and intelligence in the mammalian order. In general, after we take account of body size, mammals with larger brains tend to engage in a wider variety of behaviors that we would call *complex learned skills* (Passingham, 1982). However, many scientists have been hesitant to give credence to "size" alone as the mechanism by which nature would generate increasingly complex novel behavior. The import of something as simple as brain size has been further questioned by the finding that all mammalian brains have essentially the same number of neurons per unit of space (Rockel, Hiorns, & Powell, 1980). Consequently, rather than being more tightly packed with neurons, larger brains are in fact less densely populated than smaller brains (Tower, 1954). However, the loose packaging of larger brains permits the formation of more elaborate dendritic connections (Bok, 1959). Nonetheless, there is no clear connection between number of neurons or number of dendritic connections and intelligence (Bullock, 1977).

Now that information transmission has been established in the extracellular space, the finding that increases in brain size are typically correlated with similar increases in the depth of the neocortex takes on new meaning. Could this be one of nature's ways of handling the problems posed by the increasing needs of some organisms to integrate information and acquire behaviors that were specific to given individuals and alterable over time? The increased depth of the neocortex provides for more potential extracellular communication as well as for greater dendritic development.

Certainly, if it should prove to be the case that the integration of novel information and concept formation rely heavily, or even in part, on volume transmission rather than on synaptic transmission alone, then the apparent discrepancies between human and ape intelligence become less puzzling because the increased depth of the neocortex could provide more information capacity than has been previously recognized. In this regard, it is interesting to note that the dolphin brain, often noted for its overall size and weight, has a very thin neocortex and consequently considerably less potential for neocortical dendritic branching and volume transmission than the human cortex (Morgan, Jacobs, & Galaburda, 1986). Similarly, it should also be noted that, when the potential for volume transmission in humans is altered, as when the ventricles become pathologically enlarged, schizophrenia results (Kandel, Schwartz, & Jessell, 1991). Since volume transmission takes place in the ventricles as well, it may be that ventricle enlargement can disrupt the normal communicative processes of the cells.

While we cannot yet explain why Kanzi has so easily acquired skills that were formerly assumed to be the sole province of *Homo sapiens*, the fact that he has done so should cause us to reconsider many of our standard assumptions regarding brain development and function. Evolution may not have innervated Kanzi's peripheral speech apparatus sufficiently to make it possible for him to speak since that is not something that all members of his species typically need to do. However, his brain is capable of comprehending language and of making sense out of disparate speech events that happen infrequently and across relatively long time spans. It is also capable of integrating information in a manner that would make speech possible if Kanzi but possessed the neurological control over his vocal apparatus that is commonly seen in human beings.

Should volume transmission prove, in part, to underlie processes of information integration, then certainly we would expect the integrative learning capacities of humans and apes, indeed humans and all mammals, to be more similar in kind than currently recognized, although noticeable differences in degree of efficiency and in execution through the particular sensorimotor wiring laid down for each species in the synaptic transmission system would continue to produce different manifestations of acquired information.

References

Agnati, L. R., Bjelke, B., & Fuxe, K. (1992). Volume transmission in the brain. *American Scientist, 80,* 362–374.

Bok, S. T. (1959). *Histonomy of the cerebral cortex.* Princeton, NJ: Van Nostrand.

Bullock, T. (1977). *Introduction to nervous systems.* San Francisco: Freeman.

Constantine-Paton, M., & Law, M. I. (1982). The development of maps and stripes in the brain. *Scientific American,* **247,** 62–67.

Dudai, Y. (1989). *The neurobiology of memory: Concepts, findings, and trends.* Oxford: Oxford University Press.

Frisch, K. V. (1967). Dance language and orientation of bees. Cambridge, MA: Harvard University Press.

Greenfield, P. M. (1991). Language, tools, and brain: The ontogeny and phylogeny of hierarchically organized sequential behavior. *Behavioral and Brain Sciences,* **14,** 531–592.

Kandel, E. R., Schwartz, J. H., & Jessell, T. M. (1991). Disorders of thought: Schizophrenia. In E. R. Kandel, J. H. Schwartz, & T. M. Jessell (Eds.), *Principles of neuroscience.* Norwalk, CT: Appleton & Lange.

Killackey, H. P. (1990). Neocortical expansion: An attempt toward relating phylogeny and ontogeny. *Journal of Cognitive Neuroscience,* **2,** 1–17.

Morgan, P. J., Jacobs, M. S., & Galaburda, A. (1986). Evolutionary morphology of the dolphin brain. In R. J. Schusterman, J. A. Thomas, & F. G. Woods (Eds.), *Dolphin cognition and behavior: A comparative approach.* Hillsdale, NJ: Erlbaum.

Passingham, R. (1982). *The human primate.* San Francisco: Freeman.

Rockel, A. J., Hiorns, R. W., & Powell, T. P. S. (1980). The basic uniformity in structure of the neocortex. *Brain,* **133,** 221–244.

Tomasello, M., Savage-Rumbaugh, E. S., & Kruger, A. C. (in press). Imitative learning of action on objects by children, chimpanzees, and educated chimpanzees. *Child Development.*

Tower, D. B. (1954). Structural and functional organization of mammalian cerebral cortex: The correlation of neuron density with brain size. *Journal of Comparative Neurology,* **101,** 19–52.

CONTRIBUTORS

E. Sue Savage-Rumbaugh (Ph.D. 1975, University of Oklahoma) is professor of biology and psychology and principal investigator of the chimpanzee language project at the Language Research Center, Georgia State University. She has researched the language, social, and communicative behaviors of chimpanzees since 1970. She served as a national Sigma Xi lecturer, 1988–1990.

Jeannine S. Murphy (B.S. 1980, Auburn University) is a research technician at the Language Research Center of Georgia State University. Her interests are in how chimpanzees and children learn language. Her daughter, Alia, also made an invaluable contribution to this *Monograph* by serving as a research subject, along with Kanzi (*Pan paniscus*).

Rose A. Sevcik (Ph.D. 1989, Georgia State University) is an assistant research professor at the Language Research Center, College of Arts and Sciences, Georgia State University. Her research interests concentrate on the development of language and communication skills and their relation to cognition in great apes and in children, including youngsters with disabilities.

Karen E. Brakke (M.A. 1989, Georgia State University) is a doctoral candidate in psychology at Georgia State University. Her research interests focus on the ontogeny of components of language and object manipulation in apes and humans.

Shelly L. Williams (Ph.D. 1987, University of Montana) is assistant research professor at the Language Research Center, College of Arts and Sciences, Georgia State University. Her research efforts focus on the effects of early rearing environments on language, memory, and attention.

Duane M. Rumbaugh (Ph.D. 1955, University of Colorado) is Regents' Professor of Psychology and director of the Language Research Center, College of Arts and Sciences, Georgia State University. He is principal investigator of the NICHD grant (06016) that supported the LANA Project in 1971 and its several elaborations to the present. He is past president of Division 6 (Physiological and Comparative) of the American Psychological Association.

Elizabeth Bates (Ph.D. 1974, University of Chicago) is professor in the Departments of Psychology and Cognitive Science at the University of California, San Diego. She is the author of *From First Words to Grammar* (1988, with Inge Bretherton and Lynn Snyder) and the editor of *The Cross-Linguistic Study of Sentence Processing* (1989, with Brian MacWhinney). She has served on the editorial boards of over one dozen journals in developmental psychology and cognitive science. Her research interests focus on normal and abnormal language acquisition, cross-linguistic studies of language processing, and the brain bases of language in children and adults.

STATEMENT OF EDITORIAL POLICY

The *Monographs* series is intended as an outlet for major reports of developmental research that generate authoritative new findings and use these to foster a fresh and/or better-integrated perspective on some conceptually significant issue or controversy. Submissions from programmatic research projects are particularly welcome; these may consist of individually or group-authored reports of findings from some single large-scale investigation or of a sequence of experiments centering on some particular question. Multiauthored sets of independent studies that center on the same underlying question can also be appropriate; a critical requirement in such instances is that the various authors address common issues and that the contribution arising from the set as a whole be both unique and substantial. In essence, irrespective of how it may be framed, any work that contributes significant data and/or extends developmental thinking will be taken under editorial consideration.

Submissions should contain a minimum of 80 manuscript pages (including tables and references); the upper limit of 150–175 pages is much more flexible (please submit four copies; a copy of every submission and associated correspondence is deposited eventually in the archives of the SRCD). Neither membership in the Society for Research in Child Development nor affiliation with the academic discipline of psychology are relevant; the significance of the work in extending developmental theory and in contributing new empirical information is by far the most crucial consideration. Because the aim of the series is not only to advance knowledge on specialized topics but also to enhance cross-fertilization among disciplines or subfields, it is important that the links between the specific issues under study and larger questions relating to developmental processes emerge as clearly to the general reader as to specialists on the given topic.

Potential authors who may be unsure whether the manuscript they are planning would make an appropriate submission are invited to draft an outline of what they propose and send it to the Editor for assessment.

This mechanism, as well as a more detailed description of all editorial policies, evaluation processes, and format requirements, is given in the "Guidelines for the Preparation of *Monographs* Submissions," which can be obtained by writing to Wanda C. Bronson, Institute of Human Development, 1203 Tolman Hall, University of California, Berkeley, CA 94720.

NOTICE TO CONTRIBUTORS

As of August 1, 1993, manuscripts and inquiries should be directed to the Editor designate, Rachel K. Clifton, Department of Psychology, University of Massachusetts, Amherst, MA 01003. Current editorial policies will remain unchanged.